new Home Plans for 2000

Publisher
James D. McNair III

Chief Operating Officer
Bradford J. Kidney

Staff Writers
Debra Cochran/Sue Barile

Front & Back Cover Design
Marla Gladstone

Inside features

Photography supplied by The Meredith Corporation

Plan #19422 pg 94

GARLINGHOUSE

Library of Congress No.: 98-75666
ISBN: 0-938708-87-2

Submit all Canadian plan orders to:
The Garlinghouse Company
60 Baffin Place, Unit #5
Waterloo, Ontario N2V 1Z7

Canadian Orders Only: 1-800-561-4169
Fax No. 1-800-719-3291
Customer Service No.: 1-519-746-4169

Photography by John Ehrenclou

Plan #20100 pg 122

ordering details

VISIT OUR WEBSITE
http//www.garlinghouse.com

We Welcome Your Feedback!
Email us at: editor@garlinghouse.com

UNIQUE, EXCITING COURTYARD

The unique courtyard plan brings outdoor living into the home. The center pool and living area provides optimum privacy while creating great views from the living areas. A portico entry way opens up to the courtyard. The main entry door opens to the grand salon and rear views. The formal dining room is off the grand salon area. The family areas have a great view of the pool and courtyard area. The leisure room has a high ceiling, an entertainment center and glass doors to a covered pool side lanai. An outdoor fireplace makes gathering an enjoyable experience. The master wing has a large bedroom with a stepped ceiling, a bayed sitting area, glass doors to the rear lanai, and built-ins. Large his-n-her closets and vanities, a soaking tub, a glass shower and TV space highlight the bath. Upstairs, two bedrooms share a nice size bath. Both bedrooms have private decks. No materials list is available for this plan. Design by The Sater Design Group

**Main floor —
2,853 sq. ft.
Second floor —
627 sq. ft.
Guest house —
312 sq .ft.
Garage — 777 sq. ft.**

*Total living area:
3,792 sq. ft.*

MAIN FLOOR
No. 94246

SECOND FLOOR

Refer to **Pricing Schedule F** on the order form for pricing information

Elegant and Inviting

Traditional and modern elements unite to create an outstanding plan for the family that enjoys outdoor entertaining. Wrap-around verandas and a three-season porch insure the party will stay dry, rain or shine. You may want to keep guests inside, in the elegant parlor and formal dining room, separated by a half-wall. The adjoining kitchen can be closed off to keep meal preparation convenient, but removed from the bustle. The family will enjoy informal meals at the island bar, or in the adjoining breakfast nook. Even the fireplaced gathering room, with its soaring ceilings and access to the porch, is right nearby. You'll appreciate the first floor master suite, and the upstairs laundry location. Design by The Garlinghouse Company

First floor — 1,580 sq. ft.
Second floor — 1,164 sq. ft.
Basement — 1,329 sq. ft.
Garage — 576 sq. ft.

Total living area: 2,744 sq. ft.

Refer to **Pricing Schedule E** on the order form for pricing information

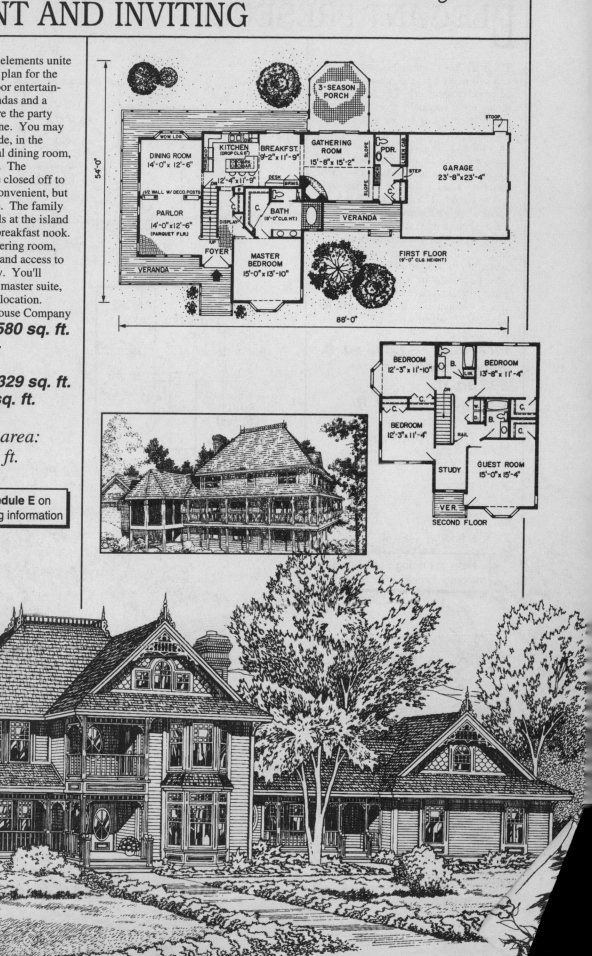

ELEGANT PRESENCE

The entry has a ceiling height of 13'7", and will make a first impression you'll be proud to show off. The formal dining room is equally worthy of envy as it features a tray ceiling and columns. The large living area has a 18' vaulted ceiling and a view of the backyard. The fireplace is shared with a hearth room, one of today's favorite features. The kitchen has a corner sink and an island. The master suite is a personal, private retreat. The upstairs has a game room that overlooks the living area. The fourth bedroom has an 11' vaulted ceiling, giving it versatility to be used as a study. The other bedrooms are adjacent to the game room and have ample closet space. No materials list is available for this plan. Design by Ryan & Associates

**First floor — 1,893 sq. ft.
Second floor — 893 sq. ft.
Garage — 632 sq. ft.**

Total living area: 2,786 sq. ft.

60-8

Hearth
15-0 × 17-10

Porch

Liv
19-3 × 17-8

18-0 Vault

Kit
10 × 13

Mbr
13-0 × 17-4

11-7 Coffer

R

P   F   W   D

59-8

Clo

Entry

Din
12 × 13

9-0 Tray

Bath

Porch

3-Car Gar
20-4 × 27-8

1st Floor Plan

Open

Rec Rm
13 × 17

Br #2
12 × 11

Br #3
12-0 × 11-8

Clo

Attic

Br #4
12 × 11

2nd Floor Plan
No. 91133

Refer to **Pricing Schedule E** on the order form for pricing information

NATURAL LIGHT GIVES BRIGHT SPACES

The generous use of windows throughout this home creates bright living spaces. The welcoming covered front porch and lovely bay window give this home great curb appeal. Notice the separate entrance close to the den making a third bedroom a practical possibility. The kitchen has a great center island and large pantry. There is a bright sunny breakfast nook to start your day. The formal dining area is close by to make entertaining easy. The living room has a fireplace to add atmosphere to the room as well as warmth. There is access to the optional patio from the dining room to add living space. The master bedroom has a private bath and double closets. The second bedroom has ample closet space and shares a full, compartmented hall bath with the possible third bedroom. Design by The Garlinghouse Company

Main floor — 1,620 sq. ft.

Total living area: 1,620 sq. ft.

Refer to **Pricing Schedule B** on the order form for pricing information

50'-0"

55'-8"

M Br
14 x 15

Living
13-10 x 21-5

Optional Patio

Br 2
12 x 11-2

linen

DN

railing

Dining
11-2 x 9

Den / Br 3
13 x 11-4

pantry

Kit.
13-6 x 13

Nook

Garage
19-4 x 19-8

Main Floor
No. 24317

Design 99086

CLASSIC GOOD LOOKS

The classic good looks of this two-story home are enhanced by the use of stucco and are accentuated by an arch topped window over the entrance door and living room which leads into a dramatic two-story vaulted foyer. The L-shaped kitchen, dinette and family room all flow together into one large area, giving this home a feeling of spacious-ness. Throughout the upstairs, four bedrooms accommodate all your needs. The master bedroom boasts a tray ceiling with a large walk-in closet and a master bath that features an oversized stall shower, a garden tub and a dual vanity. Three additional bedrooms share a full hall bath. No materials list is available for this plan. Design by National Home Planning Service

First floor — 1,731 sq. ft.
Second floor — 1,426 sq. ft.

Total living area: 3,157 sq. ft.

Refer to **Pricing Schedule E** on the order form for pricing information

FIRST FLOOR

FAMILY ROOM 20'-0" x 16'-8"
DINETTE 9'-8" x 12'-4"
KITCHEN
13'-0" x 16'-0"
DINING ROOM 13'-4" x 16'-0"
W | D
LDY
2 CAR GARAGE 20'-0" x 21'-4"
LIBRARY 10'-4" x 9'-10"
FOYER
LIVING ROOM 14'-8" x 16'-0"
CL

57'-2"
39'-0"

SECOND FLOOR
No. 99086

BATH
MASTER BEDROOM 16'-0" x 16'-0"
BEDROOM 11'-10" x 11'-8"
BEDROOM 14'-8" x 13'-8"
BALCONY
CLOSET | CLOSET
WALK IN CLOSET
BATH
WALK IN CLOSET
BEDROOM 12'-8" x 13'-4"
OPEN TO BELOW
OPEN TO BELOW

SPACE TO SPARE

Design 91130

Convenience and class come together to achieve the smooth flow this plan exhibits. The entry is impressive as it opens with a 12' high ceiling, plant ledges, a built-in bookshelf and hardwood floor. The dining and living areas are combined and share a 12' vaulted ceiling to add an open feel. The kitchen has a snack bar and ledge overhead to display plants and other treasures. On the practical side, there is plenty of counter space, a pantry, and a separate utility room with freezer space. Lots of space is the theme of this house, as all the bedrooms have large, walk-in closets. The second bedroom also has a desk in the corner. On the second floor, the first room can be left open as a game room or framed in for another bedroom and closet. There is even more storage space under the stairs and in the garage. No materials list is available for this plan. Design by Ryan & Associates

First floor — 2,173 sq. ft.
Second floor —
637 sq. ft.
Garage & storage —
452 sq. ft.

Total living area:
2,810 sq. ft.

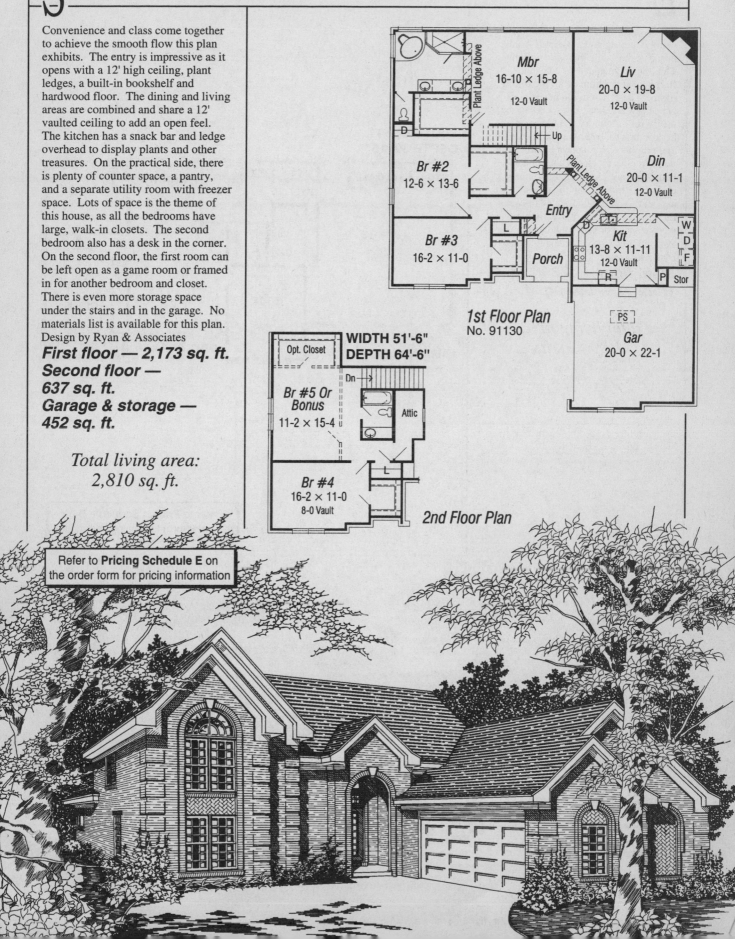

1st Floor Plan
No. 91130

WIDTH 51'-6"
DEPTH 64'-6"

2nd Floor Plan

Refer to **Pricing Schedule E** on the order form for pricing information

Design 92557

ELEGANT BRICK EXTERIOR

This home exudes elegance and style, using detailing and a covered front porch accented by gracious columns. The den is enhanced by a corner fireplace and adjoins with the dining room. The efficient kitchen is well-appointed and has easy access to the utility room/laundry. The master bedroom is topped by a vaulted ceiling and pampered by a private bath and a walk-in closet. The two secondary bedrooms are located at the opposite end of the home from the master suite and share a full bath located between the rooms. This plan is available with a crawlspace or slab foundation. Please specify when ordering. Design by Rick Garner

Main floor — 1,390 sq. ft.
Garage — 590 sq. ft.

Total living area:
1,390 sq. ft.

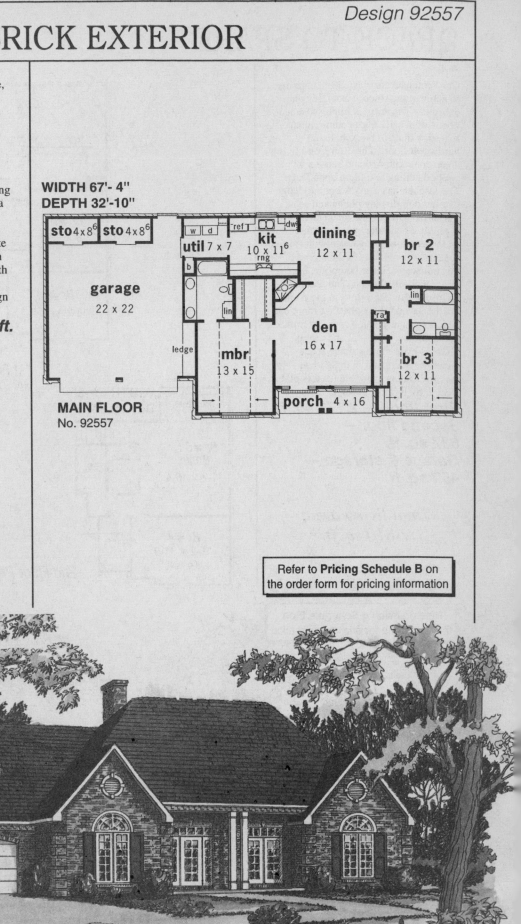

WIDTH 67'- 4"
DEPTH 32'-10"

sto 4 x 8⁶ sto 4 x 8⁶

util 7 x 7   kit 10 x 11⁶   dining 12 x 11   br 2 12 x 11

garage 22 x 22

mbr 13 x 15   den 16 x 17   br 3 12 x 11

ledge

porch 4 x 16

MAIN FLOOR
No. 92557

Refer to **Pricing Schedule B** on the order form for pricing information

MAGNIFICENT PRESENCE

The entry enjoys many different vistas. A curved staircase leads to an elevated study characterized by its arched opening, eighteen foot ceiling and very detailed block paneling. Looking forward there is a two-story living room with amazing glass to bring the outdoors in. A dramatic dining room is available for elegant entertaining. The expansive family room is open to the kitchen and breakfast bay, providing a vast informal family living area. Luxurious features and a spacious layout highlight this impressive home. No materials list is available for this plan. Design by Design Basics, Inc.

First floor — 2,897 sq. ft.
Second floor —
1,603 sq. ft.
Basement — 2,897 sq. ft.
Garage — 793 sq. ft.

Total living area:
4,500 sq. ft.

Refer to **Pricing Schedule F** on the order form for pricing information

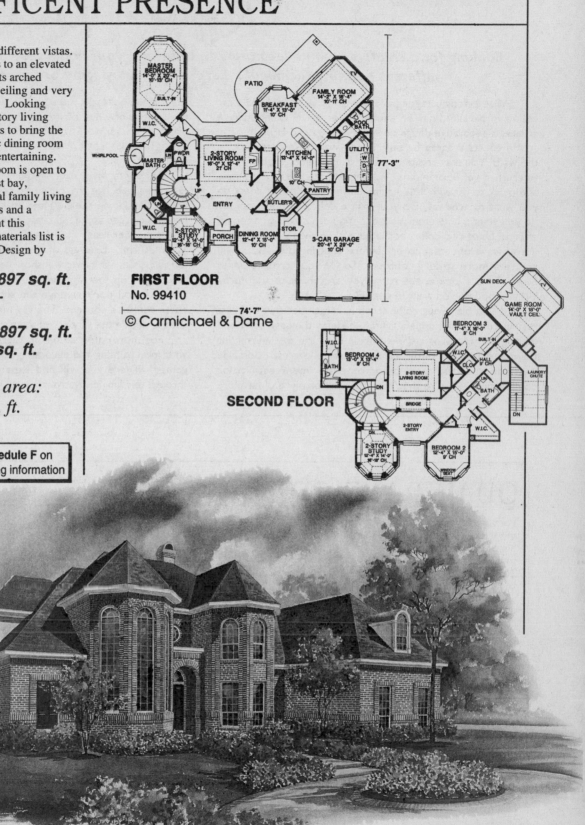

FIRST FLOOR
No. 99410
© Carmichael & Dame

SECOND FLOOR

DECORATING TIPS:
Ragging or Rag Rolling

Looking for a creative idea in decorating to transform your home's look? How about a different painting technique? Let's talk about ragging or rag rolling.

What exactly is ragging or rag rolling? A scrunched up rag rolled in parallel lines or dabbed over a wet paint surface creates a decorative design on walls, ceilings and furniture. The subtle effects created by ragging add warmth and texture to the walls. You may create an effect that resembles fabrics such as crushed velvet or moire. Ragging and rag rolling are simple and quick to do with little equipment needed. What effect do you want to achieve? Do you want a delicate, subtle look or do you want a bold dramatic look? You can create a variety of effects. Using two colors at the same time gives a subtle effect. If you leave one coat to dry before applying the next it will create a more striking contrast. So let your creative juices flow. Take a look at the room you are about to transform. What mood do you want to create?

As you plan your color scheme, remember that the best results come when using a lighter shade as the base color and ragging or rag rolling a darker shade over the top. Reversing the colors in some of the areas can create interest. Combine two tones of the same color or experiment with color combinations. You're the artist, the wall or piece of furniture is your canvas. Make sure you do some samples. You could use a piece of white poster board and experiment. Tape the effect to the surface to be decorated and check the effect during the daylight and the night before you decide on the technique.

Ragging involves dabbing the wet glaze with the rag while rag rolling requires the rag to be rolled up the wall in vertical lines, overlapping the pervious mark on the wet wall. Rags become clogged and need replacing as you work so you should have a number ready cut. An ideal size is about 8 in (20 cm) x 12 in (30 cm). Use rags of the same material to complete the job as a change in fabric will show up in the design. When you are cutting up the rags remove all hems, seams and stitched areas. If you don't remove the stitching, your finished paint effect could be spoiled. The rag material and the colors you choose decide the subtlety of the pattern.

For more information on ragging or rag rolling consult your local painting and decorating store or home improvement center. There you will find experts on hand to guide you through this fun, innovative project.

Design 99878

QUAINT AND COZY

Porches front and back adorn this three-bedroom country home. Featured, is a large Great room with cathedral ceiling. The kitchen has an angled counter open to the breakfast area. The master bedroom has a cathedral ceiling and an optional spa. A bonus room over the garage makes expanding easy. This plan is available with a basement or crawl space foundation. Please specify when ordering. Design by Donald A. Gardner Architects, Inc.

**Main floor —
1,864 sq. ft.
Garage & storage —
614 sq. ft.
Bonus room —
420 sq. ft.**

*Total living area:
1,864 sq. ft.*

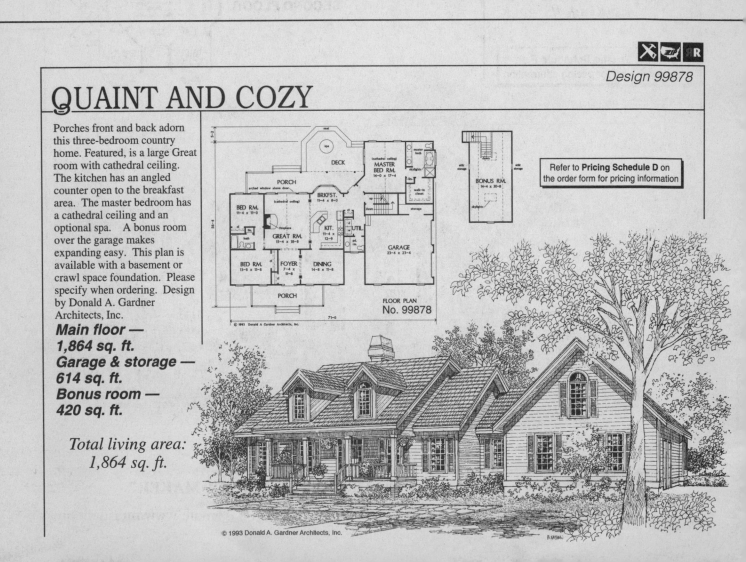

Refer to **Pricing Schedule D** on the order form for pricing information

FLOOR PLAN
No. 99878

© 1993 Donald A. Gardner Architects, Inc.

Design 10780

CLASSIC VICTORIAN

This elegant Victorian with a modern twist celebrates the classic beauty of turn-of-the-century architecture. The huge foyer, flanked by the formal parlor and dining room, leads to the island kitchen with adjoining pantry, the breakfast bay, and sunken gathering room at the rear of the house. Walk upstairs two ways: from the expansive great hall or the sunny alcove with wrap-around rear deck. Double doors open to the master suite and the booklined master retreat with a dormer sitting area. Pamper yourself in the elegant master bath, which features a raised tub and an adjoining cedar closet. Design by The Garlinghouse Company

First floor — 2,108 sq. ft.
Second floor — 2,109 sq. ft.
Basement — 1,946 sq. ft.
Garage — 764 sq. ft.

Total living area: 4,217 sq. ft.

Refer to **Pricing Schedule F** on the order form for pricing information

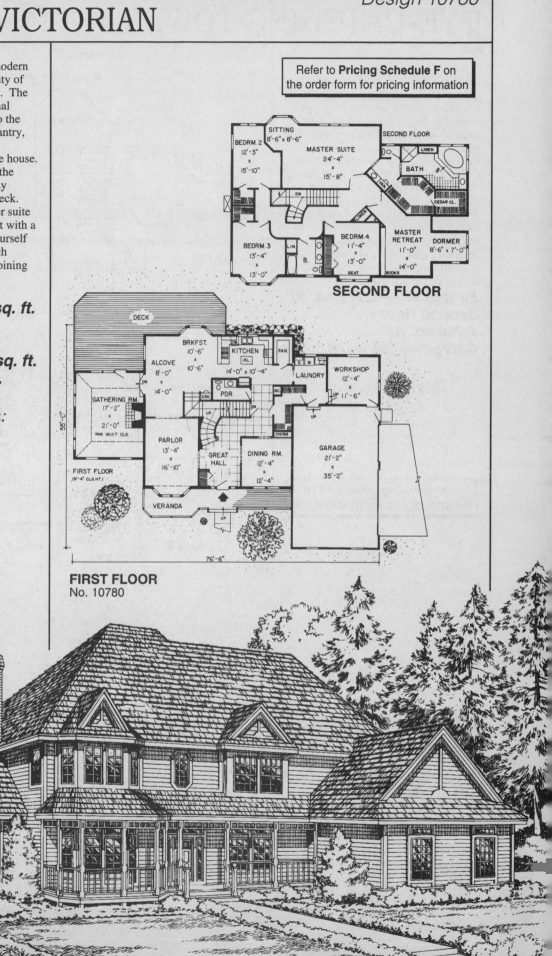

SECOND FLOOR

FIRST FLOOR
No. 10780

Design 99438

EYE-CATCHING TOWER

A look of softened brick are summarized in details like a narrow silhouette of pointed glass around the front door and a thick tower that gives a boost to the elevation. The notable impression in the entry comes from the brilliant placement of the staircase balcony and dining room that openly saturate the view. An additional back staircase lightly skips to the second floor where a sun deck awaits outside the game room. The master suite includes two walk-in closets and a whirlpool bath. The secondary bedrooms either enjoy private access to a bath or close proximity to one. Design by Design Basics, Inc.

First floor — 2,117 sq. ft.
Second floor —
1,206 sq. ft.
Garage — 685 sq. ft.

Total living area:
3,323 sq. ft.

Refer to **Pricing Schedule E** on the order form for pricing information

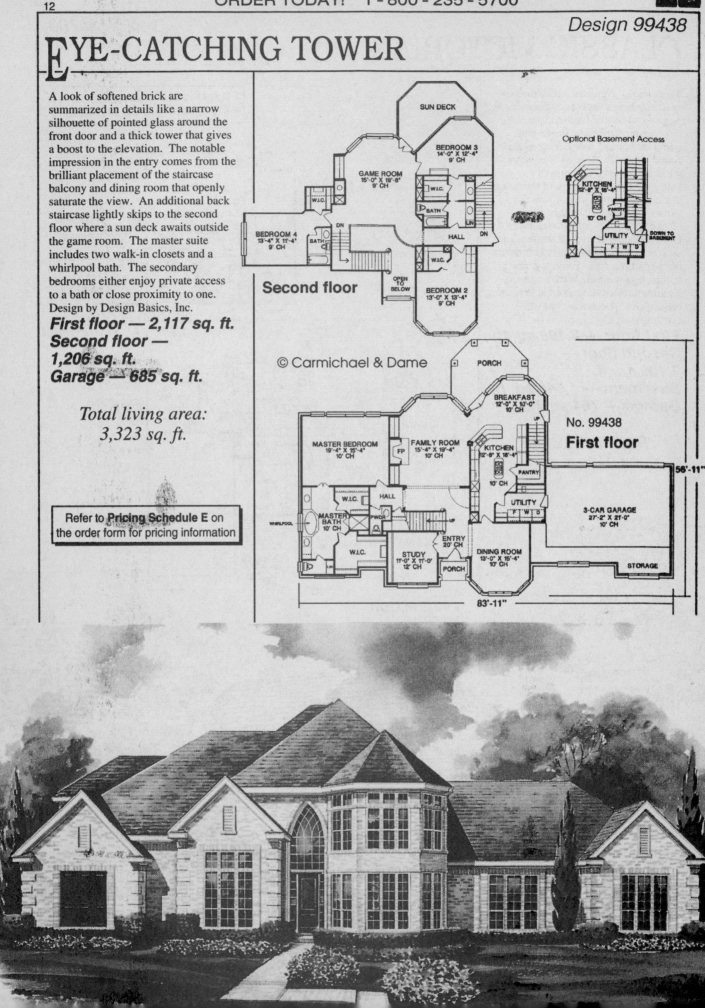

© Carmichael & Dame

Design 24718

A PORCH WITH GAZEBO

Refer to **Pricing Schedule A** on the order form for pricing information

A summer's breeze and a cool refreshing drink are all you need to add to this cozy front porch on a hot afternoon. The unique gazebo area gives this home a style all its own. Inside, the breakfast area overlooks the porch. The kitchen's peninsula counter extends the work space. There is a pass-through from the kitchen into the Great room for convenience in serving, and a built-in pantry for added storage. The garage enters through the laundry room. The Great room and the formal dining room are enhanced by a two sided fireplace. The three bedrooms are located on the left side of the home. The master suite pampers the owner with a whirlpool tub and a walk-in closet. The two additional bedrooms share the full bath in the hall. No materials list is available for this plan. Design by The Garlinghouse Company

Main floor — 1,452 sq. ft.
Garage — 584 sq. ft.

Total living area:
1,452 sq. ft.

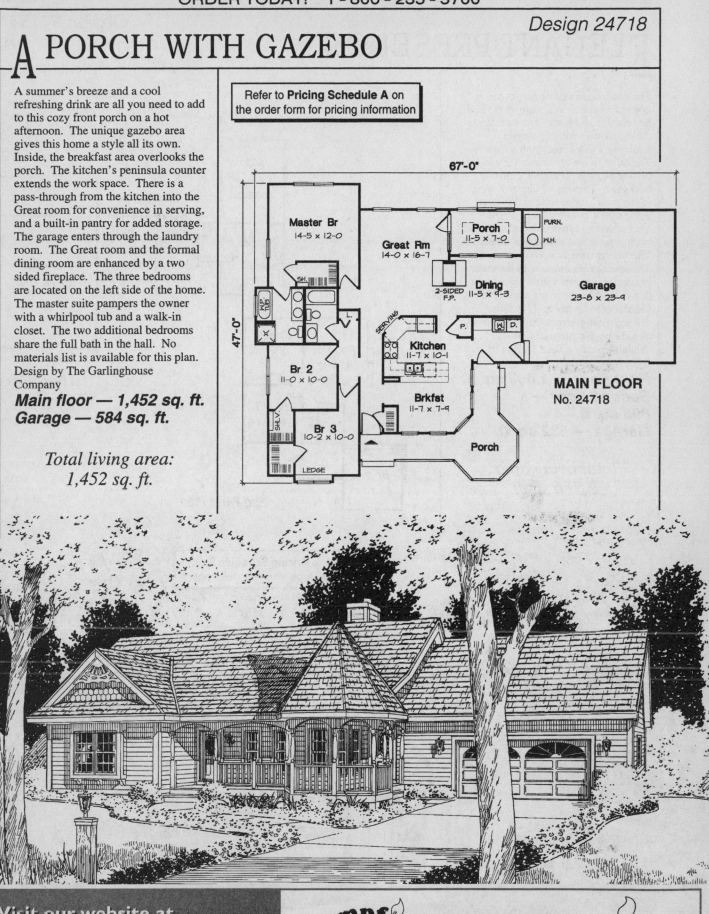

MAIN FLOOR
No. 24718

Design 91134

ELEGANT PRESENCE

The entry has a ceiling height of 13'7", and will make a first impression you'll be proud to show off. The formal dining room is equally elegant, featuring a tray ceiling and columns. The large living area has a 18' vaulted ceiling and a great review of the backyard. There is all kinds of room in the utility room and the three-car garage for a growing family. The kitchen has a corner sink and an island, both popular and convenient amenities. The master suite is a private retreat. The upstairs continues with the theme of special requests with a game room that overlooks the living area. The fourth bedroom has an 11' vaulted ceiling, giving it versatility to be used as a study. No materials list is available for this plan. Design by Ryan & Associates

**First floor — 1,893 sq. ft.
Second floor — 893 sq. ft.
Garage — 632 sq. ft.**

*Total living area:
2,786 sq. ft.*

1st Floor Plan
No. 91134

60-8

Hearth
15-0 × 17-10

Porch

Kit
10 × 13

Liv
19-3 × 17-8
18-0 Vault

Mbr
13-0 × 17-4
11-7 Coffer

P R
F W D

Entry

Clo

Din
12 × 13
9-0 Tray

3-Car Gar
20-4 × 27-8

Bath

Porch

59-8

2nd Floor Plan

Rec Rm
13 × 17

Open

Br #2
12 × 11

Br #3
12-0 × 11-8

Clo

Attic

Br #4
12 × 11

Refer to **Pricing Schedule E** on the order form for pricing information

AN ESTABLISHED FEELING

Design 93337

An established, stable feeling is created with this plan. The foyer is graced by a staircase with an attractive wooden rail. The formal living room uses a tray ceiling and pocket doors as accents. The family room is separated by a half wall from the informal dining room. An island kitchen, with a built-in pantry and ample storage, efficiently serves both formal and informal dining areas. A stepped ceiling tops the first floor master suite. Three additional bedrooms and a full bath are located on the second floor. No materials list is available for this plan. Design by Patrick Morabito A.I.A.

First floor — 1,788 sq. ft.
Second floor — 707 sq. ft.

Total living area: 2,495 sq. ft.

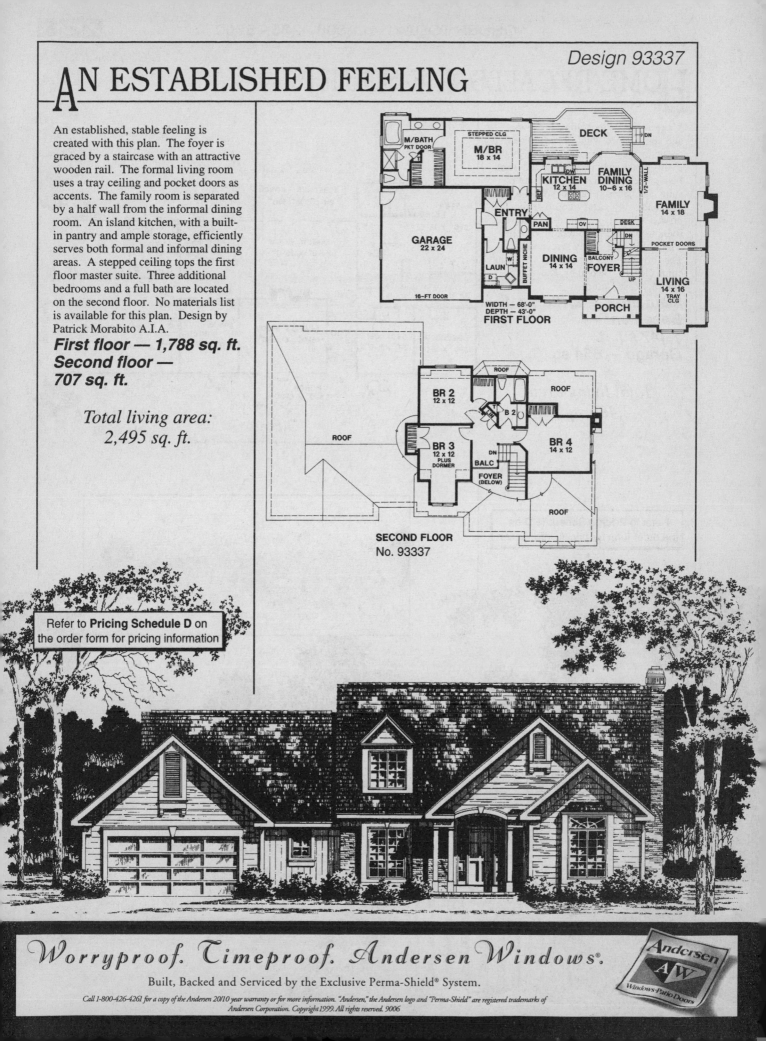

FIRST FLOOR

WIDTH — 68'-0"
DEPTH — 43'-0"

SECOND FLOOR
No. 93337

Design 9850

HOME RECALLS THE SOUTH

Magnificent white columns, shutters, and small paned windows combine to create images of the antebellum South in this generously proportioned design. Inside, the opulent master bedroom suite, with plentiful closet space, a full bath and study, offers comfort and privacy. Fireplaces enhance the formal living room and sizable family room, which skirts the lovely screened porch. The formal dining room boasts built-in china closets. Design by The Garlinghouse Company

**Main area — 2,466 sq. ft.
Basement — 1,447 sq. ft.
Garage — 664 sq. ft.**

Total living area: 2,466 sq. ft.

Refer to **Pricing Schedule D** on the order form for pricing information

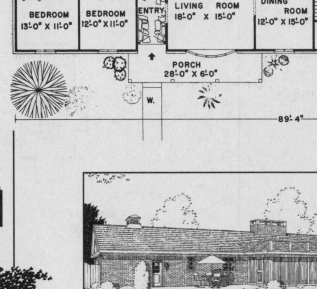

MAIN AREA
No. 9850

Design 91597

YOUR OWN SPACE

This home spreads out the living area so everyone has his or her own space. However, the spacious informal areas are arranged to encourage family interaction. The foyer leads easily into the living room and the dining room. The expansive informal family living area includes a kitchen with an island and a nook area, and a family room with a vaulted ceiling and a two-sided fireplace shared with the living room. The master suite includes another fireplace, a large private bath and a walk-in closet. There are two additional bedrooms, a bonus room and a full double vanity bath on the second floor. A three-car garage has been placed on a convenient angle to the house. No materials list is available for this plan. Design by Alan Mascord Design Associates

**First floor —
2532 sq. ft.
Second floor —
650 sq. ft.
Bonus room —
383 sq. ft.**

*Total living area:
3,182 sq. ft.*

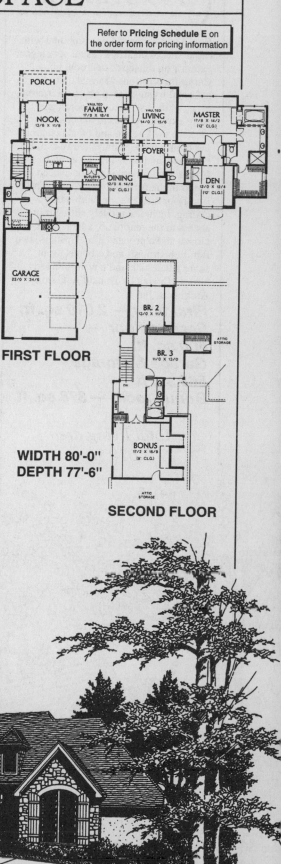

Refer to **Pricing Schedule E** on the order form for pricing information

FIRST FLOOR

PORCH

NOOK 13/6 X 11/8

VAULTED FAMILY 17/8 X 18/6

VAULTED LIVING 14/0 X 15/6

MASTER 17/8 X 14/2 (12' CLG.)

FOYER

BUTLER'S PANTRY

DINING 12/0 X 14/8 (12' CLG.)

DEN 12/0 X 12/4 (12' CLG.)

GARAGE 22/0 X 34/6

SECOND FLOOR

BR. 2 13/0 X 11/8

BR. 3 11/0 X 13/0

ATTIC STORAGE

BONUS 17/2 X 16/9 (8' CLG.)

ATTIC STORAGE

**WIDTH 80'-0"
DEPTH 77'-6"**

Refer to **Pricing Schedule E** on the order form for pricing information

Design 98067

CASUAL YET ELEGANT

Board and batten siding combined with cedar shakes creates a casual yet elegant exterior on this three bedroom home. Carefully positioned formal and informal living spaces make entertaining easy, while a screened-in porch and patio expand options to the outdoors. Open to the kitchen and breakfast area, the family room features a tray ceiling, fireplace, and built-ins. A second fireplace with flanking built-ins can be found in the formal living room. The first floor master suite, with a tray ceiling, includes a lovely sitting room, access to the rear patio, a large walk-in closet, and a private bath. Upstairs, two family bedrooms and a bonus room share a hall bath and a walk-in linen closet. Design by Donald A. Gardner Architects, Inc.

First floor — 2,010 sq. ft.
Second floor — 600 sq. ft.
Garage & storage — 568 sq. ft.
Bonus room — 378 sq. ft.

Total living area:
2,610 sq. ft.

FIRST FLOOR PLAN
No. 98067

© 1998 Donald A Gardner, Inc.

Refer to **Pricing Schedule F** on the order form for pricing information

New Design

HOT OFF THE DRAWING BOARD

SECOND FLOOR PLAN

B. NATHAN

Design 96600

ELEGANT ARCHED OPENING

An elegant arched opening graces the entrance of this classic design. The dramatic arch detail is repeated at the dining room entrance. The use of eleven-foot ceilings in the foyer, dining room and living room gives the home a distinctive appeal. The kitchen, breakfast room and family room are open to one another. Two rear porches are accessed from this area. The kitchen has all the amenities including a walk-in pantry, double ovens and an eating bar. The master suite is designed apart from the other bedrooms for privacy. The luxurious master bath includes a centerpiece whirlpool tub, a separate shower stall with seat, his-n-her vanities and walk-in closets. Two additional bedrooms share a bath and have walk-in closets. A powder room is located off the rear hall. No materials list is available for this plan. Design by Larry E. Belk

Main floor — 2,678 sq. ft.
Garage — 474 sq. ft.

Total living area:
2,678 sq. ft.

Refer to **Pricing Schedule E** on the order form for pricing information

© Larry E. Belk

New Design
HOT OFF THE DRAWING BOARD

MAIN FLOOR
No. 96600

WIDTH 70-2

DEPTH 67-9

BEDRM 4
14-8 X 12-8
9 FT CLG

COVERED PORCH
9 FT CLG

FAMILY ROOM
13-6 X 16-6
9 FT CLG

FP

PORCH
9 FT CLG

MASTER BEDRM
15-0 X 17-4
11 FT TRAY CLG

HERS   HIS
STEP
MASTER BATH
11 FT TRAY CLG
SEAT

BATH 2

LIVING ROOM
18-4 X 18-6
11 FT CLG

KITCHEN
13-6 X 11-4
9 FT CLG

BRKFST RM
10-8 X 11-6
9 FT CLG

42" LEDGE

PWDR

UTIL
12-6 X 5-8
9 FT CLG

PAN

BEDRM 3
11-0 X 13-4
9 FT CLG

BEDRM 2/
STUDY
11-6 X 13-0
11 FT TRAY CLG

FOYER
11 FT CLG

ARCH

DINING ROOM
14-0 X 13-6
11 FT CLG

GARAGE

PORCH
9 FT CLG

Design 93097

COUNTRY FRENCH STYLING

Country French appointments give this home an elegant, Old World look. The foyer opens to the well-proportioned dining room with a twelve-foot ceiling. Stairs are conveniently located in the home to provide access to the basement and the attic. A double French door with a transom leads off the living room to the rear porch. The kitchen, breakfast room and family room are open. Both the breakfast room and family room feature fourteen-foot ceilings. The fireplace provides a lovely focal point for the room. The master bedroom features a trey ceiling and a luxururious master bath. No materials list is available for this plan. Design by Larry E. Belk

Main floor — 2,757 sq. ft.
Garage — 484 sq. ft.

Total living area: 2,757 sq. ft.

Refer to **Pricing Schedule E** on the order form for pricing information

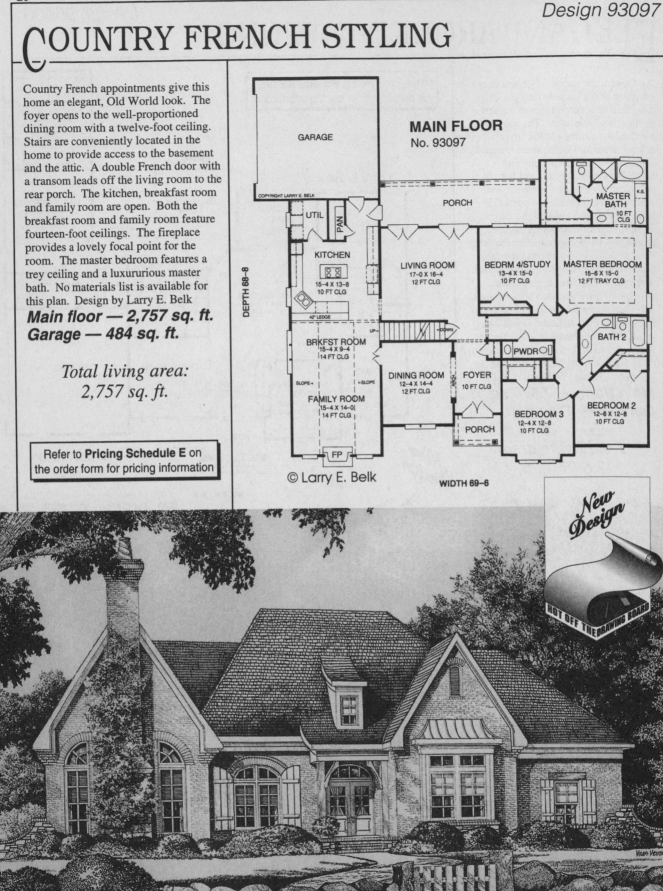

MAIN FLOOR
No. 93097

COPYRIGHT LARRY E. BELK

© Larry E. Belk

DEPTH 68-8

WIDTH 69-6

GARAGE

PORCH

UTIL

PAN

KITCHEN
15-4 X 13-8
10 FT CLG

42" LEDGE

BRKFST ROOM
15-4 X 9-4
14 FT CLG

UP

FAMILY ROOM
15-4 X 14-0
14 FT CLG

SLOPE

FP

LIVING ROOM
17-0 X 16-4
12 FT CLG

DOWN

DINING ROOM
12-4 X 14-4
12 FT CLG

FOYER
10 FT CLG

PORCH

BEDRM 4/STUDY
13-4 X 15-0
10 FT CLG

MASTER BEDROOM
15-6 X 15-0
12 FT TRAY CLG

MASTER BATH
10 FT CLG

K.S.

BATH 2

PWDR

BEDROOM 3
12-4 X 12-8
10 FT CLG

BEDROOM 2
12-6 X 12-8
10 FT CLG

New Design
HOT OFF THE DRAWING BOARD

Design 96602

WITH A EUROPEAN INFLUENCE

The Old World Country French influence in this home is evident. The foyer opens to the well-proportioned dining room. A double French door with a transom leads off the living room to the rear porch. The spacious kitchen is adjacent to the breakfast and family room. A vaulted ceiling tops the breakfast room and family room. A see-through fireplace serves both the formal and informal living areas. All the bedrooms are conveniently arranged. The master bedroom features a trey ceiling and a luxurious master bath. This plan is available with a basement, crawl space or slab foundation. Please specify when ordering. No materials list is available for this plan. Design by Larry E. Belk

Main floor — 2,745 sq. ft.
Garage — 525 sq. ft.

Total living area:
2,745 sq. ft.

Refer to **Pricing Schedule E** on the order form for pricing information

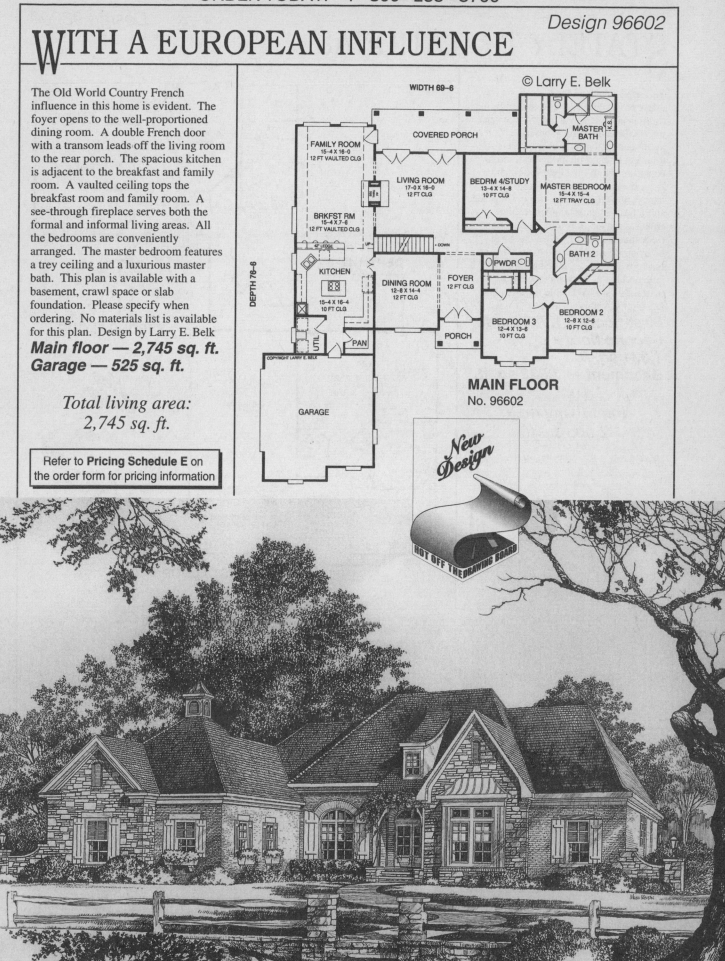

© Larry E. Belk

WIDTH 69–6

DEPTH 76–6

MAIN FLOOR
No. 96602

New Design
HOT OFF THE DRAWING BOARD

Design 98200

STATELY TRADITIONAL

The spacious foyer leads to an impressive staircase. The formal living room is accented by a bay window and the traditional dining room has efficient, direct access to the kitchen. The gourmet kitchen includes an island, a pass-through to the Great room, and a large breakfast area with access to a backyard deck. A cozy corner fireplace and a built-in entertainment center enhance the Great room. The second floor includes a loft, as well as three bedrooms that share two baths. The master suite has a vaulted ceiling, lavish bath and his-n-her walk-in closets. No materials list is available for this plan. Design by Archival Designs

First floor — 1,332 sq. ft.
Second floor — 1,331 sq. ft.
Basement — 1,332 sq. ft.

*Total living area:
2,663 sq. ft.*

Refer to **Pricing Schedule E** on the order form for pricing information

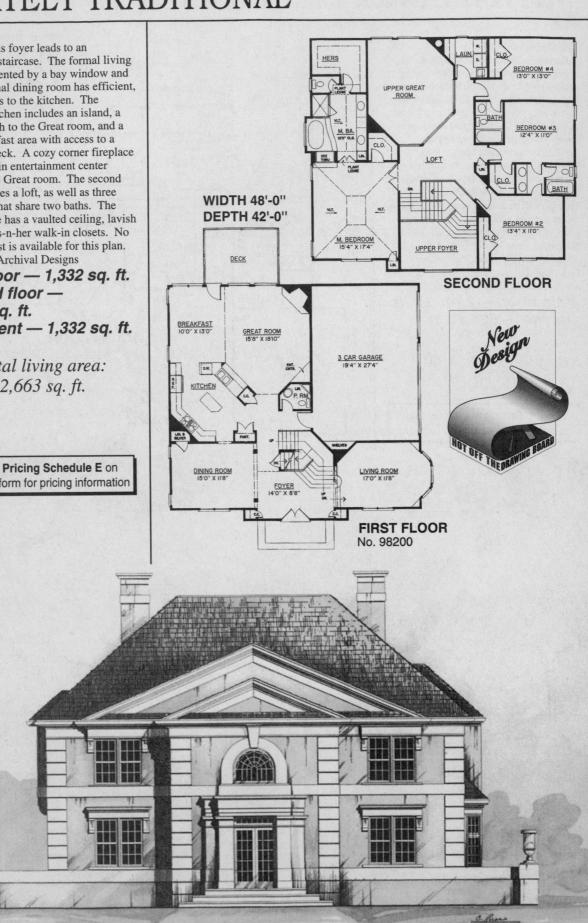

WIDTH 48'-0"
DEPTH 42'-0"

SECOND FLOOR

FIRST FLOOR
No. 98200

EUROPEAN STYLE HOME

Design 93099

Old World ambiance characterizes this European style home. The elegant stone entrance opens to the two-story foyer. A well-proportioned dining room is viewed through an arch flanked by columns. The oversize Great room features a coffered ceiling and a see-through fireplace that can be seen from the kitchen, breakfast room and Great room. A second bedroom downstairs acts as nursery, guestroom or study. Upstairs two roomy bedrooms share a bath. An expandable area is available for future use. No materials list is available for this plan. Design by Larry E. Belk

First floor — 2,050 sq. ft.
Second floor — 561 sq. ft.
Bonus — 272 sq. ft.
Garage — 599 sq. ft.

Total living area: 2,611 sq. ft.

© Larry E. Belk

WIDTH 64-10
DEPTH 64-0

SECOND FLOOR

BEDROOM 4
13-4 X 10-4

EXPANDABLE
17-4 X 18-0

BATH 3
LIN
UP

BEDROOM 3
13-0 X 11-6

OPEN TO FOYER BELOW

PLANT LEDGE

FIRST FLOOR
No. 93099

MASTER BEDRM
13-4 X 16-4
10 FT TRAY CLG

MASTER BATH

BRKFST RM
11-4 X 13-0
10 FT TRAY CLG

PORCH

KITCHEN
16-6 X 13-4
9 FT CLG

GREAT ROOM
17-4 X 20-4
10 FT TRAY CLG

DESK

BATH 2

LIN

UTIL
11-4 X 6-0
9 FT CLG

PAN

STORAGE

ARCH

BEDROOM 2
12-6 X 13-6
9 FT CLG

GARAGE

DINING ROOM
12-6 X 15-4
10 FT CLG

FOYER
2 STORY CLG

COPYRIGHT LARRY E. BELK

PORCH

New Design

HOT OFF THE DRAWING BOARD

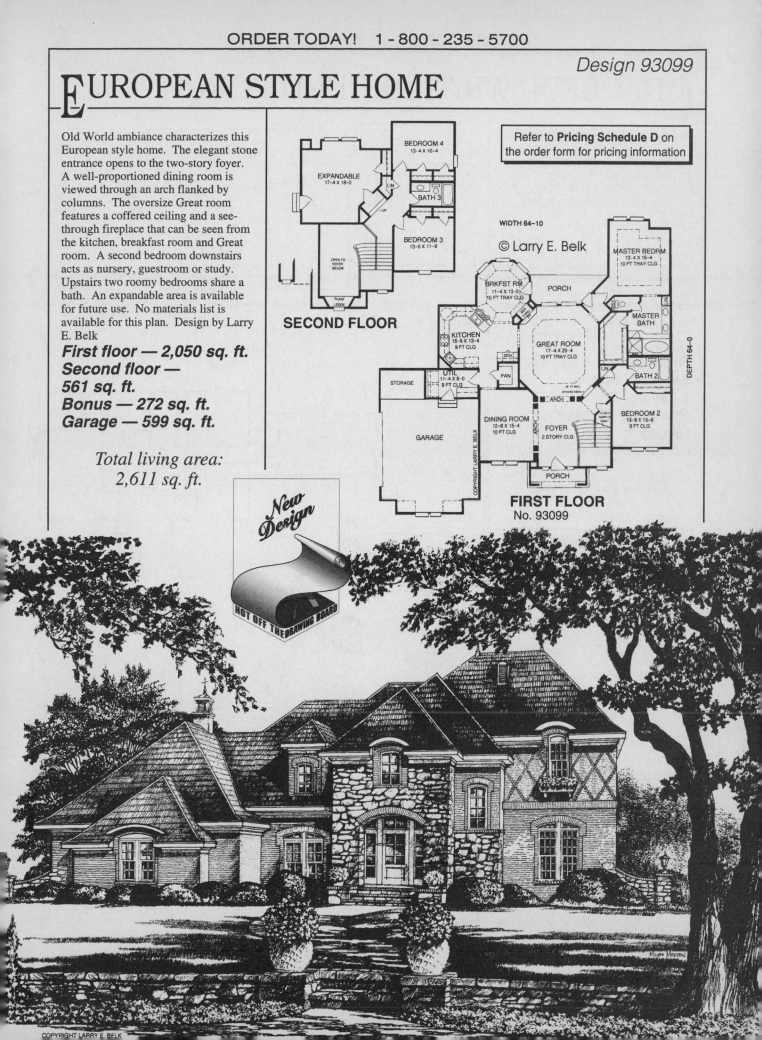

Design 98065

GRACEFUL WRAP-AROUND PORCH

Surrounded by a graceful wrap-around porch, this home boasts formal rooms in the front and an open casual area at the rear for family togetherness. The foyer, living room, and dining room welcome you into this gracious four bedroom farmhouse. The island kitchen and breakfast area with a bay window, are open to the family room with a fireplace and built-ins. The master suite features a tray ceiling, two walk-in closets, and a marvelous master bath. The recreation room/bedroom offers an optional fourth wall or railing for added openness. This plan also has a bonus room. Design by Donald A. Gardner Architects, Inc.

First floor — 1,454 sq. ft.
Second floor — 1,258 sq. ft.
Garage & Storage — 484 sq. ft.
Bonus room — 401 sq. ft.

Total living area: 2,712 sq. ft.

Refer to **Pricing Schedule F** on the order form for pricing information

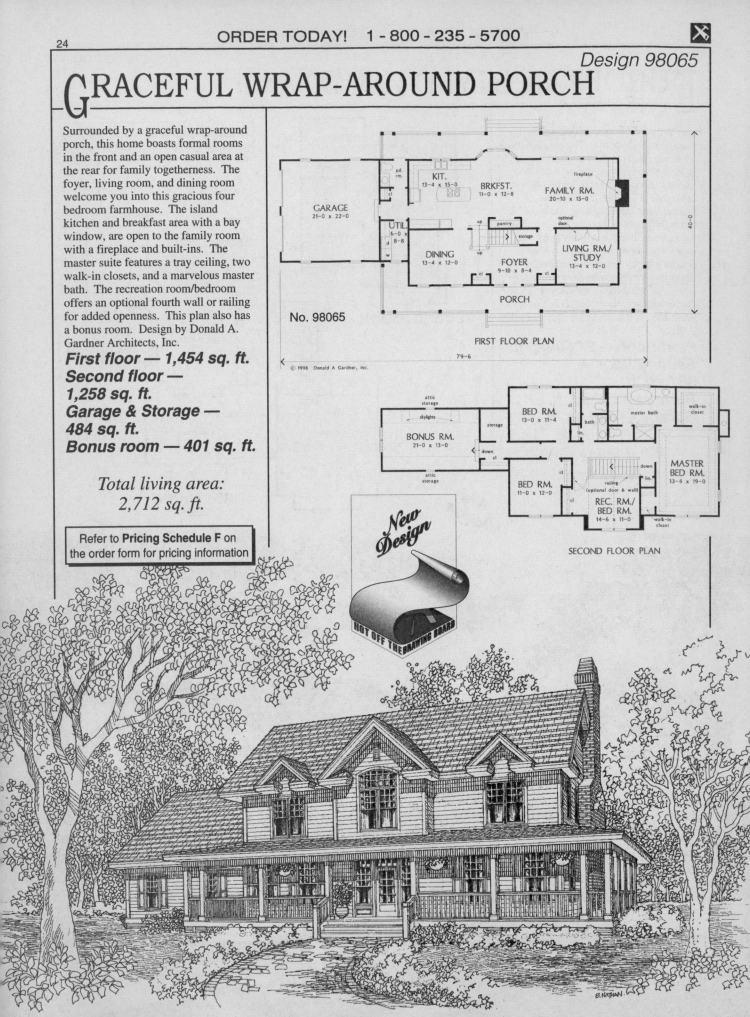

Design 97800

EASY, STEP-SAVING FLOOR PLAN

Stone and brick combine to create an elevation of distinction. The tiled entry directs traffic effortlessly into the living room or formal dining room. A short hall provides access to the study, three-quarter bath and master suite. The informal area, which is comprised of the kitchen, dining, and family room, is laid out in an open, airy format with an easy traffic flow between the rooms. The large fireplace in the family room is flanked by bookshelves. The master suite is located on the opposite side of the home from the secondary bedrooms for privacy. No materials list is available for this plan. Design by Fillmore Design Group

Main floor — 2,393 sq. ft.
Garage — 622 sq. ft.

Total living area:
2,393 sq. ft.

Refer to **Pricing Schedule D** on the order form for pricing information

New Design

HOT OFF THE DRAWING BOARD

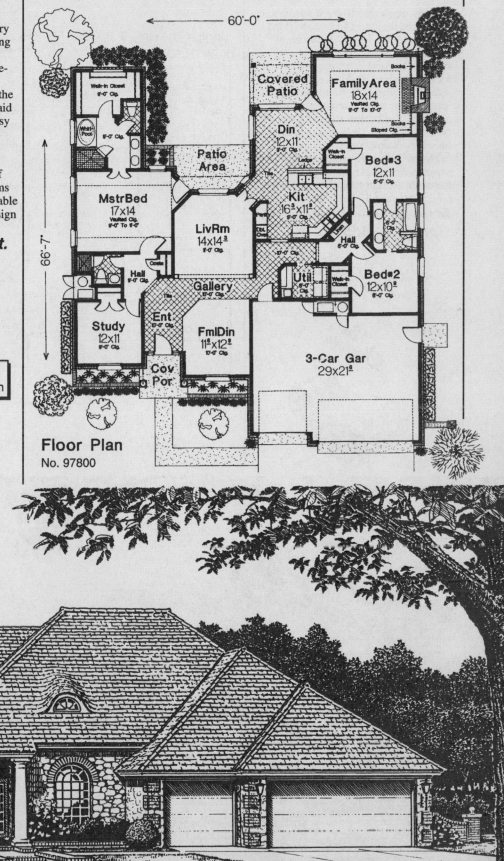

Floor Plan
No. 97800

Design 96601

FRENCH INFLUENCED DESIGN

Elegant appointments grace this French-influenced design. The interior of the home features a formal dining room with a ten-foot coffered, decorative ceiling. The oversize living room includes built-in bookcases on either side of the fireplace. An angled bar separates the kitchen and breakfast room and opens the kitchen to the living room beyond. The master bedroom includes a luxurious master bath with a huge walk-in closet, his-n-hers vanities, and separate whirlpool tub and shower. No materials list is available for this plan. Design by Larry E. Belk

Main floor — 1,890 sq. ft.
Garage — 565 sq. ft.

Total living area:
1,890 sq. ft.

New Design

HOT OFF THE DRAWING BOARD

WIDTH 65'-10"
DEPTH 53'-5"

© Larry E. Belk

Refer to **Pricing Schedule C** on the order form for pricing information

MASTER BATH

SEAT

PORCH

BRKFST RM
10-8 X 11-8
10 FT CLG

UTIL
8-0 X 5-8

STORAGE

STORAGE

MASTER BEDRM
14-4 X 15-6
10 FT CLG

FP

BUILT INS

BUILT INS

SLOPE

LIVING ROOM
17-4 X 15-8
10 FT CLG

KITCHEN
10-8 X 13-6
10 FT CLG

PAN

42" EDGE

GARAGE

COPYRIGHT LARRY E. BELK

BATH 2

LIN

PORCH

SLOPE

BEDROOM 2
12-6 X 11-6

BEDROOM 3
12-0 X 13-4
10 FT CLG

FOYER
10 FT CLG

DINING ROOM
11-0 X 13-0
10 FT COFFERED CLG

PORCH

No. 96601
MAIN FLOOR

Design 93096

EUROPEAN STYLED HOME

Designed for a pie-shaped or corner lot, this European styled home is a stunner from every angle. The two-story foyer opens to the spacious two-story Great room beyond. The kitchen features an angled sink with a window above for views to the rear yard. A large gourmet island has room for a cooktop and plenty of workspace. The breakfast room is a sunny bay. The master suite opens to a covered rear porch and includes a luxury bath with his-n-her closets, a corner whirlpool tub and a separate shower. A second bedroom and bath are conveniently located on the first floor and can be used as a guest suite, nursery or home office/study. An expandable area is available over the two-car garage. No materials list is available for this plan. Design by Larry E. Belk

First floor — 2,009 sq. ft.
Second floor — 913 sq. ft.
Bonus room — 192 sq. ft.
Garage — 622 sq. ft.

Total living area:
2,922 sq. ft.

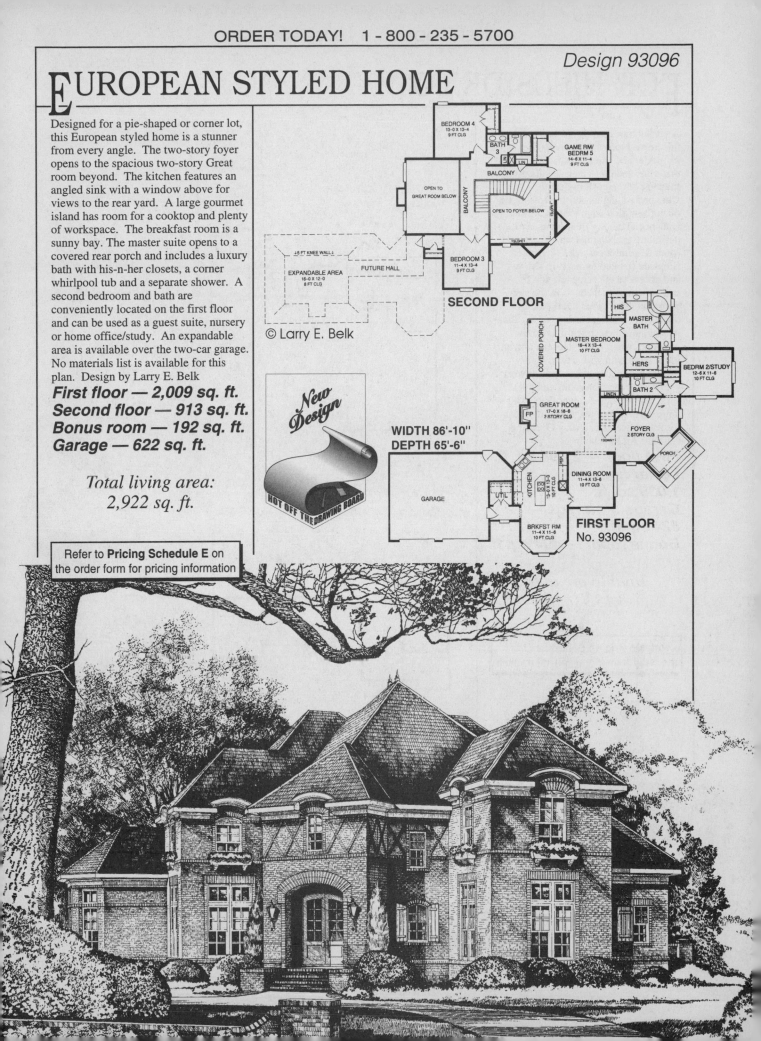

SECOND FLOOR

BEDROOM 4
13-0 X 13-4
9 FT CLG

BATH 3

GAME RM/ BEDRM 5
14-6 X 11-4
9 FT CLG

BALCONY

OPEN TO GREAT ROOM BELOW

OPEN TO FOYER BELOW

BEDROOM 3
11-4 X 13-4
9 FT CLG

5 FT KNEE WALL

EXPANDABLE AREA
16-0 X 12-0
8 FT CLG

FUTURE HALL

© Larry E. Belk

New Design
HOT OFF THE DRAWING BOARD

WIDTH 86'-10"
DEPTH 65'-6"

FIRST FLOOR
No. 93096

COVERED PORCH

HIS

MASTER BATH

MASTER BEDROOM
16-4 X 13-4
10 FT CLG

HERS

BEDRM 2/STUDY
12-6 X 11-6
10 FT CLG

LINEN

BATH 2

GREAT ROOM
17-0 X 18-6
2 STORY CLG

FP

FOYER
2 STORY CLG

PORCH

GARAGE

UTIL

KITCHEN
13-0 X 13-6
10 FT CLG

DINING ROOM
11-4 X 13-6
10 FT CLG

BRKFST RM
11-4 X 11-6
10 FT CLG

Design 98070

FOR HILLSIDE LOTS

A partial basement foundation makes this home perfect for hillside lots, while its mixture of exterior building materials and craftsman details give it the look of the custom design. Unexpected angles add interest to the open floor plan where interior columns and special ceiling treatments create definition and distinction. The Great room features a cathedral ceiling, a fireplace flanked by built-in shelves, and access to the screened porch. A convenient pass-through in the step-saving kitchen keeps everyone connected. A tray ceiling refines the master suite, which features a bay window, twin walk-in closets, and an impressive bath with a dual vanity, garden tub and an oversized shower. A generous recreation room and guest suite comprises the lower floor, and a large bonus room provides ample space for future use. Design by Donald A. Gardner Architects, Inc.

First floor — 2,094 sq. ft.
Lower floor — 1,038 sq. ft.
Garage & storage — 624 sq. ft.
Bonus room — 494 sq. ft.

Total living area:
3,132 sq. ft.

Refer to **Pricing Schedule G** on the order form for pricing information

FIRST FLOOR PLAN

SCREEN PORCH 15-6 x 14-0

DECK

BRKFST. 10-0 x 9-0

KITCHEN 12-0 x 12-0

GREAT RM. 19-0 x 16-0 (cathedral ceiling)

MASTER BED RM. 16-4 x 13-4

BED RM./STUDY 12-4 x 12-10

walk-in closet   walk-in closet

DINING 12-0 x 14-0

FOYER 6-0 x 11-10

master bath

BED RM. 12-4 x 11-0

UTIL. 8-4 x 9-0

PORCH

GARAGE 22-8 x 22-6

storage

© 1998 Donald A Gardner, Inc.

attic storage   down

BONUS RM. 16-4 x 24-10

BASEMENT FLOOR PLAN
No. 98070

PATIO

SITTING 11-1 x 8-0

REC. ROOM 26-9 x 16-2

STORAGE (unfinished)

BED RM. 16-5 x 11-6

fireplace

walk-in closet

bath

MECHANICAL 36-8 x 13-4

STORAGE (unfinished)

New Design

HOT OFF THE DRAWING BOARD

©1998 Donald A. Gardner, Inc.

Design 97722

SPLENDOR AND HOSPITALITY

A screened porch combined with textured finishes on the exterior create a home that showcases the splendor and hospitality found inside. A Great room with a fireplace and an eighteen-foot ceiling height and dining room with a furniture alcove are perfect for entertaining guests; while the kitchen, breakfast area and hearth room arrangement creates an enjoyable family gathering place. The first floor master bedroom suite, with a deluxe bath is topped with a raised ceiling treatment. An open stairway decorated with a rich wood rail leads to the second floor balcony. No materials list is available for this plan. Design by Studer Residential Design, Inc.

First floor — 2,045 sq. ft.
Second floor — 919 sq. ft.
Basement — 2,045 sq. ft.
Garage — 526 sq. ft.

Total living area: 2,964 sq. ft.

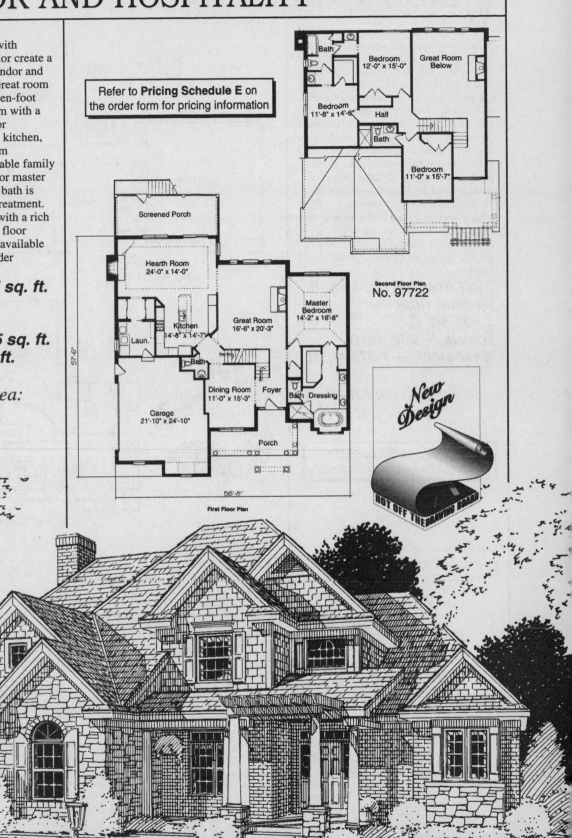

Refer to **Pricing Schedule E** on the order form for pricing information

Second Floor Plan
No. 97722

First Floor Plan

New Design
HOT OFF THE DRAWING BOARD

Design 98204

WINDOWS ABOUND

This spacious and elegant plan features four bedrooms and three full baths, including a well-appointed master suite. The foyer opens to the dining room and the grand salon, which is highlighted by a fireplace. The kitchen enjoys all amenities including a center island and a morning room. The library could easily become a guest bedroom with a bathroom just steps away. The plush master suite enjoys an abundance of storage space by having two-walk in closets, and a lavish master bath. This plan is available with a basement or slab foundation. Please specify when ordering. No materials list is available for this plan. Design by Archival Designs

First floor — 1,375 sq. ft.
Second floor — 1,087 sq. ft.
Bonus — 286 sq. ft.
Basement — 1,375 sq. ft.

Total living area: 2,462 sq. ft.

Refer to **Pricing Schedule D** on the order form for pricing information

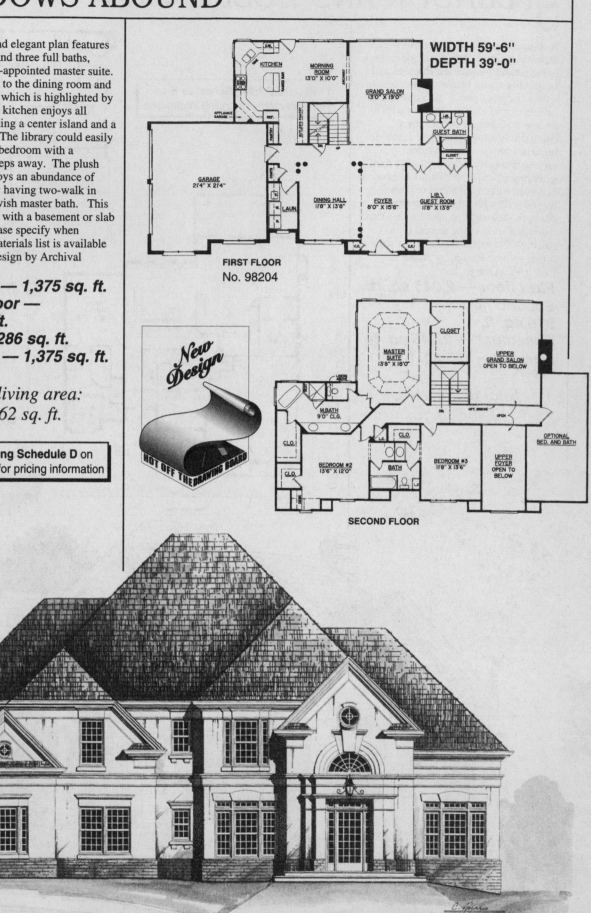

WIDTH 59'-6"
DEPTH 39'-0"

FIRST FLOOR
No. 98204

SECOND FLOOR

Design 93098

DOUBLE ARCHES ADD ELEGANCE

Double arches form the entrance to this elegantly styled home. Two palladian windows add distinction to the elevation and give the home a timeless appeal. Inside, ten foot ceilings in all major living areas give the home an expansive feeling. The kitchen features an angled eating bar that opens the kitchen to both the breakfast room and living room. The master suite includes a master bath with all the amenities including a huge walk-in closet. No materials list is available for this plan. Design by Larry E. Belk

Main floor — 1,932 sq. ft.
Garage — 552 sq. ft.

Total living area:
1,932 sq. ft.

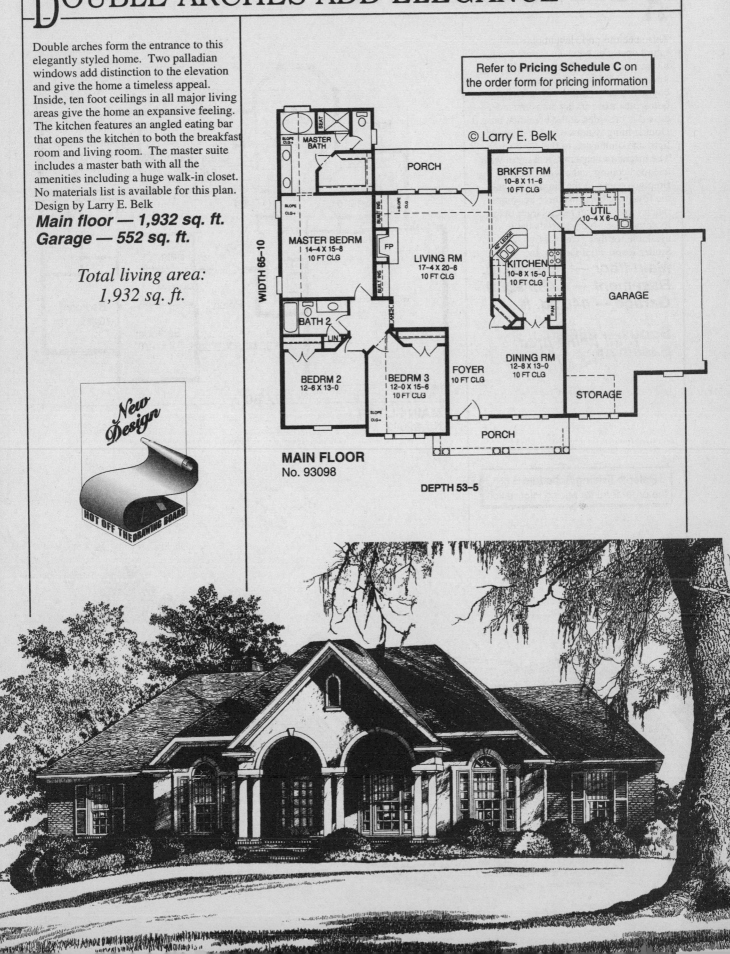

© Larry E. Belk

MAIN FLOOR
No. 93098

DEPTH 53–5

A COZY FRONT PORCH

An enchanting one level home with grand openings between rooms creates a spacious effect. The functional kitchen provides an abundance of counter space. Additional room for quick meals or serving an oversized crowd is provided at the breakfast bar. Double hung windows and angles add light and dimension to the dining area. The bright and cheery Great room with a sloped ceiling and a wood burning fireplace opens to the dining area and the foyer, making this three bedroom ranch look and feel much larger than its actual size. No materials list is available for this plan. Design by Studer Residential Design, Inc.

Main floor — 1,508 sq. ft.
Basement — 1,439 sq. ft.
Garage — 440 sq. ft.

Total living area:
1,508 sq. ft.

Refer to **Pricing Schedule B** on the order form for pricing information

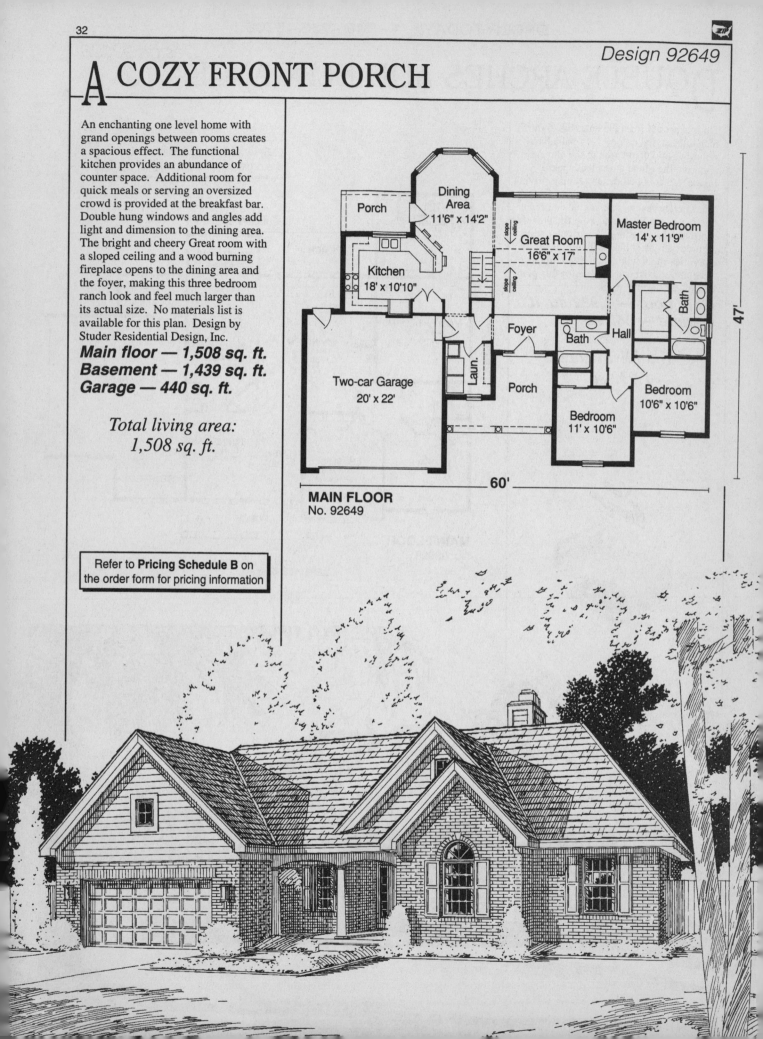

MAIN FLOOR
No. 92649

Porch

Dining Area
11'6" x 14'2"

Great Room
16'6" x 17'

Master Bedroom
14' x 11'9"

slope ceiling

Kitchen
18' x 10'10"

Bath

Two-car Garage
20' x 22'

Laun.

Foyer

Bath

Hall

Porch

Bedroom
11' x 10'6"

Bedroom
10'6" x 10'6"

47'

60'

STUCCO AND STONE EXTERIOR

Design 98419

The vaulted Great room unfolds directly in front of the entry. The kitchen includes a built-in pantry and a radius window above the double sink. The breakfast bay is crowned by a vaulted ceiling. A cozy fireplace accents the master suite. A tray ceiling adds interest to the bedroom and sitting area of the suite, while a vaulted ceiling tops the bath. An optional bonus room is included for future expansion. This plan is available with a basement, slab or crawl space foundation. Please specify when ordering. No materials list is available for this plan. Design by Frank Betz Associates, Inc.

First floor — 1,796 sq. ft.
Second floor — 629 sq. ft.
Bonus room — 208 sq. ft.
Basement — 1,796 sq. ft.
Garage — 588 sq. ft.

Total living area: 2,425 sq. ft.

WIDTH 54'-0"
DEPTH 53'-10"

© Frank Betz Associates

No. 98419

Refer to **Pricing Schedule E** on the order form for pricing information

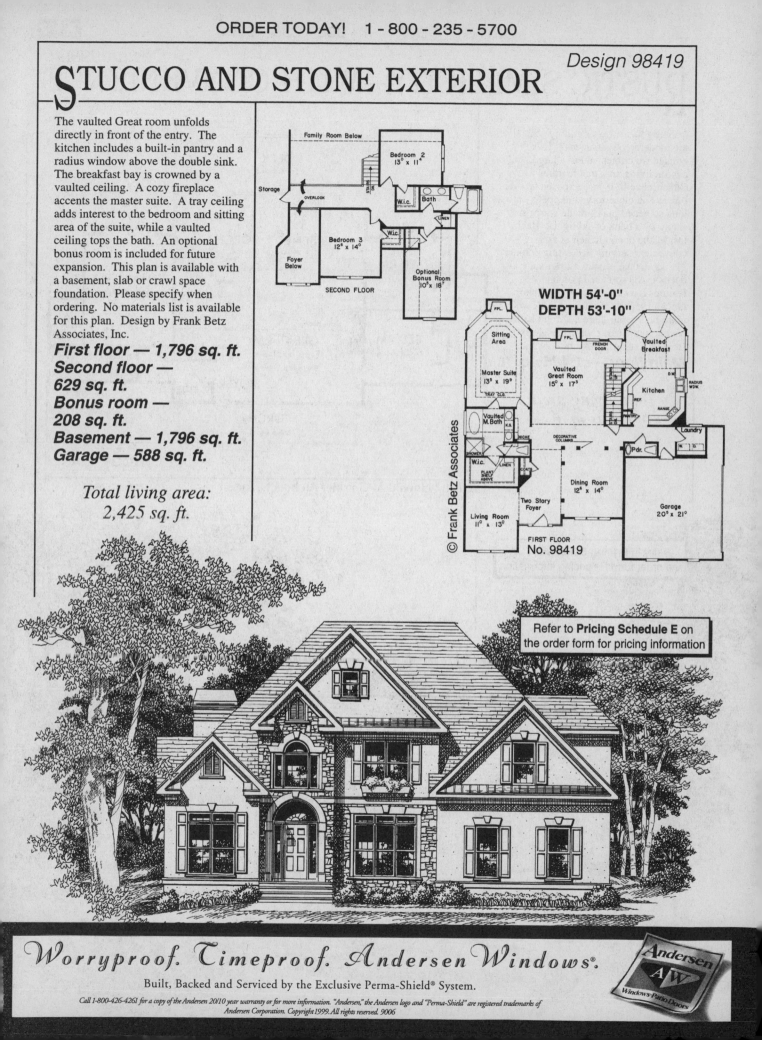

Rustic Simplicity—With Convenience

Looking for rustic simplicity with all the modern conveniences? This cottage welcomes you to a large, central living area that features a cathedral ceiling with exposed wood beams and clerestory, and opens onto a long screened porch made warm and sunny by a bank of skylights. Back inside, the open kitchen boasts a convenient serving and eating counter. The generous, private master suite also opens to the screened porch and features a walk-in closet, whirlpool tub, and separate water closet. Two more bedrooms share a second bath beyond the Great room. Design by Donald A. Gardner Architects, Inc.

Main floor — 1,426 sq. ft.

Total living area:
1,426 sq. ft.

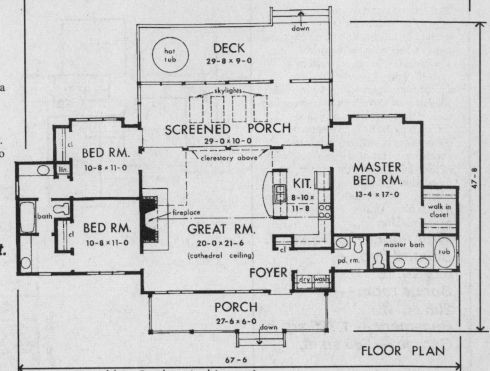

© 1987 Donald A. Gardner Architects, Inc.   No. 99864

Refer to **Pricing Schedule C** on the order form for pricing information

© 1987 Donald A. Gardner Architects, Inc.

Design 93075

TIMELESS APPEAL

Timeless appeal is the hallmark of this traditional elevation complete with a roomy front porch. Inside, ten-foot ceilings give the living room an open feel. The living room also includes a cozy corner fireplace and access to the rear yard. The dining area features a sunny bay window and is open to the kitchen. Bedrooms are conveniently grouped and include roomy closets. The master bedroom features a private bath. The garage is located at the rear and not visible from the front. This plan is available with a crawl space or slab foundation. Please specify when ordering. No materials list is available for this plan. Design by Larry E. Belk

Main floor — 1,170 sq. ft.
Garage — 478 sq. ft.

Total living area:
1,170 sq. ft.

Refer to **Pricing Schedule A** on the order form for pricing information

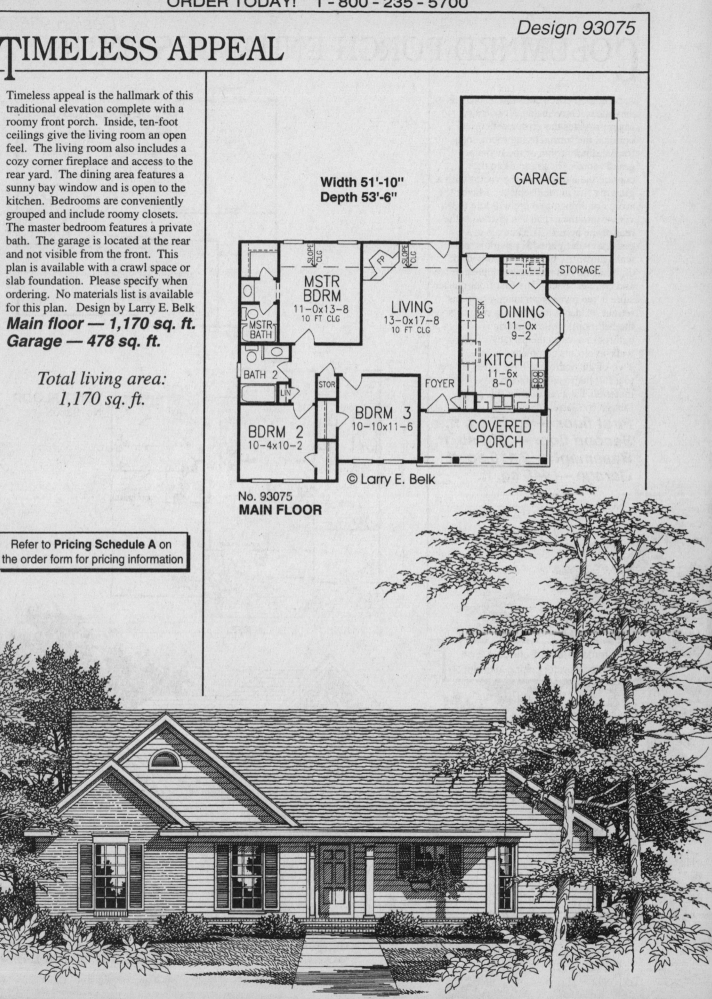

Width 51'-10"
Depth 53'-6"

GARAGE

STORAGE

MSTR BDRM
11-0x13-8
10 FT CLG

LIVING
13-0x17-8
10 FT CLG

DINING
11-0x
9-2

MSTR BATH

DESK

KITCH
11-6x
8-0

BATH 2

LIN

STOR

FOYER

BDRM 3
10-10x11-6

BDRM 2
10-4x10-2

COVERED PORCH

© Larry E. Belk

No. 93075
MAIN FLOOR

Design 93603

COLUMNED PORCH ENHANCES ENTRY

A columned porch adds interest to this elevation. Once inside, a two-story foyer provides the visitor with three options; the formal living room, the formal dining room or the two-story grand room. The grand room may capture the attention of the visitor with a glowing fire in the fireplace. Maybe the aroma of dinner cooking will lure the visitor into the expansive kitchen at the rear of the house. The kitchen is a gourmet's delight with a work island, walk-in pantry, built-in planning desk, double sink and more than ample cabinet and counter space. The first floor master suite is the owners personal, luxurious retreat. A decorative ceiling enhances the bedroom, while a luxurious bathroom adds to the privacy. Two walk-in closets complete the suite. Two of the bedrooms have direct access to a full bath with double vanity. No materials list available for this plan. Design by Garrell Associates, Inc.

First floor — 2,115 sq. ft.
Second floor — 914 sq. ft.
Basement — 2,115 sq. ft.
Garage — 448 sq. ft.

Total living area:
3,029 sq. ft.

Refer to **Pricing Schedule E** on the order form for pricing information

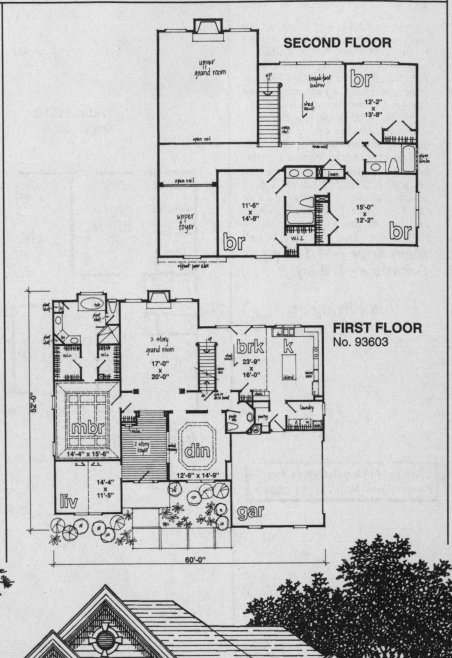

SECOND FLOOR

FIRST FLOOR
No. 93603

Design 91748

CHEERFUL AND SUNNY

The cheerful aspect comes in the form of brick planters filled with colorful flowers that flank the front walkway. Every room has at least one large window, but the sunroom is the brightest. It has seven skylights, three large windows, and French doors. In winter, when the sky is dark the tile-hearth fireplace takes over as the focal point. The large country kitchen is also skylit and vaulted. A central work island adds to the already ample counter space. One wall of shelves in the huge walk-in pantry is directly accessible from the kitchen. A small bathroom is just around the corner, conveniently close to the garage as well. Sleeping quarters are clustered together on the left side of the home. The master suite has a private bathroom with oversized shower. Other luxury features include an extra-large walk-in closet and a skylit dressing area with a vanity outside the bathroom. Design by Landmark Designs, Inc.

Main area — 2,533 sq. ft.
Garage — 724 sq. ft.

Total living area:
2,533 sq. ft.

Refer to **Pricing Schedule D** on the order form for pricing information

WIDTH 75'-0"
DEPTH 76'-0"

MASTER SUITE
17⁰ X 16⁰

FAMILY
17⁰ X 17⁰

LIVING
18⁰ X 14⁰
VAULTED CEILING

DINING
12² X 11⁰
VAULTED CEILING

PANTRY

NOOK
13⁵ X 8⁵

LINEN

F.A.U.

BED 3
11⁸ X 11⁸

BED 2
11⁰ X 13²

GARDEN WINDOW

MAIN AREA
No. 91748

GARAGE
23⁴ X 24⁰

Design 97216

TWO-STORY FAMILY ROOM

A wrap-around porch highlights the exterior of this home and adds to the curb appeal. The two-story foyer features a second floor window offering natural illumination. The living room and the dining room are located to either side of the foyer. A butler's pantry divides the dining room and kitchen. An open rail separates the family room from the breakfast room. The fireplace and French door to the porch highlight the family room while the breakfast room has another French door to the rear yard and a walk-in pantry. The second floor houses the bedrooms. The master bedroom is topped by a tray ceiling and a vaulted ceiling tops the master bath. An optional sitting room expands the suite even further. The three additional bedrooms have ample storage space and share the double vanity hall bath. No materials list is available for this plan. Design by Frank Betz Associates, Inc.

First floor — 1,351 sq. ft.
Second floor — 1,257 sq. ft.
Bonus room — 115 sq. ft.
Basement — 1,351 sq. ft.
Garage — 511 sq. ft.

Total living area: 2,608 sq. ft.

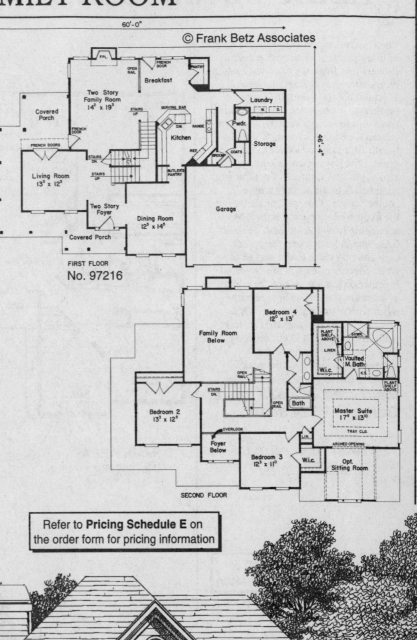

© Frank Betz Associates

FIRST FLOOR
No. 97216

SECOND FLOOR

Refer to **Pricing Schedule E** on the order form for pricing information

FAMILY HOME WITH BEDROOM TOWER

Sloping ceilings and open spaces characterize this four-bedroom home. The dining room off the foyer adjoins the breakfast room and the convenient island kitchen. The beamed living room is crowned by a balcony overlook that links the upstairs bedrooms. The vaulted first floor master suite features a private deck, a walk-in closet and a full bath with a double vanity. Design by The Garlinghouse Company

First floor — 1,496 sq. ft.
Second floor — 520 sq. ft.
Basement — 1,487 sq. ft.
Garage — 424 sq. ft.

Total living area:
2,016 sq. ft.

Refer to **Pricing Schedule C** on the order form for pricing information

FIRST FLOOR
No. 34049

SECOND FLOOR

Design 92642

AN EXTRAORDINARY HOME

Upon entering the foyer, your view will go directly to the cozy fireplace and stylish French doors of the Great room. A grand entry into the formal dining room, coupled with the volume ceiling, pulls these two rooms together for a spacious feeling. From the roomy, well-equipped kitchen, there is a pass-through to the Great room. Natural light will flood the breakfast area through large windows. Located between the first floor master bedroom suite and the garage is the laundry, adding convenience and protecting the living areas from noise and disorder. Split stairs, graced with wood railings, lead to the versatile second floor with two additional bedrooms. No materials list is available for this plan. Design by Studer Residential Design, Inc.

First floor — 1,524 sq. ft.
Second floor — 558 sq. ft.
Basement — 1,460 sq. ft.
Bonus room — 267 sq. ft.

Total living area: 2,082 sq. ft.

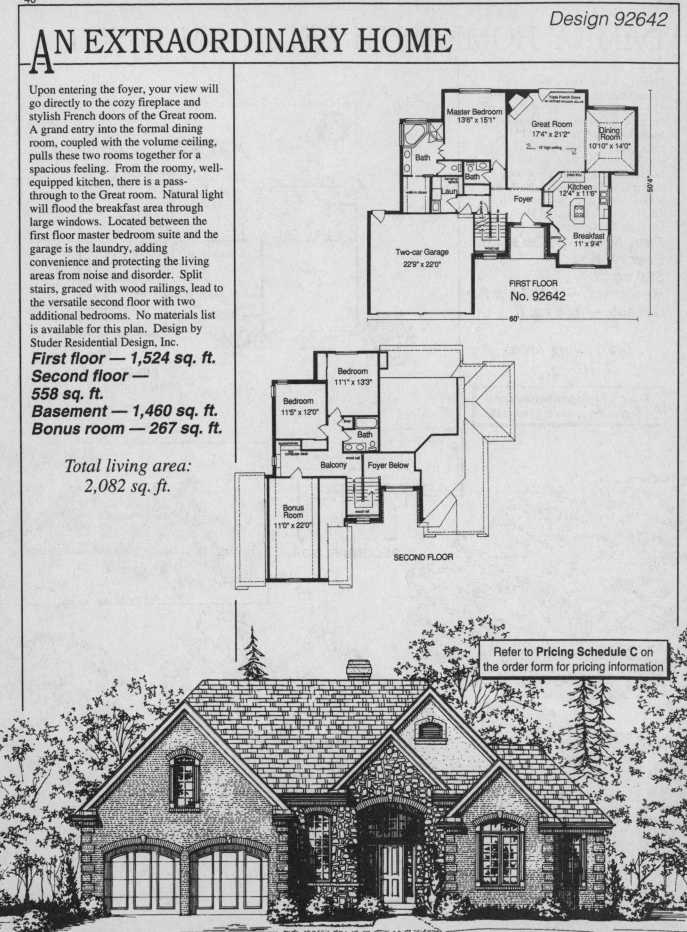

Refer to **Pricing Schedule C** on the order form for pricing information

Spectacular Volume Entry

Design 99464

The spectacular volume entry of this home has a curving staircase and defining columns leading into a sunken living room. The living room is enhanced by a fireplace, bowed window and a wetbar. There is another elegant bowed window in the formal dining room and built-in hutch space. Informal family living is highlighted in the open layout between the breakfast, kitchen and family rooms. The dramatic kitchen is equipped with a large snack bar, pantry and desk. Double doors open into the volume master suite on the main level with a private back patio door, oval whirlpool and large walk-in closet. A beautiful arched window in each secondary bedroom add natural light and elegance and completing the rooms are generous closets and bath arrangements. Design by Design Basics, Inc.

First floor — 2,617 sq. ft.
Second floor —
1,072 sq. ft
Basement — 2,617 sq. ft.
Garage — 1,035 sq. ft.

Total living area:
3,689 sq. ft.

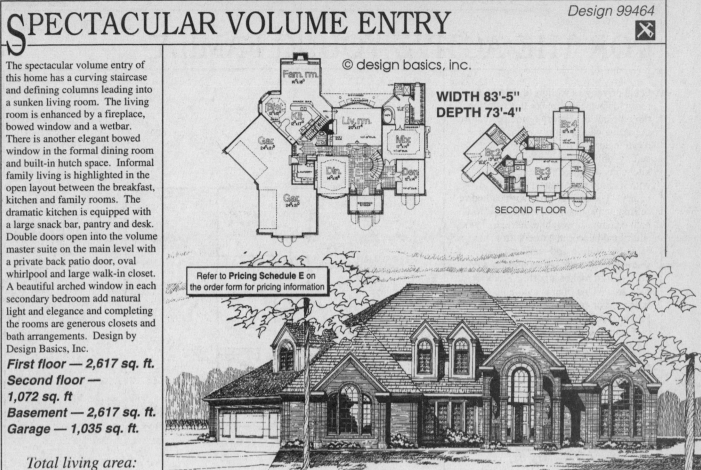

© design basics, inc.

WIDTH 83'-5"
DEPTH 73'-4"

SECOND FLOOR

Refer to **Pricing Schedule E** on the order form for pricing information

© 1990 design basics inc.

Exciting Mixture

Design 98007

An exciting mixture of styles, this home blends the wrapping porch of a country farmhouse with a brick and siding exterior, creating a unique and pleasing effect. The great room shares its cathedral ceiling with a distinctly open and unusual kitchen, while the octagonal shaped formal dining room is complemented by a splendid tray ceiling. Built-ins flank the Great room's fireplace for added convenience. The master suite is decked out with a tray ceiling, arched picture window, back porch access, private bath, and sizable walk-in closet. Another full bath with linen closet is shared by two bedrooms and a bedroom/study that shines with a palladian window and a graceful tray ceiling. Design by Donald A. Gardner Architects, Inc.

Main floor — 2,273 sq. ft.
Bonus room —
342 sq. ft.
Garage — 528 sq. ft.

Total living area:
2,273 sq. ft.

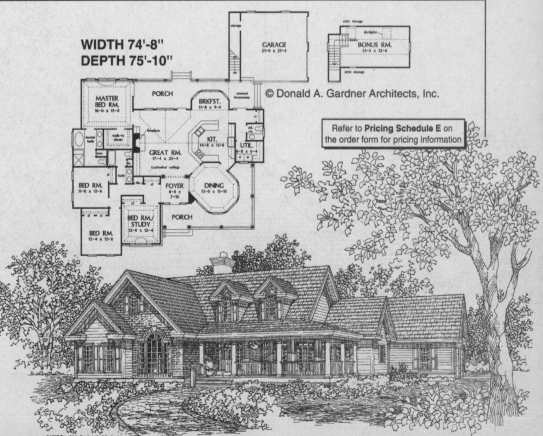

WIDTH 74'-8"
DEPTH 75'-10"

© Donald A. Gardner Architects, Inc.

Refer to **Pricing Schedule E** on the order form for pricing information

Design 99805

FOR THE ACTIVE YOUNG FAMILY

Great privacy as well as an open Great room for gathering make this exciting three bedroom country home perfect for the active young family. The Great room features a fireplace, cathedral ceiling, and built-in bookshelves. The kitchen is designed for efficient use with its food preparation island and pantry. The master suite with cathedral ceiling, walk-in closet, and a luxurious bath provides a welcome retreat. Two additional bedrooms, one with a cathedral ceiling and walk-in closet, share a skylit bath. A second floor bonus room makes a perfect study or play area. This plan is available with a basement or crawl space foundation. Please specify when ordering. Design by Donald A. Gardner Architects, Inc.

Main floor — 1,787 sq. ft.
Garage — 521 sq. ft.
Bonus room—
326 sq. ft.

Total living area:
1,787 sq. ft.

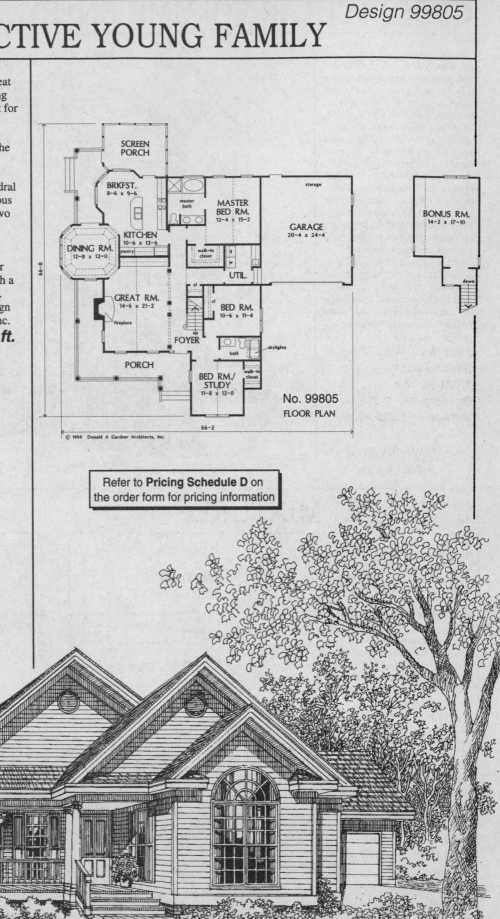

No. 99805
FLOOR PLAN

© 1994 Donald A Gardner Architects, Inc.

Refer to **Pricing Schedule D** on the order form for pricing information

© 1994 Donald A Gardner Architects, Inc.

PLENTY OF ROOM TO SPREAD OUT

This bright and spacious, five-bedroom, two-story home provides plenty of room to spread out. Family living areas, the master suite and an office are downstairs. Four more bedrooms and the utility room are on the upper level. In the kitchen, a work island with grill and vegetable sink provides additional counter space. The eating nook is brightened by the adjacent skylit sun room. Windows fill most of the back wall of the family room. The master suite has a huge walk-in closet, oversized shower, and twin basins in a long vanity. French doors open onto a small private deck. Design by Landmark Designs, Inc.

First floor — 2,037 sq. ft.
Second floor — 1,178 sq. ft.
Basement — 2,037 sq. ft.
Garage — 955 sq. ft.

Total living area: 3,215 sq. ft.

Refer to **Pricing Schedule F** on the order form for pricing information

WIDTH 89'-0"
DEPTH 61'-0"

SECOND FLOOR
No. 91764

FIRST FLOOR

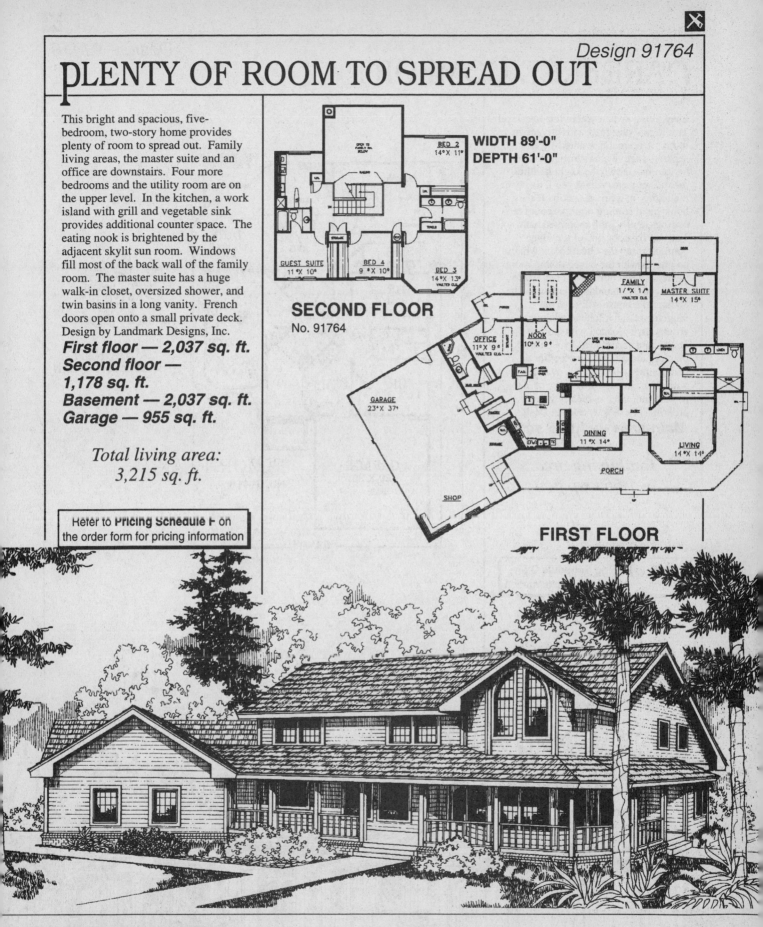

CAREFREE COMFORT

Easy living awaits you in this one-level Traditional designed with privacy in mind. A dramatic, vaulted-foyer separates active areas from the three bedrooms. Down the skylit hall lies the master suite, where you'll discover the luxury of a private patio off the book-lined reading nook, decorative ceilings, and a well-appointed bath. The soaring roof line of the foyer continues into the Great room, which combines with the bayed dining room to create a celebration of open space enhanced by abundant windows. The cook in the house will love the rangetop island kitchen and nook arrangement, loaded with storage inside, and surrounded by a built-in planter outside that's perfect for an herb garden. This plan is available with a basement, crawl space or slab foundation. Please specify when ordering. Design by Sun-tel Design

Main area — 1,665 sq. ft.

Total living area:
1,665 sq. ft.

Refer to **Pricing Schedule B** on the order form for pricing information

FLOOR PLAN
No. 91418

- PATIO
- READING
- BOOKS
- VAULTED MBR 16/6 X 14 AVG
- W1 CLO
- MB
- BR 11 X 9/6
- BATH
- BR 11 X 9/6
- UTIL
- VAULTED FOYER
- COVERED PATIO
- VAULTED GREAT ROOM 22 X 24 AVG
- DINE 10 X 12 AVG
- KIT
- BAR
- NOOK 10/6 X 9/6
- PLANTER
- GARAGE 20 X 20

65'-0"
44'-0"

ALTERNATE BASEMENT PLAN
UTIL

HIGH IMPACT TWO STORY

Gracious living abounds in this four bedroom upscale 1-1/2 story home, where the family room becomes the focus of intersecting activities. Its high impact effect comes from its two story entry with double doors and transom. As you enter you see the fireplace/window walls of the large two story family room. The master suite is quite spacious and unique with curved glass block behind the tub in the master bath. The sitting area in the master suite has a semi-circular window wall and see-thru fireplace, perfect for romantic, cozy evenings. Entertaining is a joy in the gourmet kitchen and breakfast area that opens to a covered lanai. If your guest decides to stay the night, the guest suite is more than accommodating. It is not only spacious, but features a private deck and walk-in closet. The secondary bedrooms share a bath. Design by Lifestyles Home Design

Main floor — 3,158 sq. ft.
Upper floor —
1,374 sq. ft.
Garage — 758 sq. ft.

Total living area:
4,532 sq. ft.

Refer to **Pricing Schedule F** on the order form for pricing information

Upper Floor
No. 99373

Deck
open to below
Guest Br 14x19
Br 3 14x15
Br 2 13x14

Main Floor

112'-0"
83'-8"

Sitting 15-4x13
Family Room 33-8x23 2 story dlg
Kitchen 17-4x14
Lanai
Master Suite 16x21-4
shelves
Living Rm 14x16-4
Brkfst 11x16
Dining 15x15-8
service entrance
Garage 35x21-8

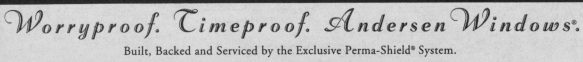

Design 99806

TREMENDOUS CURB APPEAL

This one-story home offers tremendous curb appeal and many extras usually found in much larger homes. From the friendly front wrap porch, you enter an open, volume space that takes in the Great room with fireplace, dining room, and kitchen. The kitchen features a pantry, skylight, and peninsula counter for easy food preparation and service to the screened porch and deck. The master suite opens up with a cathedral ceiling, and is pampered by walk-in and linen closets, a private bath including garden tub and a double vanity. The front swing room topped by a cathedral ceiling makes a stunning first impression. Design by Donald A. Gardner Architects, Inc.

Main floor — 1,246 sq. ft.
Garage — 420 sq. ft.

Total living area:
1,246 sq. ft.

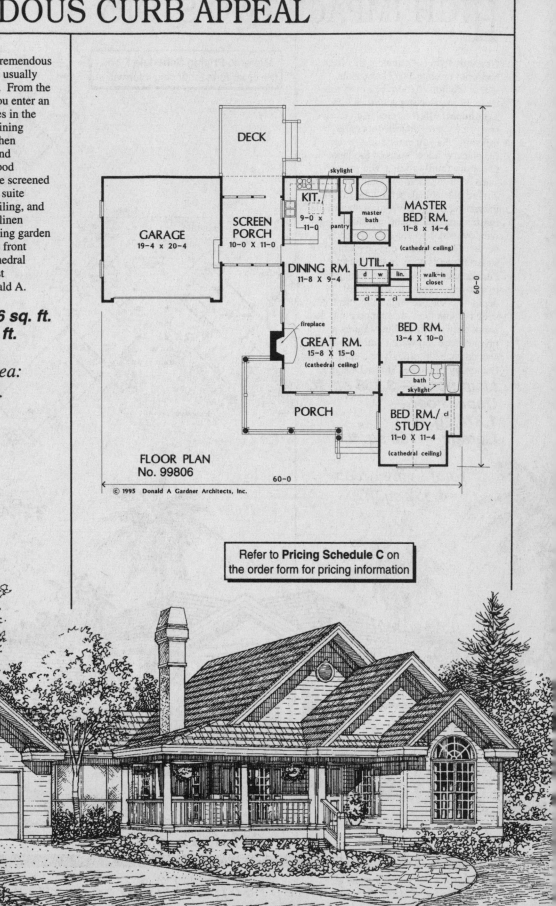

FLOOR PLAN
No. 99806

© 1995 Donald A Gardner Architects, Inc.

Refer to **Pricing Schedule C** on the order form for pricing information

B. NATHAN

© 1995 Donald A Gardner Architects, Inc.

OPEN AND AIRY

Design 93413

A Country porch leads to a foyer naturally lit by a dormer window above. The family room is to the right of the foyer. A fireplace and two front windows highlight the room. The kitchen features an angled extended counter/snack bar and an abundance of counter and cabinet space. The dining area is open to the kitchen. The roomy master suite is located on the first floor and includes a private five-piece bath and a walk-in closet. The laundry room can easily be used as a mudroom from the side entrance. No materials list is available with this plan. Design by Greg Marquis and Associates

First floor — 1,271 sq. ft.
Second floor —
537 sq. ft.
Basement — 1,271 sq. ft.
Garage — 555 sq. ft.

Total living area:
1,808 sq. ft.

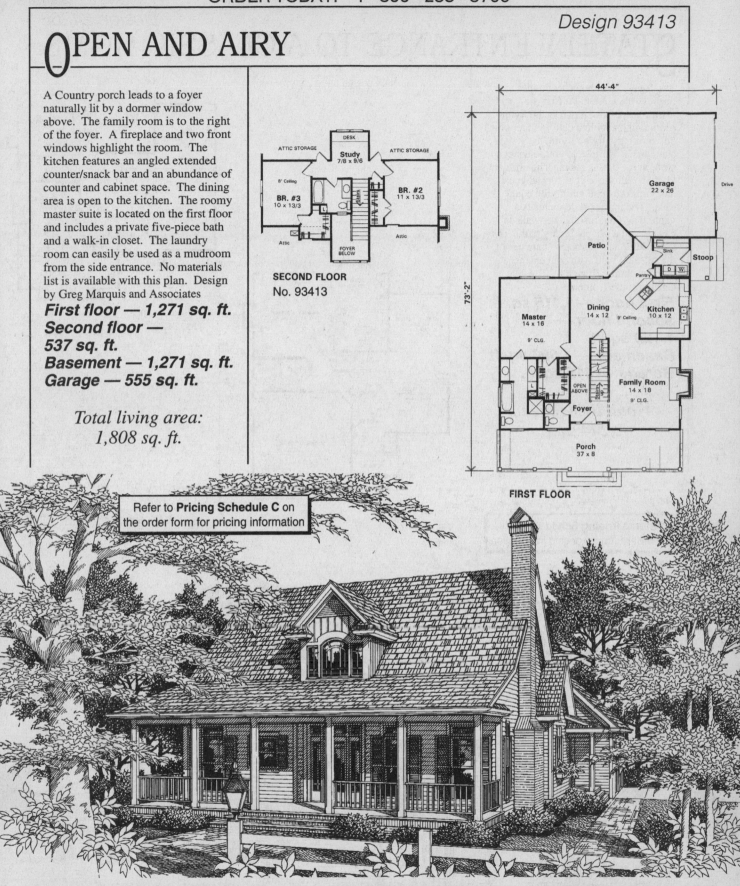

SECOND FLOOR
No. 93413

FIRST FLOOR

Refer to **Pricing Schedule C** on the order form for pricing information

Design 24268

STATELY ENTRANCE TO A CLASSIC HOME

The foyer of the house continues to impress the visitor. At first the visitor's eyes are drawn to the living room and its vaulted ceiling. Stepping down into the living room, the visitor can catch a glimpse of your elegant table in the dining room. The efficient kitchen will serve your formal guest and your informal guest with equal ease. The master suite includes a vaulted ceiling, his-and-her walk-in closets and a private luxury bath. The two additional bedrooms share use of the full hall bath with convenient laundry chute. Design by The Garlinghouse Company

First floor — 1,115 sq. ft.
Second floor — 1,129 sq. ft.
Basement — 1,096 sq. ft.
Garage — 415 sq. ft.

Total living area: 2,244 sq. ft.

Refer to **Pricing Schedule D** on the order form for pricing information

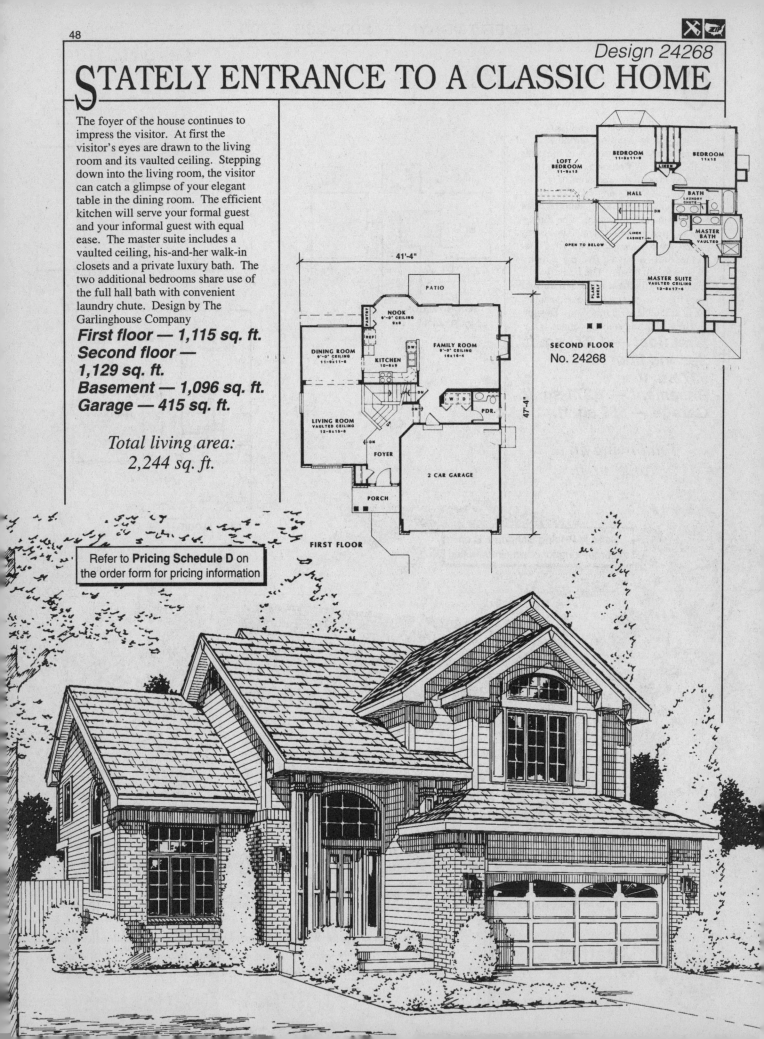

SECOND FLOOR
No. 24268

LOFT / BEDROOM 11-9x13

BEDROOM 11-9x11-8

BEDROOM 11x12

HALL

BATH

MASTER BATH VAULTED

OPEN TO BELOW

LINEN CABINET

MASTER SUITE VAULTED CEILING 12-8x17-6

PLANT SHELF

FIRST FLOOR

41'-4"

47'-4"

PATIO

NOOK 9'-0" CEILING 9x8

DINING ROOM 9'-0" CEILING 11-9x11-6

KITCHEN 10-6x9

FAMILY ROOM 9'-0" CEILING 19x16-4

LIVING ROOM VAULTED CEILING 12-8x15-8

FOYER

PDR.

2 CAR GARAGE

PORCH

RANCH PROVIDES GREAT KITCHEN

There's a lot of convenience packed into this affordable design. Flanking the kitchen to the right is the dining room which has a sliding glass door to the backyard, and to the left is the laundry room with an entrance to the garage. The master bedroom boasts its own full bathroom and the additional two bedrooms share the hall bath. An optional two-car garage plan is included. Design by The Garlinghouse Company

Main area — 1,400 sq. ft.
Basement — 1,400 sq. ft.
Garage — 528 sq. ft.

Total living area:
1,400 sq. ft.

Refer to **Pricing Schedule A** on the order form for pricing information

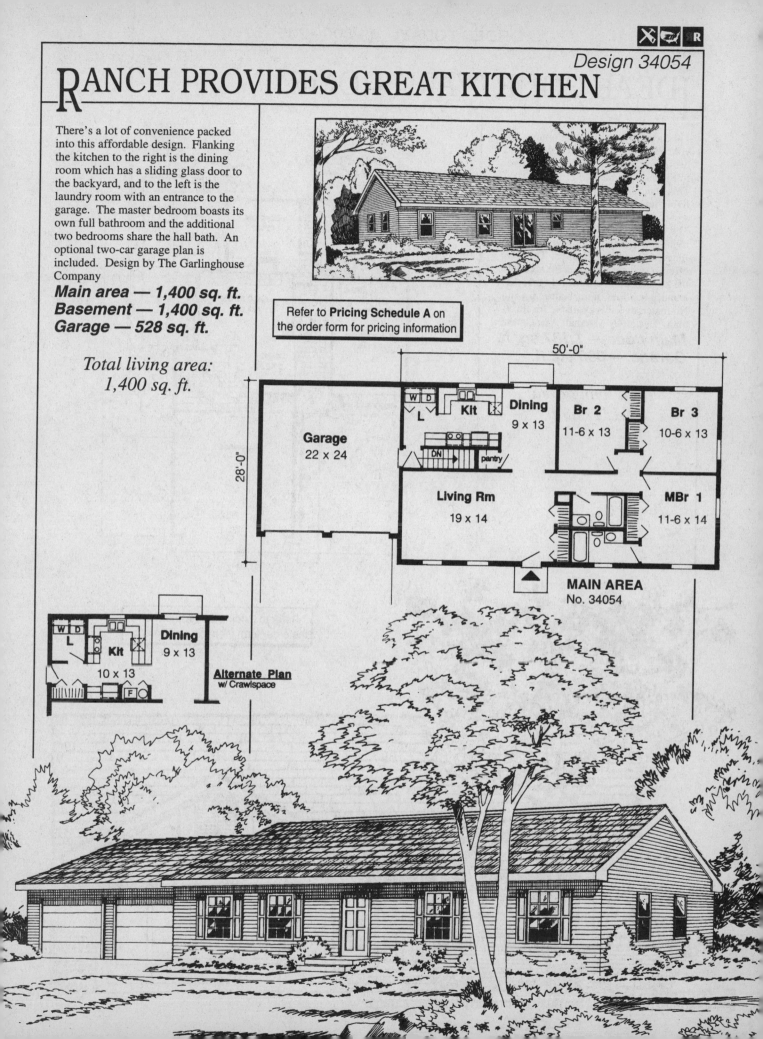

MAIN AREA
No. 34054

50'-0"
28'-0"

Garage
22 x 24

W D
L
Kit
Dining
9 x 13
Br 2
11-6 x 13
Br 3
10-6 x 13
DN
pantry
Living Rm
19 x 14
MBr 1
11-6 x 14

W D
L
Kit
10 x 13
Dining
9 x 13
F
Alternate Plan
w/ Crawlspace

IDEAL COURTYARD HOME

This home offers plenty of options for your living needs. If you need a three bedroom charmer, complete with two full baths, then plan #94302 is for you! This plan features a roomy fireplaced living room, with plenty of windows and access to the large outdoor terrace. The kitchen areas flow into the main living areas/dining rooms via a roomy four stool snackbar counter. This plan offers a two-car garage, with access to the kitchen, and conveniently located laundry facilities in the bedroom wing. No materials list is available for this plan. Design by Marshall Associates

Main floor — 1,137 sq. ft.
Garage — 390 sq. ft.

Total living area:
1,137 sq. ft.

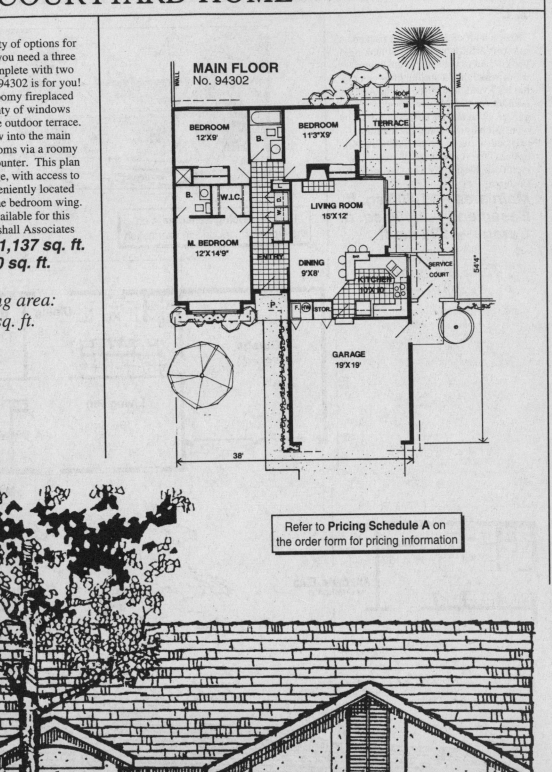

MAIN FLOOR
No. 94302

Refer to **Pricing Schedule A** on the order form for pricing information

DESIGNED FOR ENTERTAINING

Design 94247

With a large, open floor plan and an array of amenities, every gathering will be a success. The foyer embraces the living areas accented by a glass fireplace and a wetbar. The living and dining rooms each access a screened entertainment center for outside enjoyment. The gourmet kitchen delights with its openness to the rest of the house. A morning room also adds a nice touch. Two bedrooms and a den radiate from the first floor living area. Climb up the stairs or use the elevator to reach the lovely master suite. It contains a huge walk-in closet, a whirlpool tub and a private sun deck. No materials list is available for this plan. Design by The Sater Design Group

First floor — 2,066 sq. ft.
Second floor —
809 sq. ft.
Bonus — 1,260 sq. ft.
Garage — 798 sq. ft.

Total living area:
2,875 sq. ft.

Refer to **Pricing Schedule E** on the order form for pricing information

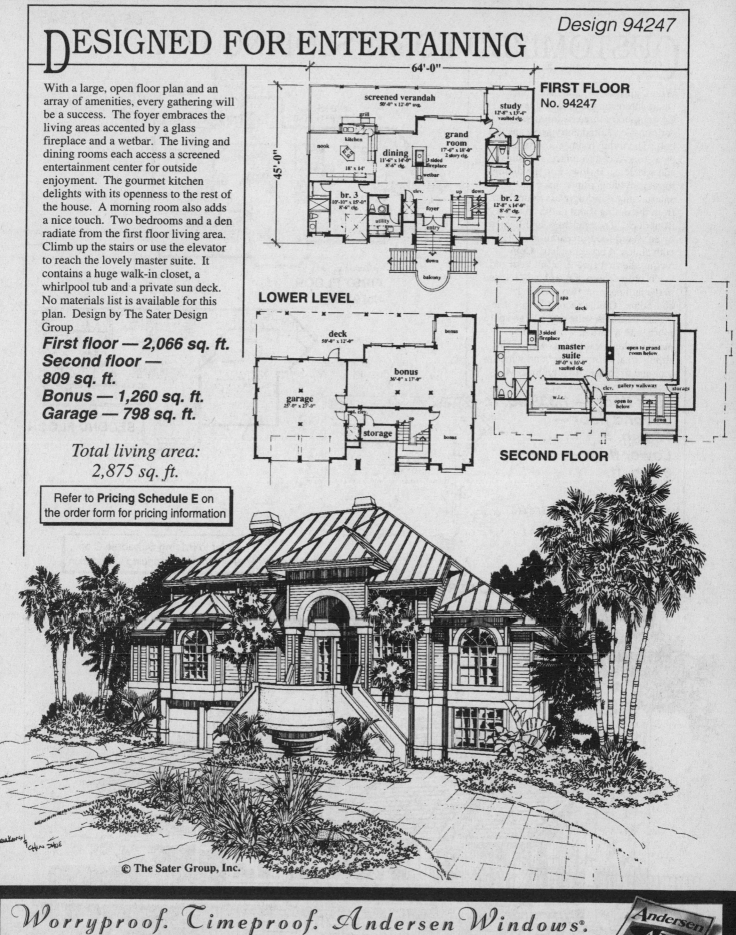

FIRST FLOOR
No. 94247

64'-0"
45'-0"

screened verandah
50'-0" x 12'-0" avg.
grill
kitchen
nook
dining
11'-6" x 14'-0"
8'-6" clg.
18' x 14'
study
12'-8" x 13'-4"
vaulted clg.
grand room
17'-6" x 18'-0"
2 story clg.
3 sided fireplace
wetbar
br. 3
10'-10" x 15'-0"
8'-6" clg.
utility
elev.
up down
foyer
entry
br. 2
12'-8" x 14'-0"
8'-6" clg.
down
balcony

LOWER LEVEL

deck
50'-0" x 12'-0"
bonus
garage
25'-0" x 27'-0"
opt. elev.
storage
bonus
36'-0" x 17'-0"
up
bonus

SECOND FLOOR

spa
deck
3 sided fireplace
master suite
20'-0" x 16'-0"
vaulted clg.
open to grand room below
w.i.c.
elev.
gallery walkway
storage
open to below
down

© The Sater Group, Inc.

CUSTOMIZED FOR A SLOPING LOT

Wood, glass and sloping roof lines create interesting appeal in this Contemporary three bedroom home. A dramatic vaulted entry serves as the hub. The living room, complimented by a stone-faced fireplace, is vaulted and spacious. It flows into the dining room providing ample space for entertaining. Sliding glass doors lead from the dining room to the adjacent front deck. The kitchen is highlighted by an island food-preparation center with sink and breakfast bar. Completing the first floor is a full bath and skylit utility room conveniently located in the hall near the two secondary bedrooms. On the second floor is the master bedroom suite and a large spare room with a garden window. The master suite is vaulted, as well as the sitting area, with wrap-around window seat and fireplace. Design by L.M. Brunier & Associates

**First floor — 1,338 sq. ft.
Second floor —
763 sq. ft.
Lower floor —
61 sq. ft.**

*Total living area:
2,162 sq. ft.*

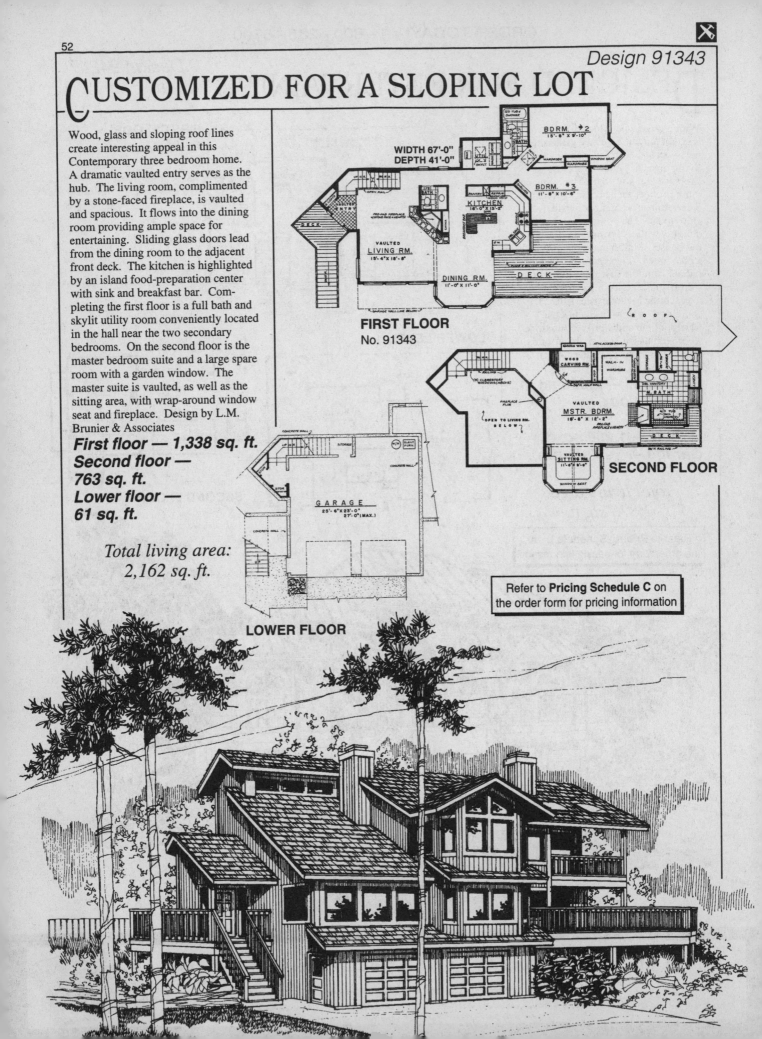

FIRST FLOOR
No. 91343

**WIDTH 67'-0"
DEPTH 41'-0"**

SECOND FLOOR

LOWER FLOOR

Refer to **Pricing Schedule C** on the order form for pricing information

EXECUTIVE DIGS

Design 99463

The entry of this home views the formal rooms and the beautiful staircase. The family room features an elegant bowed window and shares a showy three-sided fireplace with the breakfast room and kitchen. An island/snack bar, built-in desk and pantry highlight the kitchen. The bayed breakfast area is a bright place to start your day. The master suite features a tiered ceiling and an irresistible oval whirlpool tub in the luxurious bath. All secondary bedrooms have access to a Hollywood bath or a private bath. Bedroom two is elegantly accented by a beautiful arched window. Design by Design Basics, Inc.

First floor — 1,583 sq. ft.
Second floor — 1,331 sq. ft.
Garage — 676 sq. ft.

Total living area: 2,914 sq. ft.

Refer to **Pricing Schedule E** on the order form for pricing information

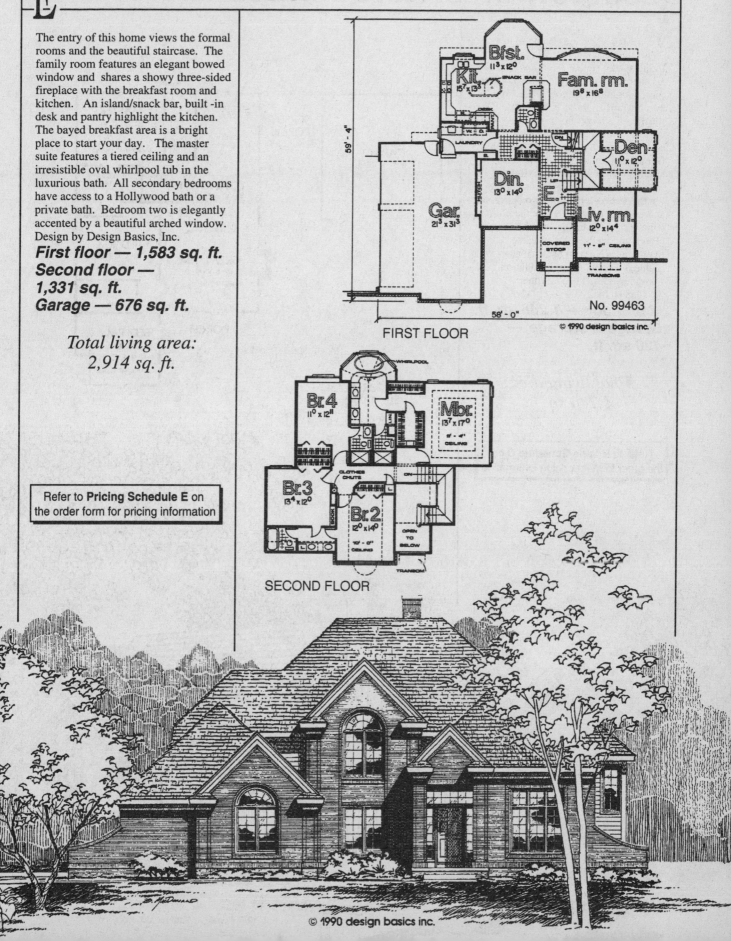

FIRST FLOOR

No. 99463

© 1990 design basics inc.

SECOND FLOOR

Design 96484

ILLUSION OF SPACIOUSNESS

We created a spacious home in just 1,246 square feet by opening up the living spaces so that they flow into one another and vaulting the ceilings in key rooms for added volume. The front porch wraps slightly, giving the illusion of a larger home on the outside, while inside a cathedral ceiling maximizes space in the open Great room and dining room. The kitchen features a center skylight, breakfast bar, and access to a garage via the screened porch. Two bedrooms share a bath up front, while the master suite with cathedral ceiling, walk-in closet, and well-equipped bath maintains privacy in back. Plan includes a crawl space foundation. Design by Donald A. Gardner Architects, Inc.

Main floor — 1,246 sq. ft.
Garage & storage — 420 sq. ft.

Total living area: 1,246 sq. ft.

Refer to **Pricing Schedule C** on the order form for pricing information

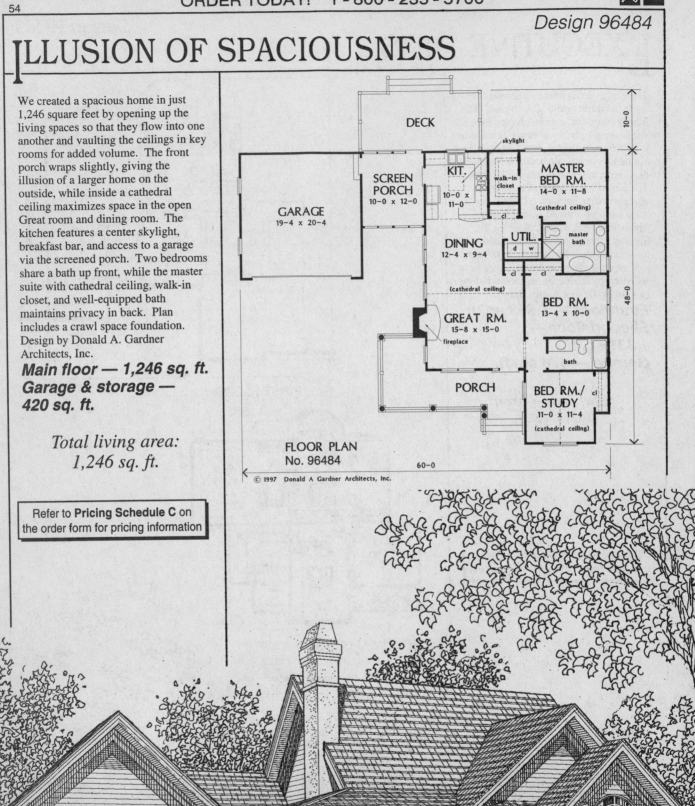

FLOOR PLAN
No. 96484

© 1997 Donald A Gardner Architects, Inc.

G. NATHAN.

© 1997 Donald A. Gardner Architects, Inc.

COVERED FRONT AND REAR PORCHES

Design 92560

If you are looking for traditional country styling, this is the home for you. The dining room is to the right of the foyer and includes direct access to the kitchen and built-in cabinets. The kitchen is made more efficient by the peninsula counter/eating bar extending counter space and provides a perfect place for meals on the go. The den is enhanced by a vaulted ceiling and a lovely fireplace. The master suite is tucked into a private corner and pampered by a five-piece master bath. The two additional bedrooms are on the opposite side of the home and share the full bath located in the hall. This plan is available with a crawl space or slab foundation. Please specify when ordering. Design by Rick Garner

Main floor — 1,660 sq. ft.
Garage — 544 sq. ft.

Total living area:
1,660 sq. ft.

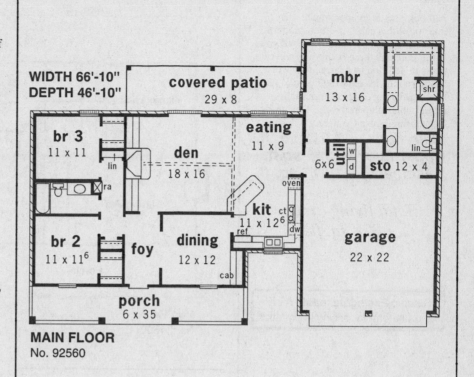

WIDTH 66'-10"
DEPTH 46'-10"

covered patio 29 x 8

mbr 13 x 16

br 3 11 x 11

den 18 x 16

eating 11 x 9

shr

6 x 6

sto 12 x 4

w/d

br 2 11 x 11⁶

foy

dining 12 x 12

kit 11 x 12⁶

oven

ct

ref

dw

cab

garage 22 x 22

porch 6 x 35

MAIN FLOOR
No. 92560

Refer to **Pricing Schedule C** on the order form for pricing information

"AMERICA'S CABINET MAKER"

tel. 1-800-575-8763, ext. 6498 ◆ email: www.merillat.com

Design 34600

RUSTIC EXTERIOR; COMPLETE HOME

Although rustic in appearance, the interior of this cabin is quiet, modern and comfortable. Small in overall size, it still contains three bedrooms and two baths in addition to a large, two-story living room with exposed beams. As a hunting/fishing lodge or mountain retreat, this compares well. Design by The Garlinghouse Company

Main floor — 1,013 sq. ft.
Upper floor — 315 sq.ft.
Basement — 1,013 sq. ft.

Total living area:
1,328 sq. ft.

Refer to **Pricing Schedule A** on the order form for pricing information

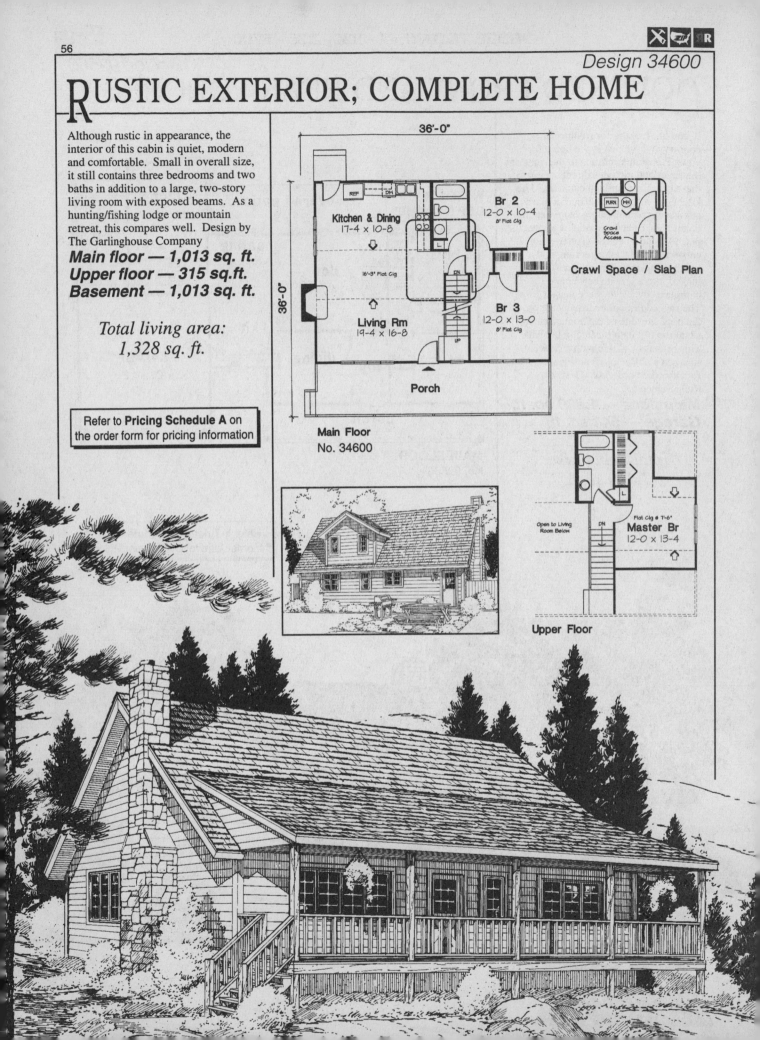

36'-0"

36'-0"

REF DW

Kitchen & Dining
17-4 x 10-8

16'-3" Flat Clg

Living Rm
19-4 x 16-8

Br 2
12-0 x 10-4
8' Flat Clg

DN

UP

Br 3
12-0 x 13-0
8' Flat Clg

Porch

Main Floor
No. 34600

FURN HH

Crawl Space Access

Crawl Space / Slab Plan

Open to Living Room Below

DN

Flat Clg @ 7'-6"

Master Br
12-0 x 13-4

L

Upper Floor

Design 91707

GOOD USE OF SPACE

With only the two bedrooms and a bathroom upstairs, this medium sized home is equally well-adapted to a family with older children, or empty nesters who wish to have space to accomodate grandchildren, and to entertain without feeling cramped. The entryway and formal living room are vaulted to the second floor giving a feeling of vastness to visitors and family alike. In fact, the landing at the top of the curving stairway, overlooks the living room. The kitchen, with both a garden window and a bay window, is spacious and bright. This design makes excellent use of oddly shaped spaces. A hutch is tucked into an angle in the dining room, a fireplace in another in the family room, and a small angled half-bath is conveniently close to everything. The master suite has an oversized tub and a shower, both brightened by a skylight and glass blocks. The two-car garage includes extra space for a workbench and/or storage space. Design by Landmark Designs, Inc.

First floor — 1,940 sq. ft.
Second floor — 552 sq. ft.
Garage — 608 sq. ft.

Total living area: 2,492 sq. ft.

WIDTH 66'-0"
DEPTH 54'-6"

FIRST FLOOR
No. 91707

MASTER SUITE 13⁸ x 14⁰

DEN / OFFICE 9⁶ x 13⁸

SHOP / STORAGE 6⁰ x 13⁸

GARAGE 21⁶ x 23⁴

TUB
SKYLIGHT
WALK-IN CLOSET

WSH DRY
SINK
UTILITY
IRON BD.
FAU

DECK

NOOK 10⁰ x 9⁸
OVEN & MW
REF

GARDEN WINDOW

KITCHEN
FIREPLACE

PANTRY
HUTCH
STAIRS TO BASEMENT OR CLOSET
UP

ENTRY

PORCH
DN

FAMILY ROOM 14⁰ x 17¹⁰

DINING ROOM 11² x 13⁶

LIVING ROOM 15² x 14⁰

DN

SECOND FLOOR

BEDROOM 2 12⁶ x 10⁸

OPEN TO ENTRY

STORAGE
DN

BEDROOM 3 12⁶ x 12⁰

LINEN

OPEN TO LIVING ROOM

Design 93041

TWO-STORY ENTRY ADDS GRACE

A stucco design is used to accent the arched, two-story entry of this pleasing design. Inside, all major living areas are located with views to the rear grounds, which makes this plan a winner for a golf course, pool or lake site. The kitchen, breakfast room and family room are adjacent and open to one another. The master suite has all the extras with an angled whirlpool tub, separate shower and his-n-her vanity. The second floor includes three bedrooms, an in-home office or bedroom and a bath. No materials list is available for this plan. Design by Larry E. Belk

First floor — 1,974 sq. ft.
Second floor —
1,060 sq. ft.
Garage — 531 sq. ft.

Total living area:
3,034 sq. ft.

Refer to **Pricing Schedule E** on the order form for pricing information

WIDTH 64'-4"
DEPTH 53'-4"

FIRST FLOOR
No. 93041

© Larry E. Belk

SECOND FLOOR

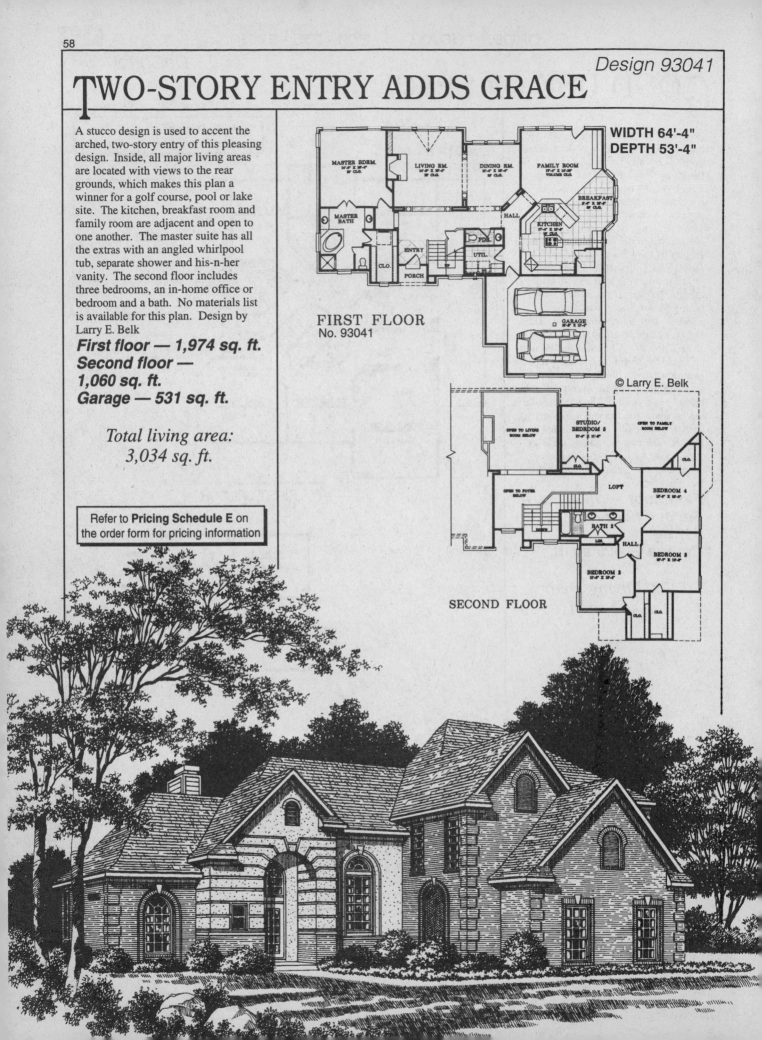

FAMILY STYLE

Design 93349

The family room crowned by a vaulted ceiling and accented by a fireplace, is sure to be the hub of activity for this home. The efficient kitchen has by a built-in pantry and an extended counter/eating bar for added comfort. A bay window highlights the dinette which serves informal meals while the formal dining room is accented by a boxed bay window. The wood deck is accessed from the dinette. A secluded first floor master suite pampers the owners with a private bath and ample closet space. A full bath and two additional bedrooms on the second floor complete the floor plan. No materials list is available for this plan. Design by Patrick Morabito A.I.A.

First floor — 1,454 sq. ft.
**Second floor —
507 sq. ft.**
Basement — 1,454 sq. ft.
Garage — 624 sq. ft.

*Total living area:
1,961 sq. ft.*

Refer to **Pricing Schedule C** on the order form for pricing information

No. 93349

Design 92561

CLASSICALLY APPOINTED

This classically styled home features a raised twelve foot ceiling topping the den and the master bedroom. The recessed front entry leads into a formal foyer. The dining room is to the right with direct access to the kitchen. The kitchen is laid out in an efficient U-shape, with an extended counter eating bar. The eating bay is highly windowed for a bright setting. The den includes a focal point fireplace. A private master bath highlights the master suite, while the two additional bedrooms share the bath in the hall. This plan is available with a crawl space or slab foundation. Please specify when ordering. Design by Rick Garner

Main floor — 1,856 sq. ft.
Garage — 521 sq. ft.

Total living area:
1,856 sq. ft.

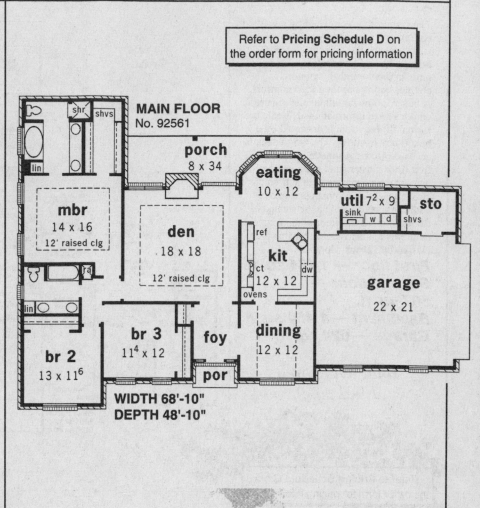

MAIN FLOOR
No. 92561

porch
8 x 34

eating
10 x 12

util 7² x 9   sto

mbr
14 x 16
12' raised clg

den
18 x 18
12' raised clg

kit
12 x 12

garage
22 x 21

br 2
13 x 11⁶

br 3
11⁴ x 12

foy

dining
12 x 12

por

WIDTH 68'-10"
DEPTH 48'-10"

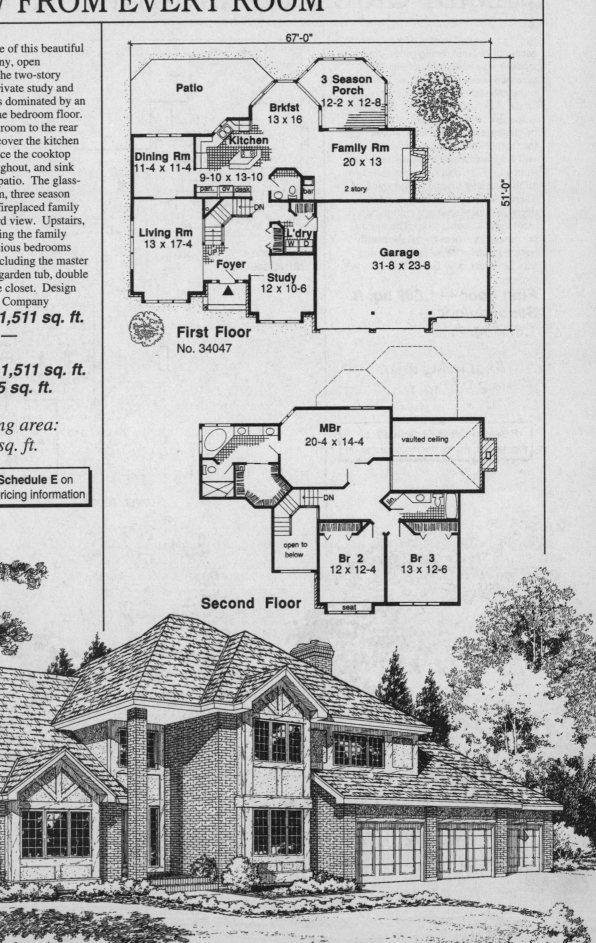

A VIEW FROM EVERY ROOM

The impressive facade of this beautiful home hints at the sunny, open atmosphere inside. The two-story foyer, flanked by a private study and formal living room, is dominated by an angular staircase to the bedroom floor. Step past the powder room to the rear of the house, and discover the kitchen of your dreams. Notice the cooktop island, built-ins throughout, and sink overlooking the rear patio. The glass-walled breakfast room, three season porch, and towering fireplaced family room share a backyard view. Upstairs, the balcony overlooking the family room links three spacious bedrooms and two full baths, including the master suite with its private garden tub, double vanity, and room-size closet. Design by The Garlinghouse Company

First floor — 1,511 sq. ft.
Second floor — 1,163 sq. ft.
Basement — 1,511 sq. ft.
Garage — 765 sq. ft.

Total living area: 2,674 sq. ft.

Refer to **Pricing Schedule E** on the order form for pricing information

First Floor
No. 34047

67'-0"
51'-0"

Patio
3 Season Porch 12-2 x 12-8
Brkfst 13 x 16
Kitchen 9-10 x 13-10
Dining Rm 11-4 x 11-4
Family Rm 20 x 13
2 story
pan. ov desk
DN
Living Rm 13 x 17-4
L'dry W D
Garage 31-8 x 23-8
bar
UP
Foyer
Study 12 x 10-6

Second Floor

MBr 20-4 x 14-4
vaulted ceiling
DN
lin.
open to below
Br 2 12 x 12-4
Br 3 13 x 12-6
seat

Design 92045

FAMILY ORIENTED AND YET PAMPERING

From the vaulted central entry you can access the formal dining room, den/study, living area and kitchen. A screened porch and first floor laundry room enhance the livability of this home. The kitchen features an island with raised counter adjacent to a bright, cheerful breakfast bay area. Up the unique double access staircase, you will find four large bedrooms and three full baths. The roomy master suite has all the features anyone would want. There is a fireplace, a huge closet, an oversized tub placed in a columned alcove and a double sink. The three car garage has room for all the family vehicles and/or "toys," whatever they may be. Design by Urban Design Group

First floor — 1,607 sq. ft.
Second floor — 1,372 sq. ft.

Total living area:
2,979 sq. ft.

Refer to **Pricing Schedule E** on the order form for pricing information

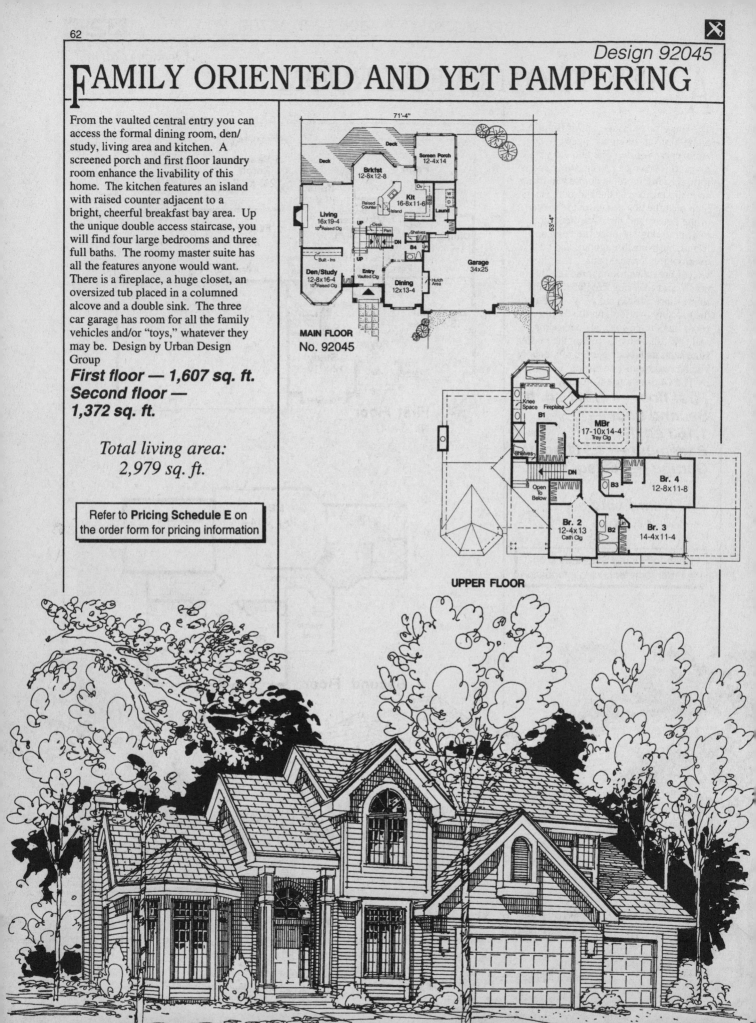

MAIN FLOOR
No. 92045

71'-4"

53'-4"

Deck

Deck

Screen Porch
12-4x14

Brkfst
12-8x12-8

Ov.

Kit
16-8x11-6

W
D
Laund

Living
16x19-4
10" Raised Clg

Raised
Counter

Island

Shelves

UP
Desk
Pan

DN

B4

Built - Ins

UP

Den/Study
12-8x16-4
10" Raised Clg

Entry
Vaulted Clg

Dining
12x13-4

Hutch
Area

Garage
34x25

UPPER FLOOR

Knee
Space   Fireplace

B1

MBr
17-10x14-4
Tray Clg

Shelves

DN

B3

Br. 4
12-8x11-8

Open
To
Below

Br. 2
12-4x13
Cath Clg

B2

Br. 3
14-4x11-4

Design 93716

ITALIAN STYLE EXTERIOR

Though it is compact in its foot print and efficient in its design, the Italian styled exterior of this home is a statement of elegance. The ten-foot ceilings add to the open feeling of the main level design. The interior columns and French doors add drama on entering the foyer from the front porch. The large covered porch at the rear extends the living area outdoors and also has an optional kitchen for outdoor entertaining. The upper level has two full baths to service three bedrooms which all have walk-in closets. No materials list is available for this plan. Design by Building Science Associates

First floor — 1,814 sq. ft.
Second floor — 884 sq. ft.
Garage — 552 sq. ft.

Total living area: 2,698 sq. ft.

Refer to **Pricing Schedule E** on the order form for pricing information

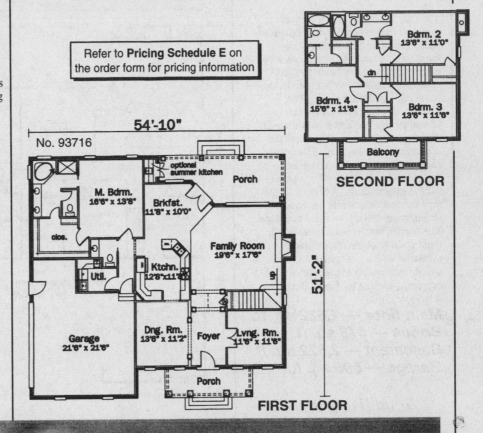

SECOND FLOOR

FIRST FLOOR

Design 98426

DELIGHTFUL DETAILING

The exterior of this home projects a polished look created by the attention paid to details. The corner quoins, keystones, arches and shutters are eye-catching. The foyer has a vaulted ceiling and flows into both the living room and the dining room. The kitchen is enhanced by a cooktop island/serving bar and a pass-through into the family room. The breakfast area adjoins the kitchen. The family room is highlighted by a vaulted ceiling and a fireplace. The master suite is outstanding. A tray ceiling tops the bedroom while the windowed sitting room has a two-sided fireplace. The master bath is luxurious with a huge walk-in closet. This plan is available with a basement or crawl space foundation. Please specify when ordering. Design by Frank Betz Associates, Inc.

Main floor — 2,622 sq. ft.
Bonus — 478 sq. ft.
Basement — 2,622 sq. ft.
Garage — 506 sq. ft.

Total living area:
2,622 sq. ft.

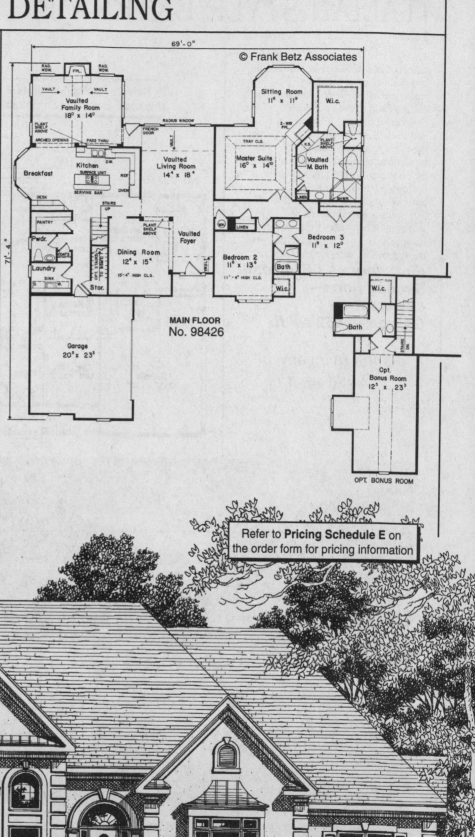

© Frank Betz Associates

MAIN FLOOR
No. 98426

Refer to **Pricing Schedule E** on the order form for pricing information

Design 32042

OUTDOOR ORIENTED LIVING

This home offers comfortable outdoor oriented vacation living as well as year round practicality. This home's curb appeal is achieved by the stone and wood cladding, and a double door entry blending with the traditional colonial style architecture. This home's features include a den and a private office. The heart of this home is the dramatic Great room with large windows. Upstairs, via a spiral staircase, there is a reading nook and an additional bedroom and bath. Design by The Meredith Corporation

Main level — 2,072 sq. ft.
Upper level — 522 sq. ft.
Lower level — 1,275 sq. ft.

Total living area: 3,869 sq. ft.

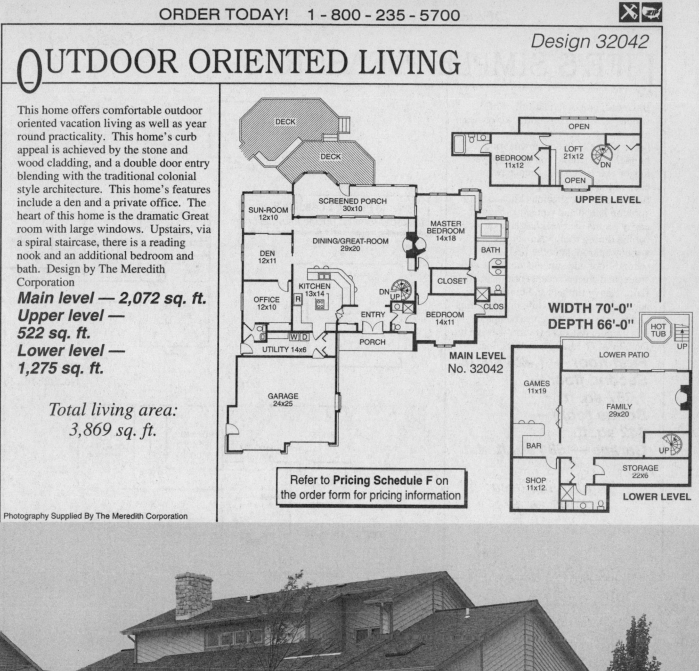

UPPER LEVEL

MAIN LEVEL
No. 32042

WIDTH 70'-0"
DEPTH 66'-0"

LOWER LEVEL

Refer to **Pricing Schedule F** on the order form for pricing information

Design 99816

LIFE'S SIMPLE PLEASURES

Balanced, graceful, and full of life's simple pleasures, this home welcomes all to a warm, inviting retreat. This will home please both homeowner and builder with simple construction, yet lots of extras like two fireplaces, one each in the study/living room and family room. A spacious kitchen with cooktop island and peninsula counter easily serves the breakfast area or the formal dining room. Numerous windows throughout the first and second floor add sun and warmth, while stone, and stucco accents bring a rustic flair. Heavy timbers and brackets accent the entrance, while metal roofing and simple gable structure complete this unique, relaxed exterior. Design by Donald A. Gardner Architects, Inc.

First floor — 1,428 sq. ft.
Second floor — 1,067 sq. ft.
Bonus room — 342 sq. ft.
Garage — 584 sq. ft.

Total living area:
2,495 sq. ft.

Refer to **Pricing Schedule E** on the order form for pricing information

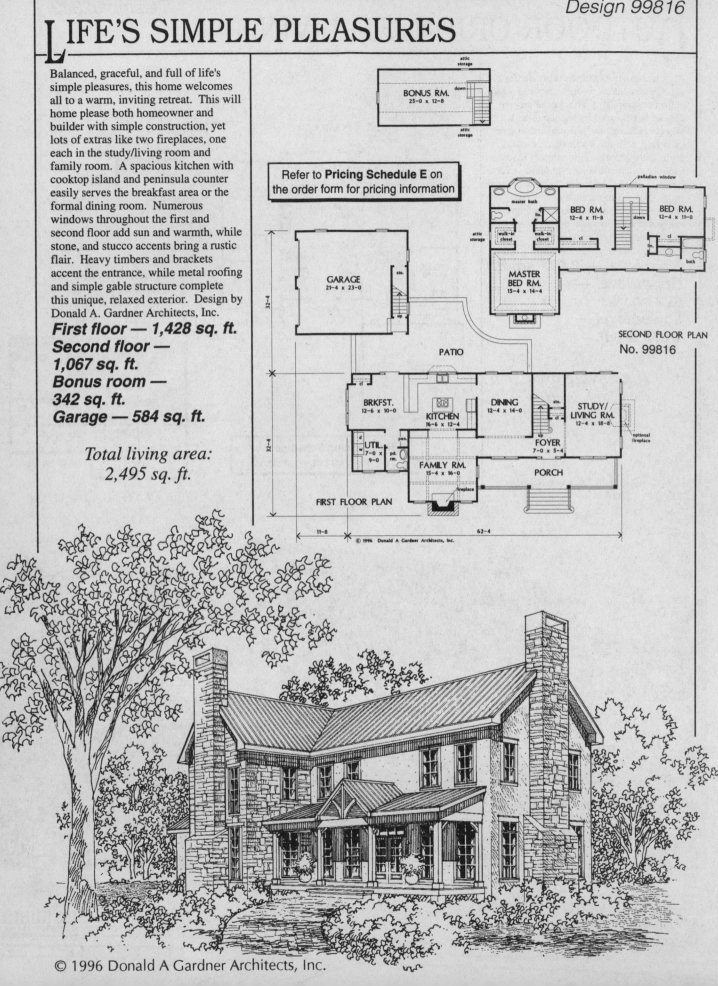

© 1996 Donald A Gardner Architects, Inc.

ATTRACTIVE GABLED DESIGN

This attractive gable has boxed front windows and uses a mixture of brick and siding giving it great curb appeal. The large spacious floor plan gives a good feeling upon entering the home. Standing in the entry you can look into the cathedral ceiling living room at the cozy fire in the fireplace. Or, maybe, your guests would like to enjoy the outdoors on your large covered patio. The island kitchen has corner windows surrounding the sink area. The master bedroom features its own master bath. The two additional bedrooms share a bath. No materials list is available for this plan. Design by Fillmore Design Group

Main floor — 1,830 sq. ft.
Garage — 759 sq. ft.

Total living area:
1,830 sq. ft.

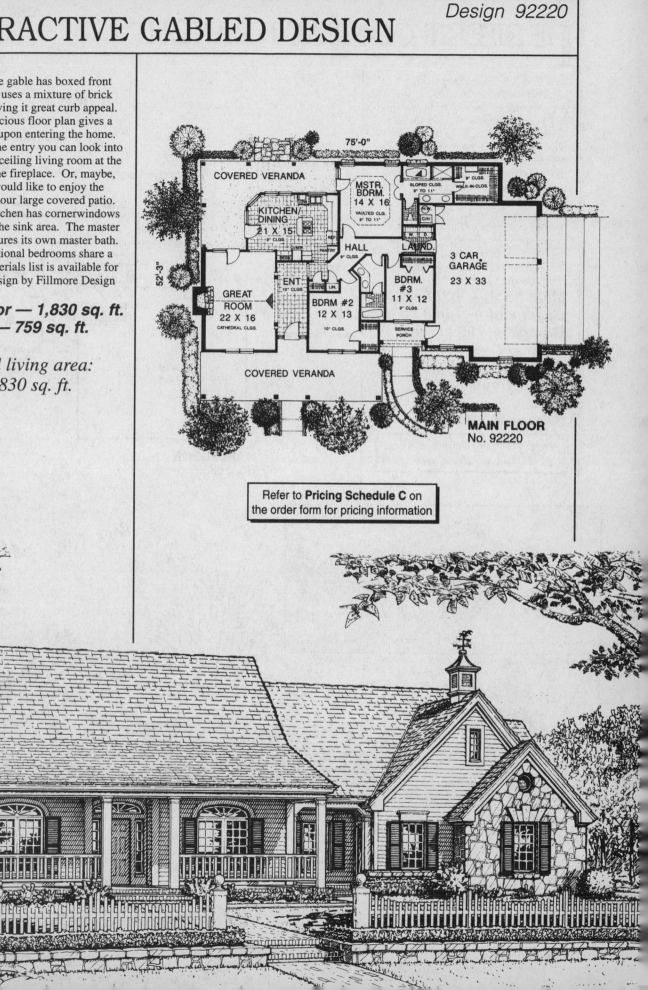

MAIN FLOOR
No. 92220

Refer to **Pricing Schedule C** on the order form for pricing information

Design 10839

PERFECT COMPACT RANCH

This Ranch home features a large sunken Great room, centralized with a cozy fireplace. The master bedroom has an unforgettable bathroom with a super skylight. The huge three-car plus garage can include a work area for the family carpenter. In the center of this home a kitchen includes an eating nook for family gatherings. The porch at the rear of the house has easy access from the dining room. One other bedroom and a den, which can easily be converted to a bedroom, are on the opposite side of the house from the master bedroom. Design by The Garlinghouse Company

Main floor — 1,738 sq. ft.
Basement — 1,083 sq. ft.
Garage — 796 sq. ft.

Total living area:
1,738 sq. ft.

Refer to **Pricing Schedule B** on the order form for pricing information

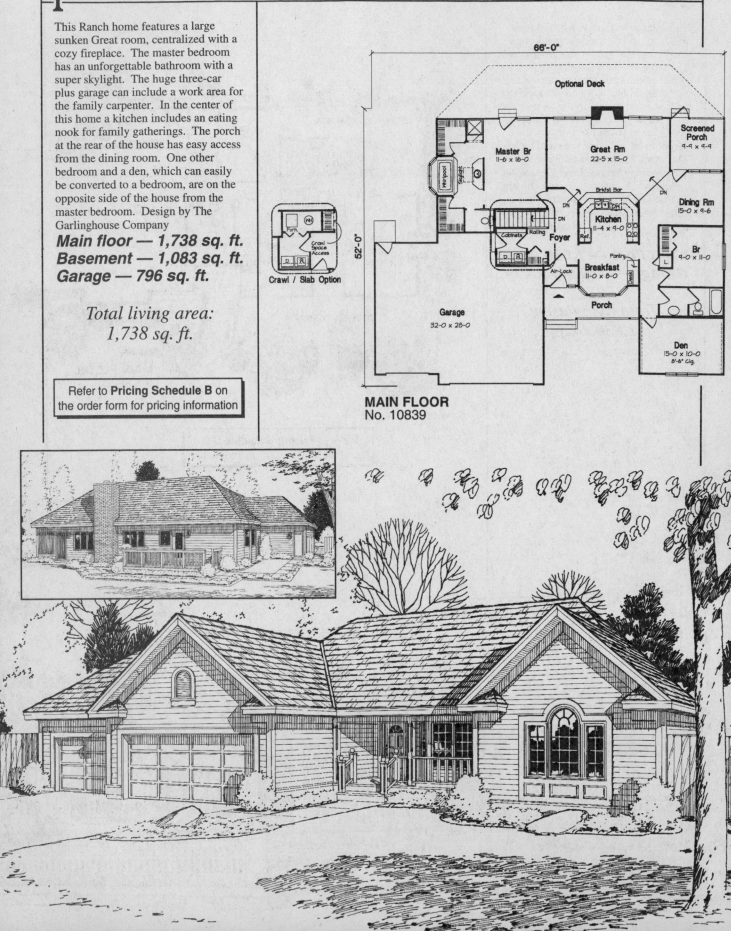

Crawl / Slab Option

MAIN FLOOR
No. 10839

SOUTHERN MANSION

Design 99485

The first and second floor of this home are enhanced by covered porches accompanied by intricate detailing and illuminating transom windows creating a splendid southern mansion appeal. The prominent entry opens to the formal dining and living rooms. The grand family room is warmed by a fireplace and views the screened porch. An efficient laundry is located near the kitchen and has an entry to the small covered side porch. The stairway in the garage leads to the bonus room on the second floor. French doors open to the master suite which is topped by a decorative ceiling. The suite contains his-n-her walk-in closets, a large dressing area, dual vanity, an oval whirlpool bath and a separate shower area. The secondary bedrooms have private access to a bath. Design by Design Basics, Inc.

First floor — 1,598 sq. ft.
Second floor — 1,675 sq. ft.

Total living area:
3,273 sq. ft.

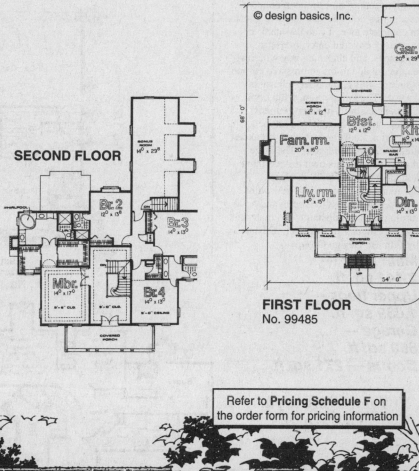

SECOND FLOOR

FIRST FLOOR
No. 99485

© design basics, Inc.

Refer to **Pricing Schedule F** on the order form for pricing information

Design 98508

COUNTRY ESTATE

Reminiscent of an European country estate, this home is sure to leave guests in complete awe. From its massive two-story covered entry, majestic chimneys, and charming bay window on the outside to the impressive curved staircase, this home offers plenty of appeal. The Great room, with wood floors and a built-in entertainment center, and the huge island kitchen, with brick floors and an open breakfast area, is truly impressive. The large master suite has its own private lanai and an enormous walk-in closet. There are three secondary bedrooms, with private access to a bath, and a future playroom upstairs. No materials list is available for this plan. Design by Filmore Design Group

**Main floor —
2,441 sq. ft.
Upper floor —
1,039 sq. ft.
Garage —
660 sq. ft.
Bonus — 271 sq. ft.**

*Total living area:
3,480 sq. ft.*

Refer to **Pricing Schedule F** on the order form for pricing information

Main Floor

No. 98508

Upper Floor

GROWING FAMILIES TAKE NOTE

Design 96479

Growing families will adore this attractive farmhouse with plenty of versatile unfinished bonus space. Today's needs are exceeded downstairs, while future needs have unlimited options upstairs. We opened up the foyer with a dormer, and columns accent the adjacent dining room. The Great room, open to the kitchen and breakfast room, is enlarged by a cathedral ceiling, while living and entertaining space expands to the deck. A tray ceiling adds interest and volume to the master bedroom. The suite includes a walk-in closet and a sunny, skylit bath with a garden tub and double vanity. A flexible bedroom/study shares a bath with another bedroom. Design by Donald A. Gardner Architects, Inc.

First floor — 1,803 sq. ft.
Second floor — 80 sq. ft.
Garage & storage — 569 sq. ft.
Bonus space — 918 sq. ft.

Total living area: 1,883 sq. ft.

Refer to **Pricing Schedule D** on the order form for pricing information

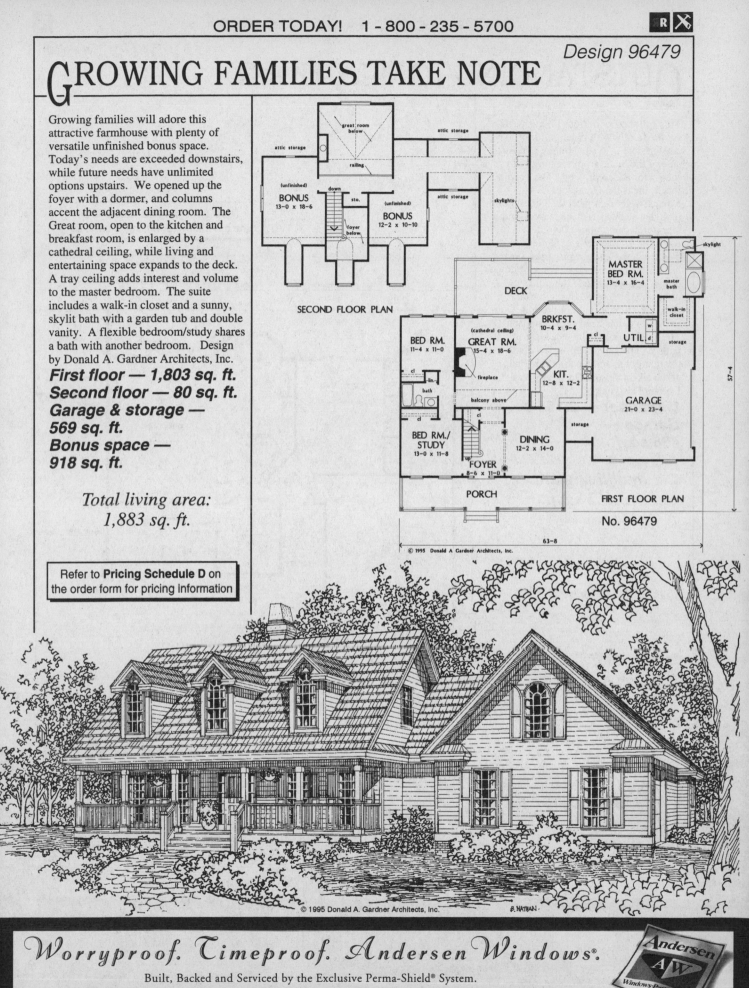

SECOND FLOOR PLAN

FIRST FLOOR PLAN

No. 96479

© 1995 Donald A Gardner Architects, Inc.

© 1995 Donald A. Gardner Architects, Inc.   B. NATHAN

72

Design 96504

Outstanding Family Home

This split bedroom floor plan is perfect for the family with older children. The master suite is located on the opposite side of the home from the children's rooms for added privacy. The heart of this home is the Great room. An expansive living space, the Great room includes a cozy fireplace, access to the rear porch and an open layout with the nook and kitchen. An extended counter in the kitchen provides a snack bar for meals or snacks. For a sit down dinner options include the informal nook and the formal dining room. Convenient access to both rooms, from the kitchen, has been accommodated. The bright nook includes a built-in pantry. The suite includes access to the rear porch and a pampering bath and walk-in closet. Design by Vaughn Lauban Designs.

Main floor — 2,162 sq. ft.
Garage —
498 sq. ft.

Total living area:
2,162 sq. ft.

Refer to **Pricing Schedule C** on the order form for pricing information

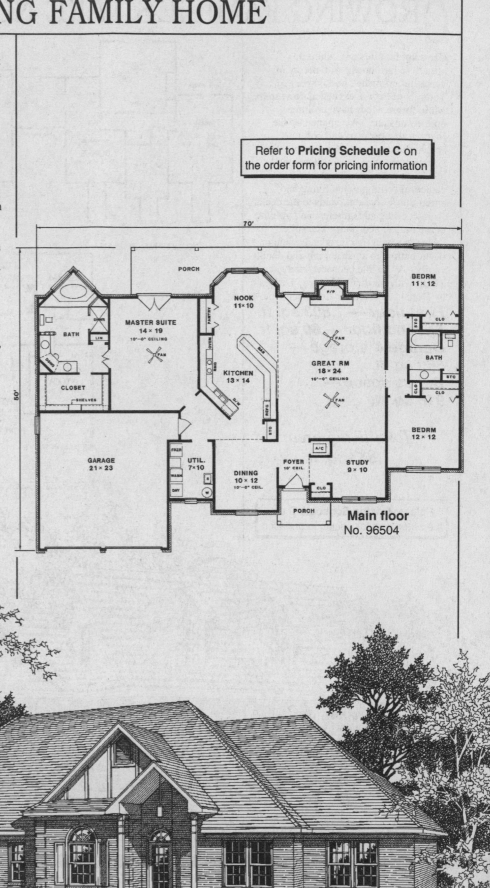

Main floor
No. 96504

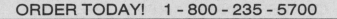

Design 94907

VICTORIAN ACCENTS

A covered porch and Victorian accents create this classical elevation. The double door entry opens to a spacious great room and elegant dining room. The gourmet kitchen features an island/snack bar and a large pantry. French doors lead to a breakfast area with access to a covered porch and kitchen. Cathedral ceilings in master bedroom and dressing area add an exquisite touch. His-n-her walk-in closets, a large dressing area with double vanity and whirlpool complement the master bedroom. A vaulted ceiling in bedroom number two accents the window seat and arched transom window. Design by Design Basics, Inc.

First floor — 905 sq. ft.
Second floor —
863 sq. ft.
Basement — 905 sq. ft.
Garage — 487 sq. ft.

Total living area:
1,768 sq. ft.

Refer to **Pricing Schedule B** on the order form for pricing information

© design basics, inc.

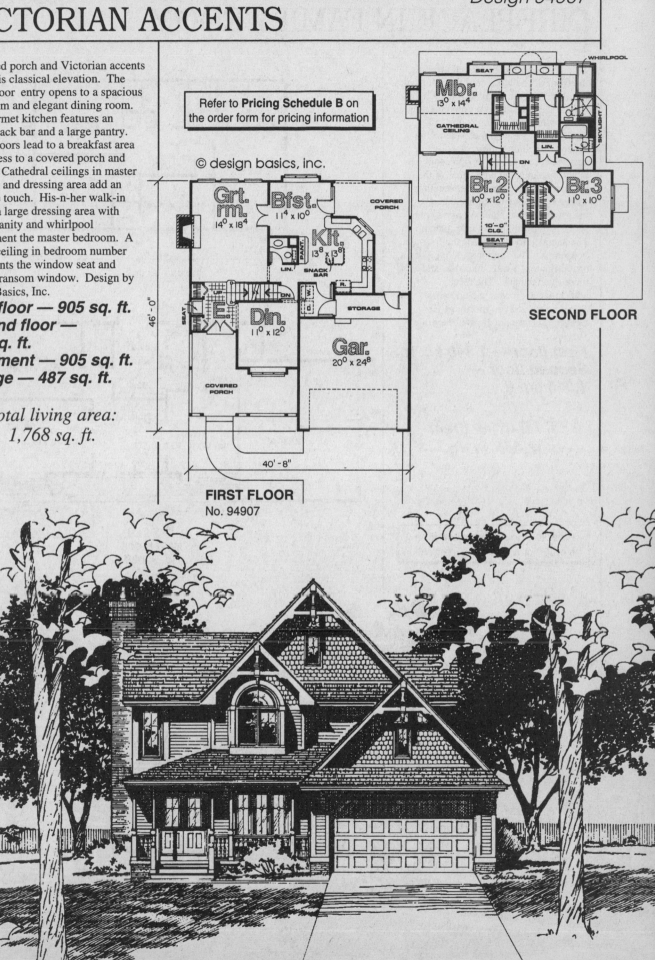

SECOND FLOOR

FIRST FLOOR
No. 94907

Design 90029

FIREPLACE IN FAMILY ROOM

This home offers the formal areas to the front of the home and the informal family living areas in the rear. The formal foyer includes a convenient coat closet. The living room and dining room are to either side of the foyer. The dining room directly accesses the kitchen. A cook top island expands the work area of the kitchen. An informal dinette with a sunny boxed bay accommodates informal meals. The expansive family room is highlighted by a fireplace. The second floor contains the four bedrooms. The master suite includes a dressing area, a walk-in closet and a three quarter bath. The three additional bedrooms include ample closet space and are roomy in size. Design by National Home Planning Service

First floor — 1,340 sq. ft.
Second floor —
1,315 sq. ft.

Total living area:
2,655 sq. ft.

Refer to **Pricing Schedule E** on the order form for pricing information

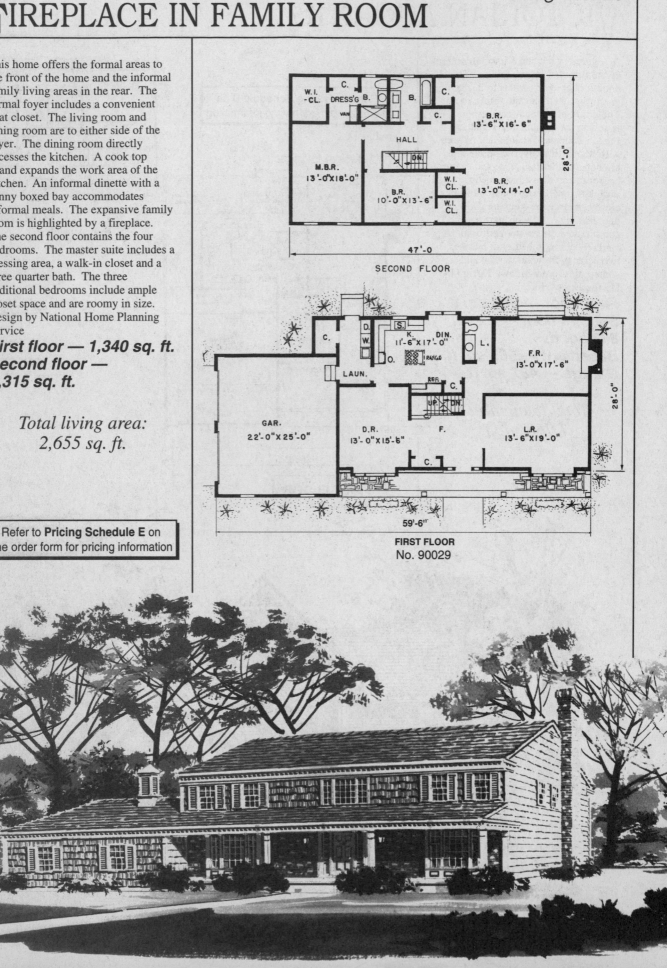

SECOND FLOOR

FIRST FLOOR
No. 90029

Design 91143

ART OF LIVING

This plan is the result of numerous requests to design a box style, two story with the master bedroom on the first floor, under 3000 sq. ft. and able to fit a 70' wide lot. This house is economical to build, while allowing plenty of room for the family. The vaulted ceiling in the Great room, the two-story entry, columns and bookshelves, all extend a warm welcome to everyone. The Master bedroom and dining room have tray ceilings. In the Master bath, a corner tub is highlighted by windows on each side. The kitchen has an open bar area for access to the breakfast nook and Great room. No materials list is available for this plan. Design Ryan & Associates

**First floor — 1,403 sq. ft.
Second floor —
1,237 sq. ft.
Garage — 431 sq. ft.**

*Total living area:
2,640 sq. ft.*

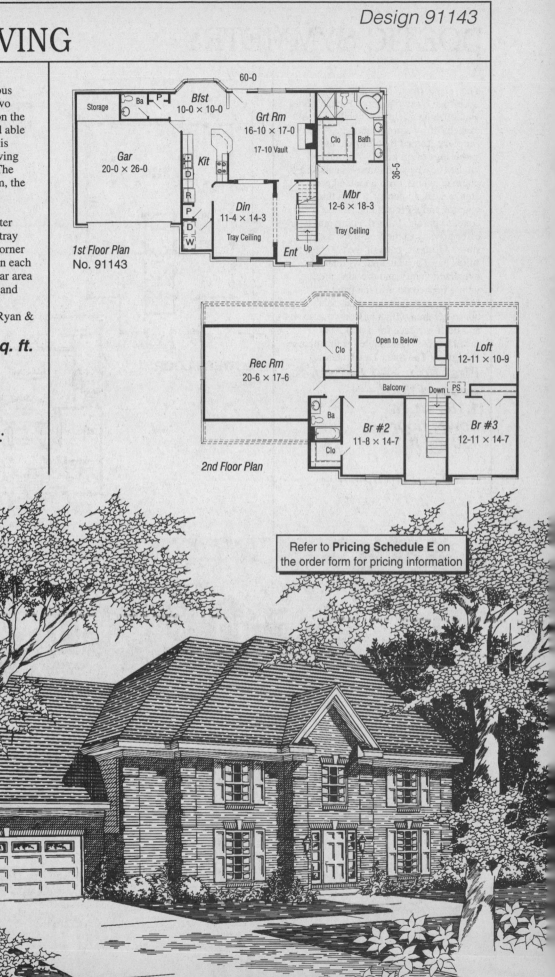

1st Floor Plan
No. 91143

2nd Floor Plan

Refer to **Pricing Schedule E** on the order form for pricing information

POETIC SYMMETRY

Design 94261

The raised, open living and dining area is defined by two pairs of French doors which frame a two-story wall of glass topped off by a graceful arch. A cozy fireplace framed by built-ins invites gatherings of all kinds. A gourmet kitchen serves both family meals and planned events, with an island prep area, a walk-in pantry, a pass-through counter and a French door to the covered porch. Split sleeping quarters offer privacy to the first floor master suite. Upstairs, each of the two guests suites has a private bath with an oversized vanity and dressing area with a French door to the front balcony. A gallery loft leads to a computer area with a balcony overlook and built-in space for a desk. No materials list is available for this plan. Design by The Sater Design Group

First floor — 1,642 sq. ft.
Second floor — 1,165 sq. ft.
Lower floor — 150 sq. ft.

Total living area: 2,957 sq. ft.

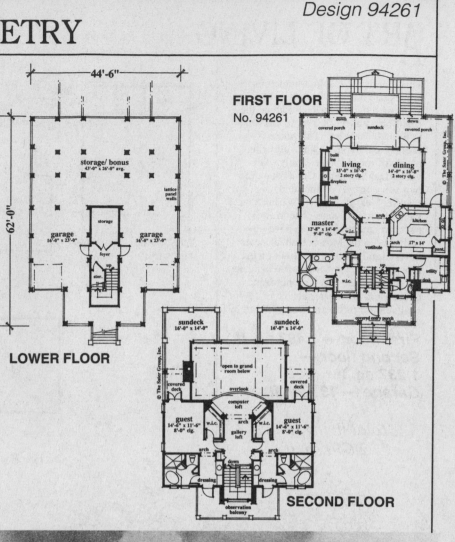

FIRST FLOOR No. 94261

LOWER FLOOR

SECOND FLOOR

Refer to **Pricing Schedule E** on the order form for pricing information

Design 98501

STUNNING FAMILY PLAN

Absolutely stunning is the only way to describe this exciting home plan with its gorgeous front elevation with bay window, huge arch window, and brick gables, to the angled family room with elegant brick fireplace and cathedral ceiling. A large angled island kitchen with bright and airy breakfast area adds to the uniqueness of this plan. A large separate master suite and bath, formal living room and dining room, and three other bedrooms complete this masterpiece of design. With its well thought out floor plan and wonderful amenities, you're sure to enjoy this home for many years to come. No materials list is available for this plan. Design by Filmore Design Group

Main floor — 2,194 sq. ft.
Garage — 462 sq. ft.

Total living area:
2,194 sq. ft.

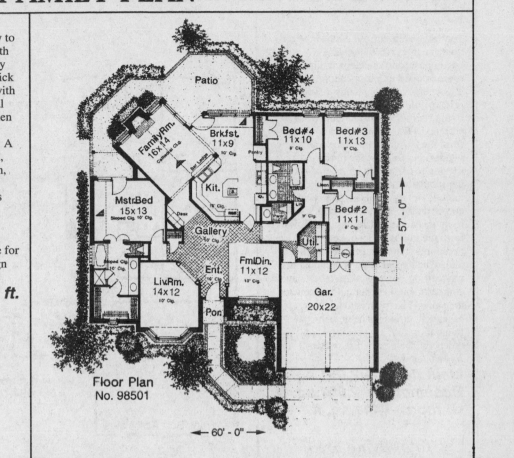

Floor Plan
No. 98501

← 60' - 0" →

57' - 0"

Weather Shield
Windows & Doors

www.weathershield.com

Weather Shield Windows and Doors offers project planning guides for your remodeling or new home project. FREE. Specify "Remodeling" or "New Home" Planning Guide by calling

1-800-477-6808

Design 98427

SPLIT BEDROOM PLAN

The large arched front window of this home is an eye-catcher. It is encompassed in the elegant dining room, topped in a tray ceiling. The master suite of this plan is assured of privacy in this split bedroom plan. The living room/den has a double door entrance. The family room is viewed from the foyer. A fireplace framed by windows highlights the room and a serving bar from the kitchen adds to the family atmosphere. The kitchen includes a large walk-in pantry and a corner double sink. The breakfast room has a vaulted ceiling and flows from the kitchen. Two secondary bedrooms share the full bath in the hall. The master suite is crowned in a tray ceiling. Two walk-in closets and a compartmental master bath complete the suite. This plan is available with a basement, crawl space or slab foundation. Please specify when ordering. Design by Frank Betz Associates, Inc.

Main floor — 2,051 sq. ft.
Basement — 2,051 sq. ft.
Garage — 441 sq. ft.

Total living area:
2,051 sq. ft.

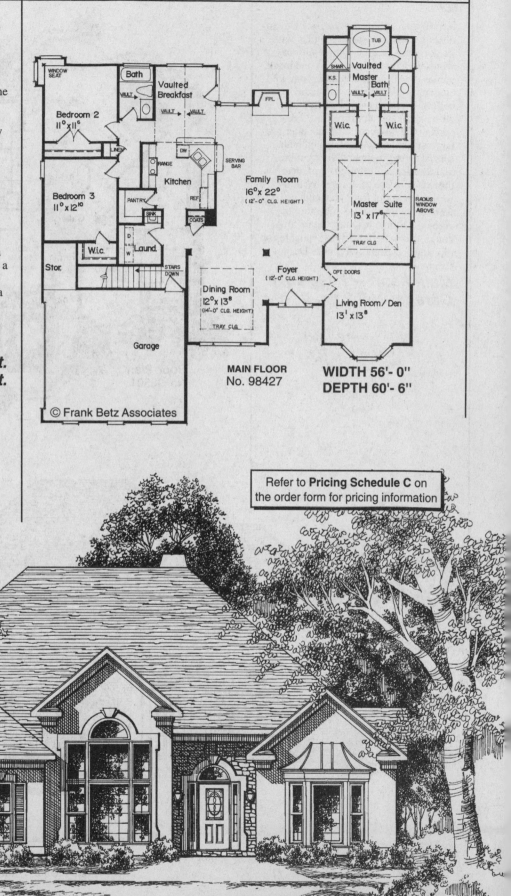

MAIN FLOOR
No. 98427

WIDTH 56'- 0"
DEPTH 60'- 6"

© Frank Betz Associates

Refer to **Pricing Schedule C** on the order form for pricing information

Design 96497

FOUR-BEDROOM TRADITIONAL

This four-bedroom traditional makes a grand impression with multiple front facing gables, elegant arched windows and a barrel vaulted entry with stately columns. The foyer is enhanced by a graceful cathedral ceiling, fulfilling the promise of grandeur created by the home's exterior. Columns add definition to the casually elegant open dining room, while the Great room's spaciousness is augmented by another cathedral ceiling. The kitchen is more than generous, featuring a center work island, pantry and breakfast counter, and the sunny breakfast bay is topped by a delightful, octagonal tray ceiling. Each of the home's four bedrooms enjoys a special ceiling treatment, as does the master bath. A lovely arched picture window accents the versatile study/bedroom, and both bedrooms upstairs boast walk-in closets. Design by Donald A. Gardner Architects, Inc.

First floor — 1,829 sq. ft.
Second floor — 479 sq. ft.
Bonus room — 228 sq. ft.
Garage — 546 sq. ft.

Total living area: 2,308 sq. ft.

FIRST FLOOR PLAN

PORCH

BRKFST.
11-0 x 10-10

UTIL.
6-0 x 10-0

KITCHEN
11-0 x 15-4

GREAT RM.
20-0 x 17-2
(cathedral ceiling)

MASTER BED RM.
14-0 x 16-0

walk-in closet

No. 96497

master bath (vaulted ceiling)

storage

GARAGE
21-0 x 22-0

DINING
12-0 x 13-0

FOYER
5-4 x 13-0

PORCH

STUDY/ BED RM.
13-0 x 11-4
(vaulted ceiling)

© 1997 Donald A Gardner Architects, Inc.

63-7

50-5

SECOND FLOOR PLAN

attic storage

BED RM.
12-0 x 11-4

bath

great room below

(cathedral ceiling)

BED RM.
12-0 x 11-0

walk-in closet

linen

walk-in closet

down

BONUS RM.
11-0 x 18-4

attic storage

attic storage

Refer to **Pricing Schedule E** on the order form for pricing information

B. NATHAN

Design 96490

STATURE & DIGNITY

Multiple gables, columns, and transoms add stature and dignity to the facade of this four bedroom traditional home. Both the foyer and the Great room have impressive two-story ceilings and clerestory windows. The Great room is highlighted by built-in bookshelves, a fireplace and French doors that lead to the back porch. The breakfast area features a bay window and a rear staircase that accesses the bedrooms and bonus room upstairs. A bedroom/study and full bath are located downstairs near the master suite. The master bath indulges with dual sinks, enclosed toilet, linen closet, separate tub and shower, and a large walk-in closet. Note the large utility room, abundant garage storage, and optional fifth bedroom in the bonus room. Design by Donald A. Gardner Architects, Inc.

First floor — 2,067 sq. ft.
Second floor —
615 sq. ft.
Bonus room —
433 sq. ft.
Garage & storage —
729 sq. ft.

Total living area:
2,682 sq. ft.

SECOND FLOOR PLAN

BED RM.
13-0 x 12-0

walk-in closet

great room below

lin.

bath

(optional bedroom)
12-4 x 10-0

down

foyer below

BED RM.
14-0 x 13-4

walk-in closet

BONUS RM.
16-8 x 15-0

attic storage

FIRST FLOOR PLAN
No. 96490

© 1997   Donald A Gardner Architects, Inc.

PORCH

MASTER BED RM.
15-0 x 14-0

GREAT RM.
15-4 x 19-6
(two story ceiling)

fireplace

BRKFST.
13-0 x 11-9

KIT.
13-0 x 12-2

UTILITY
8-0 x 10-0

storage

master bath

lin.

bath

walk-in closet

BED RM./ STUDY
12-6 x 11-0

FOYER
8-1 x 10-8

DINING
14-0 x 13-4

GARAGE
22-0 x 23-0

PORCH

storage

73-0

60-6

Refer to **Pricing Schedule F** on the order form for pricing information

B. NATHAN.

COZY AND LIVABLE RANCH

The kitchen and living area flow together for a feeling of spaciousness. Three bedrooms each have ample closet space and there is a separate washer/dryer area. The bathroom is centrally located for morning convenience. No materials list is available for this plan. Design by The Garlinghouse Company

Main area — 768 sq. ft.

Total living area:
768 sq. ft.

Refer to **Pricing Schedule A** on the order form for pricing information

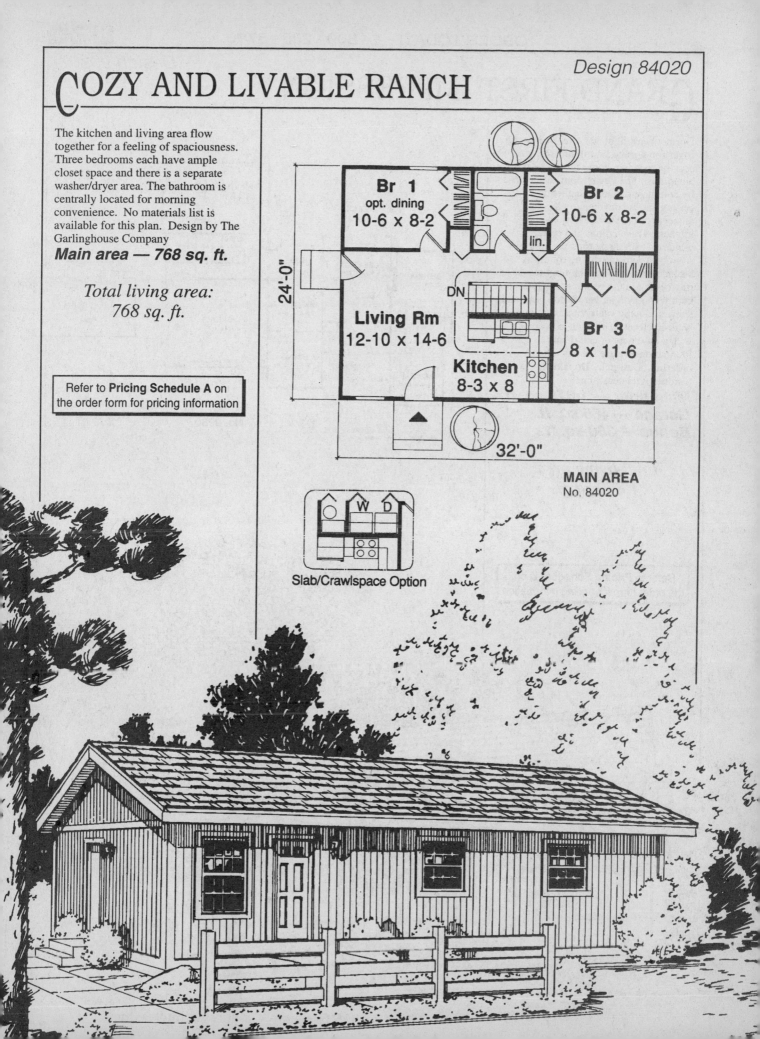

Br 1
opt. dining
10-6 x 8-2

Br 2
10-6 x 8-2

lin.

DN

Living Rm
12-10 x 14-6

Br 3
8 x 11-6

Kitchen
8-3 x 8

24'-0"

32'-0"

MAIN AREA
No. 84020

W   D

Slab/Crawlspace Option

Design 99807

GRAND FIRST IMPRESSION

Dormers cast light and interest into the foyer for a grand first impression that sets the tone in a home full of today's amenities. The Great room, articulated by columns, features a cathedral ceiling and is conveniently located adjacent to the breakfast room and kitchen. Tray ceilings and picture windows with circle tops accent the front bedroom and dining room. A secluded master suite, highlighted by a tray ceiling in the bedroom, includes a bath with skylight, garden tub, separate shower, double vanity, and spacious walk-in closet. This plan is available with a basement or crawl space foundation. Please specify when ordering. Design by Donald A. Gardner Architects, Inc.

Main floor — 1,879 sq. ft.
Garage — 485 sq. ft.
Bonus — 360 sq. ft.

Total living area:
1,879 sq. ft.

Refer to **Pricing Schedule D** on the order form for pricing information

FLOOR PLAN
No. 99807

DECK

MASTER BED RM.
14-0 x 16-0

master bath

skylight

UTILITY
7-0 x 6-4

walk-in closet

lin.

down

GREAT RM.
15-4 X 19-0

(cathedral ceiling)

BRKFST.
12-0 x 8-9

BED RM.
12-8 x 12-4

fireplace

d   w

up

storage

GARAGE
22-8 x 19-8

KIT.
12-0 x 10-5

cl

lin.

bath

FOYER
8-2 x 6-8

cl

cl

(optional door location)

BED RM.
12-0 x 11-4

PORCH

DINING
12-0 x 12-4

55-2

66-4

© 1995 Donald A Gardner Architects, Inc.

attic storage

down

BONUS RM.
22-8 X 13-0

skylights

© 1995 Donald A Gardner Architects, Inc.

DELIGHTFUL RAISED HOME

Design 94248

Inside, the entry opens right into a large grand room that is the focus for family living. The grand room has a fireplace, vaulted ceiling and double French doors to the rear deck. The kitchen and dining room are open to continue the overall feel of the style of this home. The kitchen has a large walk-in pantry, and the sink and dishwasher are in an island which creates the perfect kitchen workspace triangle. The dining room has doors to both decks while expanses of glass look out to the rear yard. Upstairs is the owner's retreat area. An overlook railing, at the top of the stairs, looks down into the grand room below. Double doors open into the suite area. To the left is the sleeping area. No materials list is available for this plan. Design by The Sater Design Group

First floor — 1,342 sq. ft.
Second floor — 511 sq. ft.
Garage — 1,740 sq. ft.

Total living area: 1,853 sq. ft.

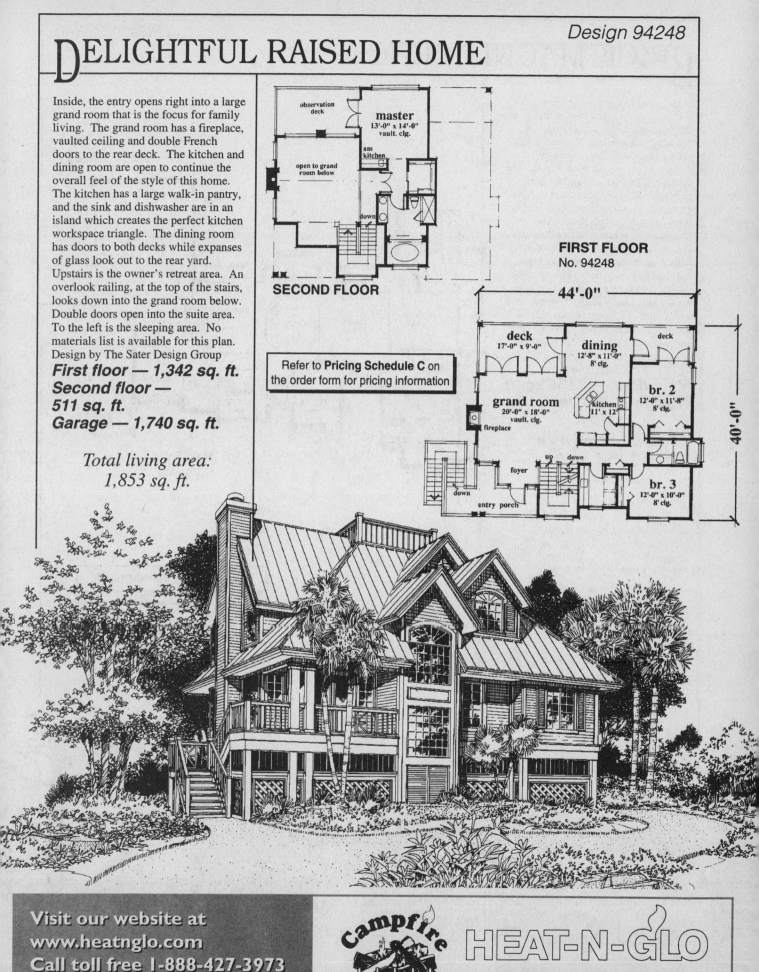

SECOND FLOOR

- observation deck
- master 13'-0" x 14'-0" vault. clg.
- open to grand room below
- am kitchen
- down

FIRST FLOOR
No. 94248

Refer to **Pricing Schedule C** on the order form for pricing information

44'-0"

40'-0"

- deck 17'-0" x 9'-0"
- dining 12'-8" x 11'-0" 8' clg.
- deck
- grand room 20'-0" x 18'-0" vault. clg.
- kitchen 11' x 12'
- fireplace
- br. 2 12'-0" x 11'-8" 8' clg.
- br. 3 12'-0" x 10'-0" 8' clg.
- foyer
- up
- down
- entry porch
- down

BRICK MAGNIFICENCE

Large windows and attractive brick detailing using segmented arches gives this home fantastic curb appeal. A convenient ranch plan allows for step-saving one floor ease. An entry/gallery greets guests upon arrival. The fireplaced living room adds a warm ambience. The island kitchen includes an extended counter/eating bar and is open to the breakfast room. The family room sports a second fireplace and built-in shelving. Two additional bedrooms include private access to a full double vanity bath. The opposite side of the home includes a luxurious master suite and a study. There is also a secondary bedroom on this side of the home that includes a walk-in closet and a private full bath. No materials list is available for this plan. Design by Fillmore Design Group

Main floor — 2,858 sq. ft.
Garage — 768 sq. ft.

Total living area:
2,858 sq. ft.

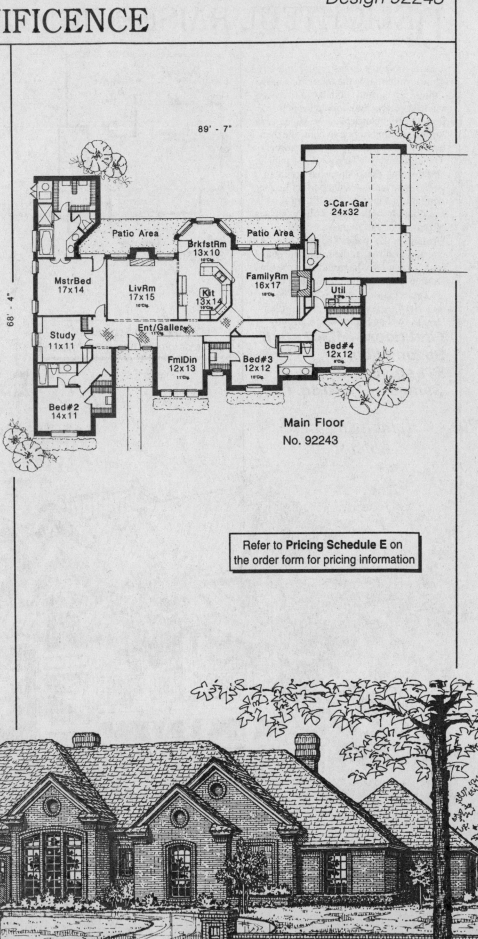

Main Floor
No. 92243

Refer to **Pricing Schedule E** on the order form for pricing information

Design 92048

Unusual and Dramatic

Unusual and dramatic would describe this 3,500 square foot two-story. When you step into the entry you are surrounded by arched doorways leading to the den on one side, the living/dining room on the other and the sunken family room straight ahead. The master bedroom is on the first floor and has two large walk-in closets and a master bath with a large sunken tub and double vanity. The kitchen area features an island with raised counter and lots of built-ins. Adjacent to the kitchen is an octagonal shaped breakfast room looking out over the deck. A first floor laundry and triple garage round out the main features of the first floor. A double curved stairway takes you upstairs to a balcony looking down over the family room, three more bedrooms and two full baths. Design by Urban Design Group

First floor — 2,646 sq. ft.
Second floor — 854 sq. ft.
Basement — 2,656 sq. ft.

Total living area: 3,500 sq. ft.

Refer to **Pricing Schedule F** on the order form for pricing information

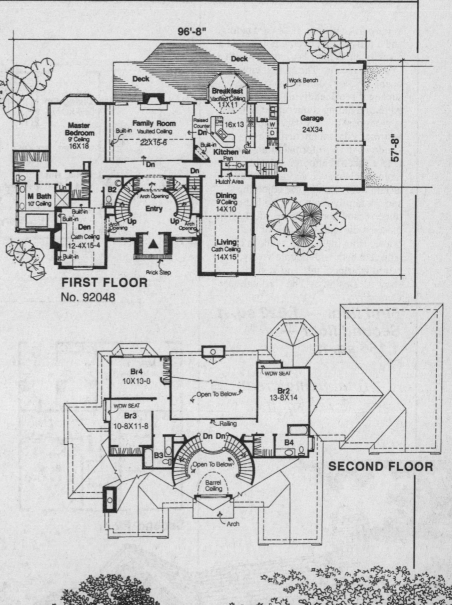

FIRST FLOOR
No. 92048

SECOND FLOOR

Design 10805

YESTERDAY'S CHARM

Wide corner boards, clapboard siding, and a full-length covered porch lend a friendly air to this classic home with a Colonial accent. The central entry opens to a cozy den on the right, a sunken, fireplaced living room with adjoining dining room on the left, and straight past the powder room to a gourmet's dream kitchen. Bay windows in the informal dining nook lend a cheerful atmosphere to the entire kitchen area, accentuated by atrium doors linking the adjoining, sunken family room with both the three-season porch and rear deck. The master suite spans the rear of the house, enjoying a huge, walk-in closet, a private bath with double vanity, a raised whirlpool tub, and step-in shower. Design by The Garlinghouse Company

First floor — 1,622 sq. ft.
Second floor —
1,156 sq. ft.

Total living area:
2,778 sq. ft.

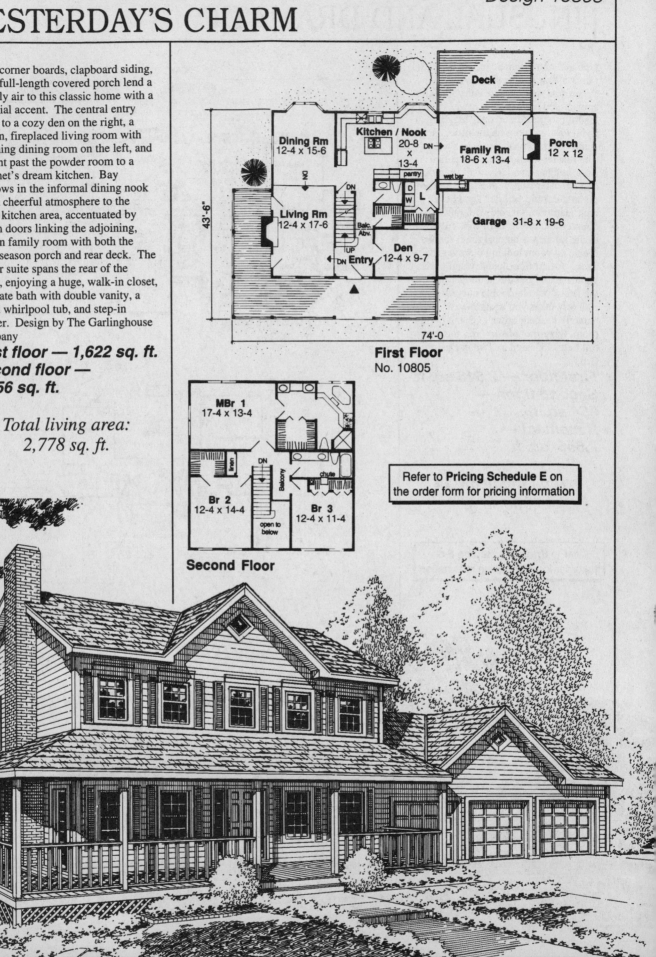

First Floor
No. 10805

Second Floor

Refer to **Pricing Schedule E** on
the order form for pricing information

Design 96513

MODERN SLANT ON A COUNTRY THEME

The Country styled front porch highlighting this home provides a country theme that has been enhanced by dormer windows. Inside is a thoroughly modern floor plan. Great open spaces give a spacious airy feeling to the entire home. The Great room is accented by a quaint, corner fireplace and a ceiling fan. The dining room flows from the Great room and the kitchen and is graced by natural light from the attractive bay window. The kitchen's snack bar conveniently serves informal snacks and meals on the go. The master suite is secluded in its own separate wing for total privacy. The two additional bedrooms share the full bath in the hallway between them. Design by Vaughn Lauban Designs

Main floor — 1,648 sq. ft.
Garage — 479 sq. ft.

Total living area:
1,648 sq. ft.

Refer to **Pricing Schedule B** on the order form for pricing information

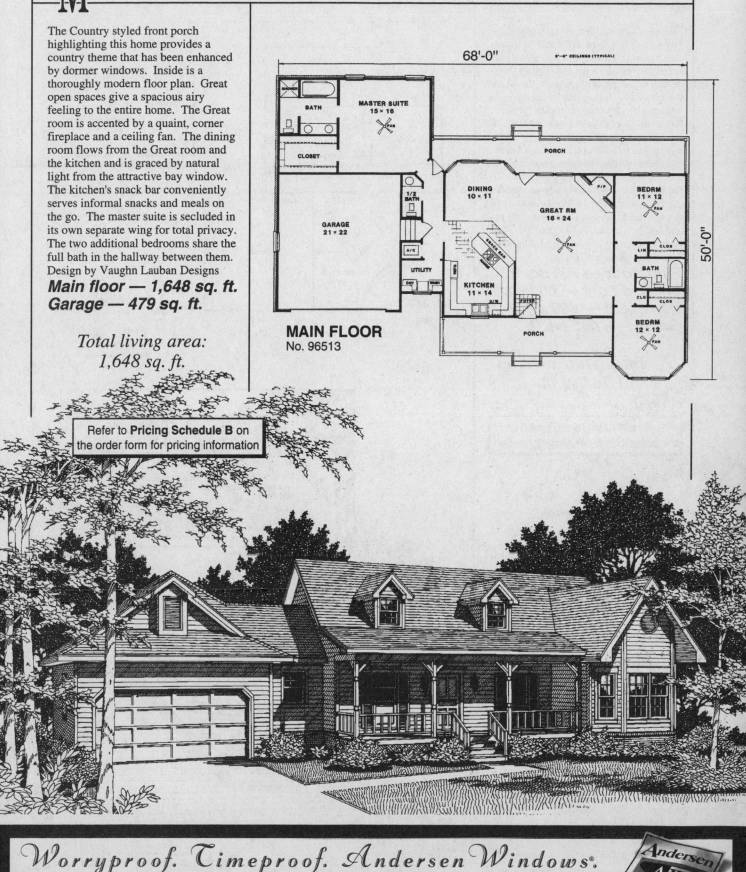

MAIN FLOOR
No. 96513

68'-0"

50'-0"

8'-0" CEILINGS (TYPICAL)

SHOWER
BATH
MASTER SUITE
15 × 16
FAN
CLOSET
GARAGE
21 × 22
1/2 BATH
A/C
UTILITY
DRY   WASH
PORCH
DINING
10 × 11
GREAT RM
16 × 24
FAN
SNACK BAR
KITCHEN
11 × 14
D/W
PORCH
F/P
BEDRM
11 × 12
FAN
LIN   CLOS
BATH
CLO   CLOS
BEDRM
12 × 12
FAN

Design 34901

FARM-TYPE TRADITIONAL

This pleasant traditional design has a farmhouse flavor exterior that incorporates a covered porch and features a circle wood louver on its garage, giving this design a feeling of sturdiness. Inside, on the first floor to the right of the foyer, is a formal dining room complete with a bay window and an elevated ceiling. To the left of the foyer is the living room with a gas-light fireplace. The kitchen is connected to the breakfast room and there is also a room for the laundry facilities. A half-bath is also featured on the first floor. The master bedroom, on the second floor, has its own private bath and walk-in closet. The other two bedrooms share a full bath. Design by The Garlinghouse Company

First floor — 909 sq. ft.
Second floor — 854 sq. ft.
Basement — 899 sq. ft.
Garage — 491 sq. ft.

Total living area:
1,763 sq. ft.

Refer to **Pricing Schedule B** on the order form for pricing information

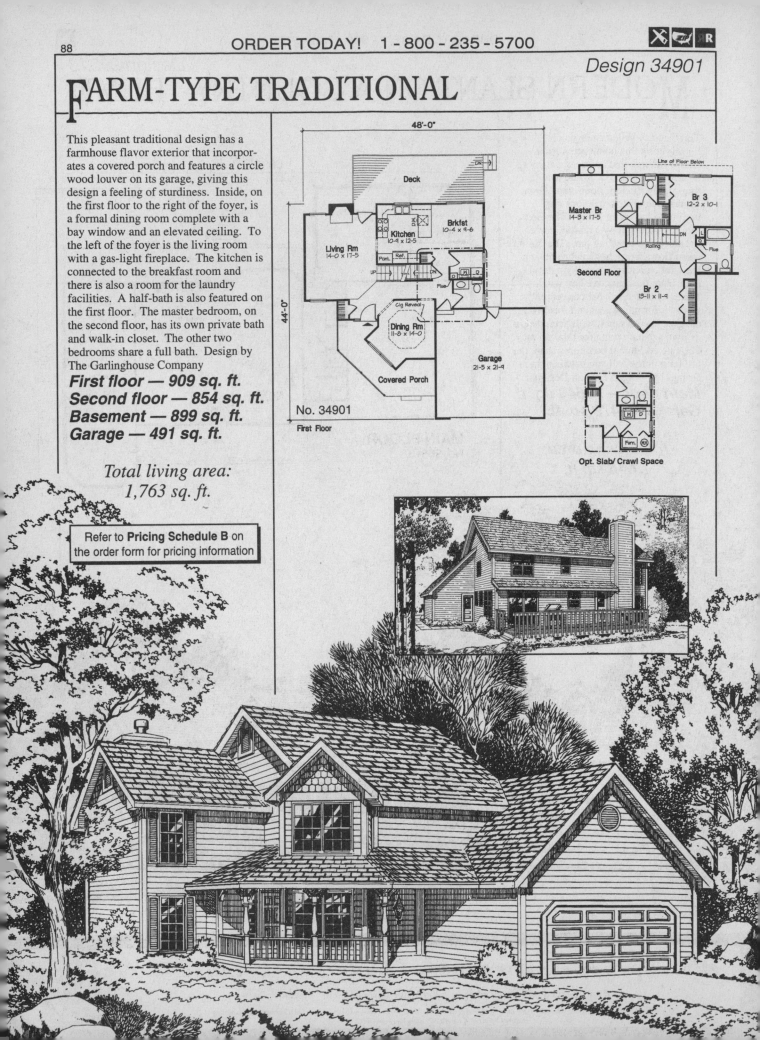

First Floor (48'-0" × 44'-0")
Deck, Living Rm 14-0 x 17-5, Kitchen 10-4 x 12-5, Brkfst 10-4 x 9-6, Pant., Ref., Dining Rm 11-8 x 14-0, Clg Reveal, Garage 21-5 x 21-4, Covered Porch, No. 34901

Second Floor
Master Br 14-3 x 17-5, Br 3 12-2 x 10-1, Br 2 13-11 x 11-9, Line of Floor Below, Railing, Flue

Opt. Slab/ Crawl Space

TRIPLE TANDEM GARAGE

The large foyer of this gracious ranch leads you back to the bright and spacious living room. The large open kitchen features a central work island with lots of extra storage space and there is also a handy laundry room with pantry and garage access. The master suite features a private master bath with oversized tub, corner shower, room-sized walk-in closet, as well as a bay shared sitting area and French doors. The two front bedrooms share a full bath. The lower level has plenty of open space for future expansion. The triple tandem garage provides space for a third car, boat, or just plenty of storage and work space. No materials list is available for this plan. Design by Ahmann Design, Inc.

Main floor — 1,761 sq. ft.
Basement — 1,761 sq. ft.
Garage — 658 sq. ft.

Total living area:
1,761 sq. ft.

Refer to **Pricing Schedule B** on the order form for pricing information

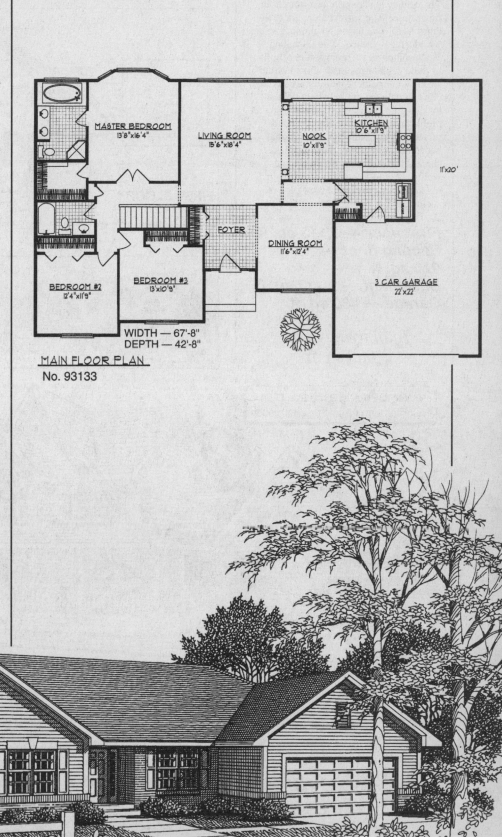

MASTER BEDROOM
13'8"x16'4"

LIVING ROOM
15'6"x18'4"

NOOK
10'x11'9"

KITCHEN
10'6"x11'9"

11'x20'

FOYER

DINING ROOM
11'6"x12'4"

3 CAR GARAGE
22'x22'

BEDROOM #2
12'4"x11'9"

BEDROOM #3
13'x10'9"

WIDTH — 67'-8"
DEPTH — 42'-8"

MAIN FLOOR PLAN
No. 93133

WRAP-AROUND COUNTRY PORCH

Design 24245

The homey feel continues throughout this house. The formal areas flank the entry hall. The living room includes a wonderful fireplace. The U-shaped kitchen includes a breakfast bar, built-in pantry, planning desk and a double sink. A convenient laundry area is close at hand in the half-bath off the mudroom. The master suite is highlighted by a walk-in closet and private master bath. Two additional bedrooms, one with a built-in desk, share a full hall bath with a double vanity. A window seat with built-in bookshelves provides a cozy place to curl up with a book. Design by The Garlinghouse Company

First floor — 1,113 sq. ft.
Second floor — 970 sq. ft.
Basement — 1,113 sq. ft.
Garage — 480 sq. ft.

Total living area: 2,083 sq. ft.

Refer to **Pricing Schedule C** on the order form for pricing information

FIRST FLOOR
No. 24245

74'-0"

41'-0"

Garage 21-5 x 21-5

Mud Room

Kitchen 12-0 x 12-5

Deck

Nook

Family 23-1 x 12-5

Pantry

Dining 12-0 x 14-2

Living 13-1 x 14-2

Porch

Crawl Space/Slab Option

SECOND FLOOR

Br 2 12-0 x 12-5

Master Br 12-0 x 15-4

Br 3 12-0 x 11-4

Bath

Bedroom 11'11" x 11'2"

Bedroom 12'5" x 11'2"

Walk-in Closet

Bonus Room 15'3" x 12'

Master Bedroom 15'4" x 12'1"

Balcony

Computer Desk

We have selected as our Home Plan of the Year a popular favorite from our collection, Plan #24245. This country style home has distinct qualities that set it apart from other homes of its genre. Take a closer look, and you will see that this is not only a great family home, but also a unique one.

HOME PLAN OF THE YEAR

Design 99820

EXTRA SPECIAL LUXURIES

Home buyers who appreciate the finer things in life will love the extras this home provides—extra living area, extra garage, storage space, and extra special luxuries. The front door opens to a central foyer that leads left to the formal dining room, right to the family bedroom wing, or straight ahead to the large Great room with cathedral ceiling, fireplace, built-ins, and access to a sun room. The kitchen with center work island and the Great room are separated only by interior accent columns. Convenient placement at the rear provides ultimate privacy for the indulgent master suite with all of today's popular amenities. Design by Donald A. Gardner Architects, Inc.

Main floor — 2,602 sq. ft.
Garage — 715 sq. ft.
Bonus room —
399 sq. ft.

Total living area:
2,602 sq. ft.

BONUS RM.
19-1 x 16-4

attic storage

skylights

attic storage

MASTER BED RM.
14-0 x 19-4

master bath

skylights

walk-in closet

(vaulted ceiling)

PATIO

storage

UTIL.

SUN RM.
16-0 x 10-0

skylights

BRKFST.
12-0 x 10-10

BED RM.
13-0 x 12-0

(cathedral ceiling)

GARAGE
24-2 x 23-0

up

GREAT RM.
16-0 x 21-0

bath

KIT.
12-0 x 17-2

fireplace

BED RM.
11-8 x 11-0

pan.

storage

FOYER
12-0 x 5-8

walk-in closet

DINING
12-0 x 14-0

PORCH

pd. rm.

BED RM./ STUDY
12-0 x 12-0

69-6

75-3

FLOOR PLAN
No. 99820

© Donald A. Gardner Architects, Inc.

Refer to **Pricing Schedule F** on the order form for pricing information

Design 32063

FOREST COTTAGE

A spacious open living area unfolds with a Great room, kitchen and separate breakfast and dining areas. The multi-purpose island includes a double sink, dishwasher, range and ample counter space. The second floor includes two bedrooms, and a master suite. The lower level includes an exercise room, guest room with a full, private bath and walk-in closet, a media room, mechanical room and storage. A steeply pitched roofline and deep eaves along with rounded windows, dormers and Craftsman-style details contribute to the curb appeal of this home. Design by The Meredith Corporation

First floor — 1,642 sq. ft.
Second floor — 1,411 sq. ft.
Lower floor — 1,230 sq. ft.
Basement — 412 sq. ft.

Total living area: 4,283 sq. ft.

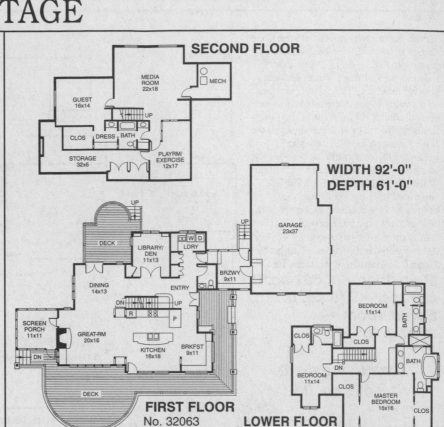

SECOND FLOOR

WIDTH 92'-0"
DEPTH 61'-0"

FIRST FLOOR
No. 32063

LOWER FLOOR

Refer to **Pricing Schedule F** on the order form for pricing information

A special custom design, Plan #32063 is being highlighted for its Architectural Impact. Behind the quaint cottage façade is an imaginative floor plan with three levels of living space. Impeccably styled with many extraordinary features like multiple windows and doors overlooking the decks this cottage is perfect.

Design 96503

COLUMNED KEYSTONE ARCHED ENTRY

This home has extra touches and attention to detail that today's home buyer is looking for. The keystone arches and arched transoms above the windows display a pleasing curb appeal. Inside, the formal dining room and the study flank the foyer while the expansive Great room looms ahead. A focal point fireplace catches the visitor's eye from the foyer. The efficient kitchen features a peninsula counter extending work space. A bayed nook offers the homeowner a bright, cheery place to start their day. The split bedroom plan gives the master suite privacy. A step ceiling and interesting master bath with a triangular area for the oval bath tub pampers the owner. The secondary bedrooms share a full bath in the hall. Design by Vaughn Lauban Designs

Main floor — 2,256 sq. ft.
Garage — 514 sq. ft.

Total living area:
2,256 sq. ft.

MAIN FLOOR
No. 96503

Refer to **Pricing Schedule D** on the order form for pricing information

MASTER RETREAT AND SPACIOUS HOME

Here's a compact beauty with a wide-open feeling. Step past the inviting front porch, and savor a breathtaking view of active areas: the columned entry with its open staircase and windows high overhead; the soaring living room, divided from the kitchen and dining room by the towering fireplace chimney; the screened porch beyond the triple living room windows. Tucked behind the stairs, you'll find a cozy parlor. Upstairs, the master suite is an elegant retreat you'll want to come home for, with its romantic dormer window seat, private balcony, and double-vanity bath.
Design by The Meredith Corporation

First floor — 1,290 sq. ft.
Second floor — 405 sq. ft.
Screened porch — 152 sq. ft.
Garage — 513 sq. ft.

Total living area: 1,695 sq. ft.

WIDTH 50'-8"
DEPTH 61'-8"

No. 19422
First Floor

Refer to **Pricing Schedule B** on the order form for pricing information

Design 98004

COMPACT COUNTRY HOME

This compact country home is economical due to its squared off design, yet remains stylish with architectural accents such as gables and arched windows. Completely open to one another, the Great room, dining room, and kitchen are combined under a grand cathedral ceiling creating a wonderfully comfortable gathering room. Built-ins flank the fireplace, making decorating easy. The split bedroom design places the master suite on one side of the house with an elegant tray ceiling, a private, fully appointed bath, and a walk-in closet. Two more bedrooms share a full bath on the opposite side of the home near the utility room and access to the bonus room. Design by Donald A. Gardner Architects, Inc.

Main floor — 1,517 sq. ft.
Bonus room —
287 sq. ft.
Garage — 447 sq. ft.

Total living area:
1,517 sq. ft.

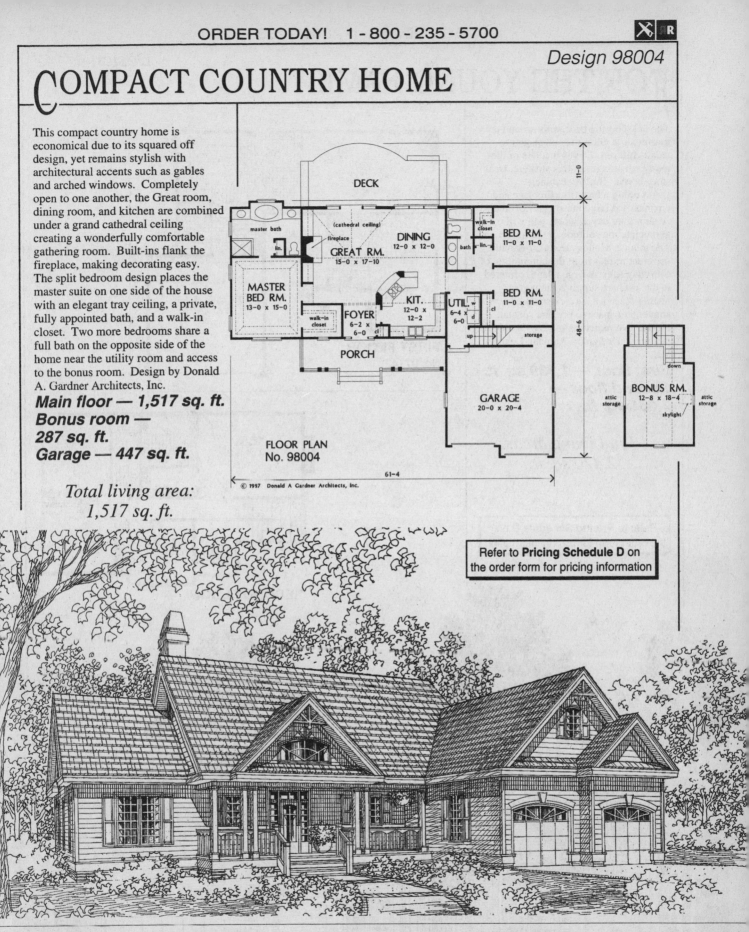

FLOOR PLAN
No. 98004

© 1997 Donald A Gardner Architects, Inc.

Refer to **Pricing Schedule D** on the order form for pricing information

Weather Shield
Windows & Doors

www.weathershield.com

Weather Shield Windows and Doors offers project planning guides for your remodeling or new home project. FREE. Specify "Remodeling" or "New Home" Planning Guide by calling

1-800-477-6808

Design 97142

FOR THE YOUNG FAMILY

The neighboring bedrooms around the master suite allows for closeness to small children. This is just one of the many advantages of this striking, two-story home. Built-in cabinets surrounding a beautiful fireplace add coziness for large family get-togethers. After a long day at work, you will appreciate the solitude of the quiet den. The unique window seat also provides the great retreat from the commotion of everyday life. A large island, centered in the kitchen, supplies the perfect resting place for a quick snack or a convenient space to prepare special meals.   No materials list is available for this plan. Design by Ahmann Design, Inc.

First floor — 1,339 sq. ft.
Second floor —
1,081 sq. ft.

Total living area;
2,420 sq. ft.

Refer to **Pricing Schedule D** on the order form for pricing information

FIRST FLOOR
No. 97142

SECOND FLOOR

Design 91750

COUNTRY STYLE

The Country style of this home sends a welcoming message. And since this home is a single level it can be easily adapted for wheelchair accessiblity. Skylights brighten a spacious vaulted family room with tall windows and a glass door that opens onto another railed deck at the rear. More vaulted ceilings add elegance to the dining room and living room. The kitchen is huge yet efficient. This is achieved by clustering the most heavily used features - cooktop, sink and refrigerator - in a triangle. A dishwasher and trash compactor are next to the sink. Bedrooms and a utility room are down the hall to the right of the entry. Amenities in the spacious owners' suite include a large walk-in closet and private bathroom with raised spa tub, oversized shower, and a dressing room with a basin in the vanity. The utility room has a fold-down ironing board and plenty of counter space for folding clothes. Design by Landmark Designs, Inc.

Main area — 3,188 sq. ft.
Porch — 560 sq. ft.
Deck — 324 sq. ft.
Garage — 705 sq. ft.

Total living area:
3,188 sq. ft.

WIDTH 84'-0"
DEPTH 73'-6"

Refer to **Pricing Schedule E** on the order form for pricing information

SHOP

GARAGE
29⁸ X 22⁰

DECK

HOBBY / OFFICE
11¹⁰ X 12²

NOOK

MASTER SUITE
15¹⁰ X 16⁸

SPA

PANTRY

FAMILY
16⁸ X 17¹⁰
VAULTED

SKYLIGHTS

BEDROOM 2
13² X 10¹⁰

DINING
15⁰ X 12⁰
VAULTED

LINEN
SHELVES

BOOKS WOOD BOX

ENTRY
VAULTED

BEDROOM 4
13⁸ X 12⁴
SKYLIGHT

BEDROOM 3
13⁸ X 12⁴
SKYLIGHT

LIVING
17⁰ X 15⁴
VAULTED

PORCH

MAIN AREA
No. 91750

PERFECT FOR A CORNER LOT

This Ranch plan is ideal for a corner lot, with a rear garage that enters from the side. The focal point of this plan is the Great room with a vaulted ceiling, and loft above. The French doors on either side of the fireplace open onto a screened porch. The large double-L kitchen is open to the breakfast room, which has a bay window. The master bedroom has a large walk-in closet, and the master bath features a corner tub, as well as double vanities. Two other bedrooms on the opposite end of the house make this split-bedroom design popular. Each of these bedrooms has a walk-in closet, and a desk for school-age children. The loft has a vaulted ceiling and overlooks the Great room with an open rail balcony. This plan is available with a basement or crawl space foundation. Please specify when ordering. Design by Corley Plan Service

Main floor — 1,996 sq. ft.
Loft — 305 sq. ft.

Total living area:
2,301 sq. ft.

Refer to **Pricing Schedule D** on the order form for pricing information

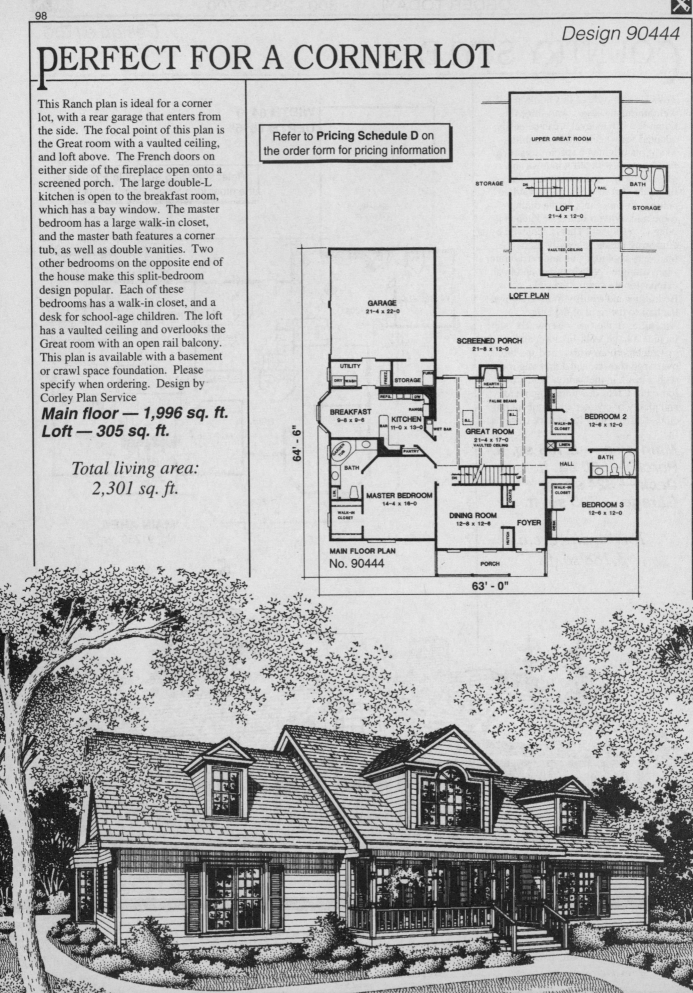

SUNNY CHARACTER

An elegant, bayed dining room adjoins the centrally located island kitchen, which features easy access to a screened porch. A short hall leads past the laundry and handy powder room to a huge, fireplaced living room that opens to a rear deck. Walk under the balcony to the first floor master suite with its walk-in closet and luxury bath. You'll love the quiet, yet convenient location of this special retreat. The second floor balcony overlooking the living room and two-story foyer links two more bedrooms, each with a huge closet, and a large divided bath.
Design by The Garlinghouse Company

First floor — 1,293 sq. ft.
Second floor — 526 sq. ft.
Basement — 1,286 sq. ft.
Garage — 484 sq. ft.
Breezeway — 180 sq. ft.

Total living area: 1,819 sq. ft.

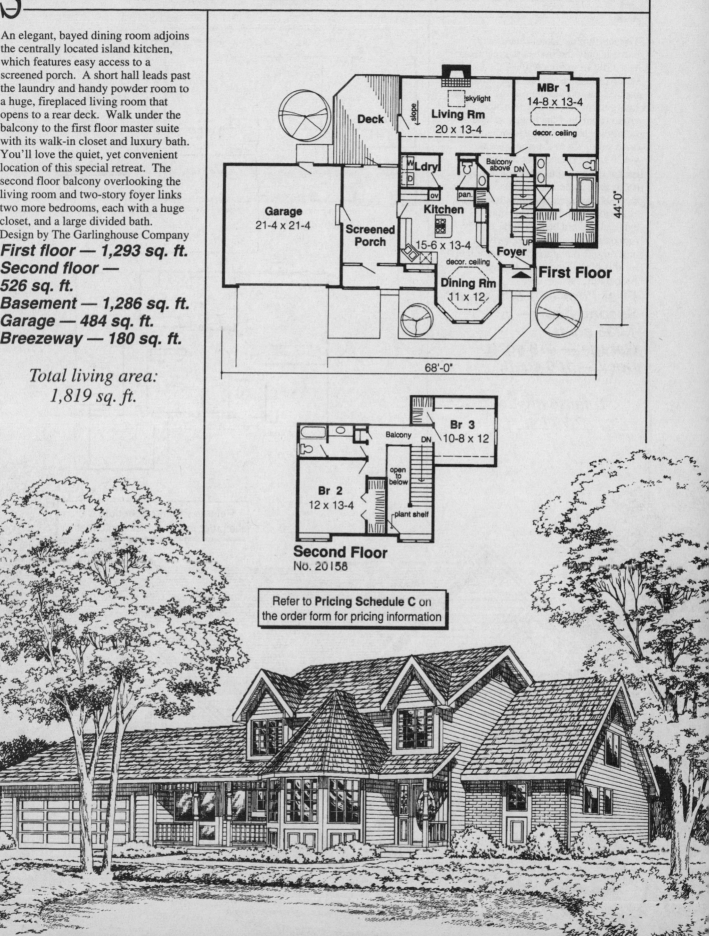

Refer to **Pricing Schedule C** on the order form for pricing information

Design 93609

AN IDEAL FAMILY HOME

The inviting facade of this stately home is only the first of the features you will fall in love with. This ideal family home has no less than three living areas on the main level, a classic living room, a dramatic two story grand room, and the highly valued family/keeping room. Heading up the open stair case to the upper level, you'll find a spectacular master bedroom suite with a private sitting room retreat and huge bath. There are three other large bedrooms, one with an optional full bath. This plan is available with a basement or slab foundation. Please specify when ordering. No materials list is available for this plan. Design by Garrell Associates, Inc.

First floor — 1,535 sq. ft.
Second floor —
1,236 sq. ft.
Garage — 418 sq. ft.
Deck — 100 sq. ft.

Total living area:
2,771 sq. ft.

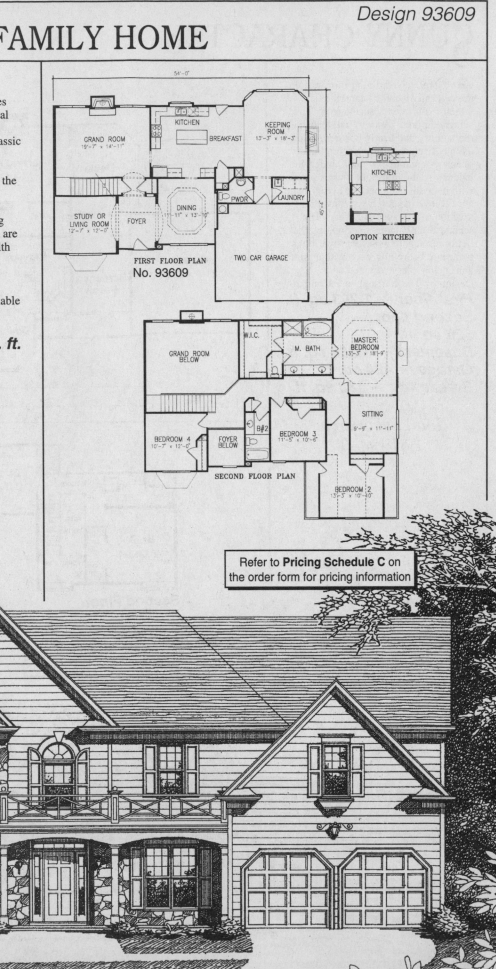

FIRST FLOOR PLAN
No. 93609

OPTION KITCHEN

SECOND FLOOR PLAN

Refer to **Pricing Schedule C** on the order form for pricing information

CLASSIC COTTAGE

Design 98014

This classic cottage offers maximum comfort for its economic design and narrow lot width. A cozy front porch invites relaxation, while twin dormers and a gabled garage provide substantial curb appeal. The foyer features a generous coat closet and niche for displaying collectibles. The Great room gains drama from two clerestory dormers and a balcony that overlooks the room from the second floor. With plenty of space for more than one cook, the kitchen services both dining room and Great room with ease. Topped by a elegant tray ceiling, the first floor master suite enjoys a private bath and a walk-in closet, while the upstairs bedrooms and bonus room share a hall bath with linen closet. Design by Donald A. Gardner Architects, Inc.

First floor — 1,336 sq. ft.
Second floor —
523 sq. ft.
Bonus room —
225 sq. ft.
Garage & storage —
492 sq. ft.

Total living area:
1,859 sq. ft.

SECOND FLOOR PLAN

- BED RM. 13-0 x 11-0
- BED RM. 11-0 x 12-0
- BONUS RM. 11-0 x 16-8
- attic storage
- great room below
- railing
- foyer below
- down
- bath
- lin.

FIRST FLOOR PLAN
No. 98014

- PORCH
- DINING 11-0 x 10-0
- MASTER BED RM. 13-0 x 15-0
- GREAT RM. 19-0 x 17-0 (cathedral ceiling) — fireplace
- KIT. 11-0 x 13-0
- master bath
- walk-in closet
- FOYER 6-0 x 11-11 up
- UTIL. 9-1 x 5-8
- pd. rm.
- storage
- pan.
- GARAGE 21-0 x 21-0
- PORCH
- 53-0
- 45-0

© 1998 Donald A Gardner, Inc.

Refer to **Pricing Schedule D** on the order form for pricing information

© 1998 Donald A. Gardner, Inc.

B. NATHAN

TERRIFIC FRONT PORCH

Design 93261

If you are looking for a Country type home with a few extra touches, this may be the house you are looking for. The country feeling comes from the front porch. Those extra touches abound in the expansive living area with a fireplace, the two front bedrooms that enjoy bay windows and the sunny breakfast area that includes a built-in pantry and access to the rear sun deck. The master suite provides the owner with a private retreat. The master bath includes a walk-in closet, oval tub, double vanity and separate shower. The two additional bedrooms are located on the opposite side of the house and have easy access to a full hall bath. The added convenience of a main area laundry is included. Design by Jannis Vann & Associates, Inc.

Main area — 1,778 sq. ft.
Basement — 1,008 sq. ft.
Garage — 728 sq. ft.

Total living area:
1,778 sq. ft.

Refer to **Pricing Schedule B** on the order form for pricing information

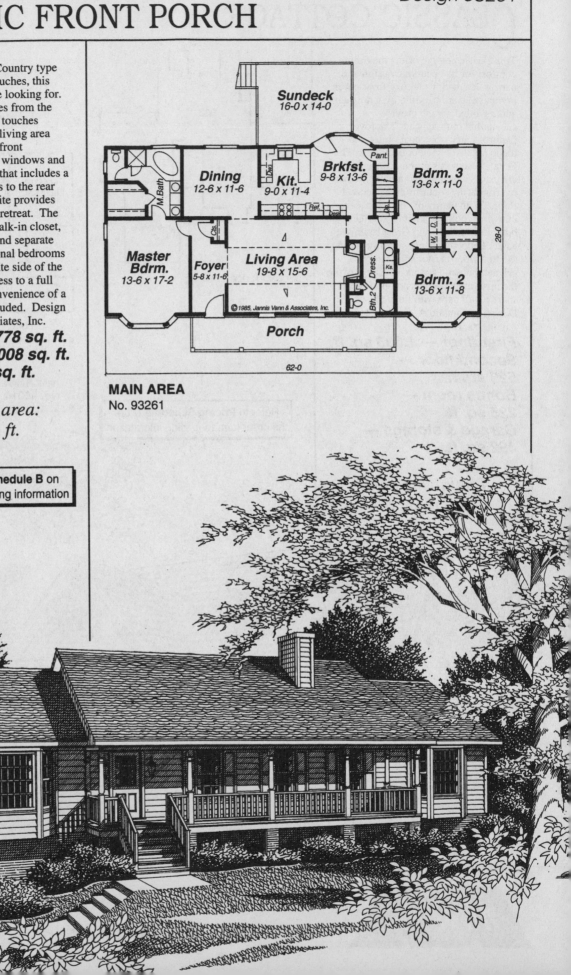

MAIN AREA
No. 93261

Design 99856

COMPACT COUNTRY COTTAGE

Multi-paned bay window, dormers, cupola, covered porch, and a variety of building materials give this compact country cottage visual impact. The foyer opens to a large Great room, with fireplace and cathedral ceiling, which flows to the open dining and kitchen area. Two front bedrooms, one with bay window, the other with walk-in closet, share an ample bath. The master suite is privately located at the rear with walk-in closet and private bath with double vanity. A partially covered deck with skylights becomes an outdoor room accessible from dining room, Great room, and master bedroom. Design by Donald A. Gardner Architects, Inc.

Main floor — 1,310 sq. ft.
Garage & Storage — 455 sq. ft.

Total living area:
1,310 sq. ft.

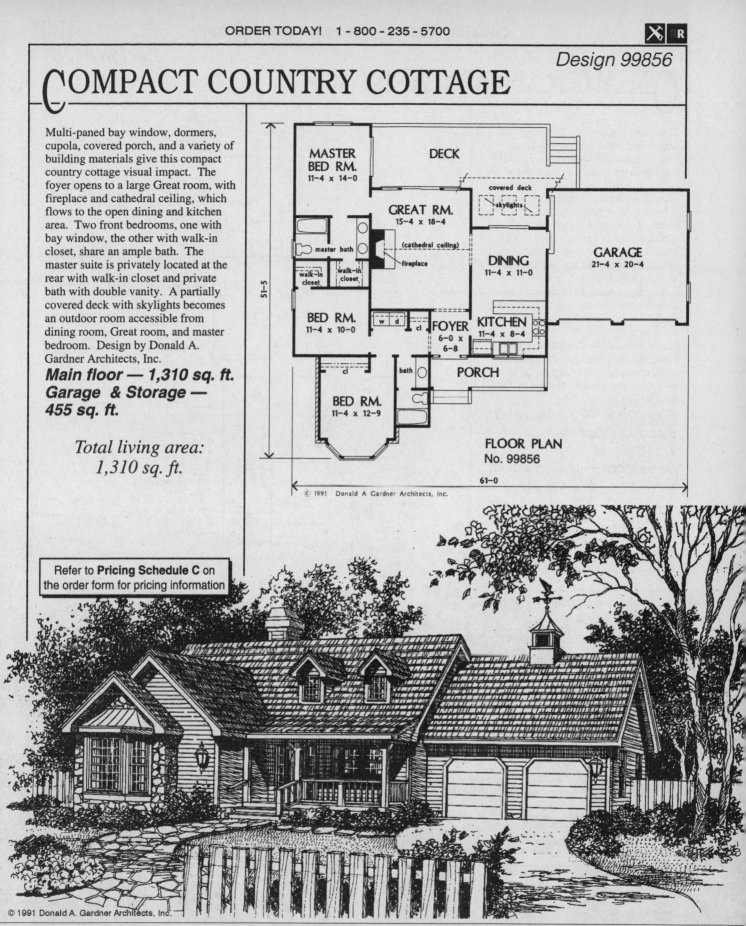

FLOOR PLAN
No. 99856

© 1991 Donald A Gardner Architects, Inc.

© 1991 Donald A. Gardner Architects, Inc.

Design 97288

ON A GRAND SCALE

This home provides a grand impression with a large two-story foyer. The dining room's entrance is defined by columns and the living room is to the right of the foyer. The family room has a two-story ceiling and a cozy fireplace. The study is tucked into the right rear corner of the home. The kitchen includes a cooktop island, a built-in pantry and plenty of counter space. The master suite is on the second floor and features a tray ceiling over the bedrooms and lavish bath. The sunny sitting room and two-walk-in closets completes the suite. The three additional bedrooms have easy access to a full bath and walk-in closets. This plan is available with a basement or crawl space foundation. Please specify when ordering. No materials list is available for this plan. Design by Frank Betz Associates, Inc.

First floor — 1,595 sq. ft.
Second floor — 1,518 sq. ft.
Basement — 1,595 sq. ft.
Garage — 475 sq. ft.

Total living area:
3,113 sq. ft.

© Frank Betz Associates

FIRST FLOOR PLAN
No. 97288

SECOND FLOOR PLAN

Refer to **Pricing Schedule E** on the order form for pricing information

© Frank Betz Associates

DRAMATIC RANCH

The exterior of this Ranch home is all wood with interesting lines. More than an ordinary ranch home, it has an expansive feeling to drive up to. The large living area has a stone fireplace and decorative beams. The kitchen and dining room lead to an outside deck. The laundry room has a large pantry, and is off the eating area. The master bedroom has a wonderful bathroom with a huge walk-in closet. In the front of the house, there are two additional bedrooms with a bathroom. This house offers one floor living and has nice big rooms. Design by The Garlinghouse Company

Main area — 1,792 sq. ft.
Basement — 818 sq. ft.
Garage — 857 sq. ft.

Total living area:
1,792 sq. ft.

Refer to **Pricing Schedule B** on the order form for pricing information

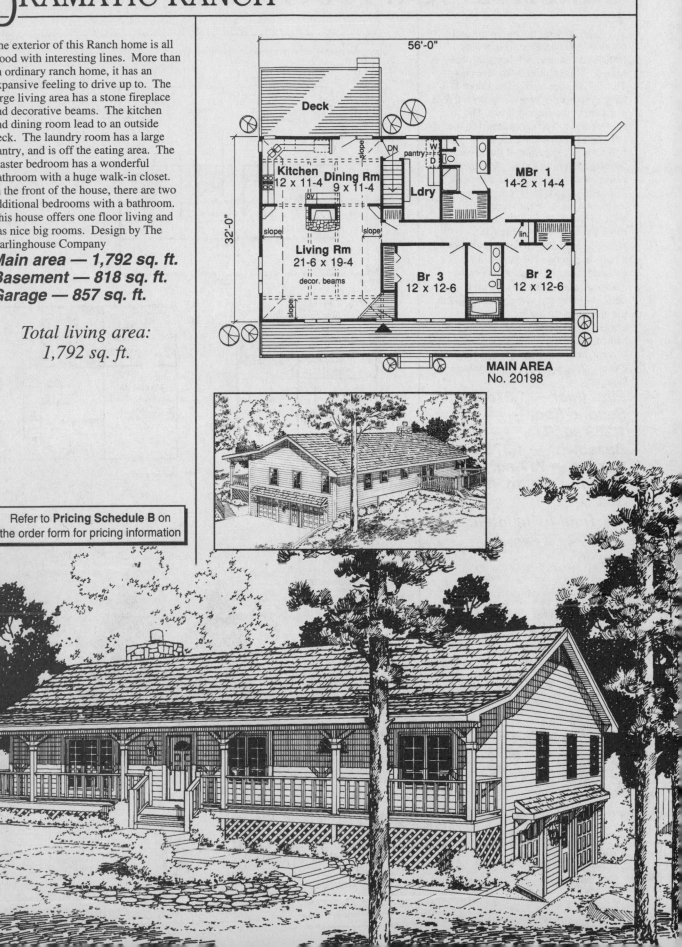

MAIN AREA
No. 20198

PORCH ADDS A TOUCH OF COUNTRY

The large, welcoming, wrap-around porch of this home exudes an old-fashioned country feel, but don't be fooled. This is a totally modern home. Through the decorative front door is a large entrance foyer with an attractive staircase to the second floor. The study/guest room is positioned to the left and has convenient access to a full hall bath. To the right of the foyer is the elegant dining room. A decorative ceiling treatment enhances the room. The family room is expansive and includes a massive fireplace with built-in bookshelves. The breakfast room has a convenient built-in planning desk and the kitchen includes a built-in pantry. The peninsula counter/eating bar separates the two rooms. A corner double sink and ample counter and storage space add to the efficiency of the kitchen. The master bedroom is crowned by a cathedral ceiling and includes a private, lavish bath with a walk-in closet. Design by The Garlinghouse Company

First floor — 1,378 sq. ft.
Second floor — 1,269 sq. ft.
Basement — 1,378 sq. ft.
Garage — 717 sq. ft.
Porch — 801 sq. ft.

Total living area:
2,647 sq. ft.

First Floor
71'-0"
45'-0"

BOOKS
Family Rm 21-4 x 15-1
Brkfst 10-6 x 15-1
Kit. 9-6 x 15-1
Shop 14-5 x 15-5
DESK
PANTRY
Study/ Guest 11-8 x 14-0
Foyer
Dining Rm 11-8 x 14-0
UP
Garage 21-5 x 22-0
DN
Porch
DN

First Floor
No. 24403

Optional Second Floor
DN
RAILING
Br 4 12-2 x 10-9
Br 3 11-8 x 13-6

Optional Second Floor

Second Floor
WLP-TUB
Mstr Bath
Br 2 15-5 x 11-4
LINEN
LINEN
Master Br 14-0 x 17-9
RAILING
DN
Sitting Area 12-2 x 10-9
Br 3 11-8 x 13-6

Second Floor

Crawl Space/Slab Option
HW
FURN
Shop 14-5 x 15-5

Crawl Space/Slab Option

Refer to **Pricing Schedule E** on the order form for pricing information

Design 99487

COLUMNS AND ARCHED WINDOWS

Beautiful columns and arched transoms are focal points of this ranch home elevation. The ten foot entry has formal views of the volume dining room and the Great room, which features a brick fireplace and arched windows. The large island kitchen offers an angled range and a pantry. The sunny breakfast room has an atrium door to the backyard, and a garage with built-in shelves accesses the home through an efficient laundry room. The separate bedroom wing provides optimum privacy. The master suite includes a whirlpool bath with a sloped ceiling, a plant shelf, a double vanity and a walk-in closet. This plan is available with a basement or slab foundation. Please specify when ordering. Design by Design Basics, Inc.

Main floor — 1,806 sq. ft.
Garage — 548 sq. ft.

Total living area:
1,806 sq. ft.

Refer to **Pricing Schedule C** on the order form for pricing information

No. 99487
MAIN FLOOR

Bfst. 11⁴ x 11⁴
Grt. rm. 15⁰ x 20⁰
10'-0" CEILING
Br. 2 11⁰ x 11⁰
Kit. 12¹⁰ x 12⁰
Br. 3 11⁰ x 11⁰
Din. 11⁰ x 14⁰
10'-0" CLG.
Mbr. 14⁰ x 15⁰
10'-0" CLG.
Gar. 23⁴ x 22⁴
SHELVES
COVERED PORCH
WHIRLPOOL
56'-0"
55'-4"

© design basics inc.

© design basics inc.

Design 32113

INTRIGUING FEATURES

Round and angular shapes blend gracefully into the eye-catching contemporary design of this home. An angled garage, an arched entry and a glass block stairway turret are just some of the intriguing features of this home. On the first floor, the foyer opens to the angled dining room and the living room, with a high ceiling, a fireplace and dramatic windows. On the second floor, there is a master suite with two walk-in closets, a private bath and access to a private deck. The exercise area is located between the bedrooms and there are two additional bedrooms with private bath access. Design by The Meredith Corporation

Main level — 2,091 sq. ft.
Upper level — 1,746 sq. ft.
Garage — 641 sq. ft.

Total living area: 3,837 sq. ft.

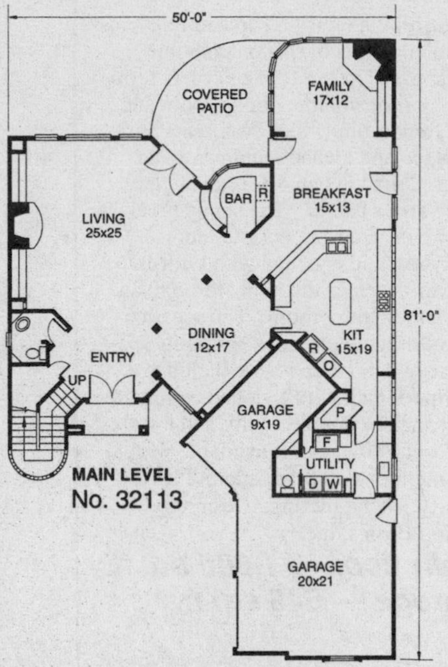

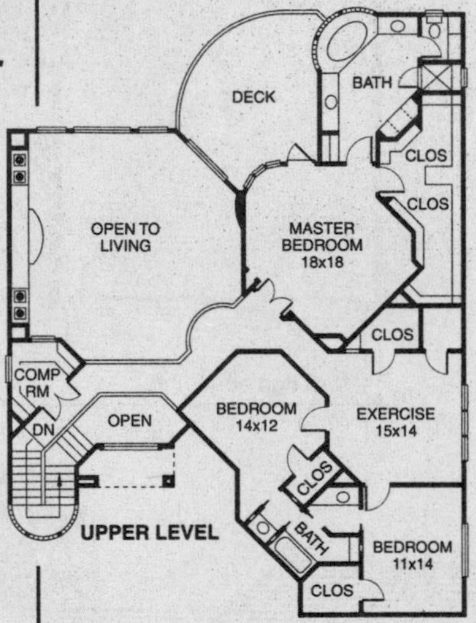

MAIN LEVEL
No. 32113

UPPER LEVEL

Refer to **Pricing Schedule F** on the order form for pricing information

Photography Supplied By The Meredith Corporation

Design 99825

STATELY AND LUXURIANT

Clerestory window, detailed square columns, and French doors lend drama to the arched and gabled grand entry of this stately home. Inside, luxury abounds with a formal living room with fireplace and box bay window as well as a formal dining room. Open to the kitchen and breakfast bay, the two-story family room boasts a fireplace with built-in cabinets on either side. The master suite includes a lovely bay window sitting area. Upstairs you'll find two generous bedrooms with walk-in closets, a full bath, and bonus room. Additionally, this plan offers a convenient second master suite on the first floor for guests, the nanny, or a live-in parent. Design by Donald A. Gardner Architects, Inc.

First floor — 2,249 sq. ft.
Second floor — 620 sq. ft.
Garage & storage — 642 sq. ft.
Bonus room — 308 sq. ft.

Total living area:
2,869 sq. ft.

First Floor Plan

PATIO

SITTING
9-4 x 4-4

MASTER BED RM.
14-0 x 16-0

FAMILY RM.
21-8 x 19-10
(two story ceiling)
fireplace

BRKFST.
9-4 x 10-4

BED RM./OFFICE
12-4 x 12-0

KITCHEN
16-4 x 10-4

balcony above

master bath

walk-in closet

up

pan.

UTIL
7-0 x 8-8

storage

bath

LIVING RM./STUDY
14-0 x 12-0
fireplace

DINING
12-8 x 13-4

FOYER
8-6 x 9-8

(two story ceiling)

GARAGE
24-4 x 23-0

PORCH

FIRST FLOOR PLAN

© 1997 Donald A Gardner Architects, Inc.

52-0

69-6

Second Floor Plan

family room below

railing

balcony

down

BED RM.
14-0 x 14-8

walk-in closet

bath

BED RM.
12-8 x 13-4

foyer below

down

walk-in closet
shelf

attic storage

BONUS RM.
14-4 x 17-0

attic storage

SECOND FLOOR PLAN
No. 99825

Refer to **Pricing Schedule F** on the order form for pricing information

© 1997 Donald A Gardner Architects, Inc.

Design 90476

SPLIT-BEDROOM RANCH DESIGN

This classic split-bedroom Ranch design features a formal foyer leading to a large Great room with a vaulted ceiling. The Great room has a fireplace and a French door to the deck. The formal dining room is enhanced by a tray ceiling. The U-shaped kitchen is open to the breakfast area. The master bedroom is accented by a tray ceiling and a French door to the deck. The master bath features a spa tub, a shower and dual walk-in closets. Two ample bedrooms and a full bath complete the main floor. The covered front porch and an open rear deck provide for outdoor living. The full basement offers lots of room for later expansion. This plan is available with a basement, crawl space or slab foundation. Please specify when ordering. Design by Corley Plan Service

Main floor – 1,804 sq. ft.
Basement – 1,804 sq. ft.
Garage – 506 sq. ft.

Total living area:
1,804 sq. ft.

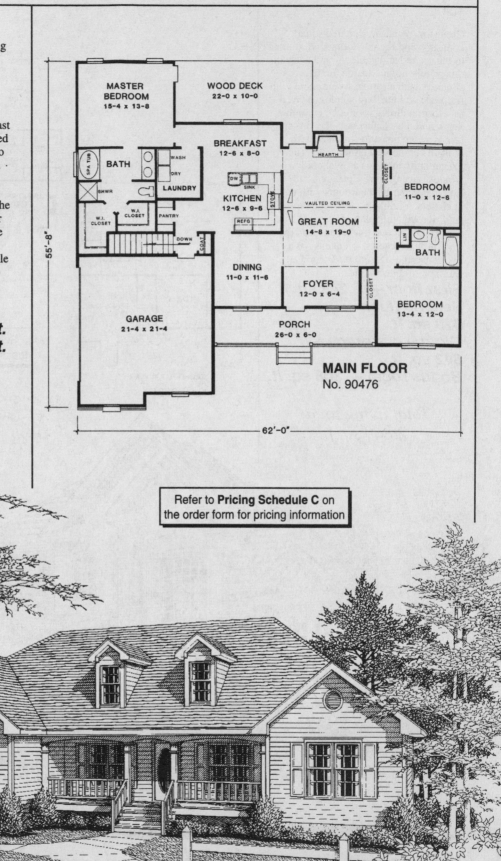

MAIN FLOOR
No. 90476

Refer to **Pricing Schedule C** on the order form for pricing information

Design 98437

OUTSTANDING CURB APPEAL

The bayed windows that highlight this home along with the keystones arched windows and attractive detailing give an eye-catching elegance to the elevation. Inside, the bayed windows are enjoyed by the formal dining and living room which flank the two-story foyer. A butler's pantry is located between the kitchen and the formal dining room for serving ease. The island kitchen has been made convenient and efficient by a large walk-in pantry and a peninsula counter/serving bar. The two-story family room is enhanced by a fireplace. The second floor master suite includes a tray ceiling topping the bedroom, and a vaulted ceiling above the sitting room and master bath. This plan is available with a basement or crawl space foundation. Please specify when ordering. Design by Frank Betz Associates, Inc.

First floor — 2,002 sq. ft.
Second floor —
1,947 sq. ft.
Basement — 2,002 sq. ft.
Garage — 737 sq. ft.

Total living area:
3,949 sq. ft.

Refer to **Pricing Schedule F** on the order form for pricing information

© Frank Betz Associates

FIRST FLOOR PLAN
No. 98347

SECOND FLOOR

Design 99853

STATELY ELEGANCE

A double gabled roof with front and rear palladian windows give this wrap-around porch plan a stately elegance. Vaulted ceilings in the two-story foyer and Great room reinforce the visual drama of the palladian windows while a loft/study overlooks both areas. The spacious first floor master suite accesses the large sun room from a luxurious master bath with garden tub, shower, and double vanity. The covered porch and outstanding deck with seating and optional spa expand living space outdoors. Upstairs, one of the three bedrooms could be a second master with private bath. Design by Donald A. Gardner Architects, Inc.

First floor — 1,734 sq. ft.
Second floor — 958 sq. ft.

Total living area:
2,692 sq. ft.

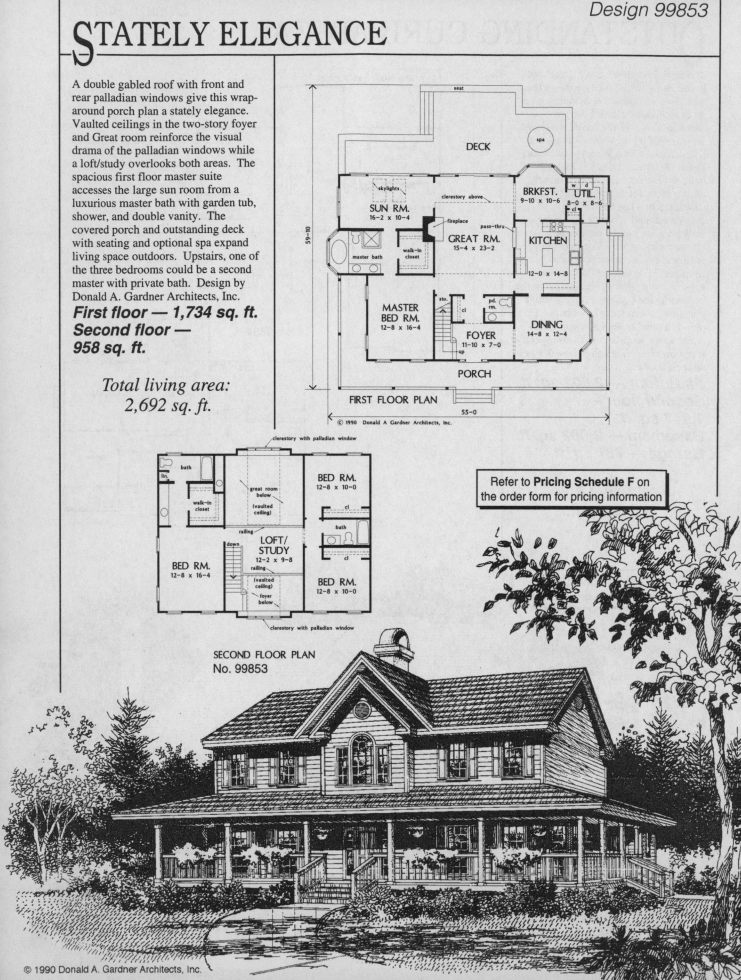

FIRST FLOOR PLAN

© 1990 Donald A Gardner Architects, Inc.

SECOND FLOOR PLAN
No. 99853

Refer to **Pricing Schedule F** on the order form for pricing information

EASY LIVING

Here's a pretty, one-level home designed for carefree living. The central foyer divides active and quiet areas. Step back to a fireplaced living room with dramatic, towering ceilings and a panoramic view of the backyard. The adjoining dining room features a sloping ceiling crowned by a plant shelf, and sliders to an outdoor deck. Just across the counter, a handy, U-shaped kitchen features abundant cabinets, a window over the sink overlooking the deck, and a walk-in pantry. The master suite boasts its own private bath with both shower and tub, a room-sized walk-in closet, and a bump-out window that adds light and space. Design by The Garlinghouse Company

Main area — 1,456 sq. ft.
Basement — 1,448 sq. ft.
Garage — 452 sq. ft.

Total living area:
1,456 sq. ft.

Refer to **Pricing Schedule A** on the order form for pricing information

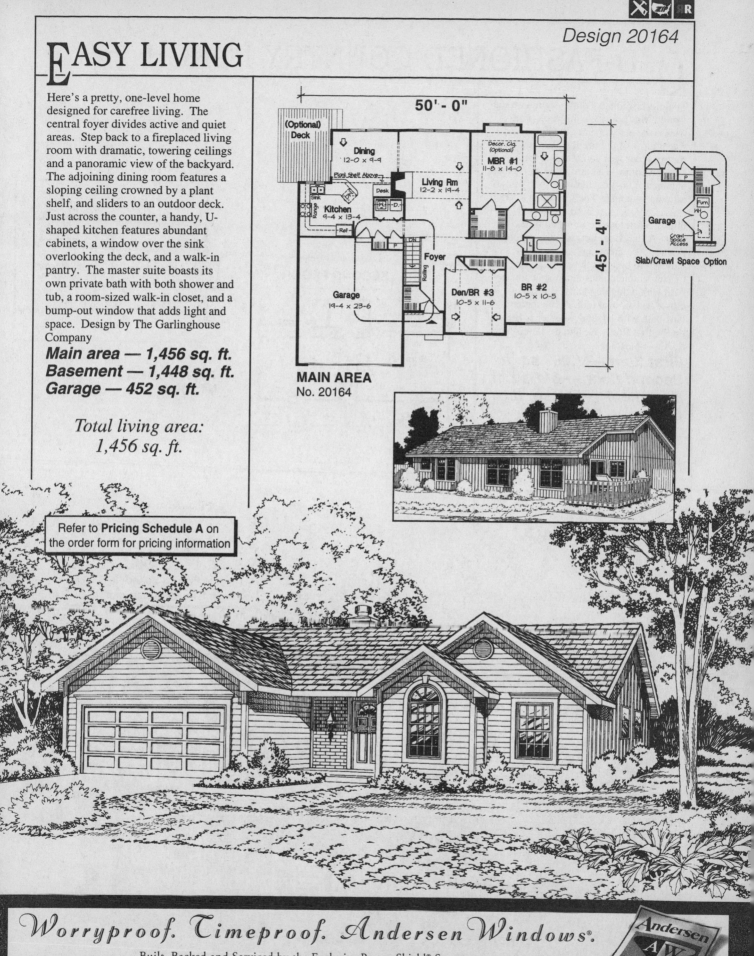

MAIN AREA
No. 20164

Slab/Crawl Space Option

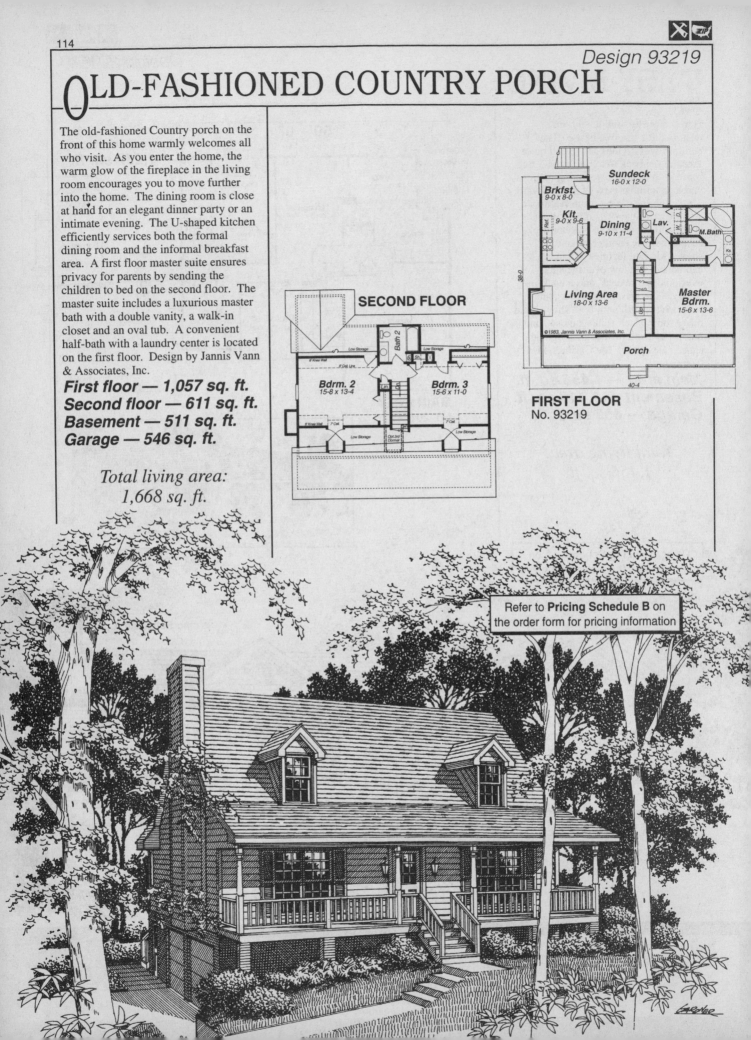

Design 93219

OLD-FASHIONED COUNTRY PORCH

The old-fashioned Country porch on the front of this home warmly welcomes all who visit. As you enter the home, the warm glow of the fireplace in the living room encourages you to move further into the home. The dining room is close at hand for an elegant dinner party or an intimate evening. The U-shaped kitchen efficiently services both the formal dining room and the informal breakfast area. A first floor master suite ensures privacy for parents by sending the children to bed on the second floor. The master suite includes a luxurious master bath with a double vanity, a walk-in closet and an oval tub. A convenient half-bath with a laundry center is located on the first floor. Design by Jannis Vann & Associates, Inc.

First floor — 1,057 sq. ft.
Second floor — 611 sq. ft.
Basement — 511 sq. ft.
Garage — 546 sq. ft.

Total living area:
1,668 sq. ft.

SECOND FLOOR

Bath 2
Low Storage
Low Storage
6' Knee Wall
3" Cel. Line.

Bdrm. 2
15-8 x 13-4

Bdrm. 3
15-6 x 11-0

Lin.
6' Knee Wall
7' Cel.
Low Storage
Opt.3rd Dormer
7' Cel.
Low Storage

FIRST FLOOR
No. 93219

Sundeck
16-0 x 12-0

Brkfst.
9-0 x 8-0

Kit.
9-0 x 9-6

Dining
9-10 x 11-4

Lav.

M. Bath

Ref.
W. D.

Living Area
18-0 x 13-6

Master Bdrm.
15-6 x 13-6

© 1983, Jannis Vann & Associates, Inc.

38-0

Porch

40-4

Refer to **Pricing Schedule B** on the order form for pricing information

ONE-STORY COUNTRY HOME

Design 99639

The entrance to the house is sheltered by the front porch that leads into the living room with its imposing high ceiling that slopes down to a normal height of eight feet focusing on the decorative heat-circulating fireplace at the rear wall. Widely open to the living room is the dining room. Its front wall is windowed from side to side. The adjoining fully equipped kitchen is also a feature of the house. The convenient

dinette can comfortably seat six people and leads to the rear terrace through six foot sliding glass doors. The master suite is arranged with a large dressing area that has a walk-in closet plus two linear closets and space for a vanity. The main part of the bedroom contains a media wall designed for TV viewing with shelving and cabinets for a VCR, radio, speakers, records and CD player. Design by Perfect Plan

Main area — 1,367 sq. ft.
Garage — 431 sq. ft.
Basement — 1,267 sq. ft.

Total living area: 1,367 sq. ft.

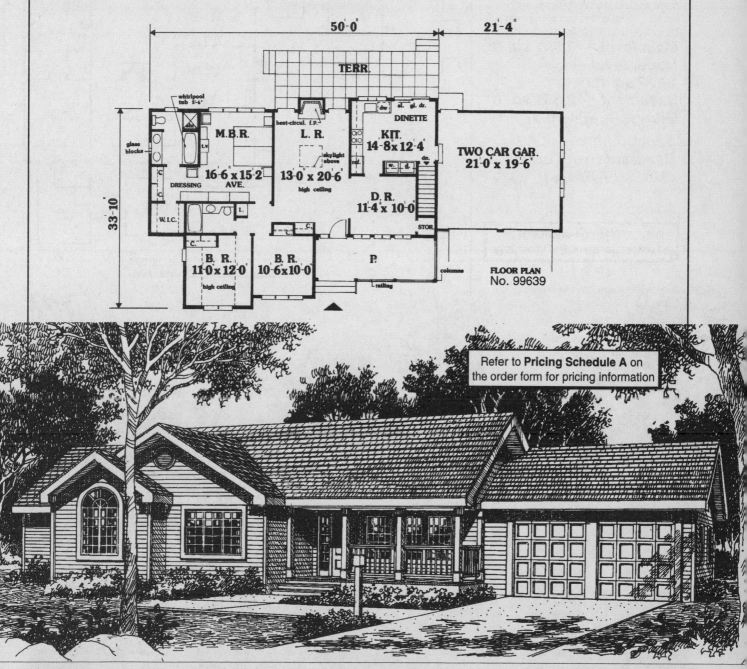

FLOOR PLAN No. 99639

Refer to **Pricing Schedule A** on the order form for pricing information

Weather Shield
Windows & Doors
www.weathershield.com

Weather Shield Windows and Doors offers project planning guides for your remodeling or new home project. FREE. Specify "Remodeling" or "New Home" Planning Guide by calling

1-800-477-6808

Design 32076

EUROPEAN STYLE

This home has a refined European-style elevation. Inside, to the right of the entry is the study made private by a double door entry. The formal dining room is to the left of the entry and is highlighted by a floor-to-ceiling bay window. The right wing of the main floor includes a study, a powder room and the master suite. The left wing includes the dining room, the family room and the kitchen with an adjacent keeping room and rear screen porch. Design by The Meredith Corporation

Main level — 2,391 sq. ft.
Upper level —
1,223 sq. ft.
Basement — 2,391 sq. ft.
Garage — 484 sq. ft.

Total living area:
3,614 sq. ft.

Refer to **Pricing Schedule F** on the order form for pricing information

Photography Supplied By The Meredith Corporation

WIDTH 61'-0"
DEPTH 68'-0"

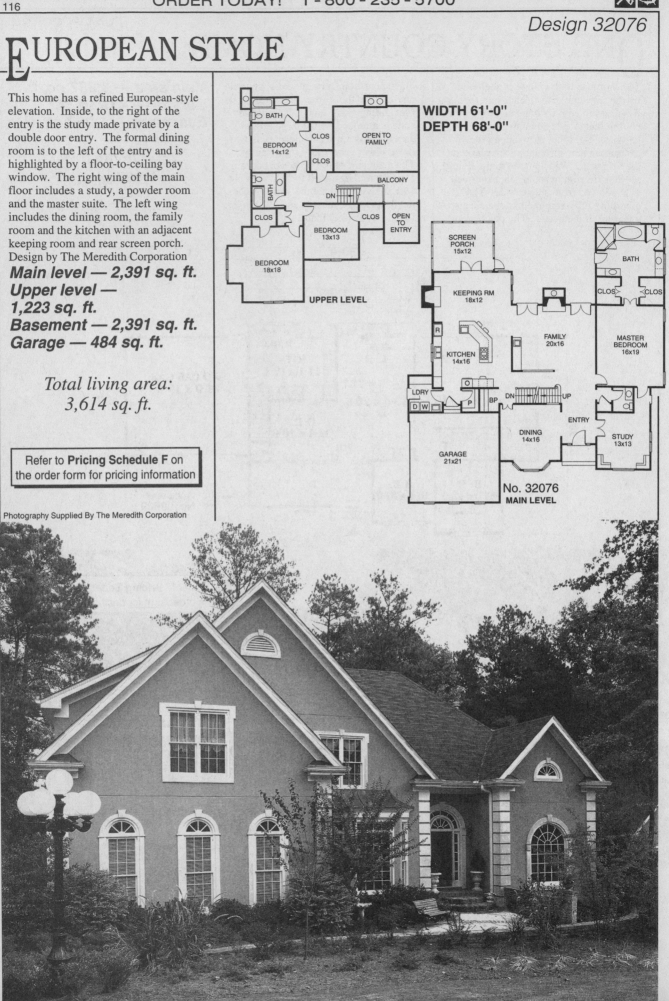

FEATURES OF A MUCH LARGER PLAN

This rustic Ranch design has only 1,811 square feet, yet it offers many amenities found in much larger homes. The large Great room has a vaulted ceiling and a stone fireplace with book shelves on either side. The kitchen is spacious with a lot of cabinet space, and is located between the large dining room with a bay on one side, and the screened porch on the other. The master suite has a large bath with a garden tub and a dual vanity. The large walk-in closet offers plenty of space. Two other large bedrooms, each with a walk-in closet, share another full bath. The utility room is located conven-iently off of the main hall. The large wood deck in the rear of the house offers a space for outdoor living. This plan is available with a basement, slab or crawl space foundation. Please specify when ordering. Design by Corley Plan Service

Main area — 1,811 sq. ft.
Basement — 1,811 sq. ft.
Garage — 484 sq. ft.

Total living area:
1,811 sq. ft.

Refer to **Pricing Schedule C** on the order form for pricing information

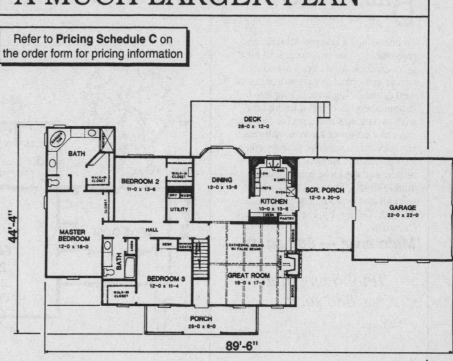

MAIN AREA
No. 90441

BEDROOMS ENJOY DECK ACCESS

To encourage a relaxed lifestyle and enjoyment of the outdoors, a 50 foot wooden deck fronts this vacation retreat and opens to two bedrooms as well as the living area. Complete but simple, the plan offers a living area with two closets and a prefab fireplace, open to a compact kitchen with rear entrance. The separate laundry room also houses the furnace and water heater, and the large bath features double sinks. The plan can be built without one or both bedrooms if desired. Design by The Garlinghouse Company

Main area — 888 sq. ft.

Total living area:
888 sq. ft.

Refer to **Pricing Schedule A** on the order form for pricing information

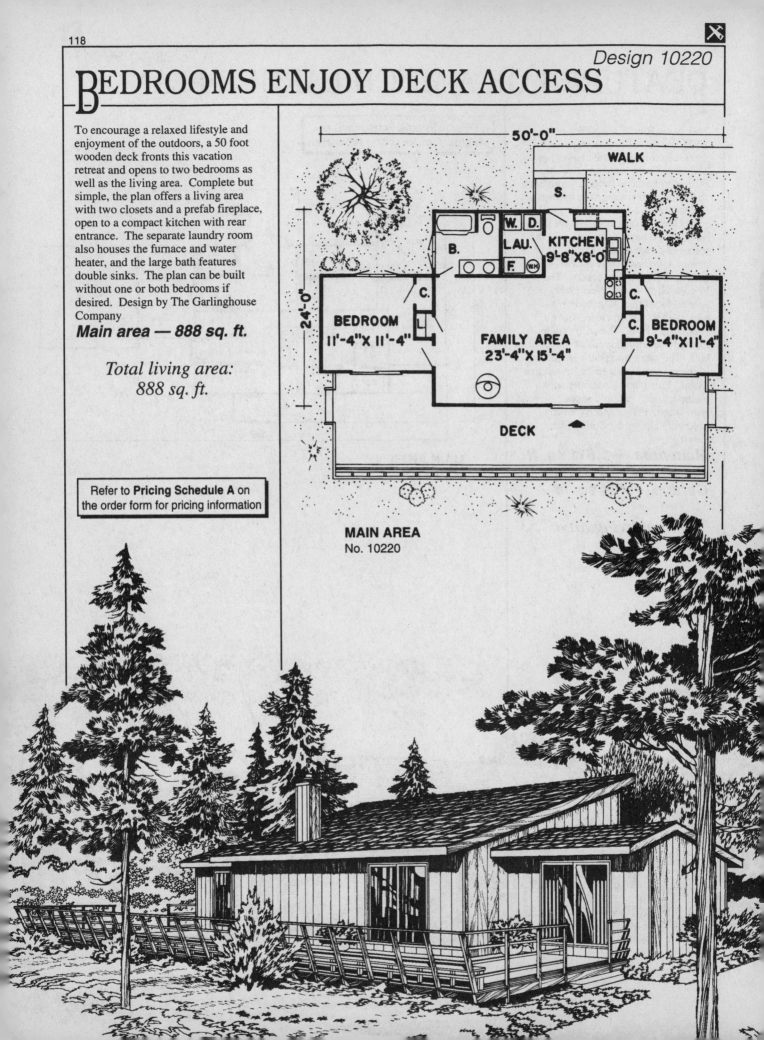

MAIN AREA
No. 10220

STATELY RANCH

This brick and siding ranch has much to offer. The foyer leads into the Great room with cathedral ceilings and direct vent corner gas fireplace. There are arched pass-throughs to the kitchen. The kitchen has all of the amenities including plenty of cupboard and counter space. The adjoining dining area has large windows and a glass door leading to the back yard, and a screen porch. The private master suite has a large walk-in closet and full bath with corner whirlpool tub and free standing shower. Two more bedrooms can be found off the Great room. Both have large closets, and share a full bath. From the two car garage, you will enter into the main floor laundry with a large closet for storage. This plan is not to be built within a 20 mile radius of Iowa City, Iowa. No materials list is available for this plan. Design by Ahmann Design, Inc.

Main floor — 1,472 sq. ft.
Basement — 1,472 sq. ft.
Garage — 424 sq. ft.

Total living area:
1,472 sq. ft.

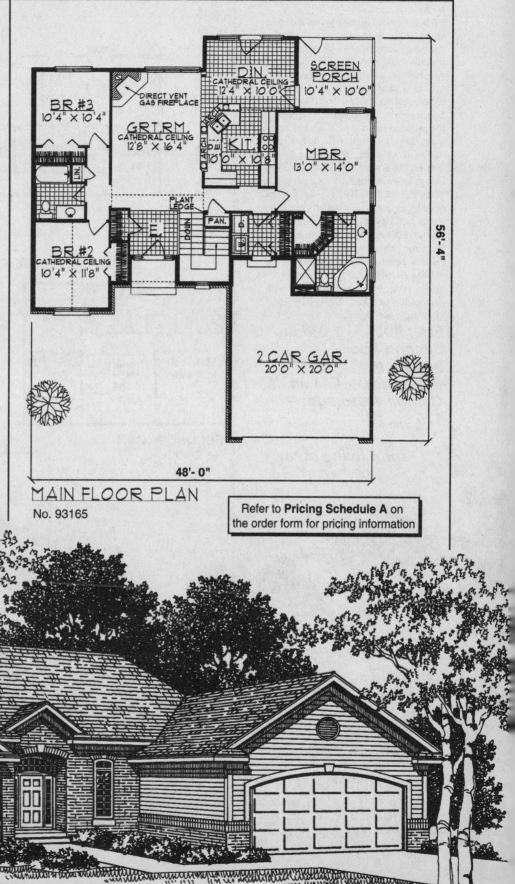

MAIN FLOOR PLAN
No. 93165

Refer to **Pricing Schedule A** on the order form for pricing information

Design 24400

NATIONAL TREASURE

This delightful home's wrap-around covered porch recalls the warmth and charm of days past — lounging in the porch swing, savoring life. Inside, a spacious foyer welcomes guests and provides easy access to the formal dining room, secluded den/guest room (which might serve as your home office), and the large living room. Ceilings downstairs are all 9' high, with decorative vaults in the living and dining rooms. The kitchen, with its island/breakfast bar, is large enough for two people to work in comfortably. Upstairs, three bedrooms, each with cathedral ceilings, share a cheery, sunlit sitting area. For privacy, the master bedroom is separated from the other bedrooms, and boasts a palatial bathroom, complete with a whirlpool tub. If room to relax is what you're after, this home is loaded with irresistible features. Design by The Garlinghouse Company

First floor — 1,034 sq. ft.
Second floor — 944 sq. ft.
Basement — 944 sq. ft.
Garage & storage — 675 sq. ft.

Total living area: 1,978 sq. ft.

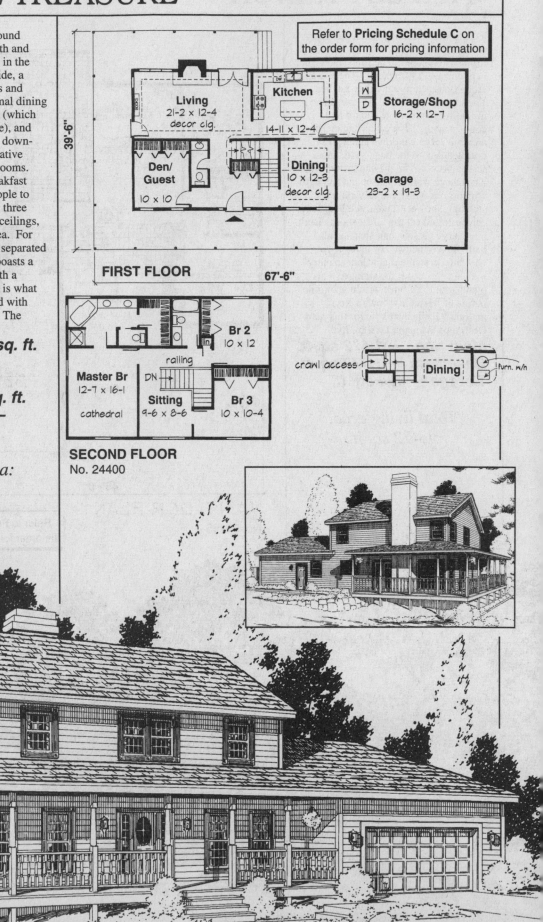

Refer to **Pricing Schedule C** on the order form for pricing information

FIRST FLOOR   67'-6"

39'-6"

Living 21-2 x 12-4 decor clg.

Kitchen 14-11 x 12-4

Storage/Shop 16-2 x 12-7

Den/Guest 10 x 10

Dining 10 x 12-3 decor clg.

Garage 23-2 x 19-3

SECOND FLOOR
No. 24400

Master Br 12-7 x 16-1 cathedral

Sitting 9-6 x 8-6

Br 2 10 x 12

Br 3 10 x 10-4

railing

DN

crawl access   Dining   furn. w/h

TWO-STORY FOYER ADDS ELEGANCE

As you enter this magnificent home the two-story entrance captures your attention. There is a cascading curved staircase directly in front of you. The foyer is flanked by the formal dining room and the formal living room, both enjoy the view of the front yard through large windows. The family room is enhanced by a fireplace and has access to a sundeck. A sunny breakfast area is directly off of the well-appointed kitchen. Upstairs, the master suite has a decorative ceiling and a large master bath. This plan comes with a basement, crawl space or slab foundation. Please specify when ordering. Design by Jannis Vann & Associates, Inc.

First floor — 1,277 sq. ft.
Second floor — 1,177 sq. ft.
Bonus room — 392 sq. ft.
Basement — 1,261 sq. ft.
Garage — 572 sq. ft.

Total living area:
2,454 sq. ft.

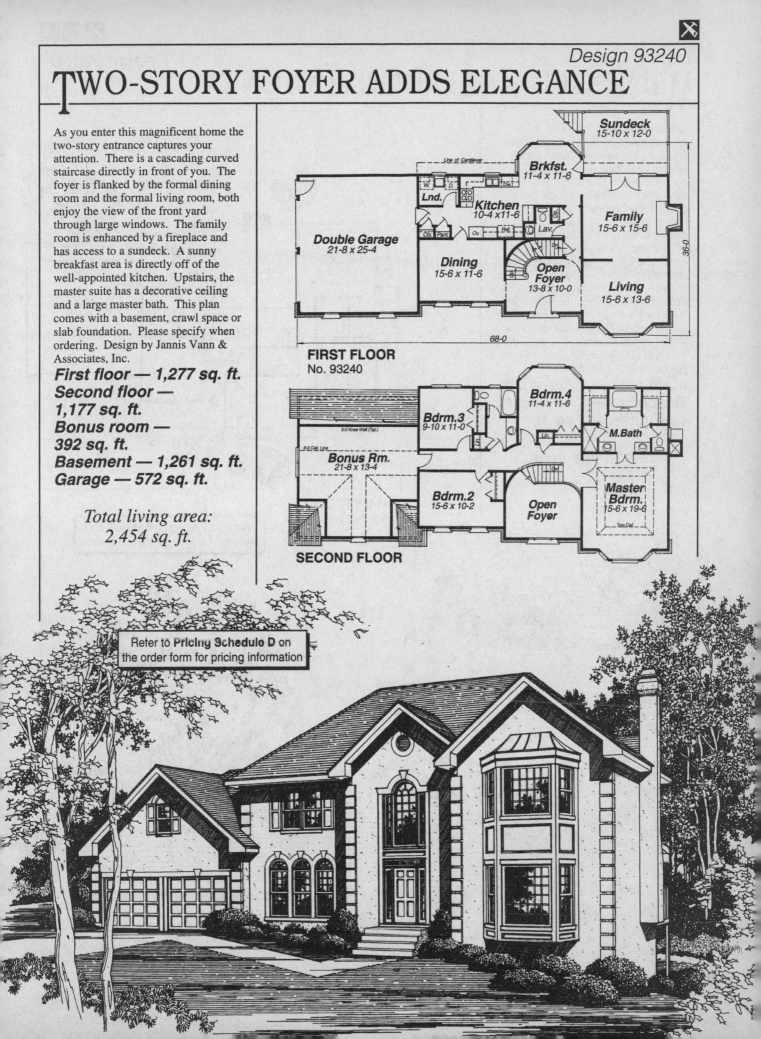

FIRST FLOOR
No. 93240

- Sundeck 15-10 x 12-0
- Brkfst. 11-4 x 11-6
- Lnd.
- Kitchen 10-4 x 11-6
- Family 15-6 x 15-6
- Double Garage 21-8 x 25-4
- Lav.
- Dining 15-6 x 11-6
- Open Foyer 13-8 x 10-0
- Living 15-6 x 13-6
- 68-0
- 36-0
- Line of Cantilever

SECOND FLOOR

- Bdrm.4 11-4 x 11-6
- Bdrm.3 9-10 x 11-0
- M.Bath
- Bonus Rm. 21-8 x 13-4
- 5-0 Knee Wall (Typ.)
- Bdrm.2 15-6 x 10-2
- Open Foyer
- Master Bdrm. 15-6 x 19-6

Refer to **Pricing Schedule D** on the order form for pricing information

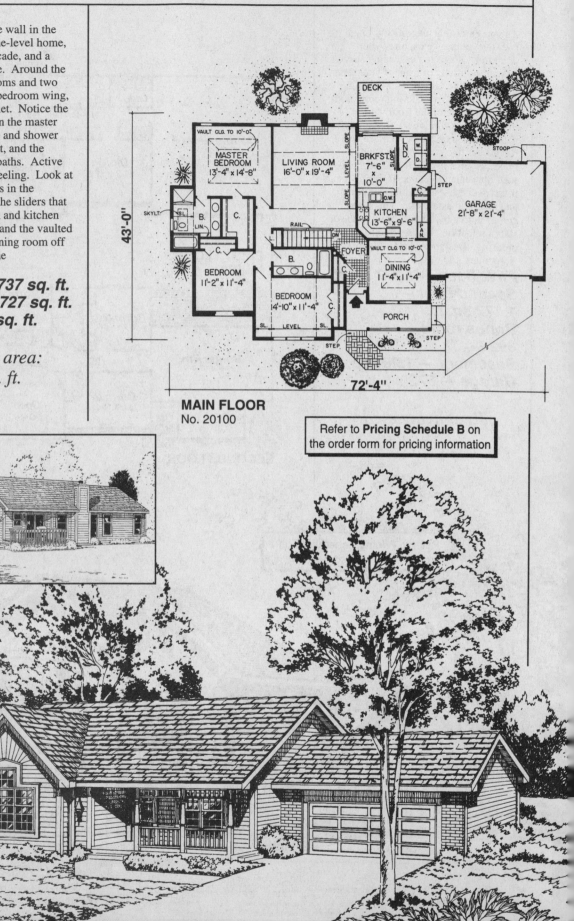

WIDE-OPEN AND CONVENIENT

Design 20100

Stacked windows fill the wall in the front bedroom of this one-level home, creating an attractive facade, and a sunny atmosphere inside. Around the corner, two more bedrooms and two full baths complete the bedroom wing, set apart for bedtime quiet. Notice the elegant vaulted ceiling in the master bedroom, the master tub and shower illuminated by a skylight, and the double vanities in both baths. Active areas enjoy a spacious feeling. Look at the high, sloping ceilings in the fireplaced living room, the sliders that unite the breakfast room and kitchen with an adjoining deck, and the vaulted ceilings in the formal dining room off the foyer. Design by The Garlinghouse Company

Main area — 1,737 sq. ft.
Basement — 1,727 sq. ft.
Garage — 484 sq. ft.

Total living area:
1,737 sq. ft.

MAIN FLOOR
No. 20100

Refer to **Pricing Schedule B** on the order form for pricing information

Design 10518

COMPACT LEISURE DESIGN

Built to be efficient, this home still has lots of living space in a three bedroom, two bath design. The trim on the deck suggests a chalet, but this modern home would be welcome anywhere. Tucked into the peak of the roof is the master bedroom with its own private bath. Two more bedrooms plus a four-piece bath are located on the first floor. The combined living/dining room opens onto the deck which extends the full width of the house. The front kitchen is easily accessible from the entry and is designed for efficient meal preparation. Design by The Garlinghouse Company

First floor — 864 sq. ft.
Second floor — 307 sq. ft.

Total living area:
1,171 sq. ft.

Refer to **Pricing Schedule A** on the order form for pricing information

SECOND FLOOR PLAN

ATTIC

MASTER BEDROOM #1
12'-2" X 12'-0"

OPEN TO LIVING ROOM BELOW

B.   C.

H.

DN

RAILING

FALSE DECK

ATTIC

FIRST FLOOR PLAN
No. 10518

36'-0"

24'-0"

DECK

UP

LIVING ROOM
11'-4" X 23'-0"

S.

C.

W/D

W.H.

FURN.

crawl access

B.

BEDROOM #3
9'-4" X 8'-11"

C.

C.

DINING AREA

KIT.
9'-0" X 7'-10"

C.

BEDROOM #2
10'-2" X 8'-11"

ENTRY

S.

UP

W.

Design 98010

Always in Style

Always in style, brick, gables, and a traditional hip roof combine with an arched entry and beautiful, arched windows for a truly elegant home. The interior offers an abundance of luxury with dramatic spaces, tray ceilings, built-ins, and a lovely picture window with an arched top in the dining room. Custom details abound. Note the wetbar, walk-in pantry, oversized laundry room with sink and cupboards, and three-car garage. A large walk-up attic and a partial basement gives added space for storage. His-n-her baths highlight the master suite, and each has its own walk-in closet. Two family bedrooms share a well-equipped bath, while a fourth bedroom makes a great guest room with a private bath. This plan is not to be built in Greenville County, SC. Design by Donald A. Gardner Architects, Inc.

Main floor — 4,523 sq. ft.
Garage — 1,029 sq. ft.

Total living area:
4,523 sq. ft.

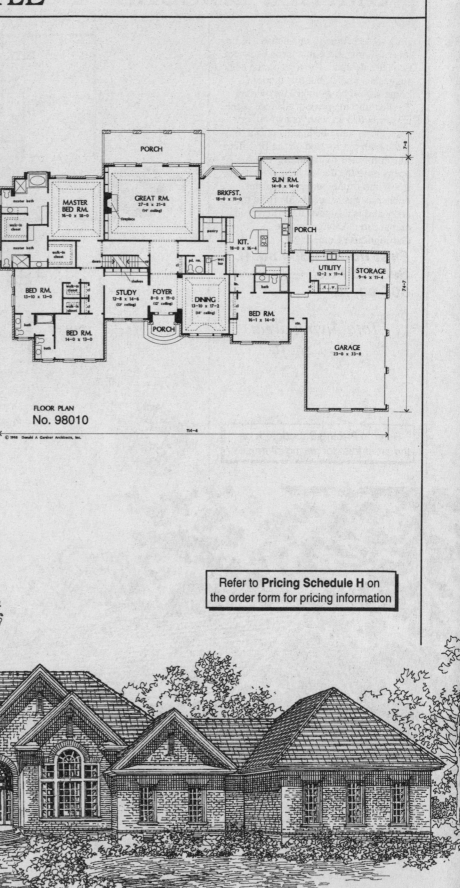

FLOOR PLAN
No. 98010

© 1998 Donald A Gardner Architects, Inc.

©1997 Donald A. Gardner Architects, Inc.

WITH ATTENTION TO DETAIL

It's the little details that make a home so much more. A window is a window, yet with the detailing around the windows of this home it becomes a multi-paned looking glass to the outside world. A door is just an entry way, yet with the curved glass crown above and detailing around the door, it becomes a grand entrance. Paying attention to details continues inside the home. Decorative and vaulted ceilings "dress-up" many of the rooms. These little touches add to the elegance and spaciousness. There is a formal living room and dining room for entertaining. Privacy is the theme of the master suite. The master bath pampers the owner in luxury. An island kitchen is waiting for the gourmet of the family to personalize. No materials list is available for this plan. Design by Garrell Associates, Inc.

First floor — 2,115 sq. ft.
Second floor — 914 sq. ft.
Basement — 2,115 sq. ft.
Garage — 448 sq. ft.

Total living area: 3,029 sq. ft.

FIRST FLOOR
No. 93604

Refer to **Pricing Schedule E** on the order form for pricing information

---

Merillat ®

"AMERICA'S CABINET MAKER"

tel. 1-800-575-8763, ext. 6498 ◆ email: www.merillat.com

COUNT YOUR OPTIONS

Design 97258

The designer of this plan has thought of these choices as well as elegant detailing, a convenient floor plan and "show stopping" curb appeal. The master suite is lavishly appointed. The kitchen includes plenty of storage and work space. The family room is enhanced by a fireplace. This plan is available with a basement or crawl space foundation. Please specify when ordering. No materials list is available for this plan. Design by Frank Betz Associates, Inc.

First floor — 1,860 sq. ft.
Second floor — 612 sq. ft.
Bonus Room — 244 sq. ft.
Basement — 1,860 sq. ft.
Garage — 460 sq. ft.

Total living area:
2,472 sq. ft.

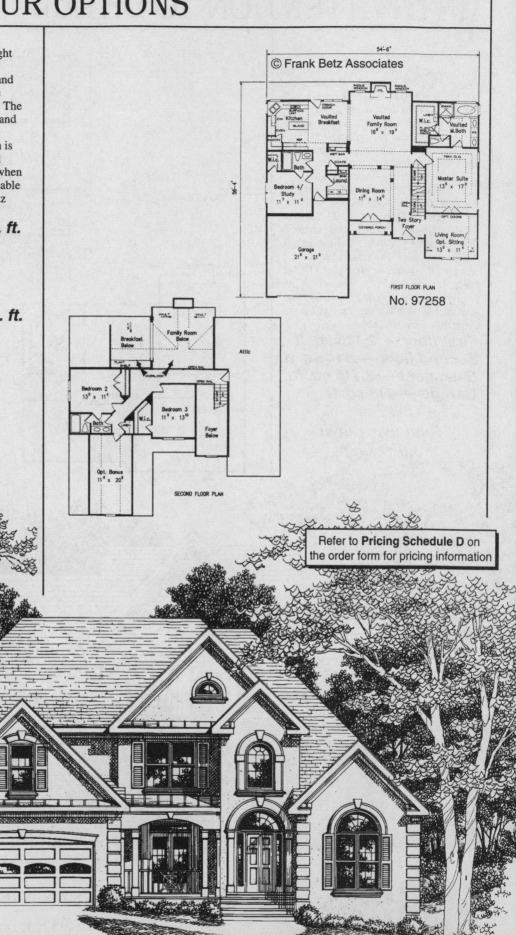

© Frank Betz Associates

FIRST FLOOR PLAN
No. 97258

SECOND FLOOR PLAN

Refer to **Pricing Schedule D** on the order form for pricing information

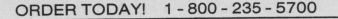

Design 98511

A NEW ANGLE ON LIFE

Are you looking for a new angle on life? Then take a look at this extraordinary home with the right angle for you. Upon entering this home, from the eyebrow arched covered entry, angles abound. From the bay window in the formal living room to the unique angled family room with a huge brick fireplace, built-in bookcases, and cathedral ceiling elegance predominates. Angles can also be found in the kitchen with built-in ovens and a pantry, as well as the master bath with a huge walk-in closet and upscale glass block shower. With four bedrooms, two living and dining areas and a three-car garage, you are sure to have found the perfect house for luxurious living. No materials list is available for this plan. Design by Filmore Design Group

Main floor — 2,445 sq. ft.
Garage — 630 sq. ft.

Total living area:
2,445 sq. ft.

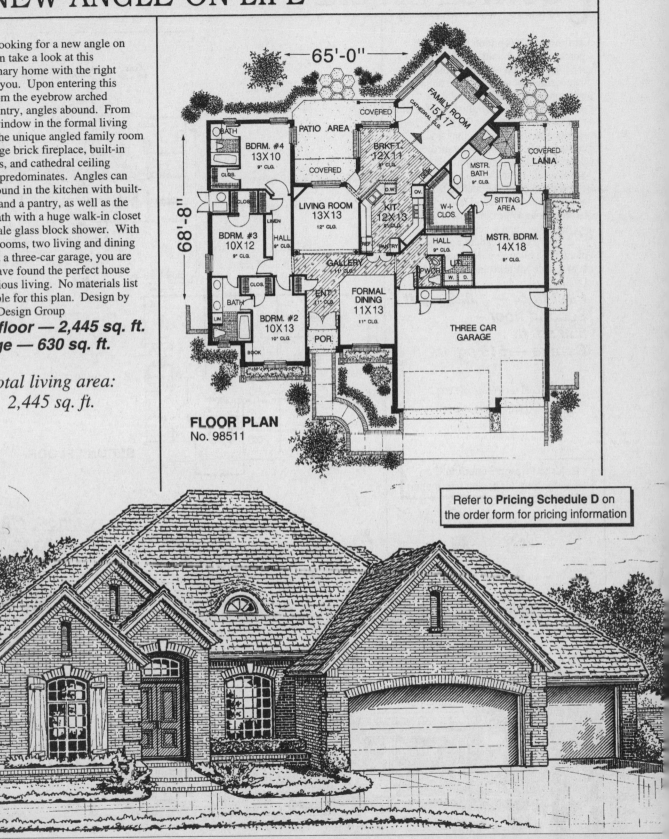

FLOOR PLAN
No. 98511

Refer to **Pricing Schedule D** on the order form for pricing information

Design 99492

COTTAGE APPEAL

This home's steep roof, two front porches and diamond-muntin windows lend the feel of a cottage by the sea. The airiness of the kitchen is enhanced with openings to the second floor, entry and dinette. A built-in buffet and two half railings warmly welcome guests into the dining room. A tall ceiling in the Great room is further dramatized when viewed from the open railing on the second floor. A computer area on the second floor accompanies the second floor bedrooms as a homework area. A large storage area accessed from the mid level staircase landing offers a place for a playroom. No materials list is available for this plan. Design by Design Basics, Inc.

First floor — 1,823 sq. ft.
Second floor —
858 sq. ft.
Garage — 515 sq. ft.

Total living area:
2,681 sq. ft.

Refer to **Pricing Schedule E** on the order form for pricing information

FIRST FLOOR
No. 99492

SECOND FLOOR

© design basics inc.

Design 98528

UNIQUE AND SPECIAL HOME

Quality abounds in this unique and special home with its arched covered entry and arched windows, to its spacious and elegant floor plan for four bedrooms. A media/study room, and two living and dining areas are also featured. Retire to the master suite with it's own fireplace, or cook a fabulous meal in the amazing kitchen with brick arched opening over the range and breakfast area open to the cozy family room. No materials list is available for this plan. Design by Filmore Design Group

Main floor — 2,748 sq. ft.
Garage — 660 sq. ft.

Total living area: 2,748 sq. ft.

WIDTH 75'-0"
DEPTH 64'-5"

Refer to **Pricing Schedule E** on the order form for pricing information

MAIN FLOOR
No. 98528

Design 96413

COMFORTABLE DESIGN

This plan's wide front porch says, "Welcome Home;" inside, its comfortable design encourages relaxation. A center dormer lights the foyer, as columns punctuate the entry to the dining room and Great room. The spacious kitchen has an angled countertop and is open to the breakfast bay. A roomy utility area is nearby. Tray ceilings add elegance to the dining room and the master bedroom. A second master suite is located on the opposite end of the home and features an optional arrangement for the physically challenged. Two additional bedrooms share a third full bath with linen closet. A skylit bonus room is located over the garage and provides room for growth. Design by Donald A. Gardner Architects, Inc.

Main floor — 2,349 sq. ft.
Bonus room —
435 sq. ft.
Garage — 615 sq. ft.

Total living area:
2,349 sq. ft.

Refer to **Pricing Schedule E** on the order form for pricing information

---

Floor Plan (No. 96413)

- DECK
- spa
- PORCH
- BED RM. (optional 2nd master) 13-8 x 14-0
- MASTER BED RM. 14-0 x 17-4
- master bath
- skylights
- walk-in closet
- BRKFST. 11-4 x 9-4
- bath
- walk-in closet
- lin.
- fireplace
- GREAT RM. 15-4 x 18-8 (cathedral ceiling)
- KIT. 11-4 x 12-6
- UTIL. 7-0 x 7-8
- storage
- BED RM. 11-6 x 13-4
- bath
- lin.
- cl
- GARAGE 23-4 x 23-8
- BED RM. 13-0 x 11-8
- cl
- FOYER 7-4 x 12-0 (dormer above)
- DINING 15-4 x 11-8
- (optional door location)
- PORCH
- No. 96413 FLOOR PLAN
- 83-2
- 56-4

© 1997 Donald A Gardner Architects, Inc.

- seat
- walk-in closet
- lin.
- (optional handicapped accessible bath)

- attic storage
- down
- attic storage
- skylights
- BONUS RM. 14-6 x 23-8

B. NATHAN.

Design 92287

STONE AND BRICK PRESENT ATTRACTION

Using an English country flavor, this home features elegance and comfort. Brick quoins accent the corners while segmental arches, shutters and window boxes add the cottage touch. The brick theme is carried inside with the use of brick pavers in the galley, kitchen and breakfast room. The Great room is enhanced by a large fireplace and direct access to the covered patio in the rear. The breakfast room adjoins the Great room, creating a more spacious, airy feel. The island kitchen includes a peninsula counter/breakfast bar and a built-in pantry. Formal dining is a breeze in the dining room directly across from the kitchen. A second fireplace is included in the cozy study. A spacious first floor master suite pampers the owner in luxury. Three additional bedrooms are on the second floor. No materials list is available for this plan. Design by Fillmore Design Group

Main floor — 2,373 sq. ft.
Upper floor — 1,242 sq. ft.
Bonus — 200 sq. ft.
Garage — 780 sq. ft.

Total living area: 3,615 sq. ft.

Refer to **Pricing Schedule F** on the order form for pricing information

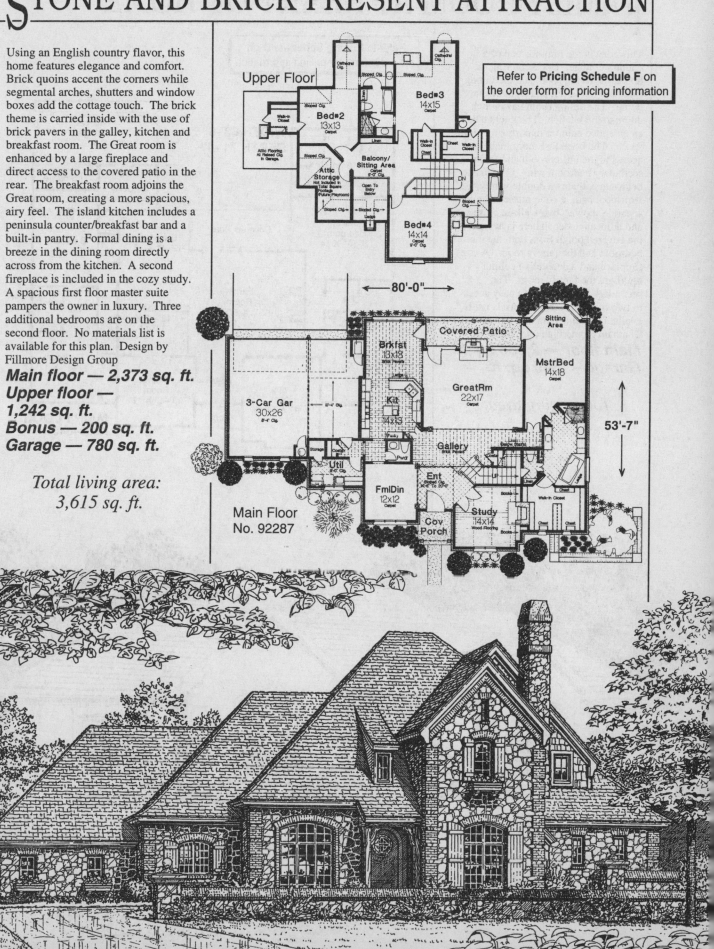

Design 94640

FAMILY ROOM AT HEART OF HOME

This cozy home reminds one of a country cottage. Upon entering the home, the living room and the dining room are to the left and right of the home. The dining room has French doors to the kitchen. The kitchen has an extended counter maximizing work space. The breakfast room includes access to the utility room and to the secondary bedroom wing. The master bedroom contains a double vanity, a whirlpool bath, a compartmental toilet, separate shower, two walk-in closets and a linear closet. There is access to the covered porch from both the master bedroom and the family room. A cozy fireplace and a decorative ceiling highlight the family room. The secondary bedrooms have easy access to two full baths. No materials list is available for this plan. Design by Chatham Home Planning, Inc.

Main floor — 2,558 sq. ft.
Garage — 549 sq. ft.

Total living area:
2,558 sq. ft.

Refer to **Pricing Schedule D** on the order form for pricing information

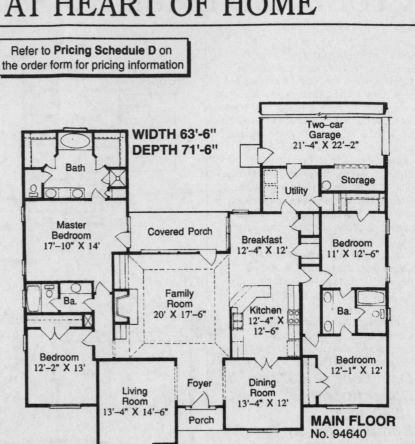

WIDTH 63'-6"
DEPTH 71'-6"

Bath

Two-car Garage
21'-4" X 22'-2"

Utility

Storage

Master Bedroom
17'-10" X 14'

Covered Porch

Breakfast
12'-4" X 12'

Bedroom
11' X 12'-6"

Ba.

Family Room
20' X 17'-6"

Kitchen
12'-4" X 12'-6"

Ba.

Bedroom
12'-2" X 13'

Living Room
13'-4" X 14'-6"

Foyer

Dining Room
13'-4" X 12'

Bedroom
12'-1" X 12'

Porch

MAIN FLOOR
No. 94640

Design 97205

FABULOUS FAMILY ROOM

The sunken family room of this home is topped by a vaulted ceiling and is overlooked from the loft above. The fireplace is a focal point for the room. The breakfast room has French doors to the rear yard and a vaulted ceiling. The dining room is enhanced by a boxed bay window. The master suite includes a tray ceiling and a lavish bath. This plan is available with a basement, crawl space or slab foundation. Please specify when ordering. No materials list is available for this plan. Design by Frank Betz Associates, Inc.

First floor — 1,488 sq. ft.
Second floor —
725 sq. ft.
Basement — 1,488 sq. ft.
Garage — 460 sq. ft.

Total living area:
2,213 sq. ft.

SECOND FLOOR PLAN

FIRST FLOOR PLAN
No. 97205

Refer to **Pricing Schedule D** on the order form for pricing information

© Frank Betz Associates

Weather Shield
Windows & Doors
www.weathershield.com

Weather Shield Windows and Doors offers project planning guides for your remodeling or new home project. FREE. Specify "Remodeling" or "New Home" Planning Guide by calling
1-800-477-6808

MAJESTIC TREASURE

Comfortable living is personified in this grand brick home. An impressive fireplace is the natural centerpiece for the two-story family room, surrounded by windows. A first floor guest bedroom can also be used as a den for the busy executive. The large kitchen has more than enough counter space, a cooktop center island, and a pantry. Upstairs are three large bedrooms separated by a catwalk overlooking the family room below. To the right are two more bedrooms with large closets and private entries to the shared full bath. No materials list is available for this plan. Design by Ahmann Design, Inc.

First floor — 1,873 sq. ft.
Second floor —
1,150 sq. ft.
Basement — 1,810 sq. ft.

Total living area:
3,023 sq. ft.

Refer to **Pricing Schedule E** on the order form for pricing information

FIRST FLOOR
No. 99109

GUEST BR./ DEN
15'4" X 13'8"

FAM. RM.
2 STORY CEILING
16'0" X 20'4"

NK.
11'0" X 10'4"

KIT.
13'8" X 13'4"

PANTRY

3 CAR GAR.
24'8" X 31'8"

LIV.
17'0" X 14'0"

E.
2 STORY CEILING

DIN.
15'4" X 13'8"

48' - 4"

77' - 0"

SECOND FLOOR

OPEN TO FAM. RM.

MBR.
13'4" X 18'8"

BR. #2
13'4" X 14'0"

LIN.

DOWN

OPEN TO E.

BR. #3
13'0" X 12'0"

PLANT LEDGE

Design 96435

STATELY HOME

This stately home effortlessly fits four bedrooms on one floor and owes its refined demeanor to its elegant brick exterior and careful detailing. Light floods through the arched window in the clerestory dormer above the foyer. The Great room with cathedral ceiling boasts built-in cabinets and bookshelves and leads directly to the sun room through glass doors capped by an arched window. Both the dining room and the bedroom/study have tray ceilings. Privately situated, the master suite has a fireplace, access to the deck, his-n-her vanities, shower and whirlpool tub. This plan is available with a basement or crawl space foundation. Please specify when ordering. Design by Donald A. Gardner Architects, Inc.

Main floor — 2,526 sq. ft.
Garage — 611 sq. ft.

Total living area:
2,526 sq. ft.

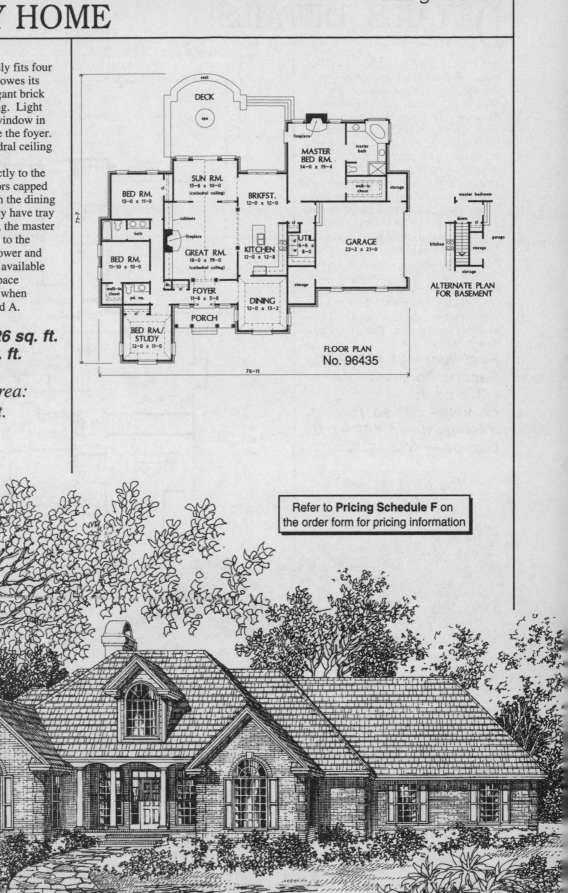

FLOOR PLAN
No. 96435

ALTERNATE PLAN
FOR BASEMENT

Refer to **Pricing Schedule F** on the order form for pricing information

B. NATHAN

DETAILS, DETAILS!

Design 98494

Attention to detail is emphasized in this home. The exterior is appointed with keystones, arches and shutters. The foyer is two-stories high for a dramatic entrance. The living room and dining room meet through an arched opening. The kitchen, breakfast and family room are open to each other. The kitchen directly accesses the dining room for ease in serving. The first floor bedroom, with a private bath, could easily become a den. The upstairs master suite features a tray ceiling over the bedroom and a vaulted ceiling over the master bath. Three additional bedrooms each have ample closet space. There is an optional bonus room for future expansion. This plan is available with a basement or crawl space foundation. Please specify when ordering. No materials list is available for this plan. Design by Frank Betz Associates, Inc.

First floor — 1,447 sq. ft.
Second floor — 1,325 sq. ft.
Bonus — 301 sq. ft.
Basement — 1,447 sq. ft.
Garage — 393 sq. ft.

Total living area:
2,772 sq. ft.

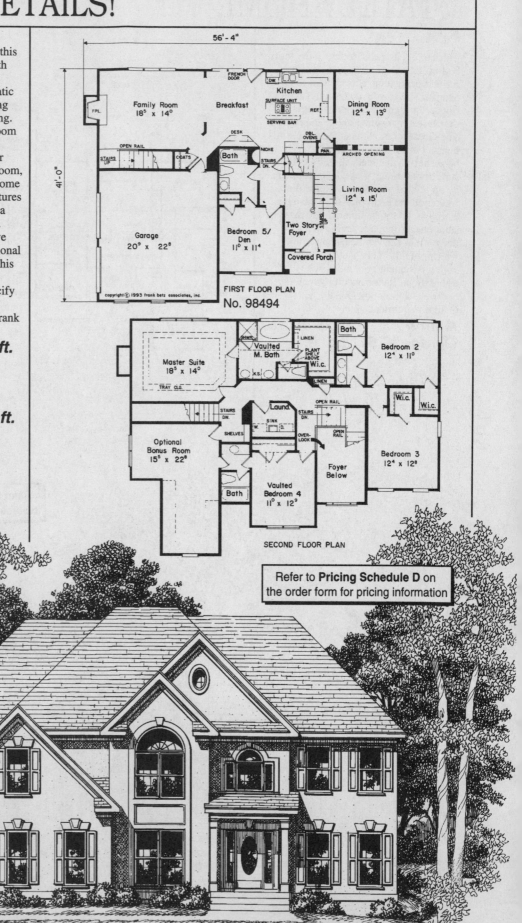

FIRST FLOOR PLAN
No. 98494

SECOND FLOOR PLAN

Refer to **Pricing Schedule D** on the order form for pricing information

EUROPEAN STYLED

This one-story European styled plan offers the ultimate in elegance and sophistication. The classic stucco exterior is accented by the use of quoins, dentil mold and arched windows, and trimmed in stucco and keyed capitals. The central foyer opens to the large den with a spacious living room on the left and an equally spacious dining room on the right. To the rear of the dining is a very large kitchen-breakfast room separated by a built in breakfast bar and accented with a large bay window. Adjacent to the breakfast area is the large den with its' flat vaulted ceiling and brick fireplace flanked by cabinets and bookshelves. To the rear of the breakfast room is the large utility room and master bedroom suite. This master suite, also, has the raised center ceiling as well as french doors opening on to the rear covered porch. The master bath is grand with his and her walk-in closets. This plan is available with a slab or crawl space foundation. Please specify when ordering. Design by Rick Garner

Main area — 2,727 sq. ft.
Garage — 569 sq. ft.

Total living area:
2,727 sq. ft.

Refer to **Pricing Schedule F** on the order form for pricing information

WIDTH 70'-10"
DEPTH 64'-5"

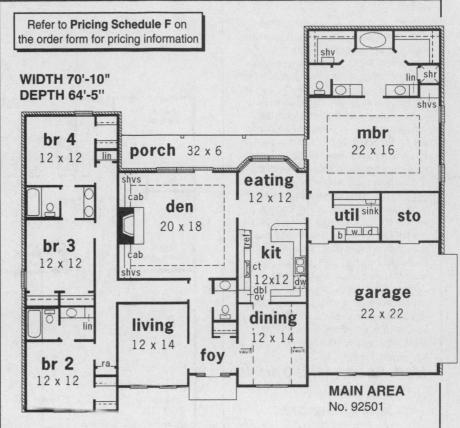

MAIN AREA
No. 92501

Design 98747

L-SHAPED FRONT PORCH

Attractive wood siding and a large L-shaped covered porch impart a nice touch of permanence to this gem. The front entry takes you into a generous, vaulted living room. with lots of space to entertain guests. The large two-car garage, not only has a side door, but direct access into the house via the utility room. Two identical bedrooms are on the left side of this floor plan. Each has a great window and adequate closet space. A full bathroom is in the hallway. The walk-through kitchen adds to the openness emphasized throughout the home. The kitchen has all the built-in appliances, plus a pantry and garden window. Adjoining the kitchen is the dining room with a vaulted ceiling. The isolated master suite completes this floor design. This appealing suite, features abundant closet space, separate vanity, linen storage and gives you the choice of two options for a private master bathroom. Design by Landmark Designs, Inc.

Main floor — 1,280 sq. ft.

Total living area: 1,280 sq. ft.

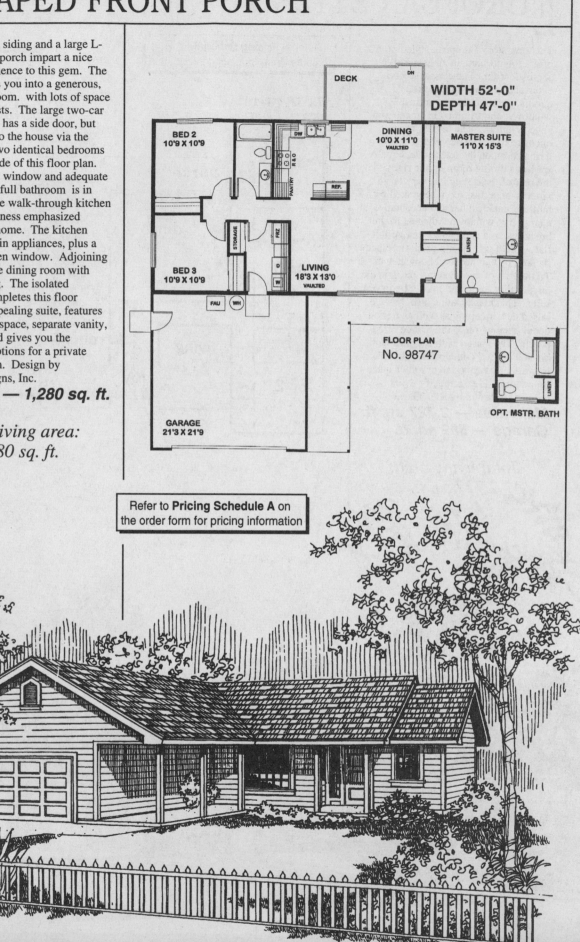

WIDTH 52'-0"
DEPTH 47'-0"

DECK

BED 2
10'9 X 10'9

DINING
10'0 X 11'0
VAULTED

MASTER SUITE
11'0 X 15'3

PANTRY

REF.

STORAGE

BED 3
10'9 X 10'9

LIVING
18'3 X 13'0
VAULTED

LINEN

FAU   WH

FLOOR PLAN
No. 98747

GARAGE
21'3 X 21'9

OPT. MSTR. BATH

LINEN

Refer to **Pricing Schedule A** on the order form for pricing information

Design 99801

TWO-STORY GREAT ROOM

A two-story Great room and two-story foyer, both with dormer windows, welcome natural light into this graceful country classic with wrap-around porch. The large kitchen, featuring a center cooking island with counter and large breakfast area, opens to the Great room for easy entertaining. Columns punctuate the interior spaces and a separate dining room provides a formal touch to the plan. The master suite, privately situated on the first floor, has a double vanity, garden tub, and separate shower. The semi-detached garage features a large bonus room. Design by Donald A. Gardner Architects, Inc.

First floor — 1,618 sq. ft.
Second floor —
570 sq. ft.
Bonus room —
495 sq. ft.
Garage — 649 sq. ft.

Total living area:
2,188 sq. ft.

FIRST FLOOR PLAN
No. 99801

© 1997 Donald A Gardner Architects, Inc.

SECOND FLOOR PLAN

Refer to **Pricing Schedule E** on the order form for pricing information

S. NATHAN

© 1997 Donald A Gardner Architects, Inc.

Design 94933

REPETITIVE PEAKS

This gracious front facade is enhanced by the repetitive peaks of the roof line. The living room and the dining room combine for formal entertaining. The interesting T-shaped staircase highlights the entry. The gourmet kitchen includes a salad sink in the island as well as a snack bar. There is a convenient back staircase off the kitchen for the family. The family room includes a wetbar and a cozy fireplace. The master suite is pampered by two walk-in closets, a private gazebo shaped sitting area, and a skylit master bath. The three additional bedrooms have private access to a full bath. Design by Design Basics, Inc.

First floor — 1,709 sq. ft.
Second floor — 1,597 sq. ft.
Basement — 1,709 sq. ft.
Garage — 721 sq. ft.

Total living area:
3,306 sq. ft.

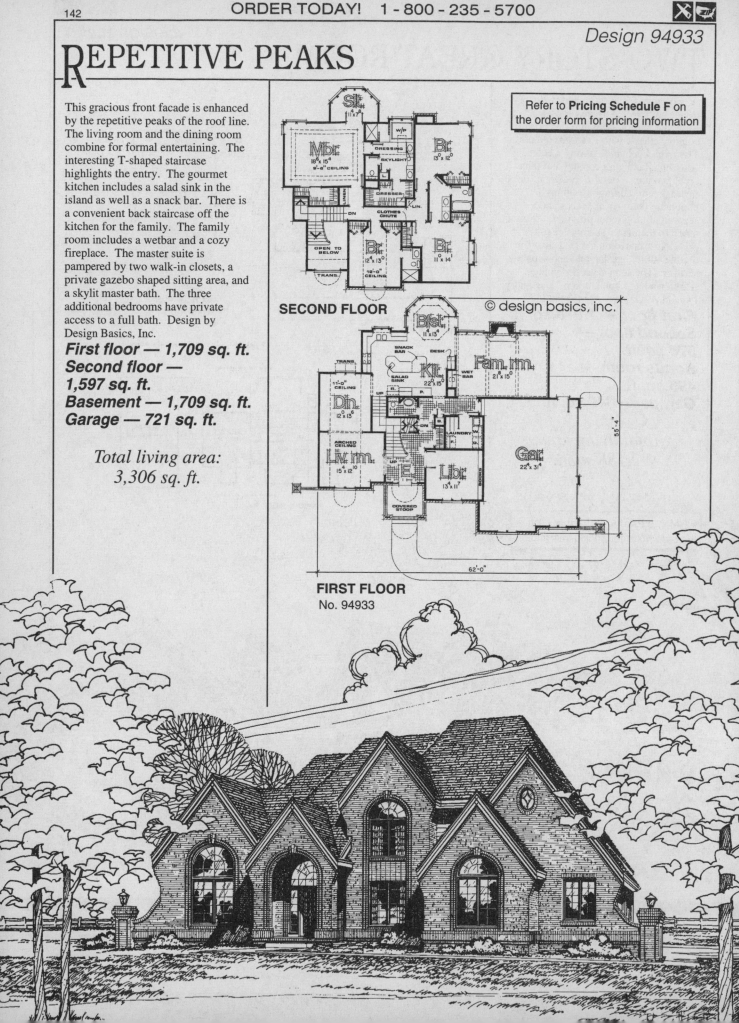

© design basics, inc.

SECOND FLOOR

FIRST FLOOR
No. 94933

SUBSTANCE AND GRACE

Design 99782

Family gathering spaces, formal and informal, dominate the main floor. The elegant master suite is here as well, its wide bay windows jutting out onto the shady porch. Features include a security system, his-n-her walk-in closets, dual basins, and a separately enclosed water closet and oversized shower. Both the living room and dining room are richly glassed to maximize light, year round. A tile-hearth fireplace provides warmth and atmosphere. The kitchen includes a raised dishwasher. Upstairs, a railing overlooks the wide foyer below. The guest suite is almost as large and well outfitted as the master suite. Design by Landmark Designs, Inc.

First floor — 1,680 sq. ft.
Second floor — 919 sq. ft.
Basement — 1,580 sq. ft.
Garage — 794 sq. ft.

Total living area:
2,599 sq. ft.

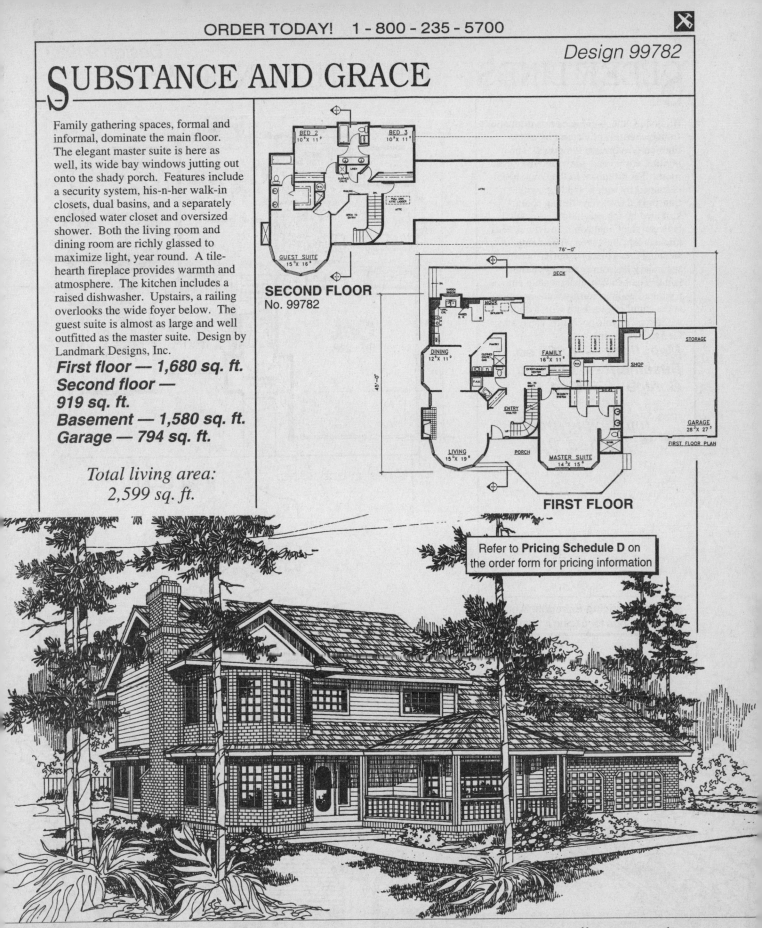

SECOND FLOOR
No. 99782

FIRST FLOOR

Refer to **Pricing Schedule D** on the order form for pricing information

Design 94923

SLEEK LINES — ORNATE WINDOWS

Brick and stucco enhance this dramatic front elevation showcased by sleek lines and decorative windows. The inviting entry has a view into the Great room. The fireplace in the Great room is framed by sunny windows with transoms above. The dining room, accented by a bay window, is nestled between the Great room and the superb kitchen/breakfast area. The design of sleeping areas places a buffer between secondary bedrooms and the master suite. The peaceful master suite enjoys a vaulted ceiling, roomy walk-in closet and a sunlit master bath with a double vanity and a whirlpool tub. Design by Design Basics, Inc.

Main floor — 1,666 sq. ft.
Basement — 1,666 sq. ft.
Garage — 496 sq. ft.

Total living area:
1,666 sq. ft.

Refer to **Pricing Schedule B** on the order form for pricing information

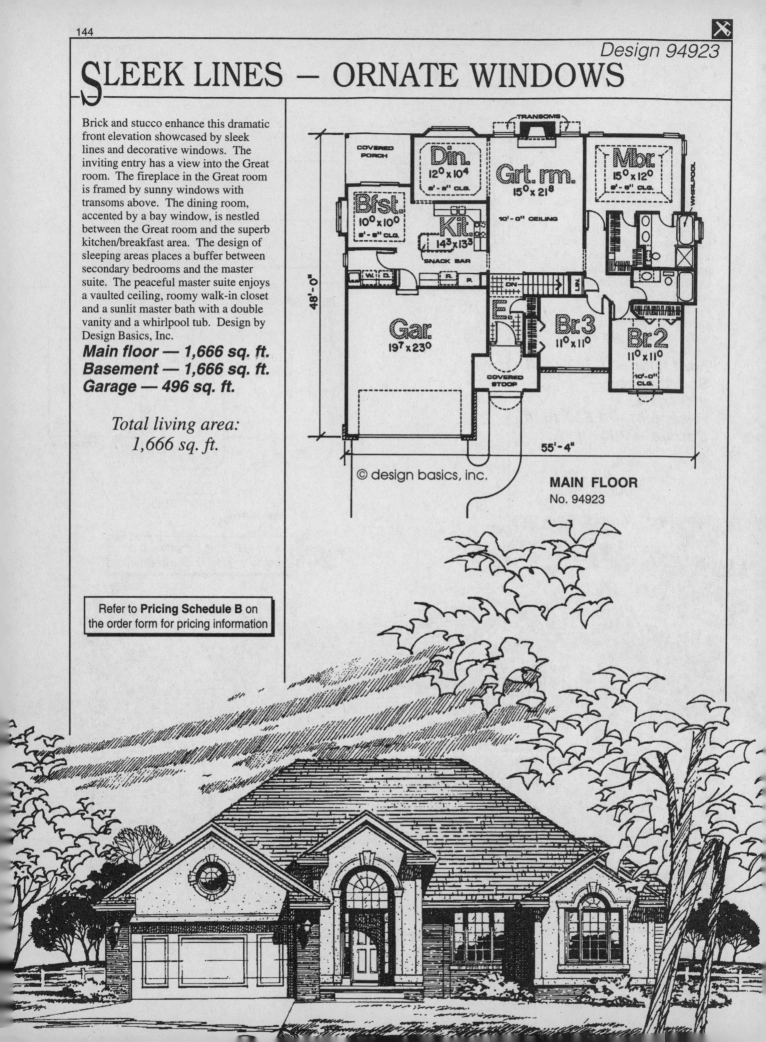

© design basics, inc.

MAIN FLOOR
No. 94923

AN EXECUTIVE ESTATE

Design 98539

A stately two-story covered entry, brick dormer window, and bay window with copper roofing, along with brick quoin corners and massive front chimney, provide a bold statement of success to all. Quality continues inside as well. A curved staircase flanked by a large living room with fireplace and adjacent to the formal dining room is sure to impress. A huge island kitchen and impressive master suite with bay window sitting area, and a luxurious bath with gigantic walk-in closet are included in this spectacular home. There other bedrooms, play room and a study are upstairs. This plan is available with a basement or slab foundation. Please specify when ordering. No materials list is available of this plan. Design by Filmore Design Group

Main floor — 2,751 sq. ft.
Upper floor — 1,185 sq. ft.
Bonus room — 343 sq. ft.
Garage — 790 sq. ft.

Total living area: 3,936 sq. ft.

Refer to **Pricing Schedule F** on the order form for pricing information

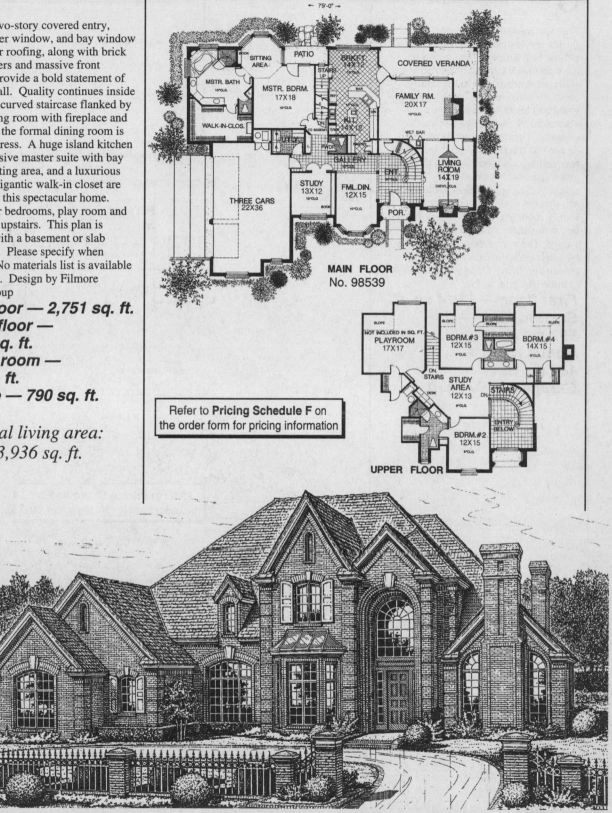

MAIN FLOOR
No. 98539

UPPER FLOOR

Design 98002

SPACIOUS FARMHOUSE

This spacious, three bedroom farmhouse features, bold, front facing gables, bay windows, and generous front and back porches. The main staircase is positioned in the family room for convenience, and both family room and breakfast bay area are optimized by exciting two-story ceilings. The master suite is privately located on the first floor and features a tray ceiling, his-n-her walk-in closets, and a splendid bath with every amenity. The second floor includes a loft that overlooks both the two-story family room and foyer, while two bedrooms share a hall bath with dual vanity. The bonus room is accessed by a second staircase as well as the upstairs hallway. Design by Donald A. Gardner Architects, Inc.

First floor — 1,914 sq. ft.

Second floor — 597 sq. ft.

Bonus room — 487 sq. ft.

Garage — 580 sq. ft.

Total living area: 2,511 sq. ft.

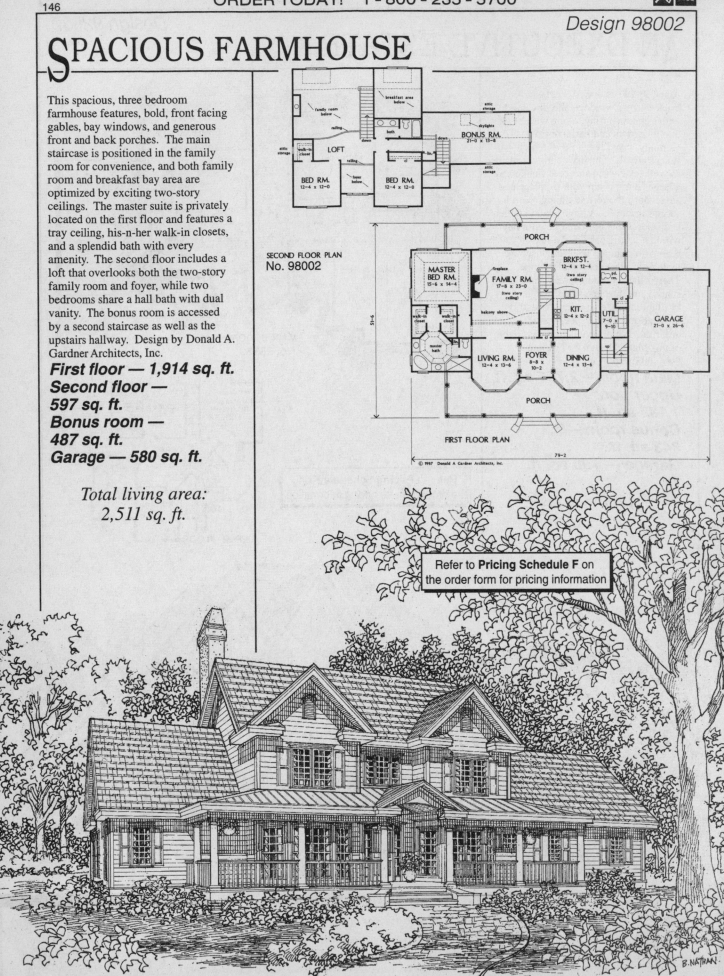

SECOND FLOOR PLAN
No. 98002

FIRST FLOOR PLAN

© 1997 Donald A Gardner Architects, Inc.

Refer to **Pricing Schedule F** on the order form for pricing information

B. NATHAN

©1997 Donald A. Gardner Architects, Inc.

Design 92657

TWO LEVELS OF ELEGANCE

Detailed stucco and stone accents provide warmth and character to the exterior of this one level home. An arched entry introduces you to the interior where elegant window styles and dramatic ceiling treatments create an impressive showplace. The extra large gourmet kitchen and breakfast room offer a spacious area for chores and family gatherings; while providing a striking view through the Great room to the fireplace wall. For convenience, a butler's pantry is located in the hall leading to the dining room. An extravagant master bedroom suite and library with built-in book shelves round out the main floor. Accented by a wood rail, an extra wide stairway leads to the lavish lower level. Two additional bedrooms with a tandem bath, a media room, billiard room and exercise room are created in the finished basement. No materials list is available for this plan. Design by Studer Residential Design, Inc.

First floor — 2,582 sq. ft.
Lower Level — 1,746 sq. ft.
Deck — 1,074 sq. ft.
Basement — 871 sq. ft.

Total living area: 4,328 sq. ft.

Refer to **Pricing Schedule F** on the order form for pricing information

Patio

Basement

Media Room 17'10" x 21'6"

Bedroom 14'1" x 12'9"

Bath

Bedroom 10'9" x 14'10"

Bath

Billiard Room 15'8" x 16'8"

Exercise Room 10'11" x 10'10"

Basement

LOWER LEVEL

Deck

Kitchen 15'1" x 18'7"

Breakfast 13'8" x 13'8"

Great Room 15'8" x 21'5"

Master Bedroom 14'4" x 19'11"

Dressing

Laun. Hall Bath

Gallery

Three-car Garage 22'2" x 29'8"

Dining Room 16'2" x 14'2"

Foyer

Library 11'8" x 12'7"

Porch

FIRST FLOOR
No. 92657

70' - 8"
64' - 4"

REWARDS OF SUCCESS

Your family may be in need of more room, and you're ready to move up to that dream home. Well, take a look at this floor plan. The open foyer is flanked by the formal areas of the home. To your left is the dining room and to your right is the living room. Hardwood floors take you to the large den. A large fireplace with a flat tiled hearth warms the room. Built-in cabinets and shelves provide an added convenience. The master suite is located on the first floor, and it includes a lavish master bath and a walk-in closet. The well-appointed kitchen serves the formal dining room and the informal breakfast area with equal ease. There is even a snack bar for those after school snacks or meals on the go. Three bedrooms and two full baths occupy the second floor. Each bedroom has more than ample storage space and direct access to a full bath. This plan is available with a crawl space or slab foundation. Please specify when ordering. Design by Rick Garner

First floor — 2,019 sq. ft.
Second floor —
946 sq. ft.
Garage — 577 sq. ft.

Total living area:
2,965 sq. ft.

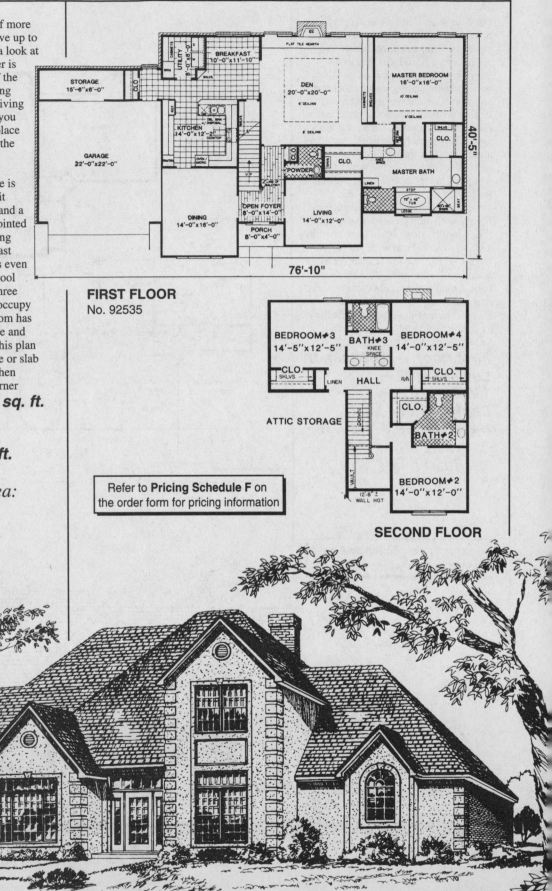

FIRST FLOOR
No. 92535

Refer to **Pricing Schedule F** on the order form for pricing information

SECOND FLOOR

FOUR DRAMATIC GABLES

Design 99841

Four dramatic gables raise this plan to new heights, while inside, vaulted and nine foot ceilings create maximum volume. Impressive and airy, this elegant executive home stays warm from two fireplaces; one in the two-story family room that warms up family gatherings, and a second in the study suggests quiet contemplation. Rear bays expand space and maximize natural light. The master suite, with an angled entrance for privacy, has it all; sitting bay, whirlpool tub, a double vanity and a separate shower. Extra room is added by a skylight bonus room and ample attic storage. Design by Donald A. Gardner Architects, Inc.

First floor — 2,162 sq. ft.
Second floor — 671 sq. ft.
Garage & storage — 587 sq. ft.
Bonus — 345 sq. ft.

Total living area: 2,833 sq. ft.

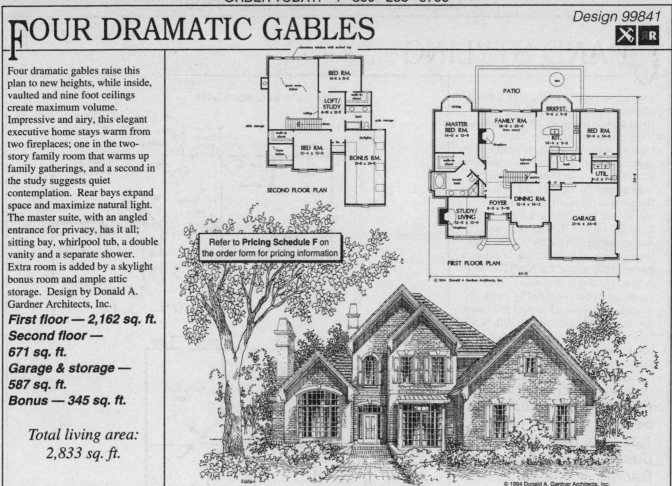

Refer to **Pricing Schedule F** on the order form for pricing information

© 1994 Donald A. Gardner Architects, Inc.

SPACIOUS ELEGANCE

Design 98455

The two-story foyer gives access to both the dining room and the family room. A convenient serving bar, double sink, built-in pantry and abundant counter space highlight the kitchen. A vaulted ceiling crowns the breakfast room while a French door gives access to the rear yard. The family room is enhanced by a fireplace flanked by windows. The master suite is privately located and decorated by a tray ceiling. A French door accesses the rear yard and a plush master bath, topped by a vaulted ceiling, and a walk-in closet are a few of the amenities in the suite. This plan is available with a basement or crawl space foundation. Please specify when ordering. Design by Frank Betz Associates, Inc.

First floor — 1,761 sq. ft.
Second floor — 588 sq. ft.
Bonus — 267 sq. ft.
Basement — 1,761 sq. ft.
Garage — 435 sq. ft.

Total living area: 2,349 sq. ft.

WIDTH 56'-0"
DEPTH 47'-6"

© Frank Betz Associates

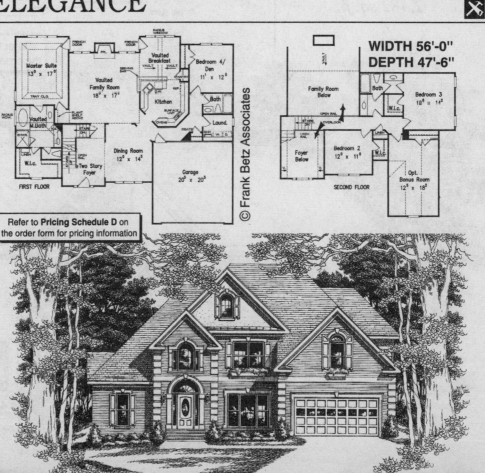

Refer to **Pricing Schedule D** on the order form for pricing information

GRAND STYLING

Design 97255

This home's eye-catching style attracts attention. Once inside, the two-story foyer retains the attention. The dining room and living room are located in traditional positions, to either side of the foyer. The family room, breakfast room, and kitchen are laid out so the open feeling prevails through-out. There is a fireplace in the family room and a serving bar between the kitchen and the breakfast room. The second floor accommodates all the bedrooms. The master suite includes a walk-in closet, a vaulted ceiling over the plush five piece bath and a cozy sitting room. The master bedroom is topped by a tray ceiling. The three additional bedrooms are roomy and share the full bath in the hall. This plan is available with a basement or crawl space foundation. Please specify when ordering. No materials list is available for this plan. Design by Frank Betz Associates, Inc.

First floor — 1,205 sq. ft.
Second floor —
1,277 sq. ft.
Basement — 1,128 sq. ft.
Garage — 528 sq. ft.

Total living area:
2,482 sq. ft.

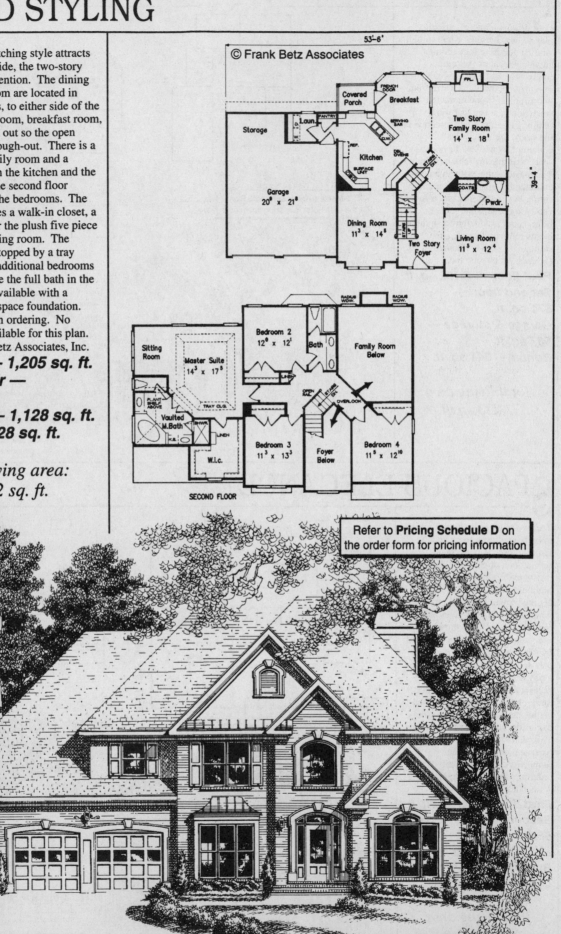

© Frank Betz Associates

Refer to **Pricing Schedule D** on the order form for pricing information

MULTIPLE GABLES

Design 97714

Exquisite columns, 13 ft. ceiling heights and detailed ceiling treatments decorate the dining room and Great room. The gourmet kitchen with island and snack bar combine with the spacious breakfast room hearth room to create a warm atmosphere. The master bedroom suite with a fireplace is complemented by a deluxe dressing room with whirlpool tub, shower and dual vanity. Blueprints come with a design for a billiard room, secondary kitchen, media area, exercise area, full bath and additional bedrooms for the lower level. A four car attached garage is an unexpected surprise. No materials list is available for this plan. Design by Studer Residential Design, Inc.

Main floor — 3,570 sq. ft.
Bonus — 2,367 sq. ft.
Lower level — 1,203 sq. ft.

Total living area: 3,570 sq. ft.

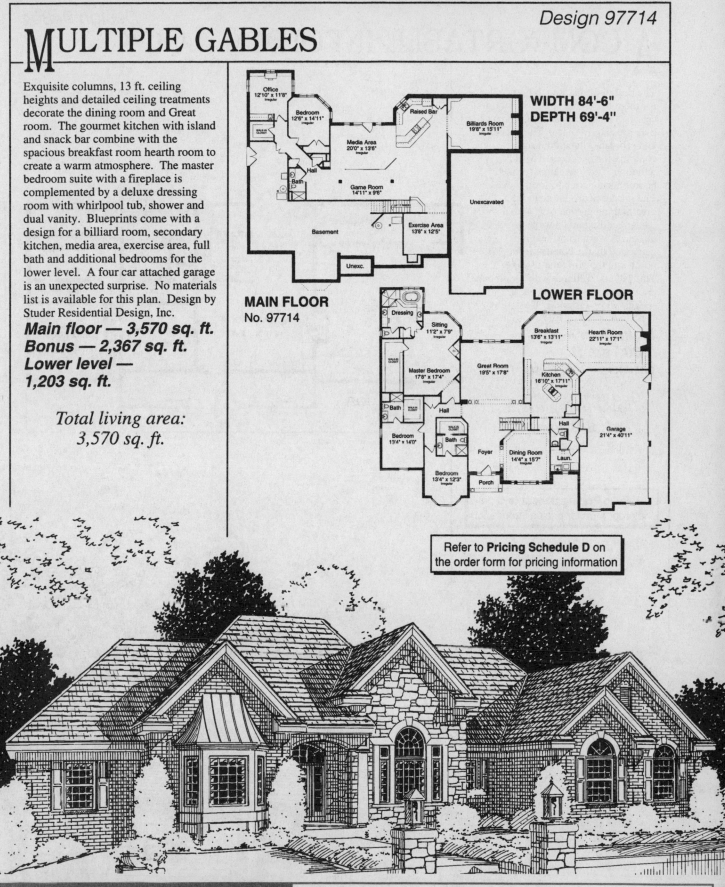

WIDTH 84'-6"
DEPTH 69'-4"

MAIN FLOOR
No. 97714

LOWER FLOOR

Refer to **Pricing Schedule D** on the order form for pricing information

Design 94801

A COMFORTABLE INFORMAL LOOK

The design of this Ranch home allows for the most practical use of interior space. The activity room is enhanced by a pre-fab fireplace. The spacious and efficient kitchen/dining combination is accented by a bay window. Three generously sized bedrooms are zoned for privacy. The master bedroom includes a breathtaking garden bath with a vaulted ceiling and a walk-in closet. A warm rural feel is generated by the country front porch and the horizontal siding. This plan is available with a slab or crawl space foundation. Please specify when ordering. Design by W.D.Farmer F.A.I.B.D.

**Main floor —
1,300 sq. ft.
Garage — 576 sq. ft.**

*Total living area:
1,300 sq. ft.*

Refer to **Pricing Schedule C** on the order form for pricing information

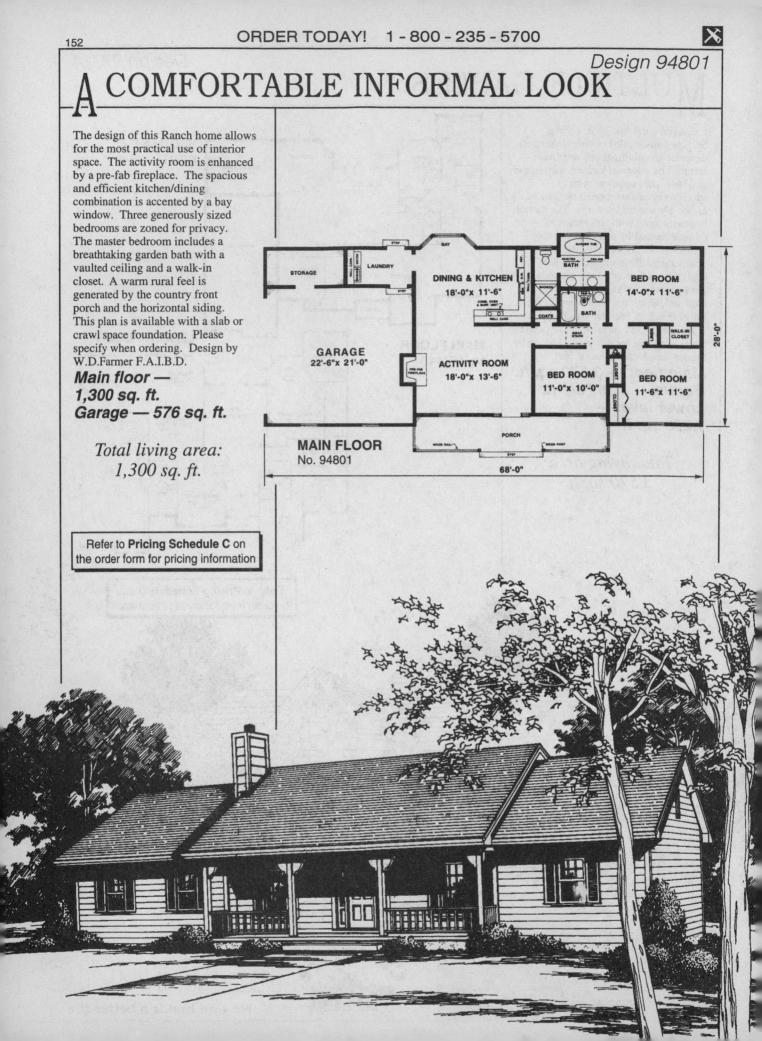

STORAGE

LAUNDRY

STEP

BAY

DINING & KITCHEN
18'-0"x 11'-6"

COMB. OVEN
& SURF. UNIT

WALL CABS.

GARDEN TUB

VAULTED CEILING

BATH

BED ROOM
14'-0"x 11'-6"

SHOWER

COATS

BATH

LINEN

WALK-IN CLOSET

GARAGE
22'-6"x 21'-0"

PRE-FAB FIREPLACE

ACTIVITY ROOM
18'-0"x 13'-6"

DISAP. STAIRS

BED ROOM
11'-0"x 10'-0"

CLOSET

CLOSET

BED ROOM
11'-6"x 11'-6"

28'-0"

MAIN FLOOR
No. 94801

WOOD RAIL

PORCH

WOOD POST

STEP

68'-0"

DIVERSITY AND STRENGTH

The diversity and strength of the exterior of this home reflects the excitement of the interior. Stairs in the foyer lead to the gallery on the first floor providing a panoramic view of the sunken Great room. The two-story high ceiling, dramatic rear wall window arrangement and the elegantly faced fireplace propel this home into a phenomenal showplace. The kitchen/breakfast area with counter seating and a spacious pantry flows easily to the cozy hearth room. A second fireplace, a furniture alcove, exciting ceiling treatment and multiple windows enhance this family gathering place. Located on the first floor and positioned for privacy, an expansive master bedroom suite provides luxury, spaciousness and relaxation for the homeowner. Rounding out the first floor is the formal dining room and a private library/retreat. No materials list is available for this plan. Design by Studer Residential Design, Inc.

First floor — 2,710 sq. ft.
**Second floor —
964 sq. ft.**
Basement — 2,700 sq. ft.

*Total living area:
3,674 sq. ft.*

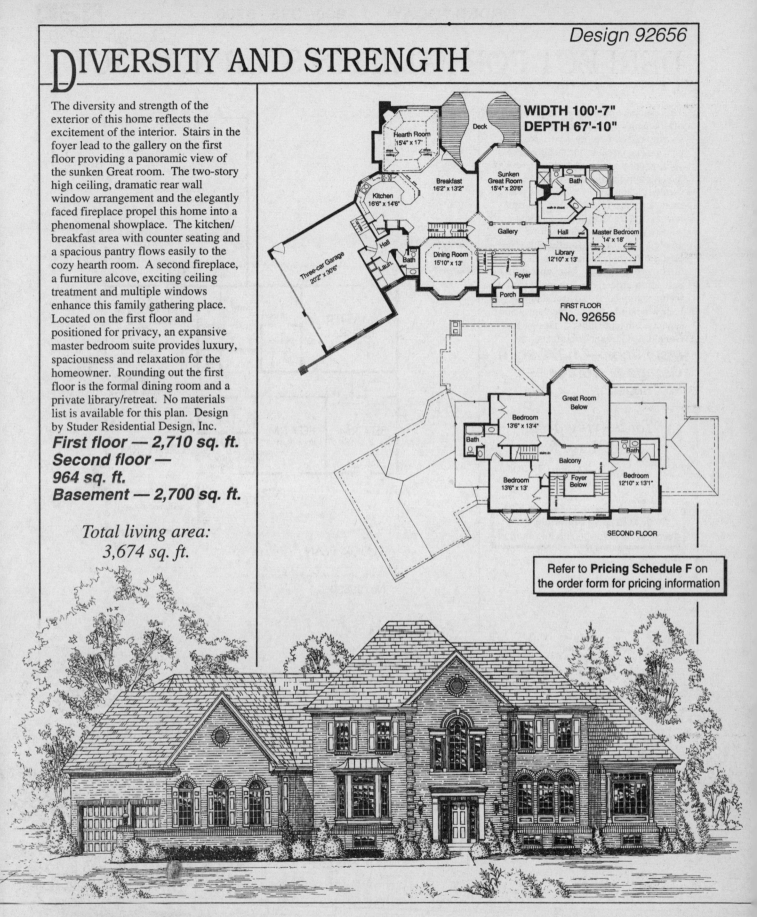

WIDTH 100'-7"
DEPTH 67'-10"

FIRST FLOOR
No. 92656

SECOND FLOOR

Refer to **Pricing Schedule F** on the order form for pricing information

Design 99830

PERFECT FOR FAMILIES STARTING OUT

This compact plan with rear garage offers plenty of room for families just starting out and empty-nester scaling down. The Great room's cathedral ceiling, combined with the openness of the adjoining dining room and kitchen, create spaciousness beyond this plan's modest square footage. The dining room is enlarged by a bay window while a palladian window allows ample light into the Great room. The efficient U-shaped kitchen leads directly to the garage, convenient for unloading groceries. The master suite features ample closet space and a skylit bath which boasts a double vanity and separate tub and shower. Design by Donald A. Gardner Architects, Inc.

Main floor — 1,372 sq. ft.
Garage & storage —
537 sq. ft.

Total living area:
1,372 sq. ft.

Refer to **Pricing Schedule C** on
the order form for pricing information

GARAGE
20-8 x 22-0
(optional)

storage

MASTER
BED RM.
14-0 x 12-4

cl

skylight   master bath

walk-in
closet

w d   lin.   cl

KITCHEN
13-4 x 9-0

walk-in
closet

DINING
13-4 x 10-8

BED RM.
10-4 x 11-0

BED RM.
10-4 x 11-0

bath

cl

FOYER
6-0 x
5-8

GREAT RM.
13-4 x 15-10

fireplace

(cathedral ceiling)

PORCH

25-2

36-8

46-0

FLOOR PLAN

© 1996 Donald A Gardner Architects, Inc.

No. 99830

MEMORIES OF YESTERDAY

Design 98518

Relive those days of yesterday with this charming Victorian home. The plant box under the utility room window, as well as the large arched window in the living room, will give a great impression. An angled country kitchen with an island range, and dining area is open to the spacious family room. The family room is highlighted by a large fireplace and wall cabinets, sure to add to a family's enjoyment. Retire to the master suite and two other bedrooms upstairs. Do not overlook the future room space for future family enjoyment. This plan is available with a basement or slab foundation. Please specify when ordering. No materials list is available for this plan. Design by Filmore Design Group

First floor — 1,447 sq. ft.
Second floor —
1,008 sq. ft.
Garage — 756 sq. ft.

Total living area:
2,455 sq. ft.

FIRST FLOOR

65'-0"
37'-11"

Patio

Kit 13x14
Din 12x11
FamRm 17x17

3 Car Garage 21x36

To Opt Basement Stairs

Gallery TILE FLOOR

LivRm 13x16 CATH. CLNG

Util

FrmlDin 14x14

Ent TILE FLOOR

Porch

SECOND FLOOR
No. 98518

Bed#2 12x12
Bed#3 12x12

STAIRS

Future Room 22x16 (Not Included in Sq. Ftg.)

Sitting Area 9x12

MstrBd 14x16

Refer to **Pricing Schedule D** on the order form for pricing information

REFINEMENT WITH BRILLIANCY

Design 97206

This home has a refinement that shines. The two-story foyer is dominated by an open rail staircase. The two-story family room is enhanced by a fireplace and is open to the breakfast room/kitchen. A French door from the breakfast room accesses the rear yard. A walk-in pantry and ample counter space highlight the breakfast room/kitchen. The secluded study easily becomes a bedroom with a private bath. The master suite features a tray ceiling, a bayed sitting area, two walk-in closets and a vaulted ceiling over the master bath. An optional bonus room is available for future expansion. This plan is available with a basement, crawl space or slab foundation. Please specify when ordering. No materials list is available for this plan. Design by Frank Betz Associates, Inc.

First floor — 1,548 sq. ft.
Second floor — 1,164 sq. ft.
Bonus room — 198 sq. ft.
Basement — 1,548 sq. ft.
Garage — 542 sq. ft.

Total living area: 2,712 sq. ft.

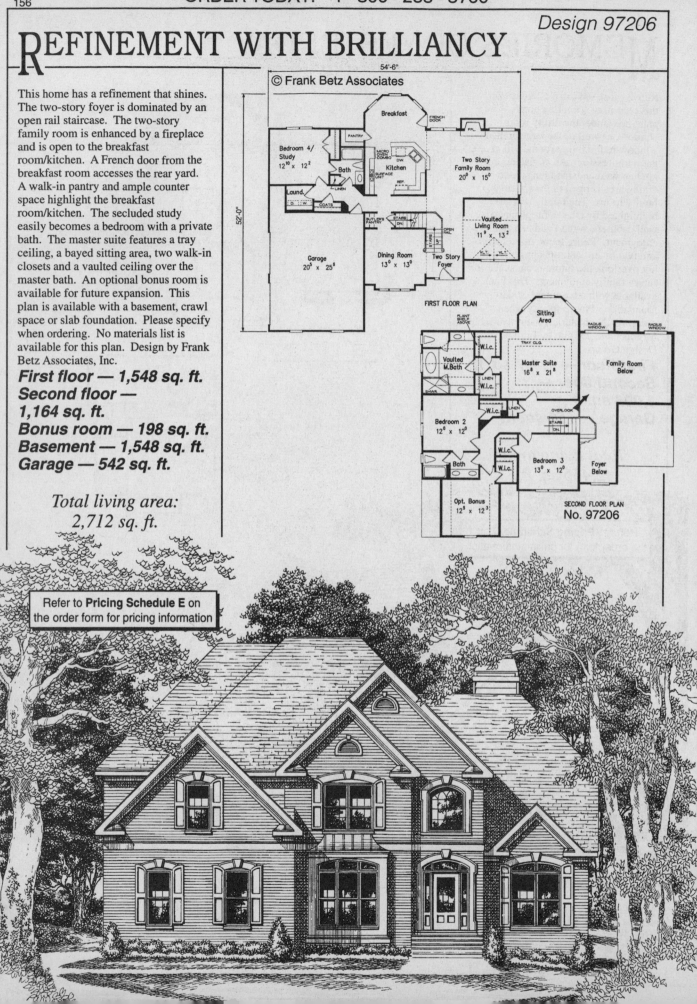

© Frank Betz Associates

FIRST FLOOR PLAN

SECOND FLOOR PLAN
No. 97206

Refer to **Pricing Schedule E** on the order form for pricing information

Design 92404

TRADITIONAL RANCH

One of today's most popular features is a master suite which is isolated from the other bedrooms. This master suite measures 14'x18' and is highlighted by a trey ceiling. Spacious his-n-her closets flank the hallway which leads to the master bath. Separate vanities and a garden tub as well as a shower and a commode closet complete this area. Double French doors lead from the master suite to a deck. The 13'x13' living room features a cathedral ceiling while an angled trey ceiling highlights the 12'x13' dining room. Stair placement is shown if a basement foundation is desired. The 16'x18' family room is a spacious gathering area with vaulted ceiling and fireplace. The breakfast area leads into the 10'x10' kitchen which includes a snack bar. Conveniently located in this bedroom wing is the laundry room. Design by Atlanta Plan Source, Inc.

Main area — 2,275 sq. ft.
Basement — 2,207 sq. ft.
Garage — 512 sq. ft.

Total living area:
2,275 sq. ft.

DECK

BR.#2
14x11

BREAKFAST

MASTER
14x18

KITCHEN
10x10

FAMILY ROOM
16X18

Trey Clg.

BR.#3
13x12

Stairs
Down

DINING
12x13

FOYER

LIVING
13x13

Cathedral

TreyClg.

Cathedral

UTILITY

WORKSHOP

MAIN FLOOR
No. 92404

GARAGE
22x19

Drive

60'

62'

Refer to **Pricing Schedule D** on the order form for pricing information

Design 99113

DISTINCTIVE RANCH

This hip-roofed ranch has an exterior that tastefully mixes brick and siding. The recessed entrance with arched transom and sidelights fills the formal entry with glowing light. The foyer opens to the large living room with a high ceiling and a fireplace, the perfect spot for family gatherings. There is a large kitchen with ample cupboard space, and a roomy dining area which leads to the back yard. The spacious master bedroom, with sweeping windows over looking the rear yard, has a large walk-in closet. The private master bath amenities include a whirlpool tub, double vanity and a large corner shower. Two additional bedrooms share a full bath and each have large closets. The laundry room is on the main floor between the three car garage and the kitchen, and has a large utility closet. No materials list is available for this plan. Design by Ahmann Design, Inc.

Main floor — 1,906 sq. ft.
Basement — 1,906 sq. ft.

Total living area:
1,906 sq. ft.

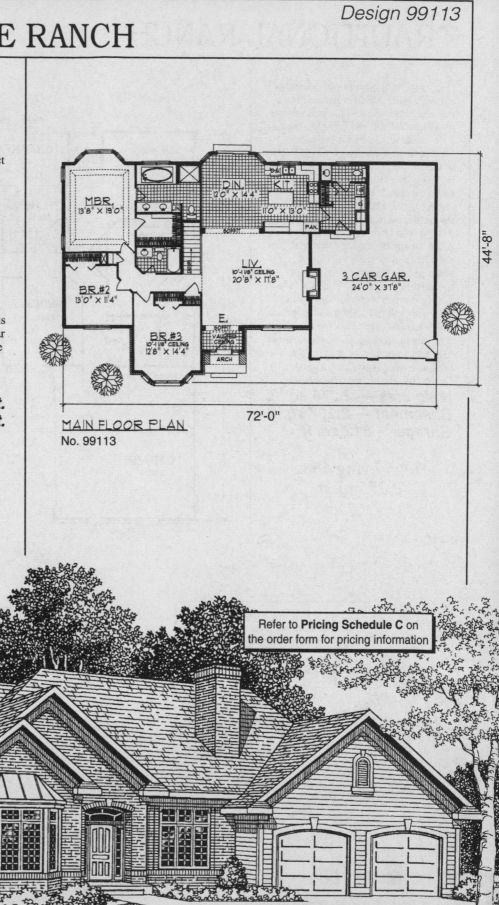

MAIN FLOOR PLAN
No. 99113

Refer to **Pricing Schedule C** on the order form for pricing information

CASUALLY ELEGANT

Design 96417

This country classic offers a casually elegant exterior with arched windows, dormers, and charming front and back porches with columns. Inside, the open, casual mood is continued in the central Great room which features a cathedral ceiling, a fireplace, and a clerestory window that splashes the room with natural light. Other special touches include a breakfast bay and interior columns. The master suite with cathedral ceiling is privately located and features a skylit bath with whirlpool tub, a shower, and a double vanity. Two additional bedrooms, share a full bath and a garage with storage completes the plan. Design by Donald A. Gardner Architects, Inc.

Main floor — 1,561 sq. ft.
Garage & storage — 346 sq. ft.

Total living area:
1,561 sq. ft.

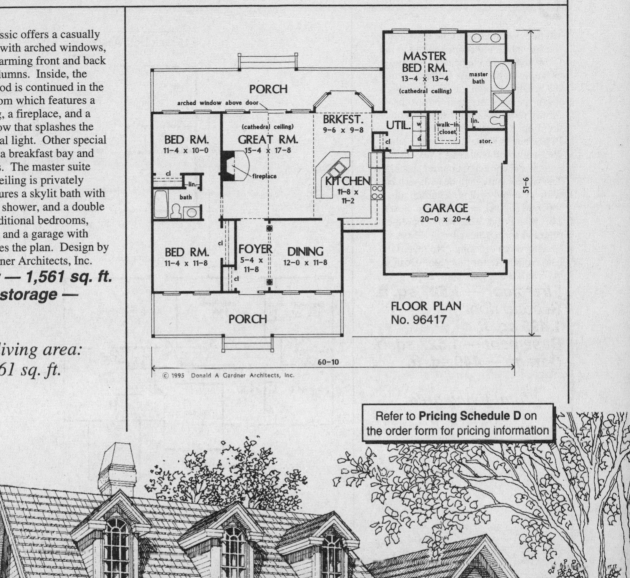

PORCH

arched window above door

BED RM.
11-4 x 10-0

cl

lin.

bath

(cathedral ceiling)
GREAT RM.
15-4 x 17-8

fireplace

BRKFST.
9-6 x 9-8

KITCHEN
11-8 x 11-2

MASTER BED RM.
13-4 x 13-4
(cathedral ceiling)

master bath

UTIL.
w d
cl

walk-in closet

lin.

stor.

GARAGE
20-0 x 20-4

BED RM.
11-4 x 11-8

FOYER
5-4 x 11-8

cl

DINING
12-0 x 11-8

PORCH

51-6

60-10

FLOOR PLAN
No. 96417

© 1995 Donald A Gardner Architects, Inc.

E. NATHAN

© 1995 Donald A. Gardner Architects, Inc.

Design 97213

LUXURIOUS APPOINTMENTS

Arched openings from the foyer into the formal dining room and the living room add to the elegance. Decorative columns highlight the entrance from the breakfast room into the family room. A two-story ceiling tops the family room, while a fireplace lends the room a cozy atmosphere. Efficiency is emphasized in the island kitchen which features a walk-in pantry and abundant counter space. The master suite includes a lavish bath with a vaulted ceiling, a garden tub, a separate shower and a walk-in closet. This plan is available with a basement or crawl space foundation. Please specify when ordering. No materials list is available for this plan. Design by Frank Betz Associates, Inc.

**First floor — 1,527 sq. ft.
Second floor — 1,495 sq. ft.
Basement — 1,527 sq. ft.
Garage — 440 sq. ft.**

Total living area: 3,022 sq. ft.

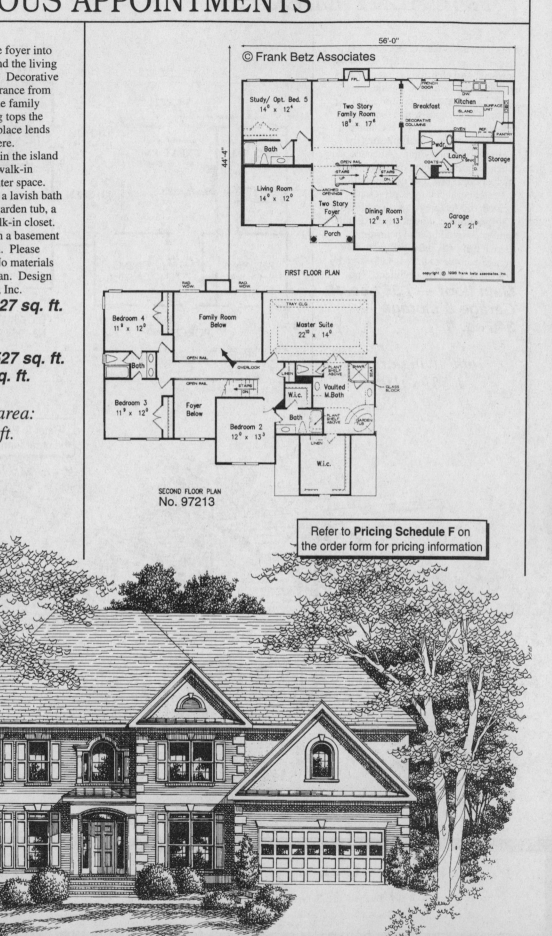

© Frank Betz Associates

FIRST FLOOR PLAN

SECOND FLOOR PLAN
No. 97213

Refer to **Pricing Schedule F** on the order form for pricing information

Design 99803

EXECUTIVE HOME

With a traditional, elegant exterior and lively interior spaces, this three bedroom executive home makes both everyday life and entertaining a breeze. A palladian window floods the foyer with light for a dramatic entrance alluding to a surprising, open floor plan. Prepare a gourmet meal in the well-planned kitchen while chatting with family and friends in the large Great room with cathedral ceiling, fireplace, and built-in cabinets. The screened porch, breakfast area, and master suite access the deck with optional spa. The large master suite features a luxurious skylit bath with separate shower and a corner whirlpool tub. A skylit bonus room above the garage adds space when needed. This plan is available with a basement or crawl space foundation. Please specify when ordering. Design by Donald A. Gardner Architects, Inc.

**Main floor — 1,977 sq. ft.
Bonus room —
430 sq. ft.
Garage — 610 sq. ft.**

*Total living area:
1,977 sq. ft.*

Refer to **Pricing Schedule D** on the order form for pricing information

seat

spa

seat

DECK

SCREEN PORCH
16-0 x 11-0

BED RM.
12-4 x 11-8

cl

lin.

bath

cl

cl

**BED RM./
STUDY**
12-0 x 12-0

GREAT RM.
18-0 x 17-4
(cathedral ceiling)

fireplace

FOYER
12-4 x 5-6

PORCH

BRKFST.
12-0 x 8-6

KIT.
12-0 x 12-8

DINING
12-0 x 13-8

storage

MASTER BED RM.
13-4 x 18-8

master bath

skylights

walk-in closet

storage

UTILITY
8-5 x 7-0

d   w

up   down

storage

GARAGE
25-8 x 20-4

5-4

63-10

**FLOOR PLAN
No. 99803**

69-8

© 1996 Donald A Gardner Architects, Inc.

attic access

down

skylights

BONUS RM.
21-9 x 16-7

Design 98032

SPLENDID COUNTRY HOME

An inviting front porch and three dormers create a welcome atmosphere for this splendid country home. The arched clerestory window in the center dormer casts natural light into the vaulted foyer and second floor bath. Beyond the foyer, the Great room is open to both breakfast and kitchen and features a cathedral ceiling and access to the rear deck. Stairs, conveniently located in the Great room, lead to a second floor balcony. The first floor master suite boasts his-n-her walk-in closets and a private bath. Upstairs, both bedrooms have walk-in closets and dormer alcoves as well as separate vanities and a linen storage in the shared bath. An abundance of attic storage is accessed easily from the second floor hall. Design by Donald A. Gardner Architects, Inc.

First floor — 1,569 sq. ft.
Second floor — 682 sq. ft.
Bonus — 332 sq. ft.
Garage— 492 sq. ft.

Total living area: 2,251 sq. ft.

Refer to **Pricing Schedule E** on the order form for pricing information

SECOND FLOOR

BED RM. 12-0 x 13-0

BED RM. 12-0 x 13-0

BONUS RM. 21-0 x 13-4

DECK

GREAT RM. 18-0 x 19-6 (cathedral ceiling)

BRKFST. 12-0 x 10-0

UTIL 9-0 x 6-0

KIT. 12-0 x 12-8

GARAGE 21-0 x 20-4

MASTER BED RM. 12-0 x 16-8

FOYER 7-4 x 12-4 (vaulted ceiling)

DINING 12-0 x 12-0

PORCH

FIRST FLOOR
No. 98032

© 1998 Donald A. Gardner, inc.

B. NATHAN.

© 1998 Donald A. Gardner, inc.

EXECUTIVE FEATURES

Design 98211

The extended staircase highlights the foyer and columns define the dining room and the grand room. The exceptionally large first floor master bedroom has a glass exterior rear wall and high ceilings. His-n-her walk-in closets and a five-piece, lavish bath highlight the suite. The island kitchen, keeping room and breakfast room create an open living space. A fireplace accents both the keeping room and the two-story grand room. The three additional bedrooms feature private bathroom access and ample closet space. A gallery is also included on the second floor. This plan is available with a basement or crawl space foundation. Please specify when ordering. No materials list is available for this plan. Design by Archival Designs, Inc.

**First floor — 2,035 sq. ft.
Second floor —
1,028 sq. ft.
Basement — 2,035 sq. ft.
Garage — 530 sq. ft.**

*Total living area:
3,063 sq. ft.*

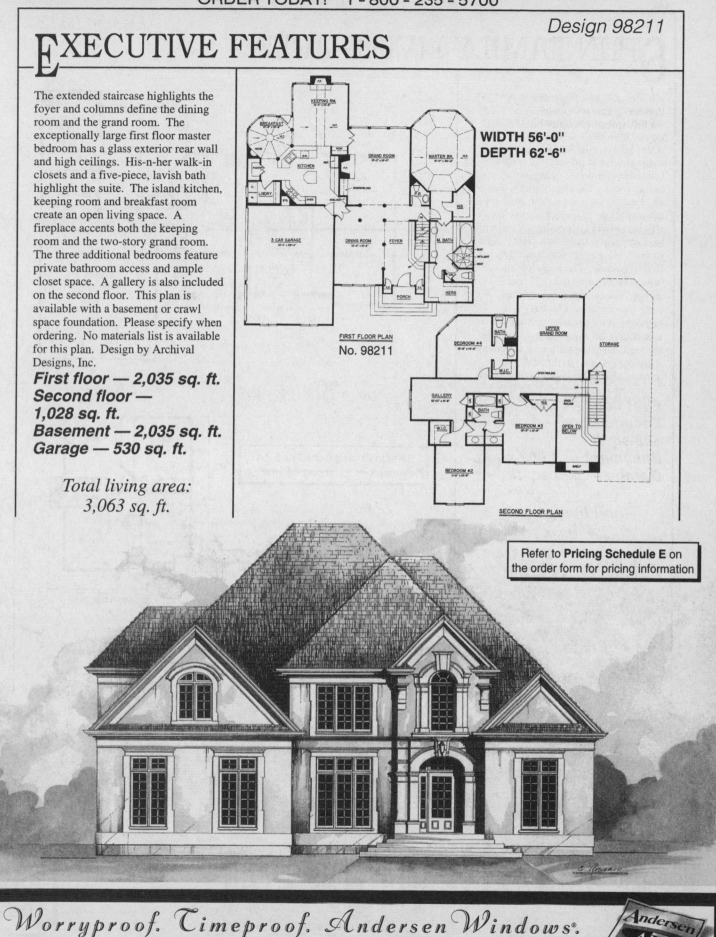

**WIDTH 56'-0"
DEPTH 62'-6"**

FIRST FLOOR PLAN
No. 98211

SECOND FLOOR PLAN

Refer to **Pricing Schedule E** on the order form for pricing information

Design 94124

OPEN FAMILY LIVING AREA

The two-story foyer gives this home an immediate spacious feeling. Flowing off the foyer is the formal living room topped by a vaulted ceiling. Pocket doors between the family room and living room add privacy. A fireplace framed by windows highlight the family room. The family room, dinette and kitchen are in an open format for a more spacious and airy feeling. The efficient island kitchen features a built-in pantry and a snack bar. The elegant formal dining room is enhanced by a bayed window. The secluded master suite is tucked into the right rear corner. Double doors provide the entry into the suite which is highlighted by a master bath and direct access into the study/office. On the second floor three additional bedrooms share the full bath in the hall. No materials list is available for this plan. Design by James Fahey, P.E., P.C.

First floor — 1,861 sq. ft.
Second floor — 598 sq. ft.
Basement — 1,802 sq. ft.
Garage — 523 sq. ft.

Total living area:
2,459 sq. ft.

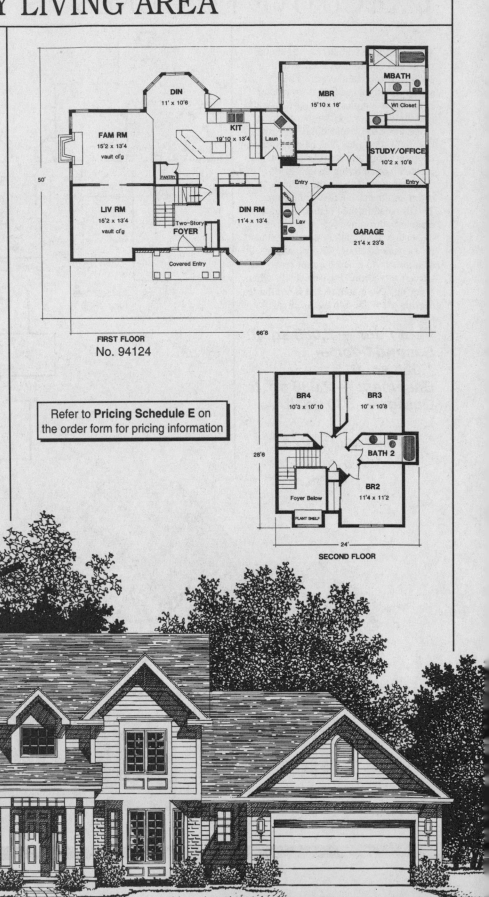

FIRST FLOOR
No. 94124

Refer to **Pricing Schedule E** on the order form for pricing information

SECOND FLOOR

Design 24594

IMPRESSIVE TWO-STORY FOYER

Natural light streams into the two-story foyer of this home from the huge window above. Windows continue to highlight living space in both the dining and living room, both accented by a bay window. The island kitchen and breakfast area are adjoined. The sunken family room is spacious and cozy with a grand fireplace. The future sun room will be accessed through French doors at either side of the fireplace. Four bedrooms and a study are located on the second floor. The master suite includes a whirlpool bath and the three additional bedrooms have easy access to the double vanity bath in the hall. The study may easily become a guest room with ample closet space. Design by The Garlinghouse Company

First floor — 1,497 sq. ft.
Second floor — 1,460 sq. ft.
Basement — 1,456 sq. ft.
Future sunroom — 210 sq. ft.
Garage — 680 sq. ft.

Total living area: 2,957 sq. ft.

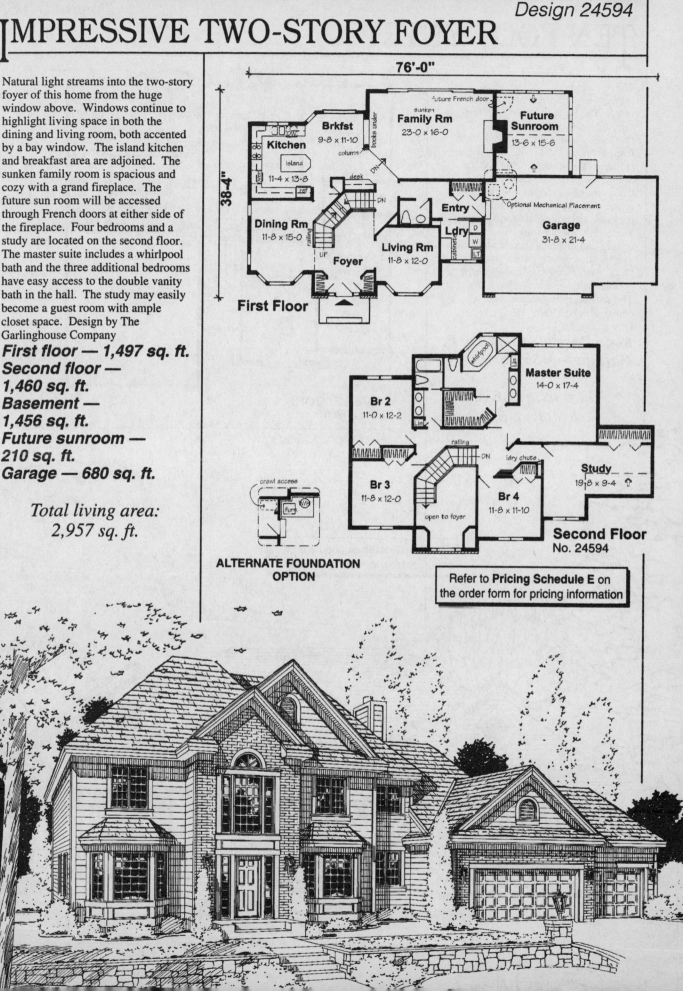

First Floor

Second Floor
No. 24594

ALTERNATE FOUNDATION OPTION

Refer to **Pricing Schedule E** on the order form for pricing information

Design 94986

TEN FOOT ENTRY

This home gives a fantastic first impression with a spacious ten foot entry. The large volume Great room is highlighted by a fireplace that is flanked by windows that can be seen from the entry. A see-through wetbar enhances the breakfast area and the dining room. A decorative ceiling treatment gives elegance to the dining room. The fully equipped kitchen includes a planning desk and a pantry. The roomy master suite has a volume ceiling and includes special amenities; a skylighted dressing/bath area with a plant shelf, a large walk-in closet, a double vanity and a whirlpool tub. The secondary bedrooms share a convenient hall bath. Design by Design Basics, Inc.

Main floor — 1,604 sq. ft.
Garage — 466 sq. ft.

Total living area: 1,604 sq. ft.

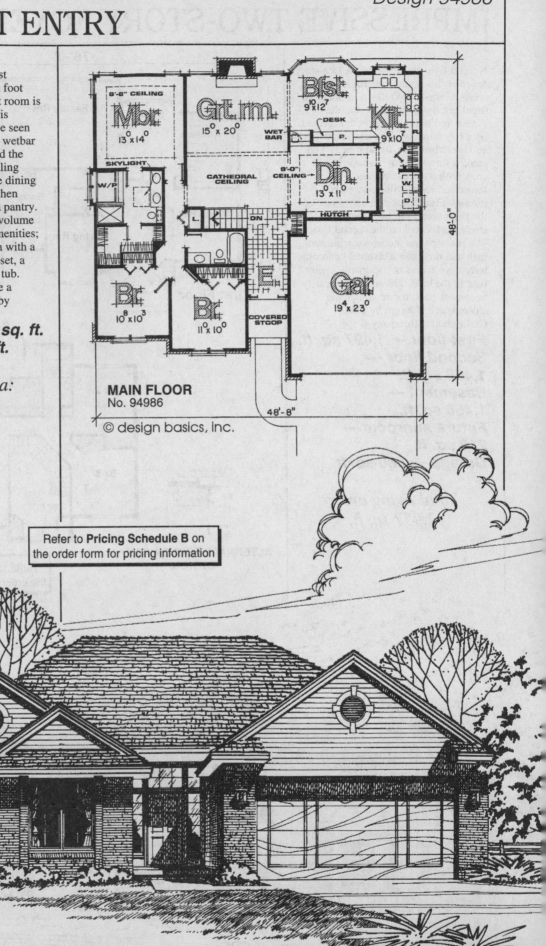

MAIN FLOOR
No. 94986

© design basics, inc.

Refer to **Pricing Schedule B** on
the order form for pricing information

SURPRISING ELEGANCE

Design 99106

No doubt about it, there is more than meets the eye in this modern ranch home. Graceful columns which support the covered entry and the multiple gables set this home apart in any neighborhood. Once inside you will be impressed with the cathedral ceiling of the Great room, and the arched pass through to the kitchen. The dining room also has a cathedral ceiling, adding to the overall impression of this plan. The unique master suite has its own fireplace and a dramatic plant ledge accentuating the decorative tray ceiling. A private bath is your evening retreat, with a spa tub, large vanity and a walk-in closet. A convenient main floor laundry separates the garage from the kitchen. Two more bedrooms share a full bath. No materials list is available for this plan. Design by Ahmann Design, Inc.

Main floor — 1,495 sq. ft.
Basement — 1,495 sq. ft.

Total living area:
1,495 sq. ft.

Refer to **Pricing Schedule A** on the order form for pricing information

MAIN FLOOR PLAN
No. 99106

ENTICING ELEVATION WITH PORCH

Design 97413

The volume entry of this home surveys the formal rooms. The parlor is enhanced by bright gazebo windows, a built in curio and direct access to the porch. The gathering room has elegant French doors at its entrance from the parlor. A bright window wall and a cozy fireplace highlight the gathering room. The kitchen has wrapping counters, a work island and an angled breakfast area with access to the rear yard. There are gazebo windows in the third bedroom and a walk-in closet in the fourth bedroom. A convenient hall bath serves these secondary bedrooms. The layout of the second floor provides privacy to the luxurious master suite which features a vaulted ceiling, his-n-her closets, a linen closet and dual vanity. No materials list is available for this plan. Design by Design Basics, Inc.

First floor — 1,183 sq. ft.
Second floor — 1,209 sq. ft.
Garage — 483 sq. ft.

Total living area: 2,392 sq. ft.

Refer to **Pricing Schedule D** on the order form for pricing information

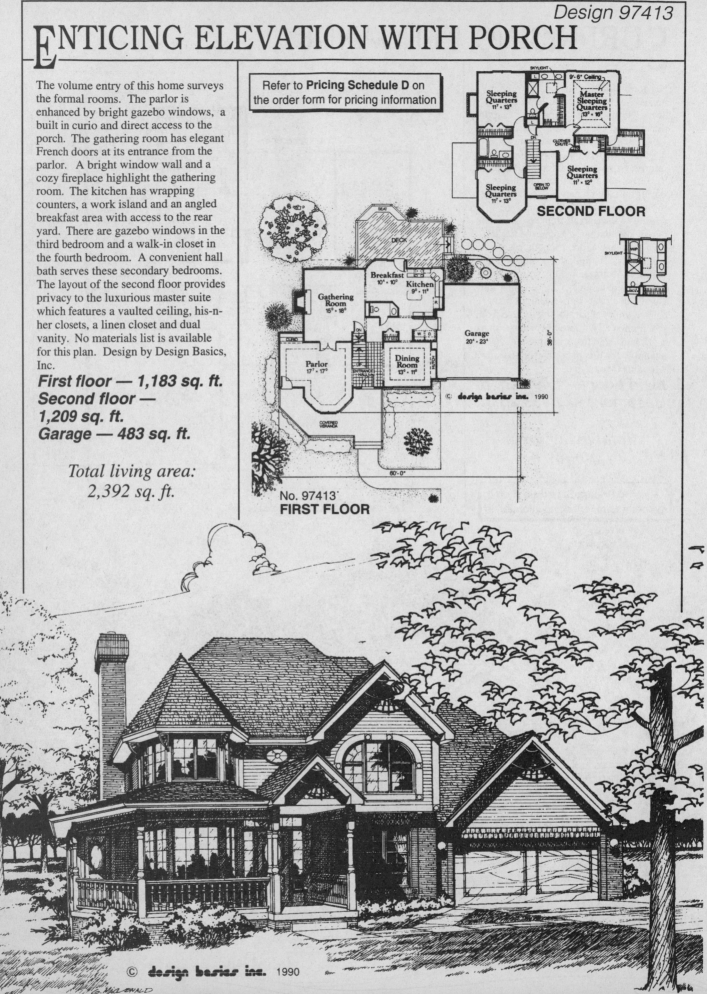

No. 97413
FIRST FLOOR

SECOND FLOOR

© design basics inc. 1990

FOR AN INFORMAL LIFESTYLE

You'll find daily living relaxed and comfortable in this stylish plan. Both the Great room and the kitchen/dining room of this home are accented by vaulted ceilings. In addition to having a conveniently arranged L-shaped food preparation center, the dining area overlooks the deck through sliding glass doors. The Great room incorporates all adjacent floor space and is highlighted by the corner placement of the fireplace. Two bedrooms are secluded from the living areas and feature individual access to the full bath. The master bedroom also includes a separate vanity in the dressing area. Design by Lifestyles Home Design

Main area — 988 sq. ft.
Basement — 988 sq. ft.
Garage — 400 sq. ft.

Total living area:
988 sq. ft.

Refer to **Pricing Schedule A** on the order form for pricing information

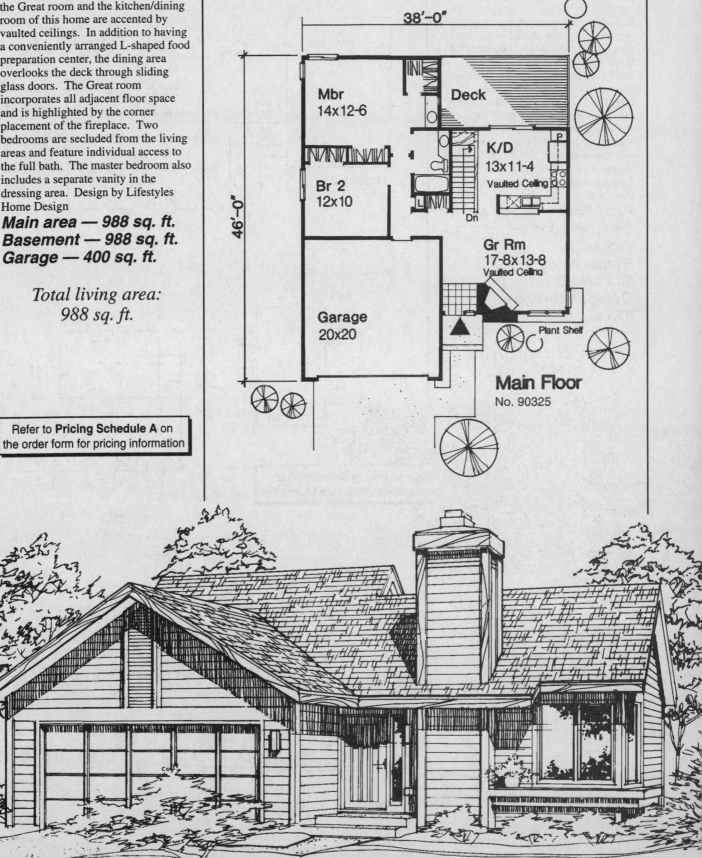

38'-0"

46'-0"

Mbr
14x12-6

Deck

Br 2
12x10

K/D
13x11-4
Vaulted Ceiling

Dn

Gr Rm
17-8x13-8
Vaulted Ceiling

Garage
20x20

Plant Shelf

Main Floor
No. 90325

Design 96443

IMRESSIVE SPACES PREVAIL

From the two-level foyer with palladian clerestory and stately stairway to the large Great room with cathedral ceiling and curved balcony, impressive spaces prevail in this open plan. A colonnaded opening from the Great room introduces a spacious family kitchen with island counter and breakfast bay. The master suite, privately located at the opposite end of the first floor, features sitting bay, extra large walk-in closet and bath with every possible luxury. A bonus room, attic storage, and an extra garage storage area provide additional space for growing families. Design by Donald A. Gardner Architects, Inc.

First floor — 2,357 sq. ft.
Second floor — 995 sq. ft.
Bonus room — 545 sq. ft.
Garage/storage — 975 sq. ft.

Total living area: 3,352 sq. ft.

Refer to **Pricing Schedule G** on the order form for pricing information

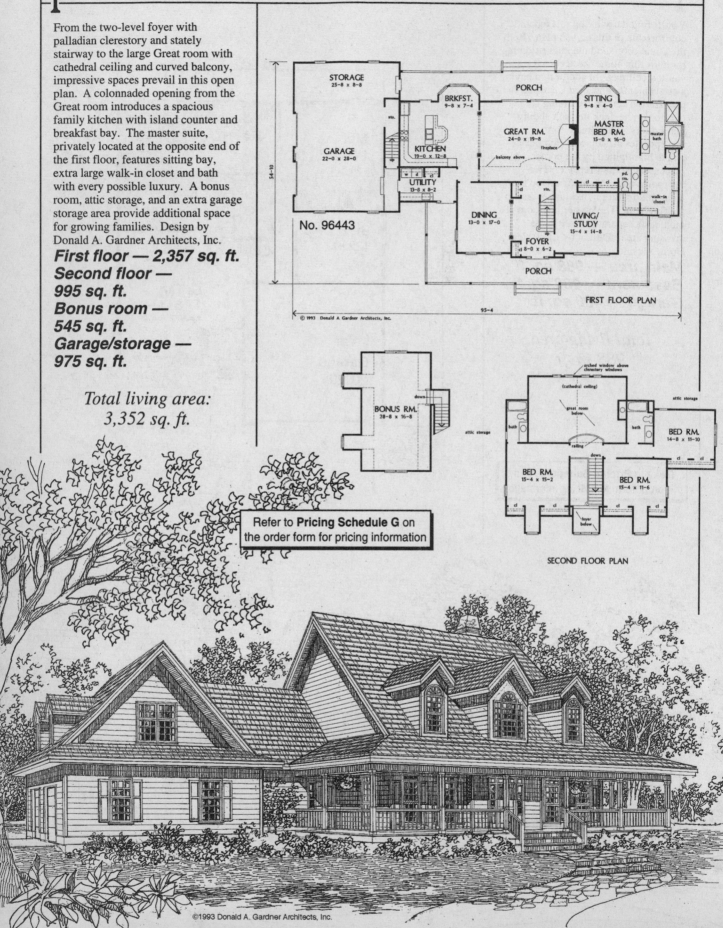

DIGNIFIED FAMILY HOME

Design 24653

A two-story foyer, benefiting from the natural light streaming through the many windows around the door, offers three choices of direction. The formal living room adjoins the formal dining room with columns between the two rooms. The U-shaped kitchen includes a built-in pantry, built-in planning desk and an island. There is room for a breakfast area for informal meals in the kitchen. The large family room flows from the kitchen and is equipped with a bright bay window and focal point fireplace. The second floor master suite includes a decorative ceiling and a lavish, private bath. A common area includes a skylight and access to the bonus room. A convenient second floor laundry is located in the common area. No materials list is available for this plan. Design by The Garlinghouse Company

First floor — 1,245 sq. ft.
Second floor — 1,333 sq. ft.
Bonus — 192 sq. ft.
Basement — 1,245 sq. ft.
Garage — 614 sq. ft.

Total living area: 2,578 sq. ft.

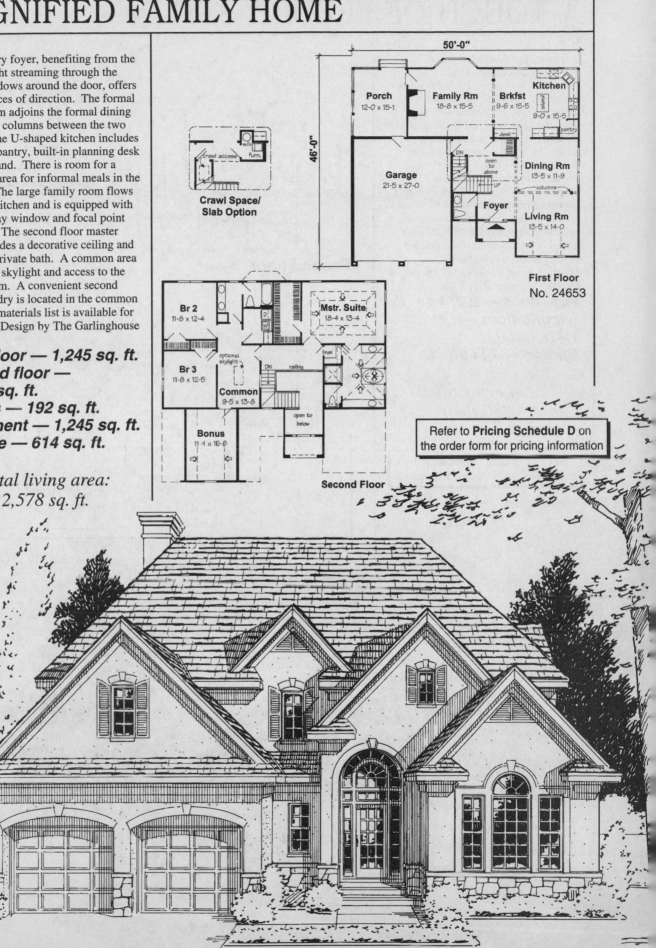

Crawl Space/
Slab Option

First Floor
No. 24653

Second Floor

Refer to **Pricing Schedule D** on the order form for pricing information

Design 99439

A TOUCH OF FRENCH STYLING

The beauty of this plan stems from its contented east-French style. The strength of this design comes from its uniform shape. The dining room protrudes into, but does not intrude, upon the entry. Arches, fluent along the gallery, disclose logically placed and invitingly restful rooms. The Great room is accented by a grand fireplace and an abundance of windows. The master suite pampers the owner with a whirlpool private bath and a large walk-in closet. Three additional bedrooms, each with easy access to a bath and a walk-in closet, and a game room are located on the second floor. No materials list is available for this plan. Design by Design Basics, Inc.

First floor — 2,274 sq. ft.
Second floor —
1,476 sq. ft.
Garage — 744 sq. ft.

Total living area:
3,750 sq. ft.

Refer to **Pricing Schedule F** on the order form for pricing information

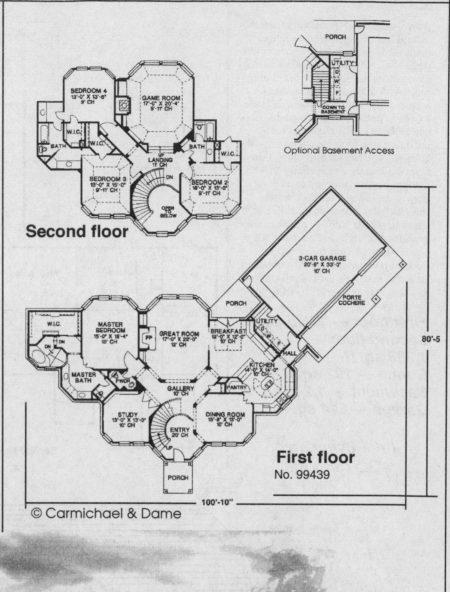

Second floor

Optional Basement Access

First floor
No. 99439

© Carmichael & Dame

Design 99045

THREE BEDROOM COUNTRY LIVING

The spacious and open interior of this delightful design, offers new vitality to this three bedroom Country style home. The oversized living room with a fireplace, leads to the sunny dining room and the U-shaped kitchen, which features abundant counter and cabinet space. There is easy access to the service entrance, the laundry, the half bath and the two-car garage. Plenty of outdoor living area is provided by the full length covered front porch. The master bedroom is complete with two closets, one a walk-in, and a private bath with a recessed tub and a full length twin basin vanity. Upstairs, the two large bedrooms share a full bath with a vanity and a recessed spa tub. No materials list is available for this plan. Design by National Home Planning Service

First floor — 1,108 sq. ft.
Second floor — 659 sq. ft.
Basement — 875 sq. ft.

Total living area: 1,767 sq. ft.

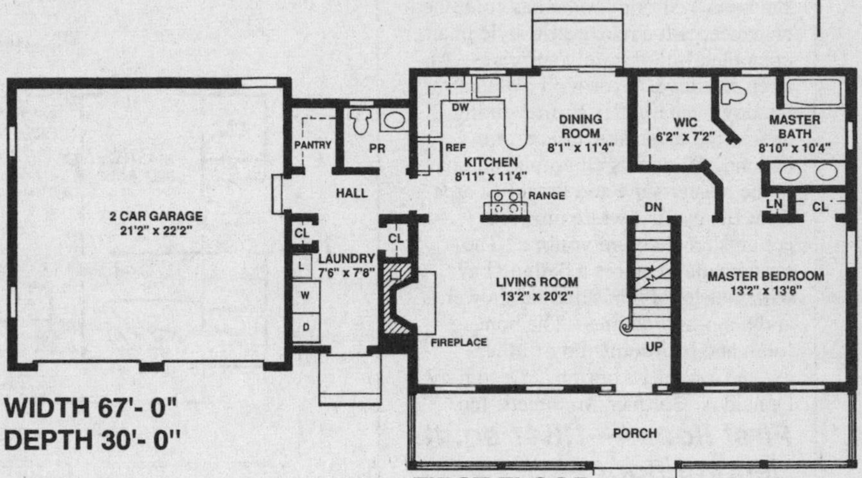

WIDTH 67'- 0"
DEPTH 30'- 0"

FIRST FLOOR
No. 99045

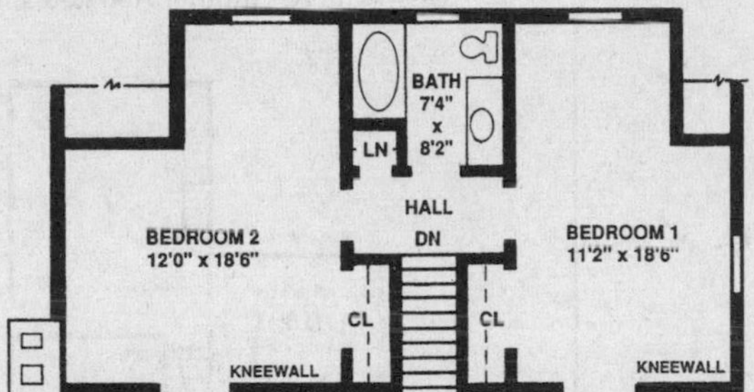

First floor plan labels:
2 CAR GARAGE 21'2" x 22'2"
PANTRY
PR
DW
REF
KITCHEN 8'11" x 11'4"
DINING ROOM 8'1" x 11'4"
WIC 6'2" x 7'2"
MASTER BATH 8'10" x 10'4"
HALL
RANGE
DN
LN
CL
CL
LAUNDRY 7'6" x 7'8"
L
W
D
LIVING ROOM 13'2" x 20'2"
MASTER BEDROOM 13'2" x 13'8"
FIREPLACE
UP
PORCH

SECOND FLOOR

Second floor plan labels:
BATH 7'4" x 8'2"
LN
HALL
DN
BEDROOM 2 12'0" x 18'6"
BEDROOM 1 11'2" x 18'6"
CL
CL
KNEEWALL
KNEEWALL

Refer to **Pricing Schedule B** on the order form for pricing information

Design 99895

ELEGANCE AND A RELAXED LIFESTYLE

This four bedroom home has combined elegance with a relaxed lifestyle in an open plan full of lovely surprises. An open two-level foyer with palladian window visually ties formal dining area to the expansive Great room beyond. Windows all around and bays in the master suite and breakfast area draw the eye out while nine foot ceilings create more volume. The master suite features a bathing bay with whirlpool tub, separate shower, and his-n-her vanities. The bonus room and bedroom/study further expand a family's options. Design by Donald A. Gardner Architects, Inc.

First floor — 1,841 sq. ft.
Second floor —
594 sq. ft.
Garage & storage —
584 sq. ft.
Bonus room —
391 sq. ft.

Total living area:
2,435 sq. ft.

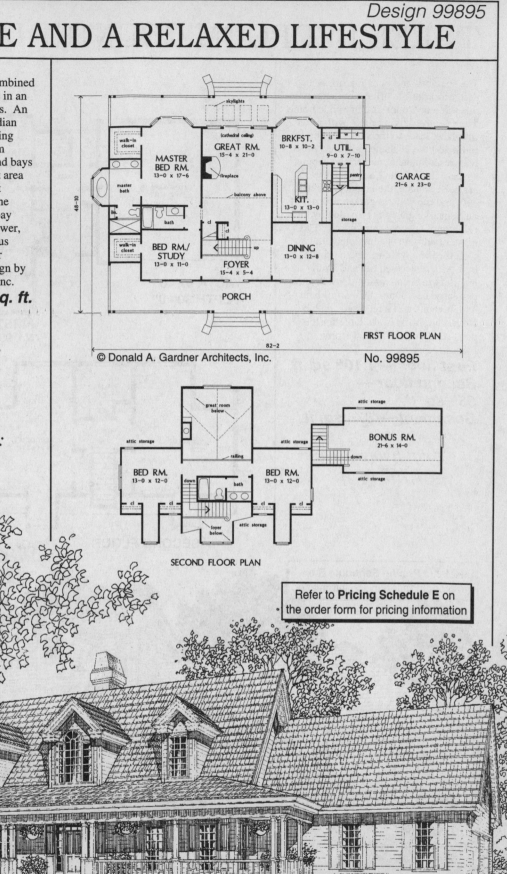

© Donald A. Gardner Architects, Inc.   No. 99895

FIRST FLOOR PLAN

SECOND FLOOR PLAN

Refer to **Pricing Schedule E** on the order form for pricing information

Design 96452

CATHEDRAL & TRAY CEILINGS

An open design heightened inside by cathedral and tray ceilings, this dormered and gabled traditional home with marvelous arched windows and brick accents wastes very little space. The foyer serves as an open hall with columns defining the entrance to the Great room. The Great room features a cathedral ceiling and opens to the contemporary island kitchen, great for large gatherings. The master suite is the ultimate retreat, separate from the rest of the house and equipped with a tray ceiling, double vanity, whirlpool tub, separate shower, and walk-in closet. The front bedroom can also be used as a study. Design by Donald A. Gardner Architects, Inc.

Main floor — 1,475 sq. ft.
Garage & storage — 478 sq. ft.

Total living area: 1,475 sq. ft.

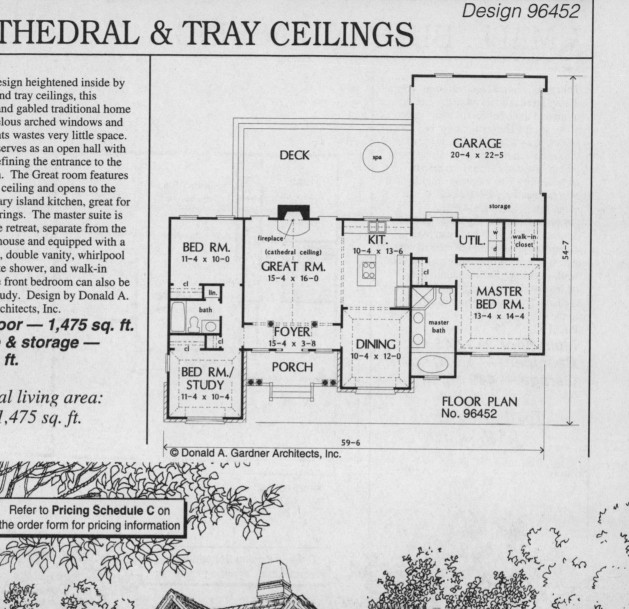

DECK

spa

GARAGE
20-4 x 22-5

storage

BED RM.
11-4 x 10-0

fireplace
(cathedral ceiling)

KIT.
10-4 x 13-6

UTIL.

walk-in closet

cl

lin.

bath

GREAT RM.
15-4 x 16-0

cl

MASTER
BED RM.
13-4 x 14-4

master bath

cl

FOYER
15-4 x 3-8

BED RM./
STUDY
11-4 x 10-4

PORCH

DINING
10-4 x 12-0

FLOOR PLAN
No. 96452

54-7

59-6

© Donald A. Gardner Architects, Inc.

Refer to **Pricing Schedule C** on the order form for pricing information

©1994 Donald A. Gardner Architects, Inc.

Design 94116

SMALL, BUT NOT LACKING

This home features a Great room, formal dining room, kitchen, dinette, laundry room and three bedrooms using only 1,546 sq. ft. The living room is enhanced by a bayed window viewing the porch and beyond. The Great room adjoins the dining room for ease in entertaining. The kitchen is highlighted by a peninsula counter/snackbar that extends work space and offers convenience in serving informal meals or snacks. The split bedroom plan allows for privacy for the master suite, which features a three-quarter bath and a walk-in closet. The two additional bedrooms share the full, family bath in the hall. The garage entry is convenient to the kitchen. Design by James Fahey, P.E., P.C.

Main floor — 1,546 sq. ft.
Basement — 1,530 sq. ft.
Garage — 440 sq. ft.

Total living area:
1,546 sq. ft.

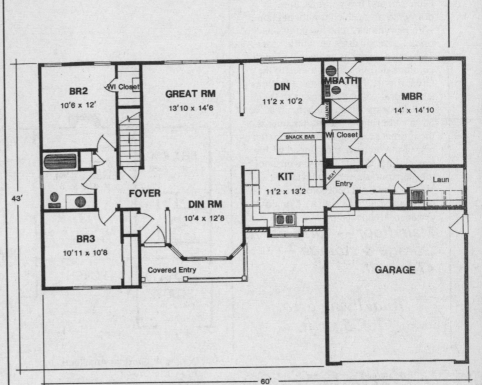

FIRST FLOOR
No. 94116

Refer to **Pricing Schedule C** on the order form for pricing information

SENSATIONAL ENTRY

Design 98404

The double door entry leads to the two-story foyer where a gracefully curving staircase continues the grandeur. The two-story living room is accented by columns and includes a massive fireplace and two sets of French doors to the rear yard. The first floor master suite, occupies the left wing of the home. Vaulted and trey ceilings add to the interest of the suite, while two walk-in closets, a sitting area and a plush, private bath provides the pampering. Another vaulted ceiling tops the family room, which is further enhanced by a fireplace. This plan is available with a basement or crawl space foundation. Please specify when ordering. Design by Frank Betz Associates, Inc.

First floor — 2,764 sq. ft.
**Second floor —
1,598 sq. ft.**
Basement — 2,764 sq. ft.
Garage — 743 sq. ft.

*Total living area:
4,362 sq. ft.*

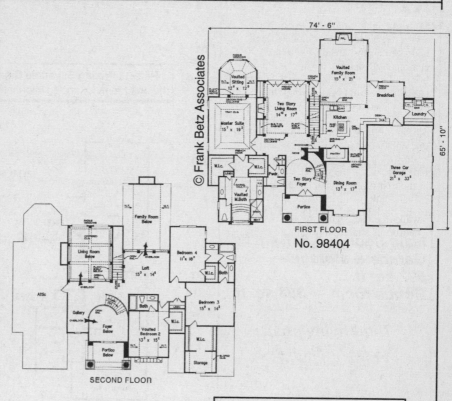

© Frank Betz Associates

FIRST FLOOR
No. 98404

SECOND FLOOR

Refer to **Pricing Schedule F** on
the order form for pricing information

180

Design 98029

MULTIPLE GABLES & DOUBLE DORMERS

Multiple gables and double dormers adorn the facade of this modest three bedroom home. Inside, even more custom style details, unexpected in a home of this size, embellish the design; cathedral ceiling, built-in shelving, ample closet and storage space, and a sizable bonus room. The Great room, dining room, and kitchen are all open to one another under a shared cathedral ceiling. Up front, two bedrooms share a hall bath, while the master suite, located at the rear of the home, features a private bath, walk-in closet, and access to the back porch. Design by Donald A. Gardner Architects, Inc.

Main floor — 1,377 sq. ft.
Garage & storage — 597 sq. ft.
Bonus room — 383 sq. ft.

Total living area: 1,377 sq. ft.

Refer to **Pricing Schedule C** on the order form for pricing information

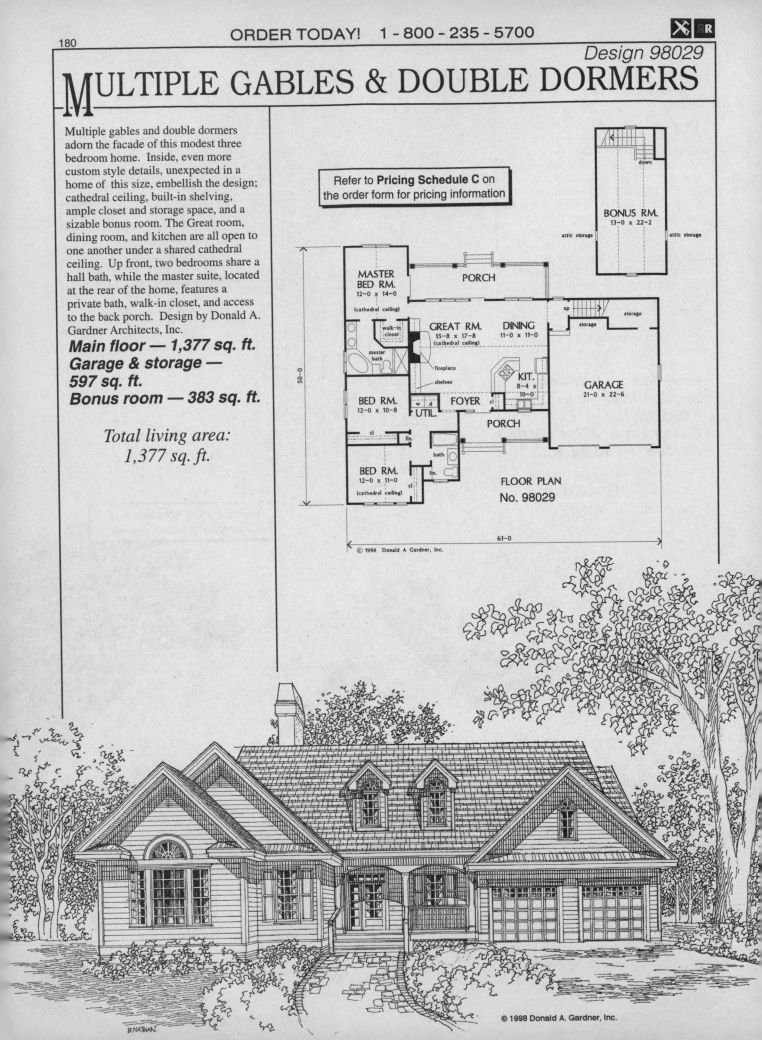

BONUS RM.
13-0 x 22-2
attic storage   attic storage

MASTER BED RM.
12-0 x 14-0
(cathedral ceiling)

PORCH

walk-in closet

master bath

GREAT RM.
15-8 x 17-8
(cathedral ceiling)

DINING
11-0 x 11-0

up   storage   storage

fireplace

shelves

KIT.
8-4 x 10-0

GARAGE
21-0 x 22-6

BED RM.
12-0 x 10-8

w d   FOYER   cl

UTIL.

PORCH

cl   lin.

bath

BED RM.
12-0 x 11-0
(cathedral ceiling)   cl   lin.

FLOOR PLAN
No. 98029

50-0

61-0

© 1998 Donald A Gardner, Inc.

© 1998 Donald A. Gardner, Inc.

B. NATHAN

Design 96442

WHIMSICAL TWO-STORY FARMHOUSE

Double gables with clerestory palladian window and a colonnaded wrap-around porch give this four bedroom, two-story farmhouse whimsical appeal. Palladian windows flood the two-level foyer and Great room with natural light. A balcony connects the two spaces on the second floor, the first floor enjoys nine-foot ceilings throughout. Both master bedroom and Great room with fireplace access the covered rear porch. The master bath features a walk-in closet, double vanity, separate shower, and whirlpool tub. One of three upstairs bedrooms enjoys a private bath and walk-in closet. Design by Donald A. Gardner Architects, Inc.

First floor — 1,346 sq. ft.
Second floor — 836 sq. ft.

Total living area: 2,182 sq. ft.

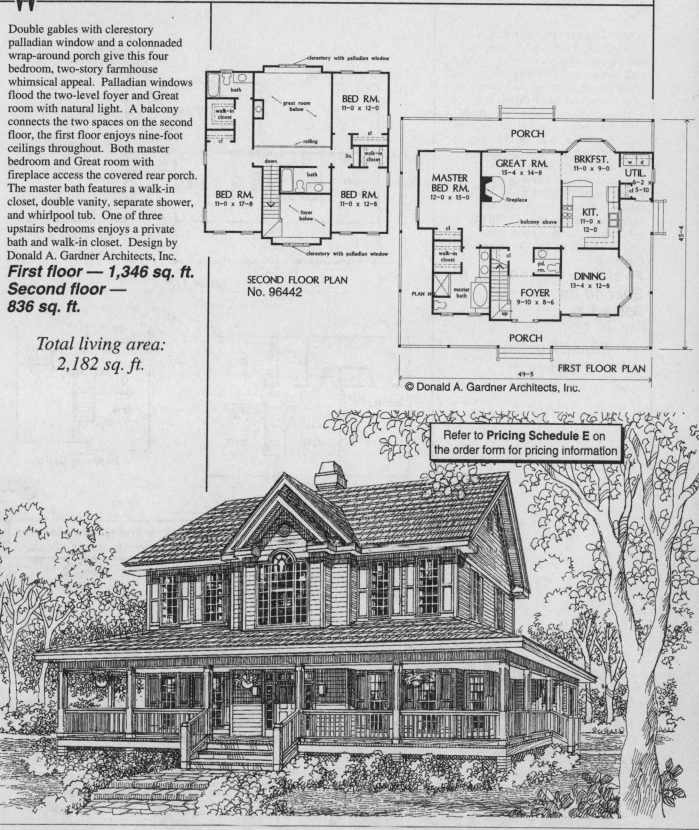

SECOND FLOOR PLAN
No. 96442

© Donald A. Gardner Architects, Inc.

Refer to **Pricing Schedule E** on the order form for pricing information

FIRST FLOOR PLAN

COMFORTABLE COUNTRY EASE

A sprawling front porch gives way to a traditional foyer area with a half bath and a graceful staircase. A tray ceiling adds elegance to the dining room, which directly accesses the kitchen. A large country kitchen with a center work island includes plenty of storage and work space. A tray ceiling accents the family room. A fireplace in the center of the rear wall of the family room adds cozy warmth to cool evenings. A vaulted ceiling and a private bath highlight the second floor master bedroom. Two additional bedrooms share the use of a full hall bath. There is a fourth bedroom option. Design by The Garlinghouse Company

**First floor — 1,104 sq. ft.
Second floor —
960 sq. ft.**

*Total living area:
2,064 sq. ft.*

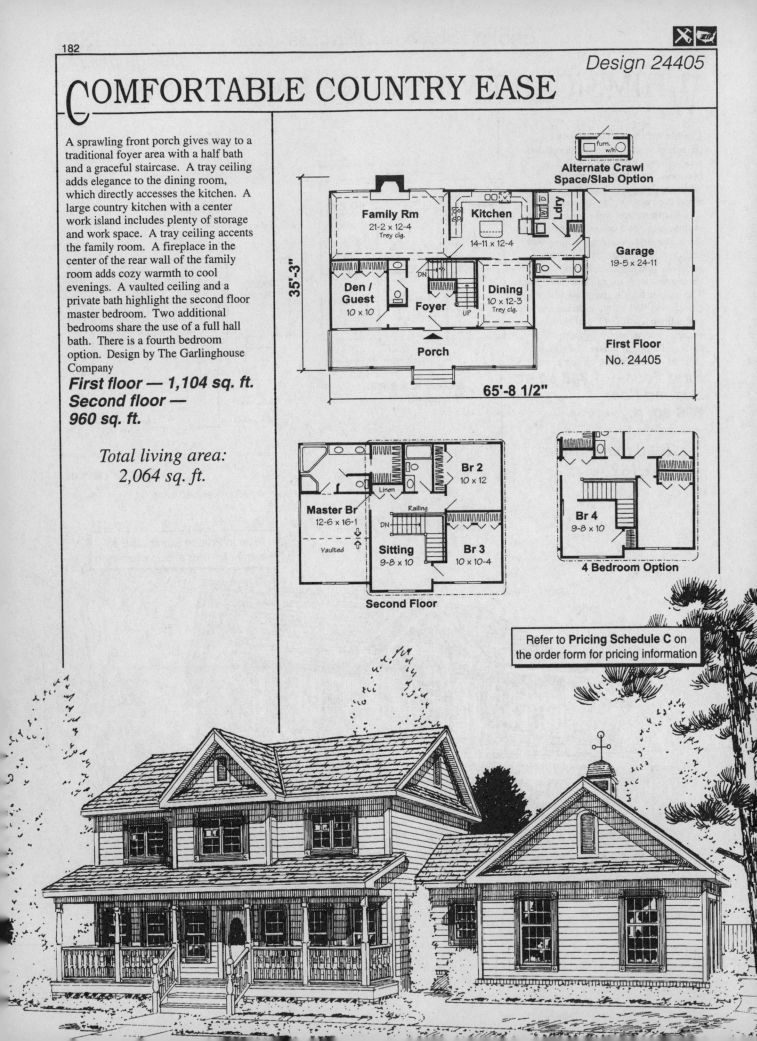

**Alternate Crawl
Space/Slab Option**

Family Rm
21-2 x 12-4
Trey clg.

Kitchen
14-11 x 12-4

Ldry

Garage
19-5 x 24-11

**Den /
Guest**
10 x 10

Foyer

Dining
10 x 12-3
Trey clg.

DN
UP

35'-3"

Porch

65'-8 1/2"

**First Floor
No. 24405**

Master Br
12-6 x 16-1

Vaulted

Br 2
10 x 12

Linen

Railing
DN

Sitting
9-8 x 10

Br 3
10 x 10-4

Second Floor

Br 4
9-8 x 10

4 Bedroom Option

Refer to **Pricing Schedule C** on
the order form for pricing information

Design 98927

GRACIOUS GEORGIAN STYLE

The gracious Georgian style ranch design is impressive with it's radius windows and quoin corners. The fourteen foot ceilings in the living room feature a paneled treatment. Eleven foot ceilings adorn the front rooms to allow for the radius window that accents the front porch. A large kitchen with a cooktop island provides space for warm gathering, as it opens to the keeping room and see through fireplace. The screen porch behind the breakfast area expands the living space to the outside, allowing for access to the sun deck. No materials list is available for this plan. Design by Jannis Vann & Associates Inc.

Main floor — 2,788 sq. ft.
Basement — 805 sq. ft.
Garage — 506 sq. ft.

Total living area:
2,788 sq. ft.

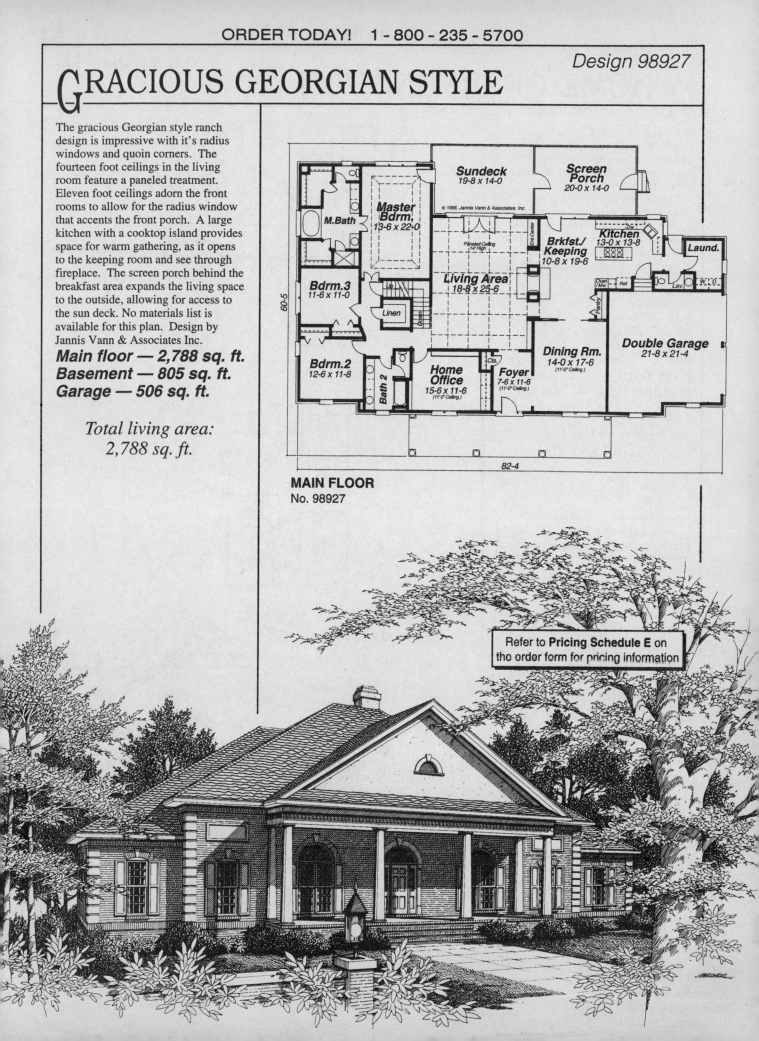

MAIN FLOOR
No. 98927

A HOME OF DISTINCTION

Design 97409

The dining room and the study are to either side of the entry. The study's entrance is at an angle with a double door entry. Columns define the dining room. The two-story family room includes a fireplace and a highly windowed rear wall. The breakfast room is open to the kitchen with a peninsula counter and a walk-in pantry. The first floor master suite includes a whirlpool tub, separate shower, and two vanities. Two walk-in closets provide for wardrobe storage. The three additional bedrooms have easy access to a full bath and ample storage space. This plan is available with a basement or slab foundation. Please specify when ordering. Design by Design Basics, Inc.

First floor — 1,844 sq. ft.
Second floor — 794 sq. ft.

Total living area:
2,638 sq. ft.

Refer to **Pricing Schedule E** on the order form for pricing information

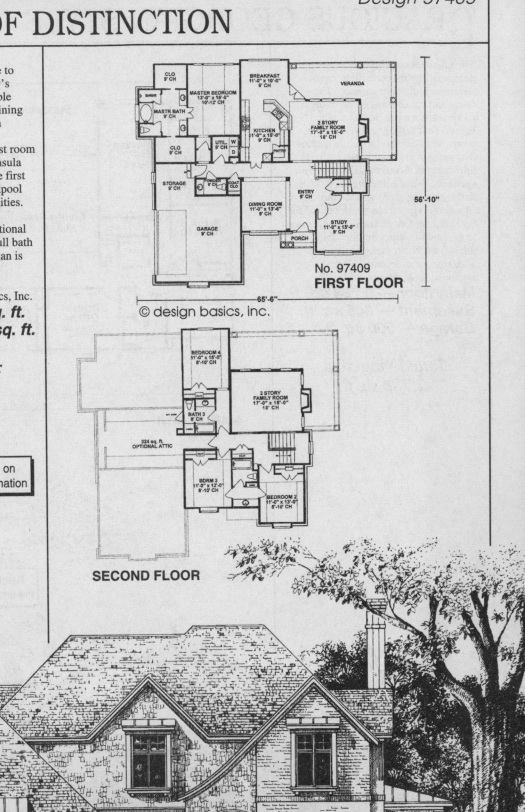

No. 97409
FIRST FLOOR

© design basics, inc.

SECOND FLOOR

THREE PORCHES OFFER CHARM

Summer fun can be enhanced by the atmosphere this beautiful home provides. It has been designed so it can be used in winter and summer. A basement is provided that could be easily eliminated if not needed at the time. Three porches offer maximum outdoor living space. A laundry room with utility sink and a stall shower are provided, plus a closet for supplies. The interior is as dramatic as the exterior. Note the oversized log-burning fireplace on the right wall. Three bedrooms and two baths can be built by finishing the second floor. Note the U-shaped kitchen with adjoining dining porch. Design by National Home Planning Service

First floor — 974 sq. ft.
Second floor — 300 sq. ft.

Total living area:
1,274 sq. ft.

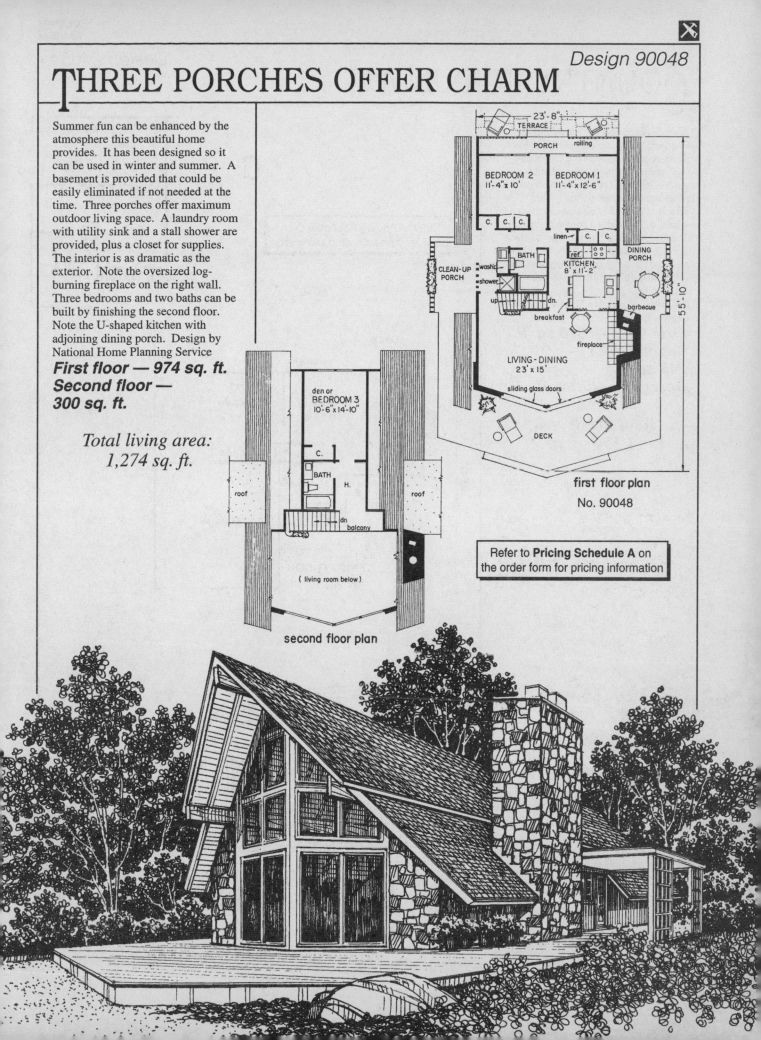

first floor plan
No. 90048

Refer to **Pricing Schedule A** on the order form for pricing information

second floor plan

COUNTRY INFLUENCE

A cozy porch sets the tone for this comfortable home. Enter into the sun room that includes a coat closet and convenient access to a half bath. A simple half wall separates the living room and the dining room. The efficient kitchen is equipped with a laundry center and a sunny bayed area. The bedrooms are on the second floor. A walk-in closet, private bath with an oval tub, a decorative ceiling and bay window highlight the master suite. The two additional bedrooms share a full bath. Design by The Garlinghouse Company

First floor — 806 sq. ft.
Second floor —
748 sq. ft.
Garage — 467 sq. ft.

Total living area:
1,554 sq. ft.

Refer to **Pricing Schedule B** on the order form for pricing information

SECOND FLOOR

Master Br
16-0 x 11-11

Br 2
11-8 x 10-8

Br 3
11-4 x 10-7

linen

DN

50'-0"

40'-0"

Deck

Living
13-4 x 17-4

1/2 wall

Dining
11-0 x 12-2

Kitchen
14-5 x 11-10

UP

W   D

Sun
Rm

Garage
21-4 x 21-8

FIRST FLOOR
No. 24654

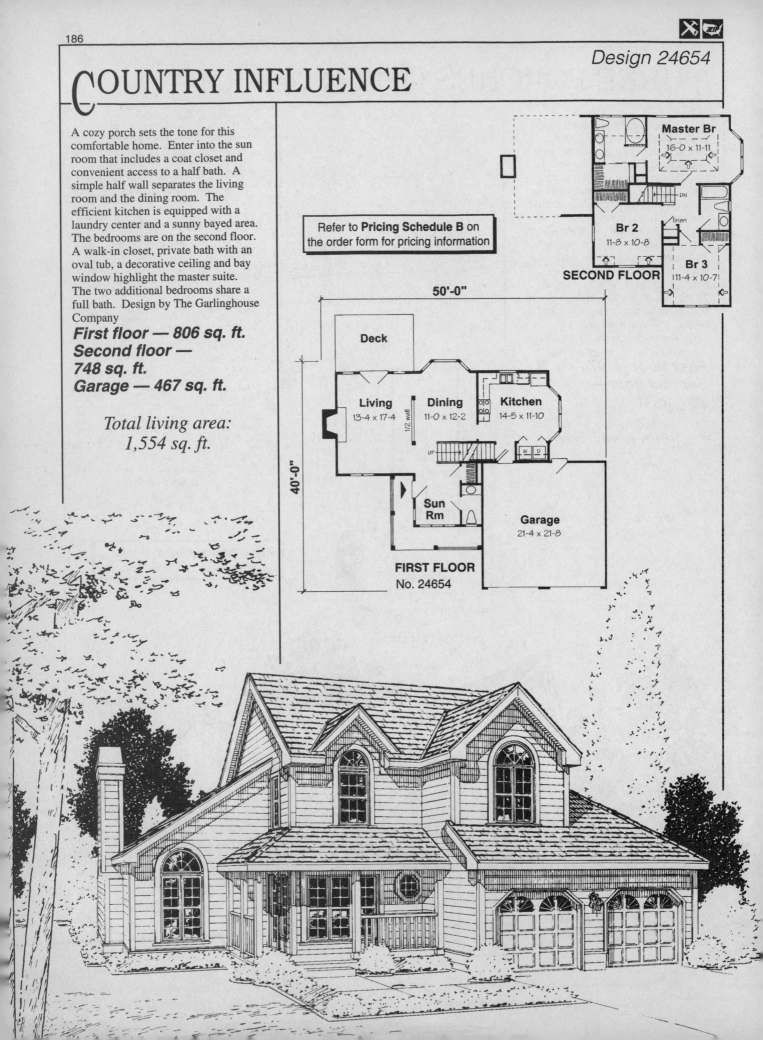

STRIKING BRICK DETAILING

A repeating arch theme and striking brick detailing complement this superb ranch. Impressive columns define the formal dining room which is crowned in a ten foot ceiling. Adding additional architectural interest, a dome ceiling tops the curved landing for the stairs to the basement. French doors open into the den from the entry hall. Built-in curio cabinets highlight the room. Beautiful arched windows bring the natural light into the Great room. A see-through fireplace is shared by the Great room and the hearth room. A built-in entertainment center and bookcases add to the convenience and coziness of the hearth room. The gazebo shaped dinette opens to the kitchen. An island cooktop, built-in desk and a snack bar add to the ease and convenience of the kitchen. The master bedroom is crowned in a vaulted ceiling and pampered by a sumptuous master bath with a whirlpool tub. Design by Design Basics, Inc.

Main floor — 2,512 sq. ft.
Garage — 783 sq. ft.

Total living area:
2,512 sq. ft.

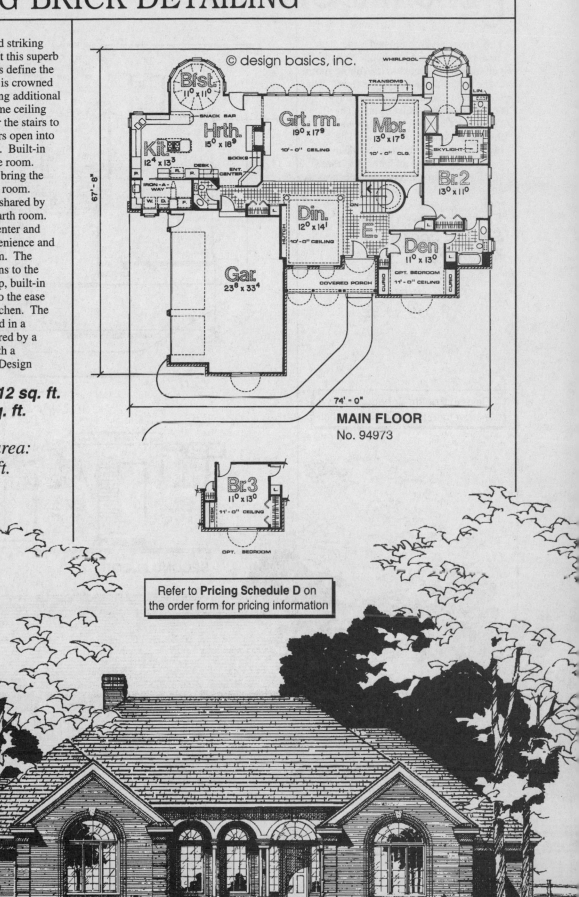

© design basics, inc.

MAIN FLOOR
No. 94973

Refer to **Pricing Schedule D** on the order form for pricing information

Design 97412

COLONIAL STYLING

This home has colonial styling and modern appointments. Inside, the tiled entrance gives access to the dining room to the left or the parlor to the right. The Great room has a fireplace and easy access to the breakfast room. The kitchen accesses the dining room and the breakfast room with ease. The master bedroom includes a walk-in closet and a whirlpool bath. The three additional bedroom have direct access to a full bath. Design by Design Basics, Inc.

First floor — 1,865 sq. ft.
Second floor — 774 sq. ft.

Total living area: 2,639 sq. ft.

Refer to **Pricing Schedule C** on the order form for pricing information

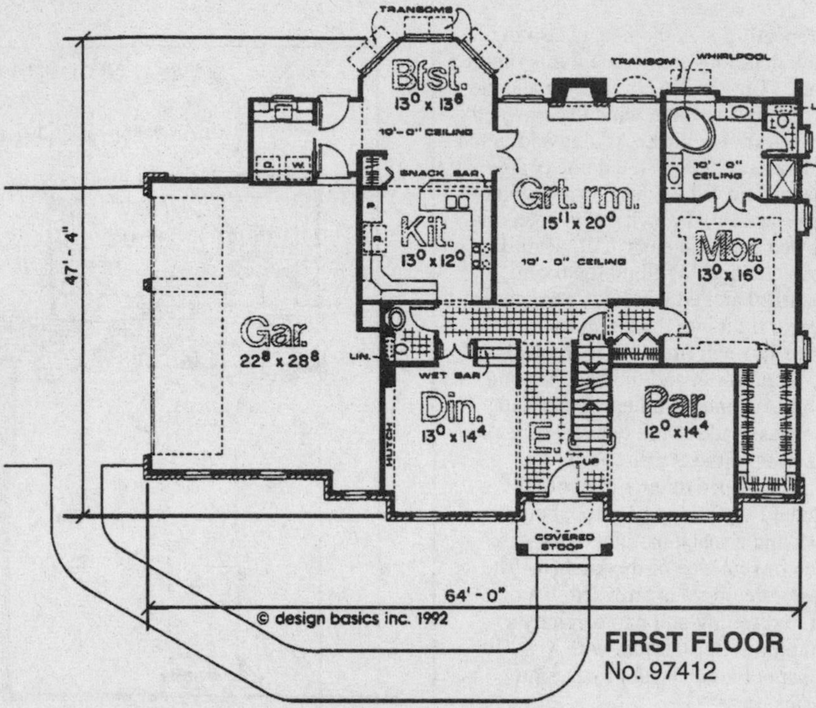

FIRST FLOOR
No. 97412

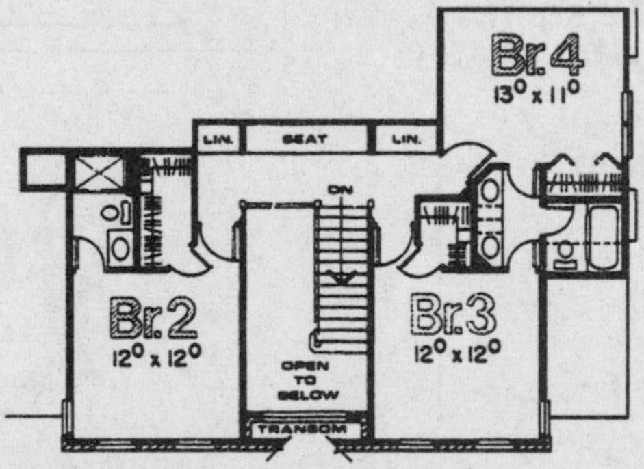

© design basics inc. 1992

SECOND FLOOR

Design 97210

NOTABLE EXTERIOR

Inside, the two-story foyer gives the feeling of volume and space. The dining room and the living room are roomy in size. The family room, directly ahead of the foyer, is topped by a vaulted ceiling and the living room to the left of the foyer, has an eleven foot high ceiling. The first floor master suite has its own wing of the home. A five-piece master bath, a large walk-in closet and a tray ceiling are some of the amenities included in the suite. The rear bedroom/study is located close to a full bath. The second floor contains two more bedrooms with a walk-in closet, a full bath and an optional bonus room. This plan is available with a basement, crawl space or slab foundation. Please specify when ordering. No materials list is available for this plan. Design by Frank Betz Associates, Inc.

First floor — 2,003 sq. ft.
Second floor — 598 sq. ft.
Bonus room — 321 sq. ft.
Basement — 2,003 sq. ft.
Garage — 546 sq. ft.

Total living area: 2,601 sq. ft.

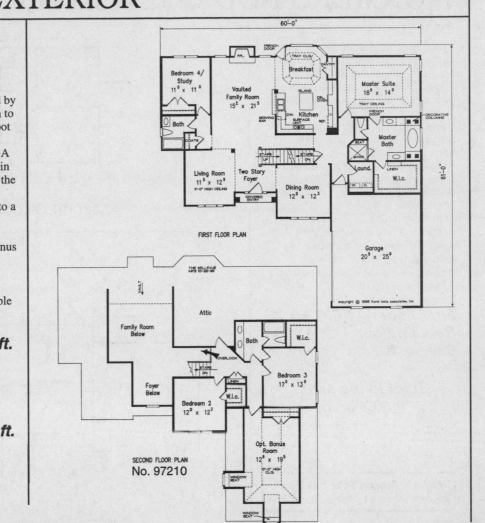

FIRST FLOOR PLAN

SECOND FLOOR PLAN
No. 97210

Refer to **Pricing Schedule E** on the order form for pricing information

Design 90218

DORMERS ADD COZY SITTING NOOKS

You'll never run out of storage room in this spacious, modified Cape. From the double closets across from the formal dining room to walk-ins in each bedroom, you'll have a place to put everything! And, there's an atmosphere of comfortable warmth throughout this cozy home, with fireplaces in both the rustic family room and formal living room, and a sunny dining nook off the kitchen. With a full bath right next door, the private study with sliders to the rear terrace can double as an extra bedroom. Three more bedrooms upstairs include a luxurious master suite with dual vanity, a private dressing room, and a full bath with step-in shower. Design by Homeplanners

**First floor — 1,632 sq. ft.
Second floor —
980 sq. ft.**

*Total living area:
2,612 sq. ft.*

Refer to **Pricing Schedule E** on the order form for pricing information

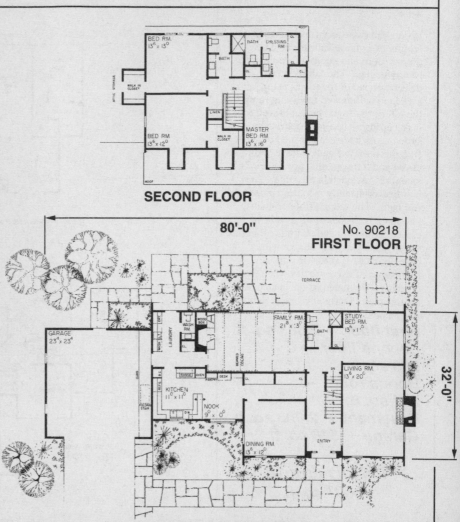

SECOND FLOOR

No. 90218
FIRST FLOOR

80'-0"

32'-0"

Design 94230

GRAND TRADITIONAL STYLE

Inside the foyer area, double arches lead into the formal living room and out to the rear through triple french doors. A two-sided fireplace is shared with the owners study. The expansive kitchen easily serves the dining room and informal nook area. The kitchen has plenty of work space, a walk-in pantry area, a cooktop island, an eating bar, and a pass-through that serves the veranda. The expansive kitchen easily serves the dining room and informal nook area. Double doors lead into the owners suite. Large his-n-her wardrobe closets framed with arches lead into the sleeping area. The bayed suite has doors to the veranda, a high stepped ceiling and a sitting area. The elegant bath is well appointed. Up the grand staircase are three secondary suites. No materials list is available for this plan. Design by The Sater Design Group

First floor — 3,546 sq. ft.
Second floor —
1,213 sq. ft.
Garage — 822 sq. ft.

Total living area:
4,759 sq. ft.

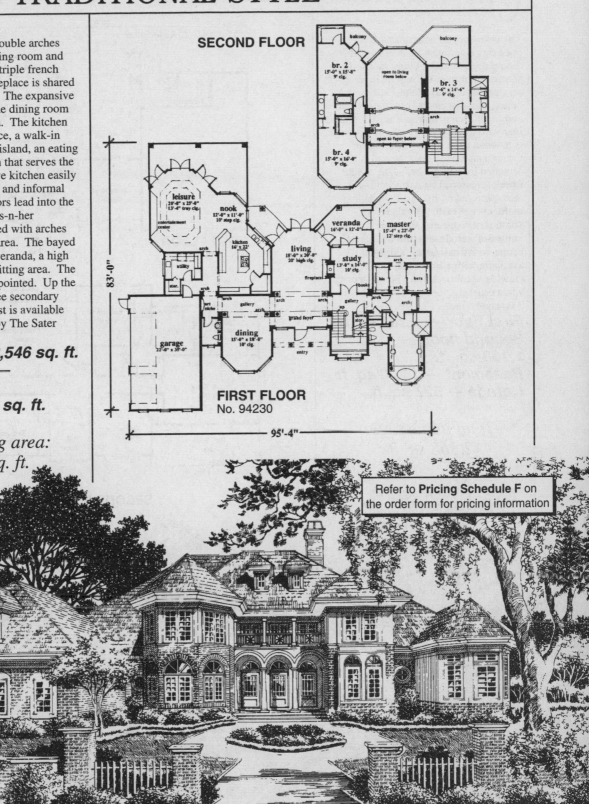

SECOND FLOOR

FIRST FLOOR
No. 94230

Refer to **Pricing Schedule F** on
the order form for pricing information

Weather Shield
Windows & Doors

www.weathershield.com

*Weather Shield Windows and Doors offers project planning
guides for your remodeling or new home project. FREE. Specify
"Remodeling" or "New Home" Planning Guide by calling*

1-800-477-6808

Design 98409

CLASSICALLY DETAILED

The two-story foyer has arched openings on either side accessing the dining room and the living room. The spacious gourmet kitchen includes a serving bar and an island. The breakfast room flows from the kitchen and includes a pantry and access to the rear yard. The two-story family room is reached from the breakfast room through an arched opening and is accented by a fireplace. The master suite is enhanced by a tray ceiling in the bedroom and by a vaulted ceiling in the master bath. The three secondary bedrooms share the full bath in the hall. Bedroom four has private access to the hall bath. This plan is available with a basement, slab or crawl space foundation. Please specify when ordering. Design by Frank Betz Associates, Inc.

First floor — 1,200 sq. ft.
Second floor — 1,168 sq. ft.
Basement — 1,200 sq. ft.
Garage — 527 sq. ft.

Total living area:
2,368 sq. ft.

© Frank Betz Associates

FIRST FLOOR
No. 98409

SECOND FLOOR

Refer to **Pricing Schedule D** on the order form for pricing information

CLASSIC EUROPEAN STYLING

Design 97716

Refer to **Pricing Schedule F** on the order form for pricing information

A grand foyer greets guests as they arrive, showcasing the exquisite dining room and Great room. Colonial columns are repeated at the entry of the Great room and a magnificent window treatment, including French doors introduces the expansive terrace. The master bedroom suite showcases a tray ceiling and fireplace. The double-sided fireplace serves the bedroom and dressing area creating a majestic setting for the whirlpool tub. The kitchen and breakfast room are creatively arranged. The cozy hearth room with fireplace promotes intimate family gatherings. No materials list is available for this plan. Design by Studer Residential Design, Inc.

**First floor — 3,392 sq. ft.
Second floor — 1,197 sq. ft.
Basement — 3,392 sq. ft.**

Total living area: 4,589 sq. ft.

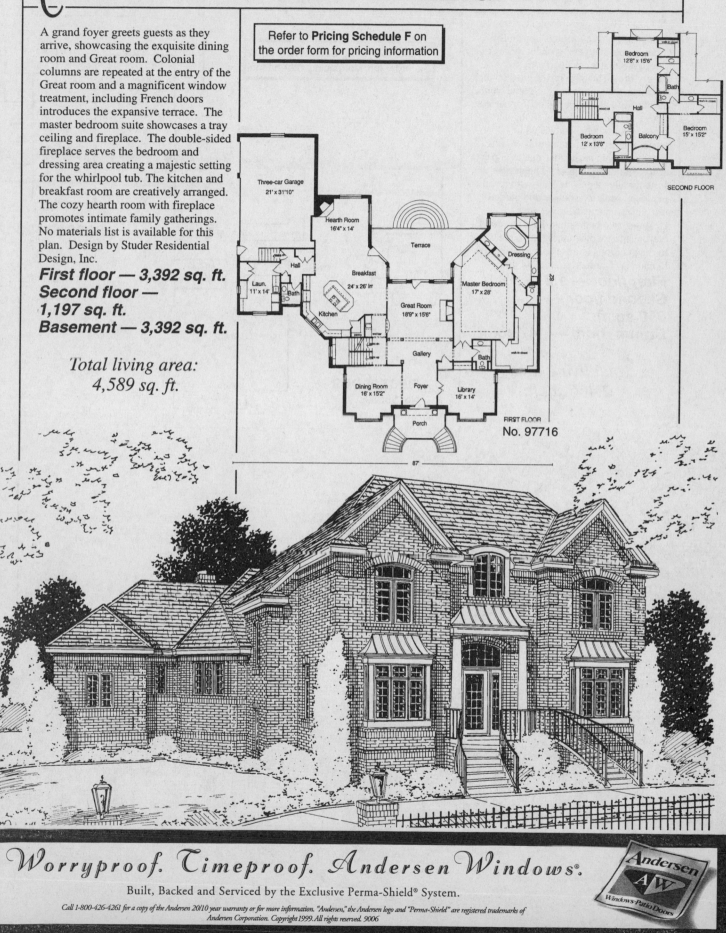

Design 98039

INNOVATIVE FLOOR PLAN

This plan holds enormous appeal for today's home buyers, with an innovative floor plan that works perfectly for family life. The plan is designed so that the main living areas of the home can be quickly and easily closed off for surprise house guests. The formal living and dining rooms stay spotless while providing privacy for the master suite. A family room at the rear makes a great, relaxed family hangout. The master suite features a private bath with a walk-in closet, separate shower and garden tub, and an enclosed toilet area. Upstairs, two bedrooms share a second bath, while extra storage flanks the entry to the generous bonus room. Design by Donald A. Gardner Architects, Inc.

First floor — 1,816 sq. ft.
Second floor —
650 sq. ft.
Bonus room — 447 sq. ft.

Total living area:
2,466 sq. ft.

Refer to **Pricing Schedule E** on the order form for pricing information

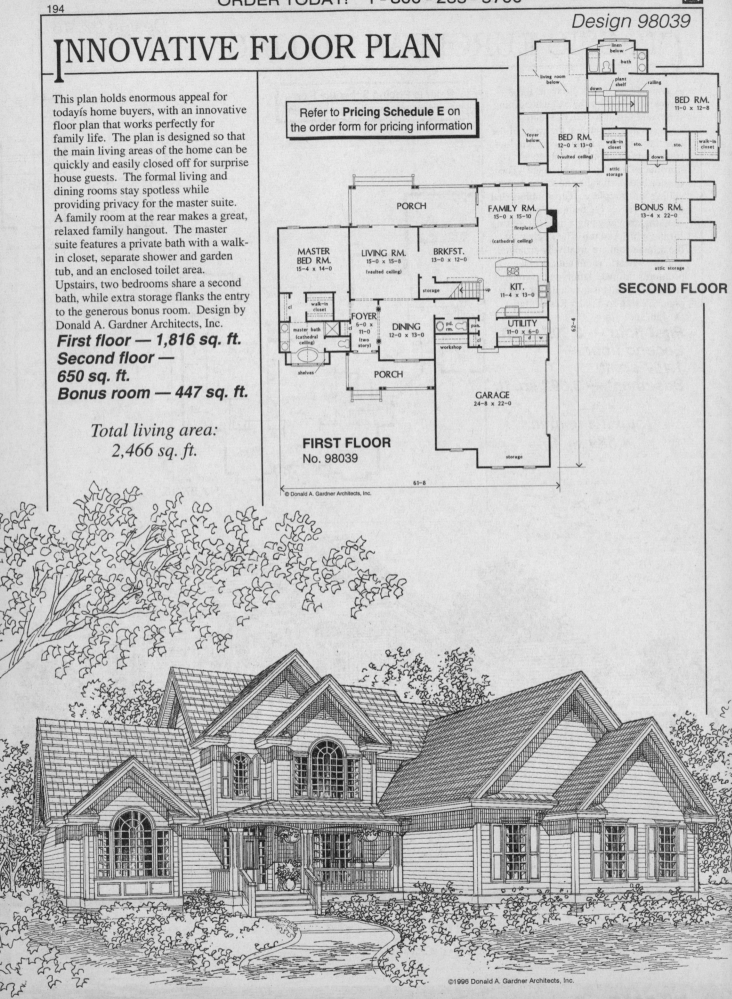

FIRST FLOOR
No. 98039

SECOND FLOOR

© Donald A. Gardner Architects, Inc.

©1996 Donald A. Gardner Architects, Inc.

VARIED ROOF HEIGHTS ADD INTEREST

This rambling one-story Colonial farmhouse packs a lot of living space into its compact plan. The covered porch, enriched by arches, columns and Colonial details, is the focal point of the facade. Inside, the house is zoned for convenience. Formal living and dining rooms occupy the front of the house. To the rear are the family room, the island kitchen, and the dinette. The family room features a heat-circulating fireplace, visible from the entrance foyer, and sliding glass doors to the large rear patio. Three bedrooms and two baths are away from the action in a private wing. Design by Perfect Plan

Main floor — 1,613 sq. ft.
Basement — 1,060 sq. ft.
Garage — 461 sq. ft.

Total living area:
1,613 sq. ft.

Refer to **Pricing Schedule B** on the order form for pricing information

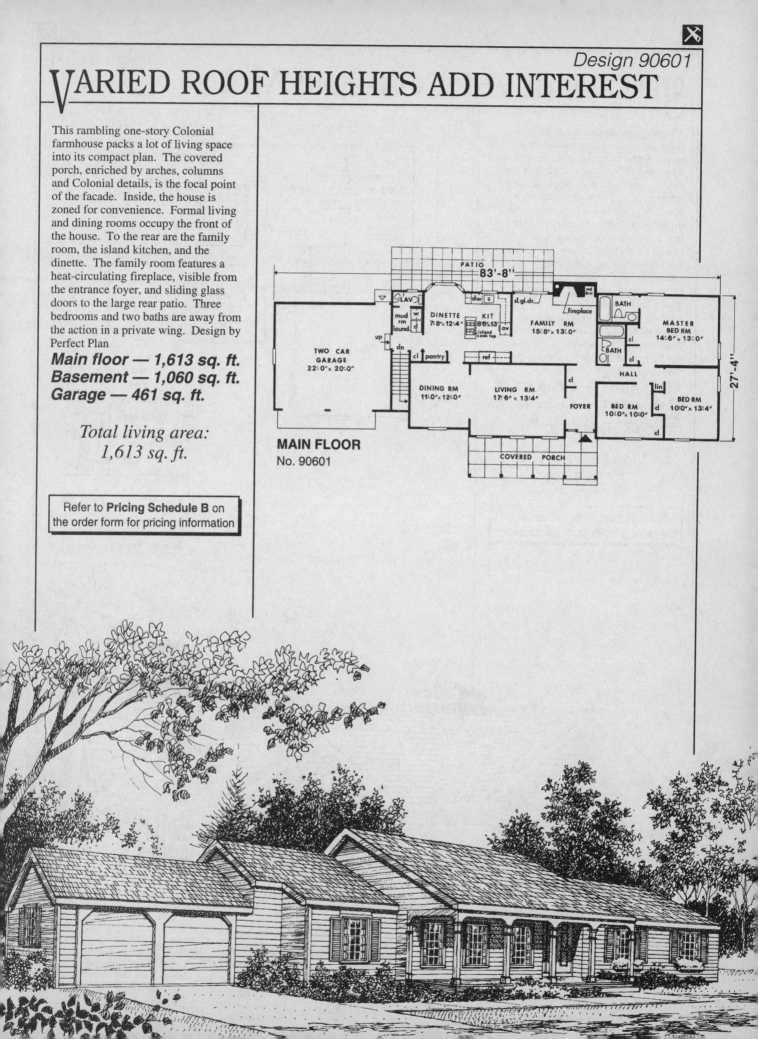

MAIN FLOOR
No. 90601

PATIO
83'-8"

TWO CAR GARAGE
22'-0" x 20'-0"

DINETTE
7'-8" x 12'-4"

KIT
8'-6" x 13'

FAMILY RM
15'-8" x 13'-0"

fireplace

BATH

MASTER BED RM
14'-6" x 13'-0"

BATH

HALL

mud rm laund.

island cook top

pantry

ref

DINING RM
11'-0" x 12'-0"

LIVING RM
17'-6" x 13'-4"

FOYER

BED RM
10'-0" x 10'-0"

BED RM
10'-0" x 13'-4"

lin

27'-4"

COVERED PORCH

SINGLE-LEVEL CONVENIENCE

This home features a well designed floor plan, offering convenience and style. The roomy living room includes a two-sided fireplace shared with the dining room. An efficient U-shaped kitchen, equipped with a peninsula counter/breakfast bar, is open to the dining room. An entrance from the garage into the kitchen eliminates tracked in dirt and affords step-saving convenience when unloading groceries. The private master suite includes a whirlpool tub, a double vanity and a step-in shower. A large walk-in closet adds ample storage space to the suite. The secondary bedroom and the den/guest room share use of the full hall bath. Design by The Garlinghouse Company

Main floor — 1,625 sq. ft.
Basement — 1,625 sq. ft.
Garage — 455 sq. ft.

Total living area: 1,625 sq. ft.

Refer to **Pricing Schedule B** on the order form for pricing information

---

Floor plan labels (Main Floor No. 24701):

54'-0"
48'-4"

- open shelves
- Dining Rm 11-9 x 12-11
- two-sided fireplace
- brkfst bar
- Kitchen 11-9 x 12-9
- utility/pantry
- Living Rm 13-8 x 17-8 9'-0" clg.
- whirlpool
- railing
- DN
- Master Br 15-9 x 11-11 9'-0" clg.
- linen
- Foy.
- Den/Guest 11-11 x 12-11
- Br 2 12-8 x 10-11
- planter
- Garage 20-5 x 21-5

Main Floor No. 24701

Alternate Foundation Plan labels:

- Living Rm 13-8 x 17-8 9'-0" clg.
- oven
- storage
- crawl access
- util./pantry
- w/h
- furn.
- Foy.

Alternate Foundation Plan

Design 99442

ARCHES ENHANCE STYLE

Just inside the entry, open rooms harmonically connect and are separated by arches. The living room is graced by a focal point fireplace and adjoins to the dining room. The expansive family room has a second fireplace and is open to the breakfast room and kitchen. From the family room there is direct access to the porch through double doors. On the second floor, the bedrooms are pampered by private access to baths and walk-in closets. The lavish master bedroom enjoys a romantic fireplace with built-in cabinets to either side and a fabulous whirlpool bath. No materials list is available for this plan. Design by Design Basics, Inc.

First floor — 1,786 sq. ft.
Second floor — 1,607 sq. ft.
Garage — 682 sq. ft.

Total living area: 3,393 sq. ft.

Refer to **Pricing Schedule F** on the order form for pricing information

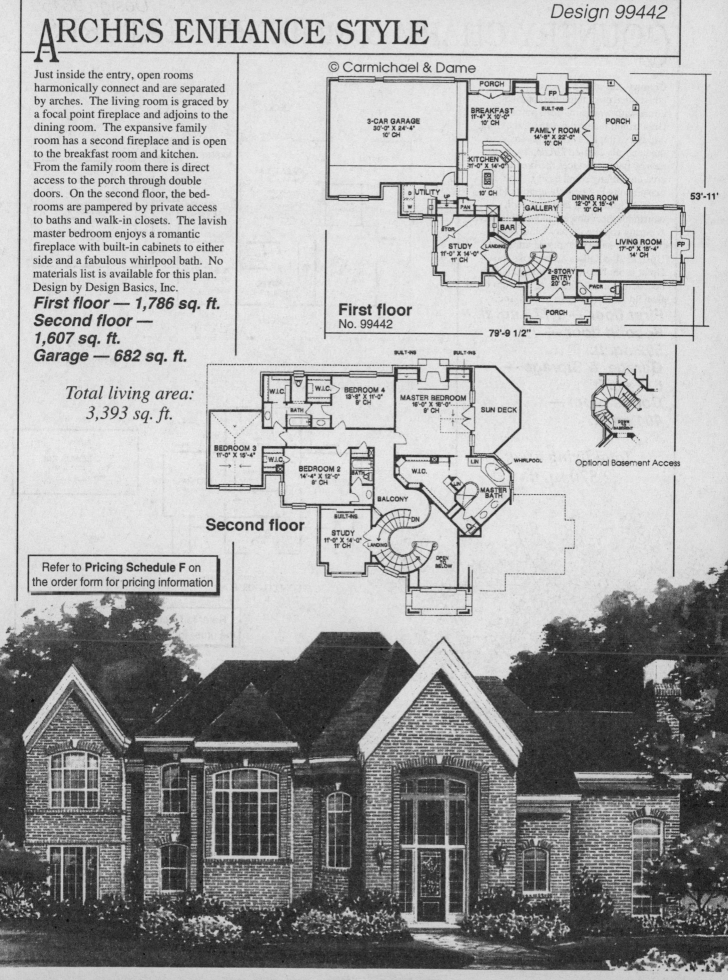

© Carmichael & Dame

First floor
No. 99442

Second floor

Optional Basement Access

Design 96459

COUNTRY CHARM & MODERN FEATURES

Country charm and modern convenience combine in this lovely home with wrapping front porch. The Great room features a cathedral ceiling and cozy fireplace with built-ins, and the centrally located kitchen with it's nearby pantry services the breakfast area and dining room easily. The master suite is elegantly appointed with walk-in closet and bath with whirlpool tub, shower, and dual vanity. A sitting room with bay window off the master suite is a special attraction. Upstairs, the hallway overlooks the Great room below, and two secondary bedrooms share a full bath. Design by Donald A. Gardner Architects, Inc.

First floor — 1,778 sq. ft.
Second floor — 592 sq. ft.
Garage & Storage — 622 sq. ft.
Bonus room — 404 sq. ft.

Total living area: 2,370 sq. ft.

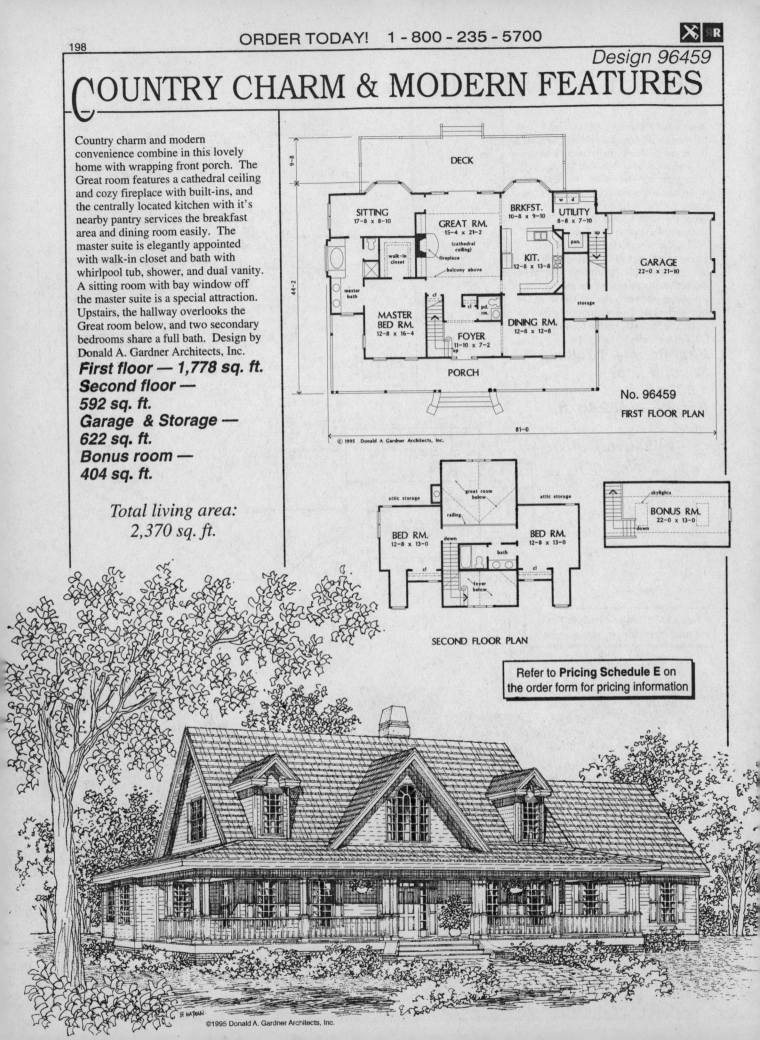

No. 96459
FIRST FLOOR PLAN

© 1995 Donald A Gardner Architects, Inc.

SECOND FLOOR PLAN

Refer to **Pricing Schedule E** on the order form for pricing information

TRADITIONAL CAPE COD

Design 97709

The Traditional style of this Cape Cod home coupled with the large front porch creates a warm and friendly atmosphere. With easy access from the foyer there is a fashionable library with built-in shelves, a formal dining room with columns and a dramatic view through the Great room to the fireplace and rear windows. Encouraging family gatherings; this spacious kitchen offers an island with seating which opens into a roomy breakfast area surrounded by windows. A master bedroom suite with deluxe bath and a spacious walk-in closet completes the first floor. For family convenience, the stairs are located close to the kitchen. No materials list is available for this plan. Design by Studer Residential Design, Inc.

First floor — 1,710 sq. ft.
Second floor — 733 sq. ft.
Bonus Room —
181 sq. ft.
Basement — 1,710 sq. ft.

Total living area:
2,443 sq. ft.

Refer to **Pricing Schedule C** on the order form for pricing information

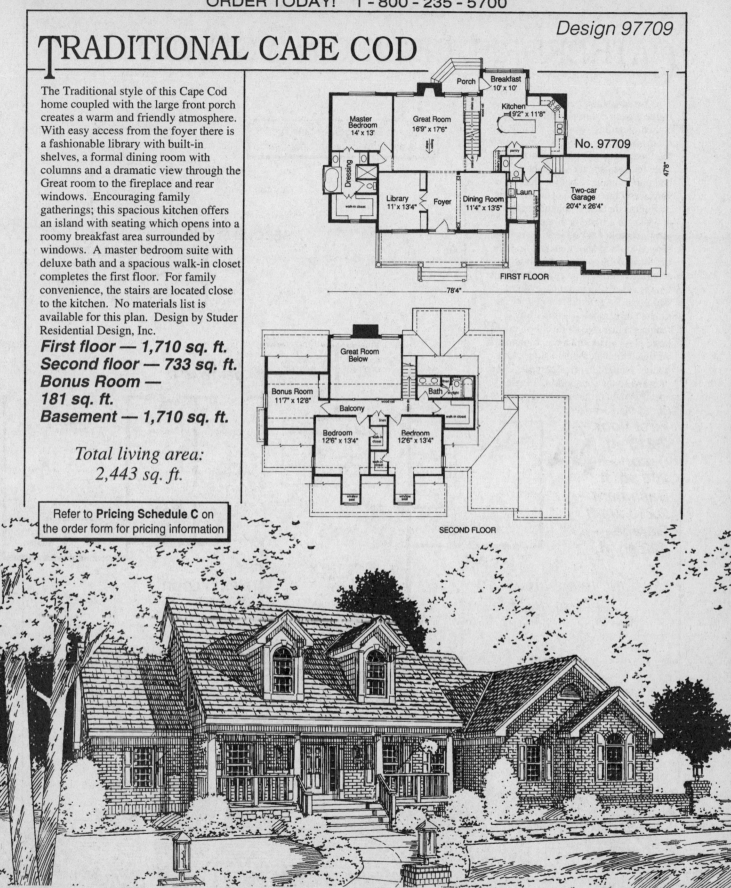

No. 97709

FIRST FLOOR

SECOND FLOOR

Design 90420

CATHERDRAL CEILING & A STUDIO

This rustic-contemporary modified A-frame design combines a high cathedral ceiling over a sunken living room with a large studio over the two rear bedrooms. The isolated master suite features a walk-in closet and compartmentalized bath with double vanity and linen closet. The two rear bedrooms include ample closet space and share a unique bath-and-a-half arrangement. On one side of the U-shaped kitchen and breakfast nook is the formal dining room which is separated from the entry by the planter. On the other side is a utility room which can be entered from either the kitchen or garage. The exterior features a massive stone chimney, large glass areas and a combination of vertical wood siding and stone. This plan is available with a basement, slab or crawl space foundation. Please specify when ordering. Design by Corley Plan Service

**First floor —
2,213 sq. ft.
Second floor —
260 sq. ft.
Basement —
2,213 sq. ft.
Garage —
422 sq. ft.**

*Total living area:
2,473 sq. ft.*

Refer to **Pricing Schedule D** on the order form for pricing information

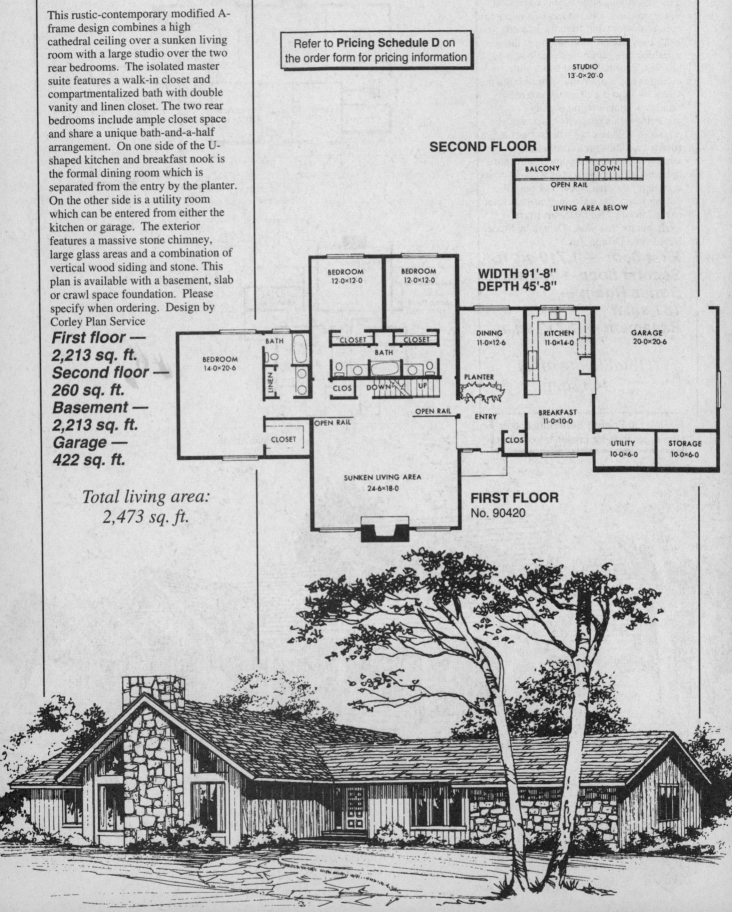

STUDIO 13-0×20-0

SECOND FLOOR

BALCONY   DOWN
OPEN RAIL
LIVING AREA BELOW

BEDROOM 12-0×12-0   BEDROOM 12-0×12-0

**WIDTH 91'-8"
DEPTH 45'-8"**

BATH
CLOSET   CLOSET
BATH
LINEN
CLOS   DOWN   UP
BEDROOM 14-0×20-6

DINING 11-0×12-6   KITCHEN 11-0×14-0   GARAGE 20-0×20-6

PLANTER

CLOSET   OPEN RAIL   OPEN RAIL   ENTRY   BREAKFAST 11-0×10-0

CLOS

SUNKEN LIVING AREA 24-6×18-0

UTILITY 10-0×6-0   STORAGE 10-0×6-0

FIRST FLOOR
No. 90420

MAGNIFICENT GRANDEUR

Design 99461

The splendor of this home is apparent from the first step into the entry hall. The decorative ceilings and the built-ins in each room both enhances and adds convenience. The island kitchen serves the dining room and the breakfast area. The Great room is topped by a valley cathedral ceiling and highlighted by a fireplace. The master suite has a decorative ceiling, a whirlpool tub and a separate shower and a walk-in closet. Three additional bedrooms are located on the second floor. A balcony overlooks the Great room below. Design by Design Basics, Inc.

First floor — 1,972 sq. ft.
Second floor — 893 sq. ft.
Garage — 658 sq. ft.

Total living area: 2,865 sq. ft.

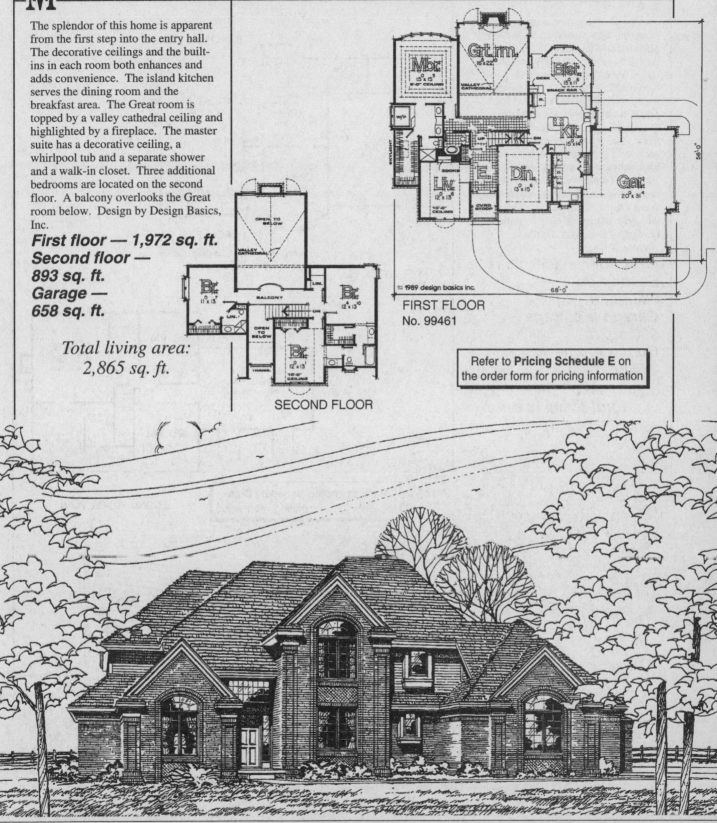

© 1989 design basics inc.

FIRST FLOOR
No. 99461

SECOND FLOOR

Refer to **Pricing Schedule E** on the order form for pricing information

Design 99836

APPEALING FARMHOUSE DESIGN

This comfortable farmhouse appeals to everyone with an easy to build floor plan that still has all of the extras. Active families will enjoy the Great room, open to the kitchen and breakfast bay, as well as the expanded living space provided by a full back porch. For narrower lot restrictions, the garage can be modified to open in front. The second floor master suite contains a walk-in closet and a private bath with garden tub and separate shower. Two more bedrooms on the second floor, one with a walk-in closet, share a full bath, and a bonus room with attic storage is just down the hall. Design by Donald A. Gardner Architects, Inc.

First floor — 959 sq. ft.
Second floor — 833 sq. ft.
Garage & storage — 500 sq. ft.
Bonus room — 344 sq. ft.

Total living area: 1,792 sq. ft.

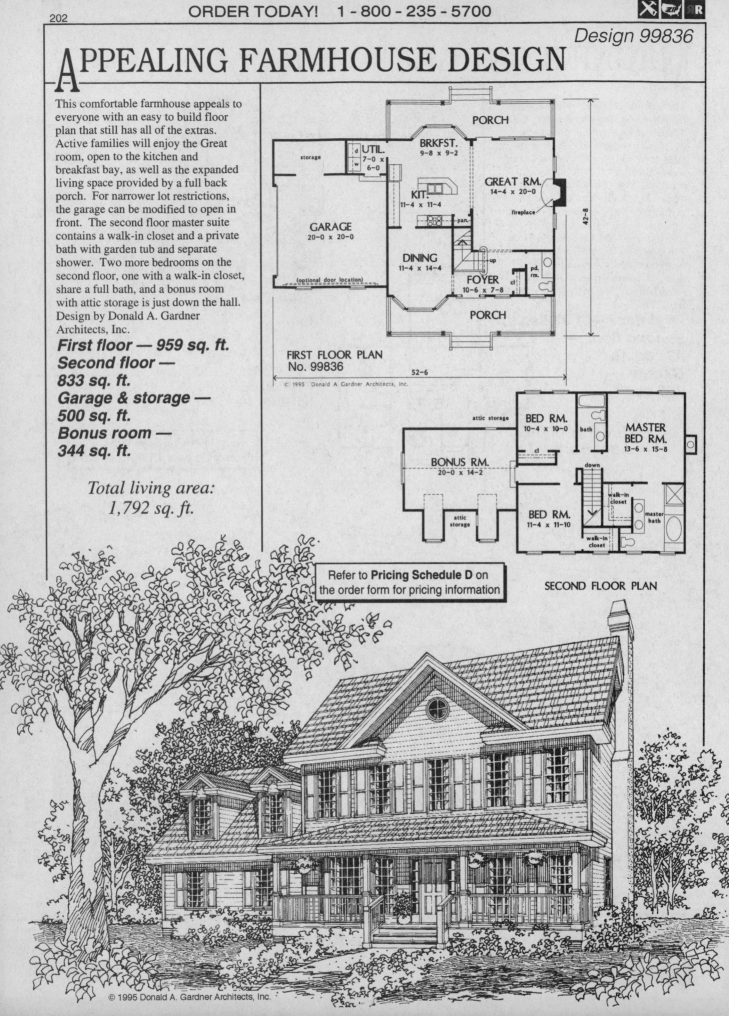

FIRST FLOOR PLAN
No. 99836

© 1995 Donald A Gardner Architects, Inc.

SECOND FLOOR PLAN

Refer to **Pricing Schedule D** on the order form for pricing information

SPACE AND PRIVACY

Design 92549

This expansive four-bedroom home offers a family a precious commodity, privacy. This spacious home allows for family togetherness at the heart of the home. The den, enhanced by a fireplace, is the perfect place to relax. The kitchen adjoins the informal eating area. The dining room adjoins the den for an easy flow when entertaining. The first floor master suite is crowned in a decorative ceiling treatment and includes a plush master bath and a walk-in closet. The first floor secondary bedroom also includes a walk-in closet and direct access to the full bath in the hall. This plan is available with a crawl space or slab foundation. Please specify when ordering. Design by Rick Garner

First floor — 1,911 sq. ft.
Second floor — 579 sq. ft.
Garage — 560 sq. ft.

Total living area: 2,490 sq. ft.

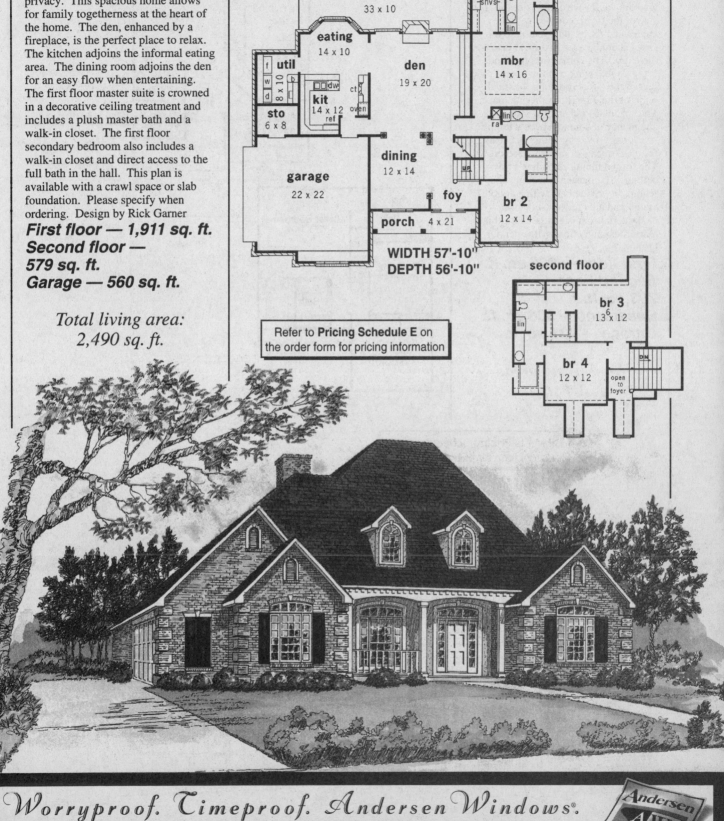

first floor
No. 92549

porch
33 x 10

eating
14 x 10

util
8 x 10

kit
14 x 12

sto
6 x 8

garage
22 x 22

den
19 x 20

dining
12 x 14

foy

porch   4 x 21

mbr
14 x 16

br 2
12 x 14

WIDTH 57'-10''
DEPTH 56'-10''

second floor

br 3
13 x 12

br 4
12 x 12

open to foyer

Refer to **Pricing Schedule E** on the order form for pricing information

Design 92695

ENCHANTING HOME WITH ATMOSPHERE

The large front porch on this charming two-story home provides an inviting atmosphere for welcomed guests. The size of the foyer, coupled with the angles and the grand opening to the Great room, gives a luxurious effect to the entry. The corner fireplace and triple double hung windows across the rear of the Great room are the focal point of this favorite gathering place. The spacious kitchen offers an abundance of counter space with the snack bar providing additional seating for quick meals or an oversized crowd. The formal dining room has a tray ceiling. The master bedroom suite features a private bath with a double vanity and a large walk-in closet. No materials list is available for this plan. Design by Studer Residential Design, Inc.

**First floor — 906 sq. ft.
Second floor —
798 sq. ft.
Basement — 906 sq. ft.
Garage — 437 sq. ft.**

*Total living area:
1,704 sq. ft.*

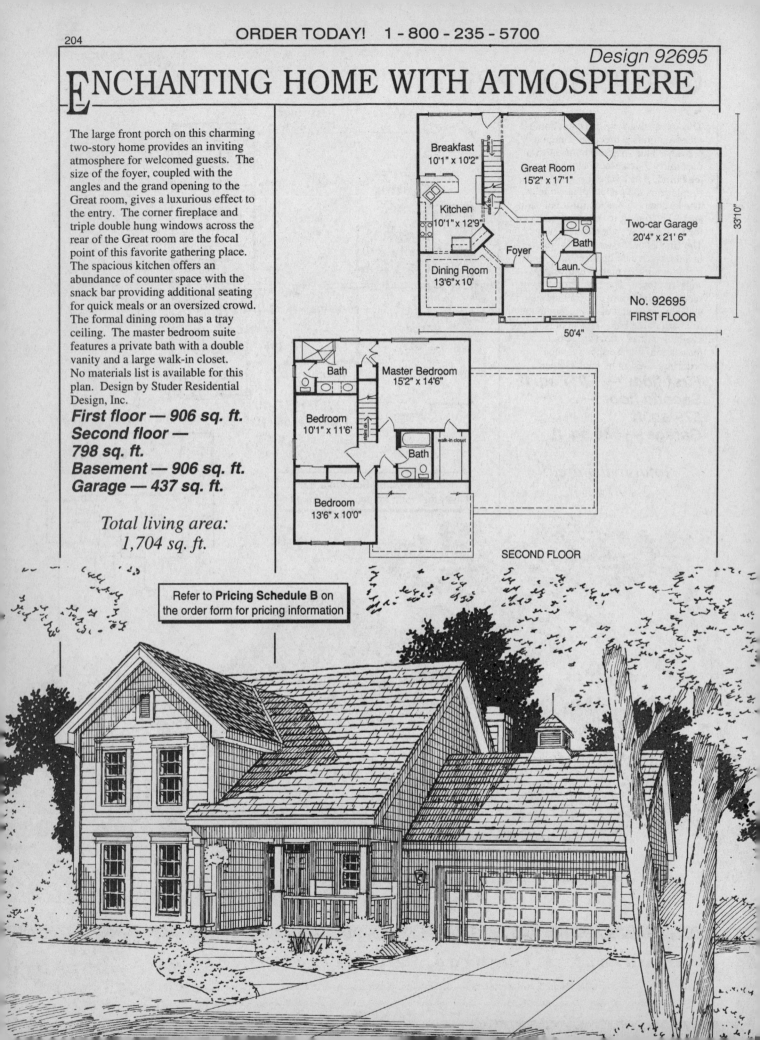

Breakfast 10'1" x 10'2"

Great Room 15'2" x 17'1"

Kitchen 10'1" x 12'9"

Two-car Garage 20'4" x 21' 6"

Foyer

Bath

Laun.

Dining Room 13'6" x 10'

No. 92695
FIRST FLOOR

33'10"

50'4"

Bath

Master Bedroom 15'2" x 14'6"

Bedroom 10'1" x 11'6"

walk-in closet

Bath

Bedroom 13'6" x 10'0"

SECOND FLOOR

Refer to **Pricing Schedule B** on the order form for pricing information

Design 90930

A-FRAME FOR YEAR-ROUND LIVING

If you have a hillside lot, this open design may be just what you've been looking for. With three bedrooms, it's a perfect plan for your growing family. The roomy foyer opens to a hallway that leads to the kitchen, bedrooms, and a dramatic, vaulted living room with a massive fireplace. A wraparound sundeck gives you lots of outdoor living space. And, upstairs, there's a special retreat — a luxurious master suite complete with its own private deck. Design by Wesplan Building Design

Main floor — 1,238 sq. ft.
Loft — 464 sq. ft.
Basement — 1,175 sq. ft.

Total living area:
1,702 sq. ft.

Refer to **Pricing Schedule B** on the order form for pricing information

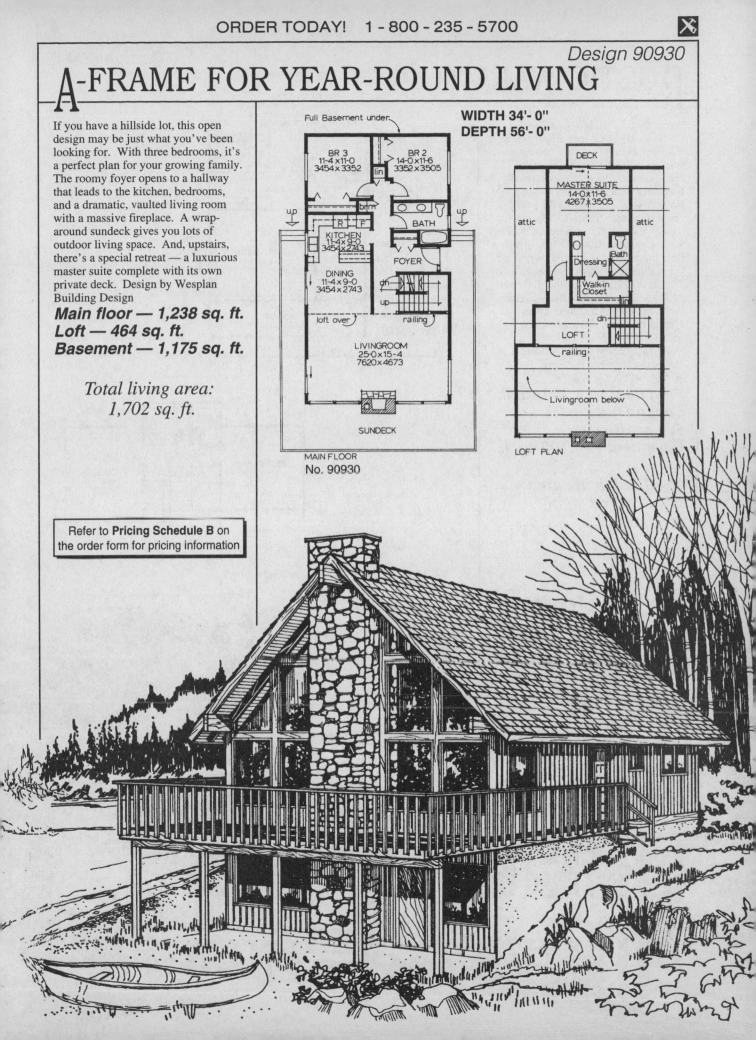

WIDTH 34'- 0"
DEPTH 56'- 0"

MAIN FLOOR
No. 90930

LOFT PLAN

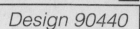

RUSTIC WARMTH

While the covered porch and huge, fieldstone fireplace lend a rustic air to this three-bedroom classic, the interior is loaded with the amenities you've been seeking. Doesn't a book-lined, fireplaced living room sound nice? Haven't you been longing for a fully-equipped island kitchen? This one adjoins a sunny dining room with sliders to a wood deck. Does the idea of a first floor master suite just steps away from your morning coffee sound good? Tucked upstairs with another full bath, two bedrooms feature walk-in closets and cozy, sloping ceilings. There's even plenty of extra storage space in the attic. This plan is available with a basement or crawl space foundation. Please specify when ordering. Design by Corley Plan Service

First floor — 1,100 sq. ft.
Second floor — 664 sq. ft.
Basement — 1,100 sq. ft.

Total living area: 1,764 sq. ft.

Refer to **Pricing Schedule B** on the order form for pricing information

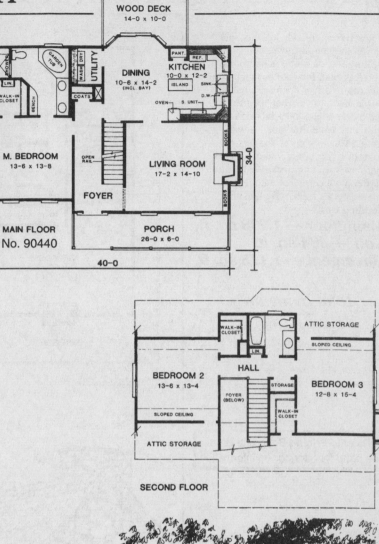

Design 99721

FOR PEOPLE WHO LIKE BOOKS

This wide, basically V-shaped home is designed especially for people who like books. Bookshelves, interspersed with windows, line the long hallway that provides access to the owners' wing. Additional built-in bookshelves are found in the kitchen, in the hallway next to the kitchen, and in the private sitting room next to the owners' sleeping quarters. Four skylights brighten an already sunny eating nook in the huge country kitchen. Other features include a walk-in pantry, range-top work island, built-in barbecue, and a sink that faces out toward the dining room. French doors here, open onto a dining deck. The living room is richly illuminated by a wide window bay on one end, and nearly an entire wall of windows along its length. The luxurious master suite features his-n-her closets, each with its own adjacent dressing area and vanity. The compartmented bath contains an oversized shower and Jacuzzi tub. Two rooms at the opposite end of the house could be used separately as bedrooms, or combined as private living space for rental or long-term guest. No materials list is available for this plan. Design by Landmark Designs, Inc.

Main area — 3,417 sq. ft.
Garage — 795 sq. ft.
Shop — 286 sq. ft.

Total living area:
3,417 sq. ft.

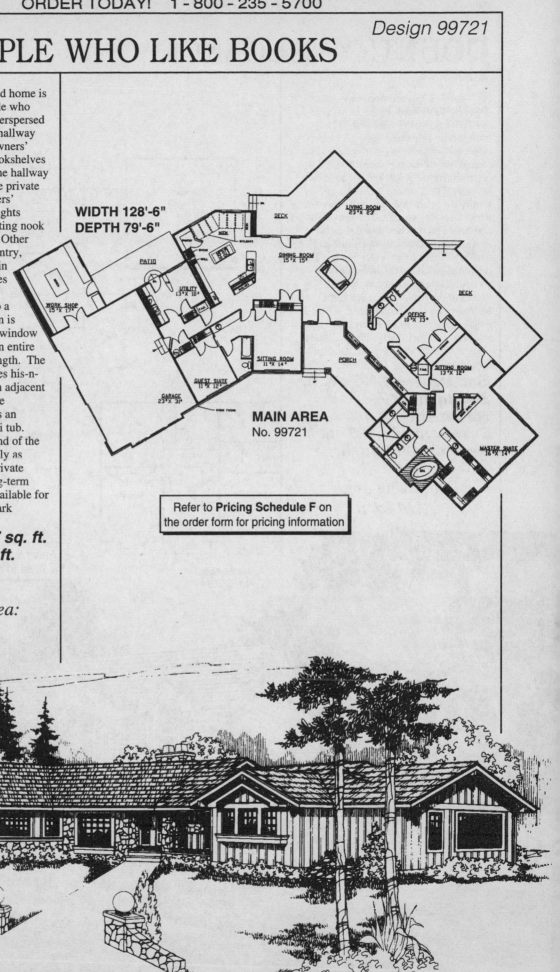

WIDTH 128'-6"
DEPTH 79'-6"

MAIN AREA
No. 99721

Refer to **Pricing Schedule F** on
the order form for pricing information

COUNTRY ELEGANCE

Design 24734

A Country porch and dormer windows highlight this charming home with an old-fashioned homey feeling. The living room is entered through French doors and accented by a fireplace. The formal dining room is directly accessed from the kitchen for ease in serving. The kitchen, breakfast and family room are open to each other for a terrific living space. The peninsula counter in the kitchen doubles as a snack bar and the built-in pantry and desk add to the room's efficiency. The breakfast bay is bright and cheery, while the family room has direct access to the deck. There are three bedrooms on the second floor. The master suite features a five-piece bath and two walk-in closets. No materials list is available for this plan. Design by The Garlinghouse Company

First floor — 1,127 sq. ft.
Second floor — 987 sq. ft.
Basement — 1,125 sq. ft.
Garage — 480 sq. ft.

Total living area: 2,114 sq. ft.

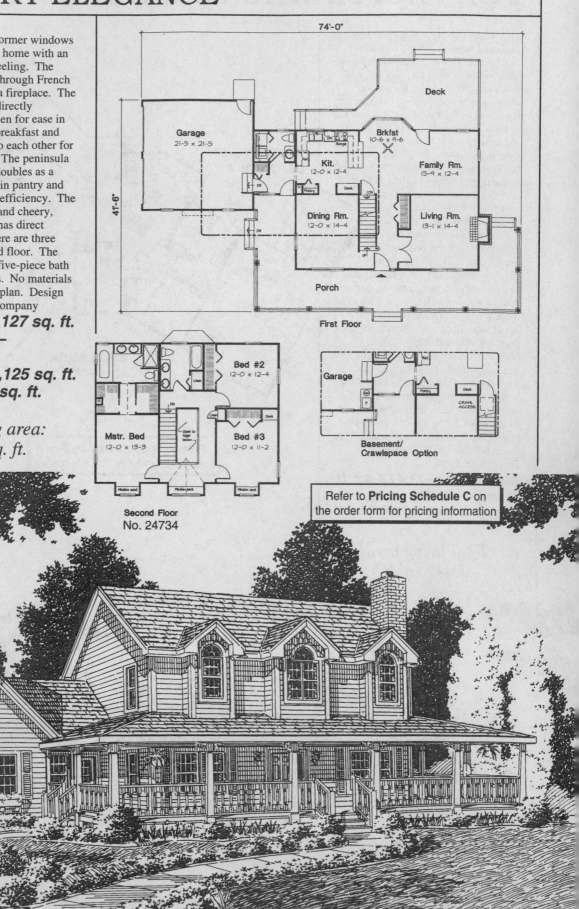

74'-0"

Garage
21-5 × 21-5

Deck

Brkfst
10-6 × 9-6

Kit.
12-0 × 12-4

Family Rm.
15-9 × 12-4

41'-6"

Pantry

Desk

Dining Rm.
12-0 × 14-4

Living Rm.
13-1 × 14-4

Porch

First Floor

Bed #2
12-0 × 12-4

Linen

Mstr. Bed
12-0 × 13-3

Open to foyer below

Desk

Bed #3
12-0 × 11-2

Window seat

Window seat

Window seat

Second Floor
No. 24734

Garage

Pantry

Desk

CRAWL ACCESS

Basement/
Crawlspace Option

Refer to **Pricing Schedule C** on the order form for pricing information

TWO-STORY CONTEMPORARY

Design 99652

A two-story foyer with an adjacent coat closet leads to the living room which has a dramatic high ceiling and a unique front facing window. A central feature of the living room is the recessed fireplace flanked by two windows. The formal dining space leads to a rear terrace through sliding glass doors. An efficient U shaped kitchen serves both the formal and informal dining areas conveniently. Three bedrooms are located upstairs. The master suite has a large walk-in closet and another linear one. The master bath includes a whirlpool tub, a separate shower and a compartmentalized toilet. Design by Perfect Plan

First floor — 810 sq. ft.
Second floor — 781 sq. ft.
Garage — 513 sq. ft.
Basement — 746 sq. ft.

Total living area: 1,591 sq. ft.

FIRST FLOOR PLAN
No. 99652

46'-2"
32'-4"

TERR.

D.R. 10'-10" x 11'
KIT. 10' x 11'
D'NET 7' x 11'
MUD RM
STOR. 7' x 11'
dw
ref.
L.R. 14'-10" x 15'
high ceiling
F.
dn.
up
2 CAR GAR. 20' x 20'
P.

SECOND FLOOR PLAN

B.R. 10'-10" x 11'
B.R. 11' x 10'
whirlpool tub
W.I.C.
cl.
lin.
H
dn.
upper part of living rm.
M.B.R. 15' x 13'
roof

Refer to **Pricing Schedule B** on the order form for pricing information

Weather Shield
Windows & Doors

www.weathershield.com

Weather Shield Windows and Doors offers project planning guides for your remodeling or new home project. FREE. Specify "Remodeling" or "New Home" Planning Guide by calling

1-800-477-6808

Design 98405

REGAL APPEAL

This home has a regal presence, accentuated by the two-story foyer. Straight ahead is the unique two-story family room, enhanced by a fireplace. The kitchen includes a cooktop island/serving bar and a walk-in pantry. A French door leads to the rear yard from the kitchen. The dining room and living room are to either side of the foyer. A guest room/study is located in close proximity to a full bath. The master suite includes a tray ceiling, a bayed sitting area and a lavish master bath with a vaulted ceiling and access to the huge walk-in closet. This plan is available with a basement or crawl space foundation. Please specify when ordering. Design by Frank Betz Associates, Inc.

First floor — 1,488 sq. ft.
Second floor —
1,551 sq. ft.
Basement — 1,488 sq. ft.
Garage — 667 sq. ft.

Total living area:
3,039 sq. ft.

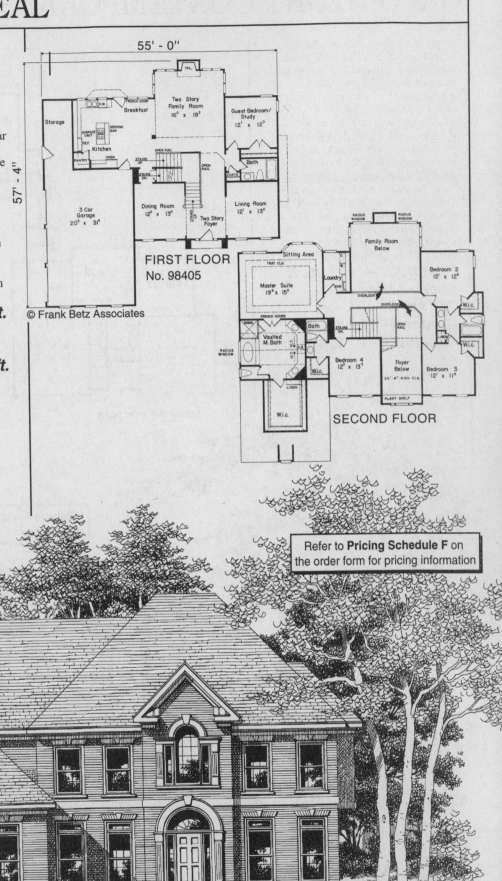

© Frank Betz Associates

FIRST FLOOR
No. 98405

SECOND FLOOR

Refer to **Pricing Schedule F** on the order form for pricing information

Design 98410

MAGNIFICENT MANOR

The two-story foyer is dominated by a lovely staircase. The formal living room is to the left. The dining room is through an arched opening to the right. The efficient kitchen directly accesses the formal dining room for ease in serving. The breakfast area is separated from the kitchen by only the extended counter/serving bar. The two-story family room is highlighted by a focal point fireplace framed by windows. A tray ceiling crowns the master bedroom while a vaulted ceiling tops the plush master bath. Two additional bedrooms share the full double vanity bath in the hall. This plan is available with a basement or crawl space foundation. Please specify when ordering. Design by Frank Betz Associates, Inc.

First floor — 1,428 sq. ft.
Second floor — 961 sq. ft.
Bonus area — 472 sq. ft.
Basement — 1,428 sq. ft.
Garage — 507 sq. ft.

Total living area: 2,389 sq. ft.

Refer to **Pricing Schedule D** on the order form for pricing information

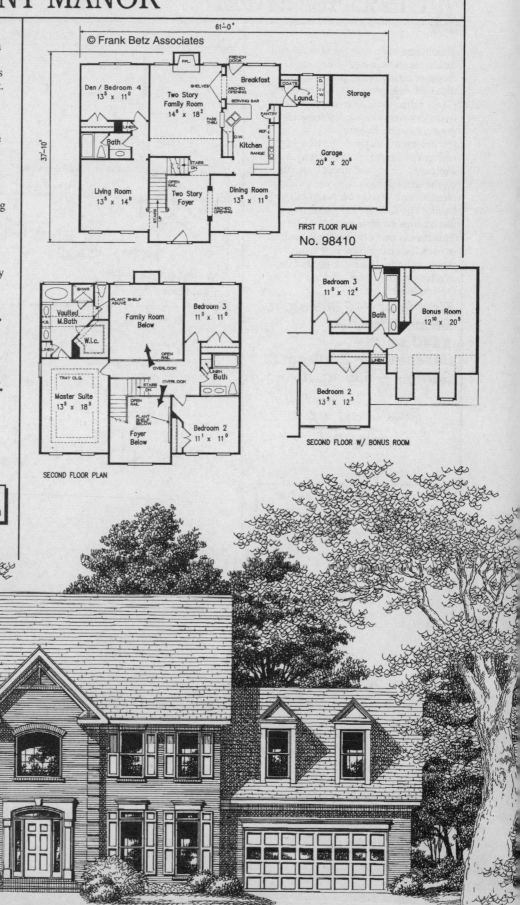

© Frank Betz Associates

FIRST FLOOR PLAN
No. 98410

SECOND FLOOR PLAN

SECOND FLOOR W/ BONUS ROOM

Design 99440

A CLASSIC HOME

This home is a classic because of its underscore of romantic freedom. The elevation features the master wing on the right. Space and light connects the entry, gallery, dining room, and the two-story living room, immediately giving this area a sense of calm. Curved glass block sets the tone in the master bath, a design inspired by the Japanese. Three additional bedrooms on the second floor, each with walk-in closets, have private access to full baths. The second floor game room has built-in cabinets and TV space. This plan is available with a basement or slab foundation. Please specify when ordering. No materials list is available for this plan. Design by Design Basics, Inc.

First floor — 2,688 sq. ft.
Second floor —
1,540 sq. ft.
Basement — 2,688 sq. ft.
Garage — 635 sq. ft.

Total living area:
4,228 sq. ft.

Refer to **Pricing Schedule F** on the order form for pricing information

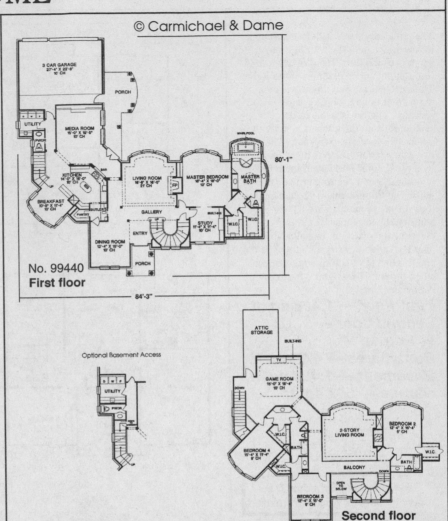

© Carmichael & Dame

No. 99440
First floor

Second floor

LAVISH ACCOMMODATIONS

From its stately exterior, to its great attention to detail, this home personifies luxury. The central den has a large fireplace and built-in cabinets and shelves. A decorative ceiling adds just the right touch to the room. Columns define the entrance to the formal dining room, adding a feeling of elegance. The island kitchen is well thought out and includes a walk-in pantry. The informal breakfast room is directly accessible from either the kitchen or the den. The master bedroom includes a decorative ceiling huge walk-in closet and a luxurious master bath. Each of the additional bedrooms have private access to a full bath. Two of the bedrooms have a walk-in closet, the other enjoys a private bath, making it the perfect guest room. This plan is available with a crawl space or slab foundation. Please specify when ordering. Design by Rick Garner

Main area — 2,733 sq. ft.
Garage and storage — 569 sq. ft.

Total living area:
2,733 sq. ft.

Refer to **Pricing Schedule F** on the order form for pricing information

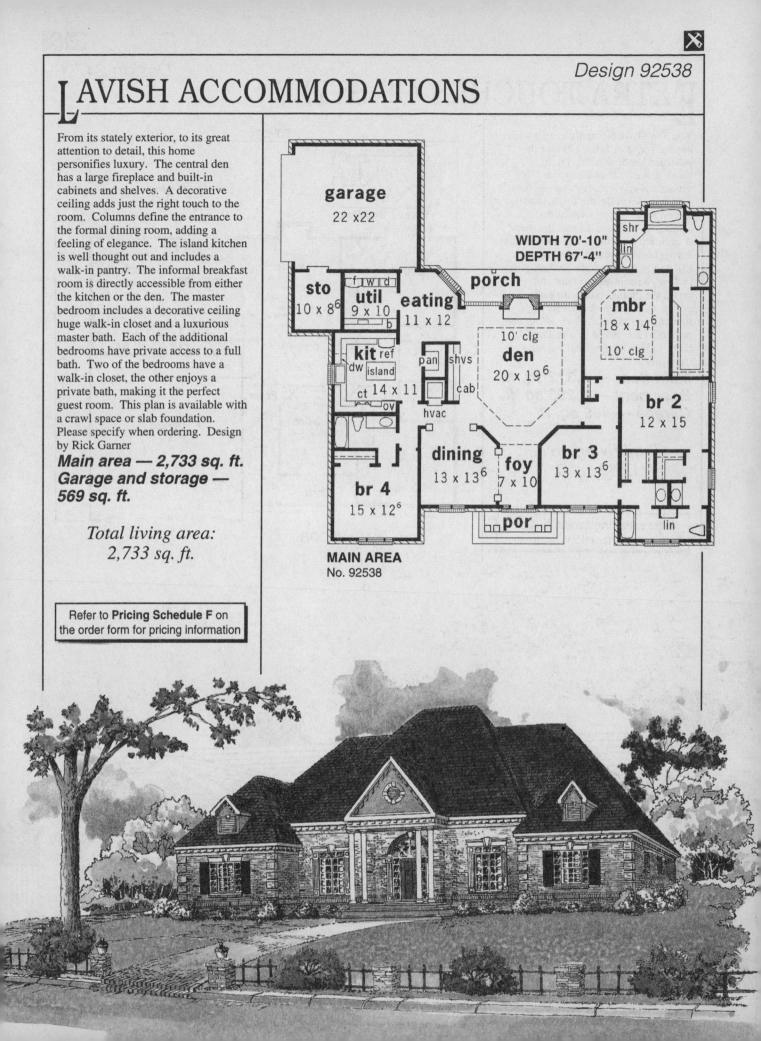

WIDTH 70'-10"
DEPTH 67'-4"

garage 22 x22

sto 10 x 8⁶ · util 9 x 10 · eating 11 x 12 · porch

mbr 18 x 14⁶ · 10' clg

kit 14 x 11 · pan · shvs · 10' clg · den 20 x 19⁶ · cab · hvac

br 2 12 x 15

dining 13 x 13⁶ · foy 7 x 10 · br 3 13 x 13⁶

br 4 15 x 12⁶ · por · lin

MAIN AREA
No. 92538

EXTRA TOUCHES OF STYLE

You don't have to sacrifice style when buying a smaller home. Notice the palladian window with a fan light above at the front of the home. The entrance porch includes a turned post entry. Once inside, the living room is topped by an impressive vaulted ceiling. A fireplace accents the room. A decorative ceiling enhances both the master bedroom and the dining room. Efficiently designed, the kitchen includes a peninsula counter and serves the dining room with ease. A private bath and double closet highlight the master suite. Two additional bedrooms are served by a full hall bath. Design by The Garlinghouse Company

Main floor — 1,312 sq. ft.
Basement — 1,293 sq. ft.
Garage — 459 sq. ft.

Total living area:
1,312 sq. ft.

Refer to **Pricing Schedule A** on the order form for pricing information

MAIN FLOOR
No. 24700

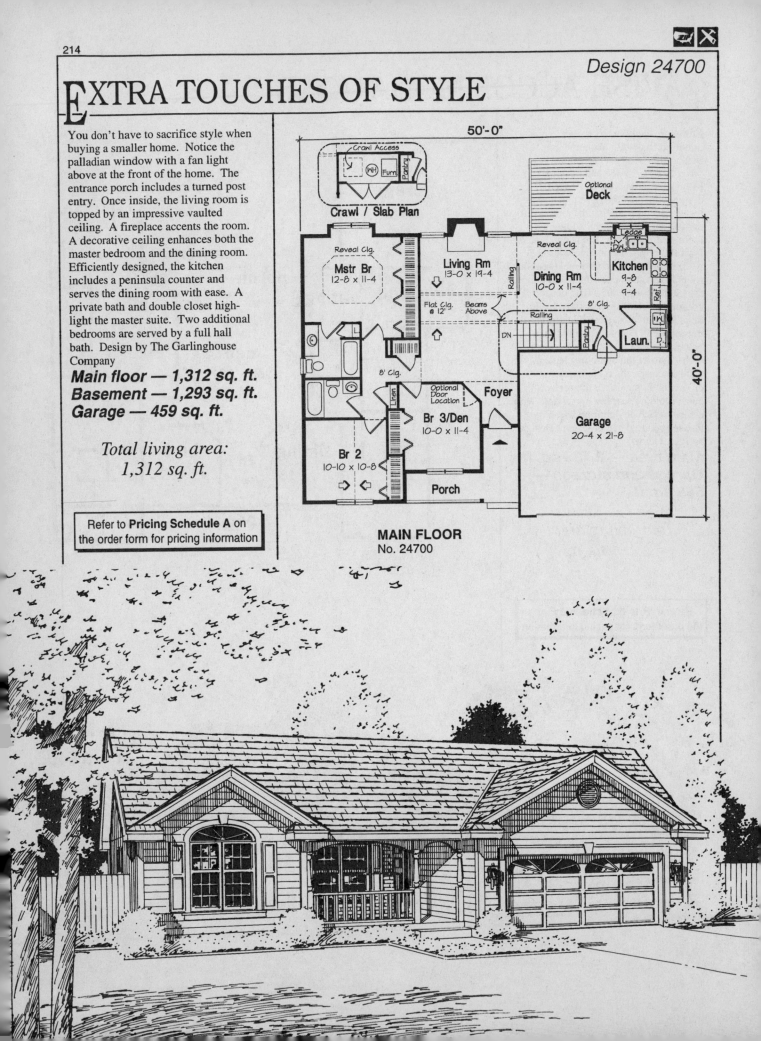

Design 92674

ABUNDANT EXTERIOR DETAILING

The ceiling in the Great room, slopes to an 11'-7" height, and coupled with the corner fireplace and multiple windows across the rear, creates a spirit of excitement. The deluxe master suite is located on the first floor. This home easily becomes a four bedroom home by accessing the second floor bonus room. The location of the rear stairs with wood banisters, a computer desk on the second floor, a spacious first floor laundry room. and screened-in porch are amenities that turn this comfortable size home into an exciting package. No materials list is available for this plan. Design by Studer Residential Design, Inc.

First floor — 1,348 sq. ft.
Second floor — 528 sq. ft.
Basement — 1,300 sq. ft.
Bonus — 195 sq. ft.

Total living area: 1,876 sq. ft.

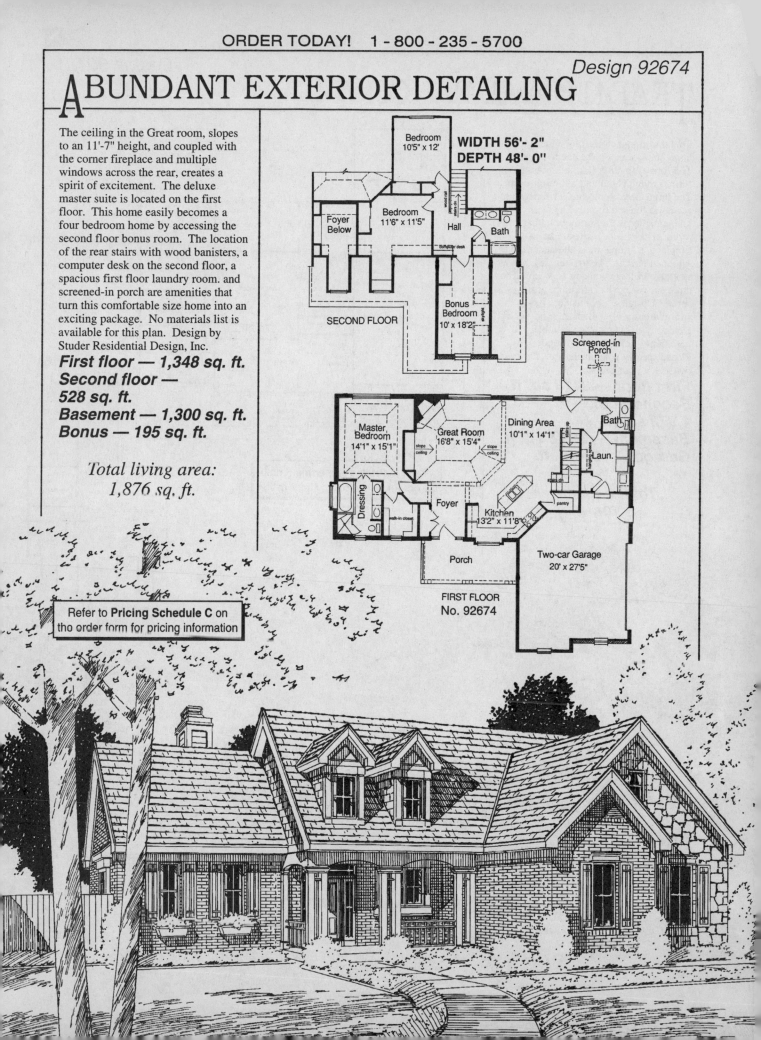

WIDTH 56'- 2"
DEPTH 48'- 0"

Bedroom 10'5" x 12'

Foyer Below

Bedroom 11'6" x 11'5"

Hall

Bath

computer desk

SECOND FLOOR

Bonus Bedroom 10' x 18'2"

Screened-in Porch

Master Bedroom 14'1" x 15'1"

Great Room 16'8" x 15'4"

slope ceiling

Dining Area 10'1" x 14'1"

Bath

Laun.

Dressing

walk-in closet

Foyer

Kitchen 13'2" x 11'8"

pantry

Porch

Two-car Garage 20' x 27'5"

FIRST FLOOR
No. 92674

Refer to **Pricing Schedule C** on the order form for pricing information

TRADITIONAL RANCH

Design 90481

This traditional style Ranch includes a large bonus area on the second floor. The formal foyer is flanked by both a formal living room and a dining room. The large Great room has a fireplace and access to the sun room. The open kitchen adjoins the sunny breakfast room. The master bedroom has a fireplace, a sitting area, and access to the screened porch. The master bath has a spa tub and large walk-in shower . The three car garage has ample parking space. Upstairs, a bonus area has a sitting areas with palladian window and a balcony. This plan is available with a basement or crawl space foundation. Please specify when ordering. Design by Corley Plan Service

First floor — 3118 sq. ft.
**Second floor —
1,078 sq. ft.**
Basement — 3,118 sq. ft.
Garage — 704 sq. ft.

*Total living area :
4,196 sq. ft.*

Refer to **Pricing Schedule F** on the order form for pricing information

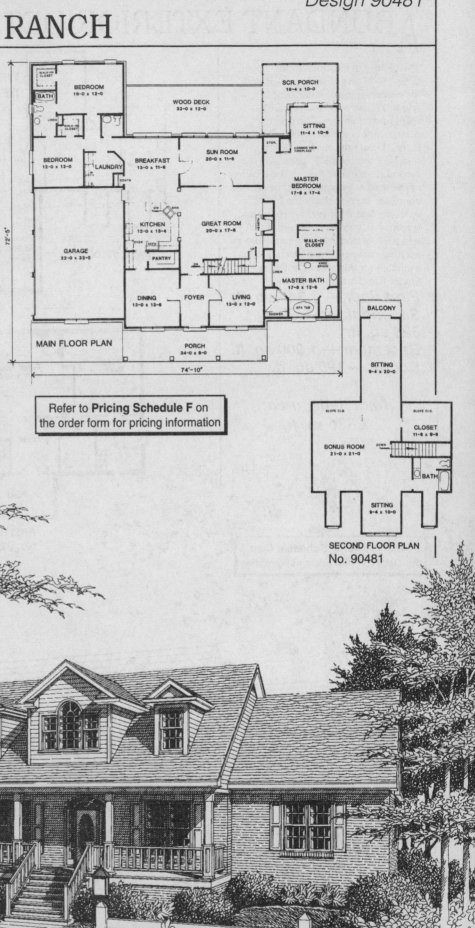

Design 99914

RUSTIC STYLING

An attractive rustic facade, complete with a field stone fireplace and plenty of outdoor living area makes a good first impression. Inside this two bedroom "A" frame, you will find a great floor plan, lots of open space and ample size closets. The large kitchen easily serves the dining area. The living room and dining area flow into each other and a gas fireplace accents the area with coziness. The master bedroom is spacious and located on the second floor with a private bath and a private deck. The secondary bedroom has easy access to a full bath. This plan is available with a basement or crawl space foundation. Please specify when ordering. Design by Wesplan Building Design.

**First floor —
1,064 sq. ft.
Second floor —
613 sq. ft.**

*Total living area:
1,677 sq. ft.*

FIRST FLOOR
No. 99914

**WIDTH 28'-0"
DEPTH 40'-0"**

BR 2
12-0x13-0

Pantry

Mud Rm/Utility

tr zr

clos.

lt W D

Bath

FOYER

Porch

up

stor

KITCHEN
12-4x12-0

dw

LR
15-0x18-6

DINING
12-0x12-0/9-9

Gas FP

Patio door

SUNDECK

attic

MBR
16-10x16-10

french

Deck

books

8'-0" clg.

lin.

attic

Whirlpool

BATH

dn

LOFT

attic

railing

LR & DR Below

SECOND FLOOR

Refer to **Pricing Schedule B** on the order form for pricing information

Weather Shield
Windows & Doors

www.weathershield.com

Weather Shield Windows and Doors offers project planning guides for your remodeling or new home project. FREE. Specify "Remodeling" or "New Home" Planning Guide by calling

1-800-477-6808

Design 99450

MAGNIFICENT PORCH ADDS APPEAL

The entry of this home surveys the formal living and dining rooms. The formal living room features two bookcases. The impressive Great room includes three large windows and a raised hearth fireplace flanked by bookcases. The gazebo dinette and island kitchen are equipped with a huge pantry and two Lazy Susans. The first floor master suite includes a porch retreat access, a roomy dressing area, his-n-her vanities and a sunlit whirlpool. This plan is available with a basement or slab foundation. Please specify when ordering. Design by Design Basics, Inc.

First floor — 1,881 sq. ft.
Second floor — 814 sq. ft.
Basement — 1,020 sq. ft.
Garage — 534 sq. ft.

Total living area: 2,695 sq. ft.

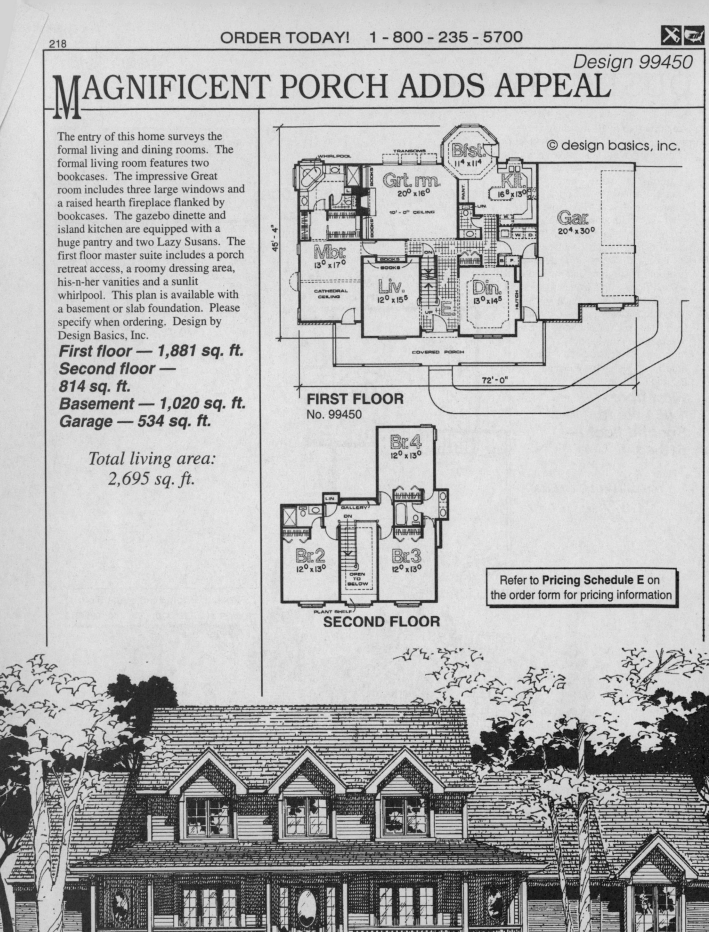

© design basics, inc.

FIRST FLOOR
No. 99450

SECOND FLOOR

Refer to **Pricing Schedule E** on the order form for pricing information

Design 96458

COUNTRY RANCH CONVENIENCE

Country charm and ranch convenience combine in this three bedroom home. The open design pulls Great room, kitchen, and breakfast bay into one common area, and cathedral ceilings give a feeling of spaciousness. A deck at the rear expands living and entertaining space, while the dining room provides a quiet place for relaxed family dinners or elegant dinner parties. The master suite is elegantly appointed with a cathedral ceiling, walk-in closet, and bath with a whirlpool tub, a shower, and a dual vanity. Two additional bedrooms, one with a cathedral ceiling and arched window, share a full bath at the front of the house. Design by Donald A. Gardner Architects, Inc.

Main floor — 1,512 sq. ft.
Garage & storage — 455 sq. ft.

Total living area:
1,512 sq. ft.

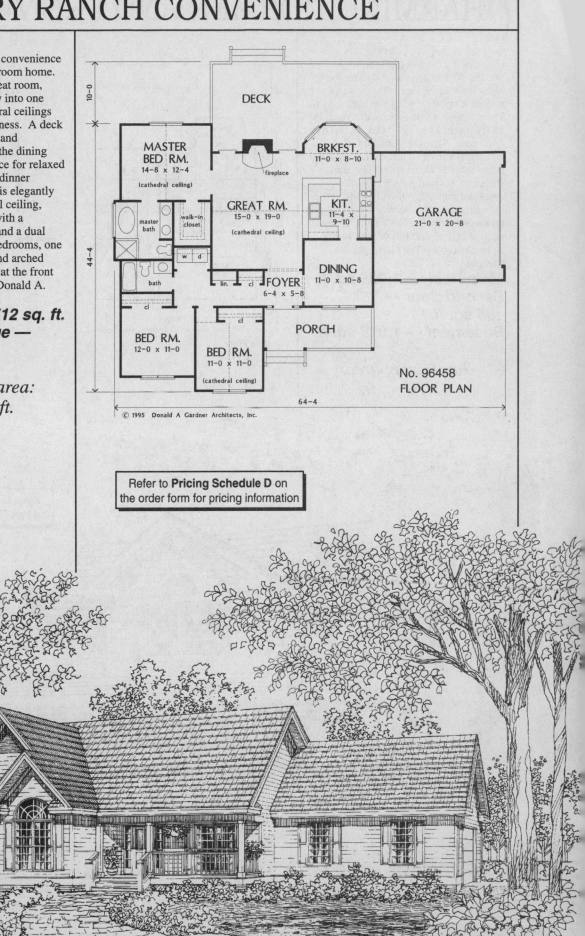

DECK

MASTER BED RM.
14-8 x 12-4
(cathedral ceiling)

master bath

walk-in closet

bath

cl

BED RM.
12-0 x 11-0

BED RM.
11-0 x 11-0
(cathedral ceiling)

fireplace

GREAT RM.
15-0 x 19-0
(cathedral ceiling)

BRKFST.
11-0 x 8-10

KIT.
11-4 x 9-10

DINING
11-0 x 10-8

FOYER
6-4 x 5-8

lin.   cl

w   d

cl

PORCH

GARAGE
21-0 x 20-8

10-0
44-4
64-4

No. 96458
FLOOR PLAN

© 1995 Donald A Gardner Architects, Inc.

Refer to **Pricing Schedule D** on the order form for pricing information

CHARMING DORMER AND FRONT PORCH

Design 24706

Country styling is evident in this elevation by the use of the front porch and the dormer above. A roomy living room with a fireplace offers a warm welcome upon entering the home. There is also a side entrance through the utility room, keeping tracked in dirt to a minimum. The island kitchen is efficiently arranged into an L-shape and flows into the cheery breakfast area. Direct access to the deck from the breakfast area conveniently adds to the living space in the warmer weather. The private master suite has a walk-in closet, vaulted ceiling and full double vanity bath. Design by The Garlinghouse Company

Main floor — 1,035 sq. ft.
Second floor —
435 sq. ft.
Basement — 1,018 sq. ft.

Total living area:
1,470 sq. ft.

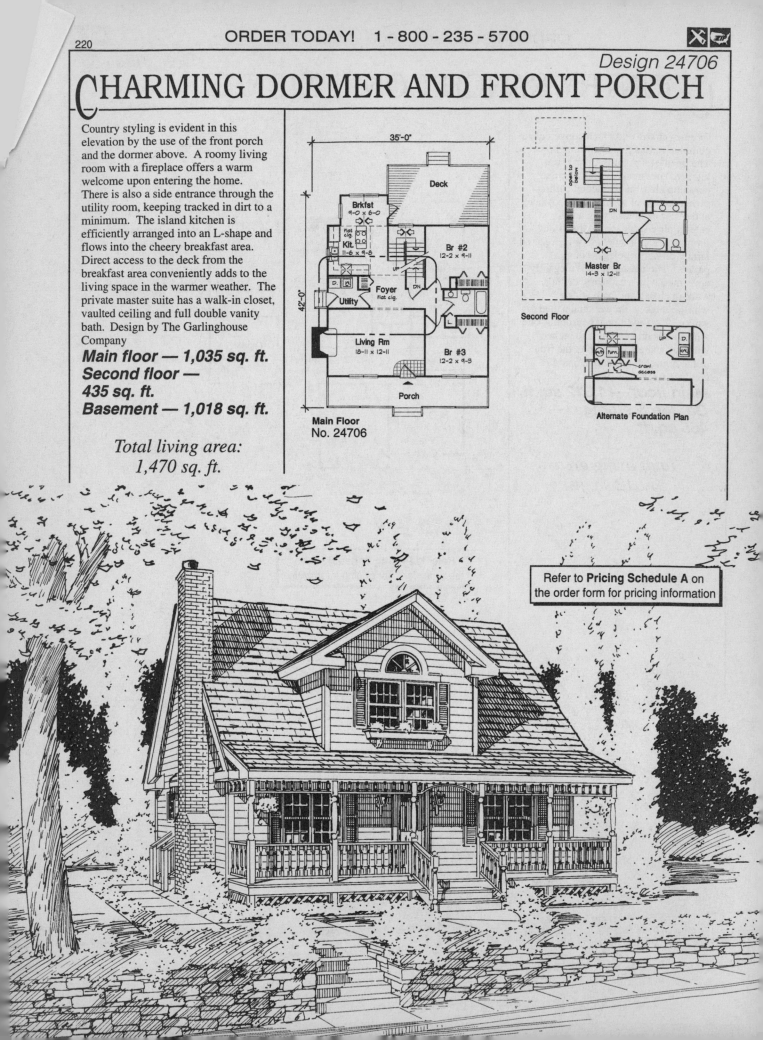

Main Floor
No. 24706

Deck

Brkfst
9-0 x 6-0

Kit.
11-6 x 9-8

Foyer

Utility

Living Rm
18-11 x 12-11

Br #2
12-2 x 9-11

Br #3
12-2 x 9-8

Porch

35'-0"
42'-0"

Second Floor

Master Br
14-3 x 12-11

Alternate Foundation Plan

Refer to **Pricing Schedule A** on the order form for pricing information

FOR A GROWING FAMILY

Design 98473

© Frank Betz Associates

Formal areas are located to either side of the impressive two-story foyer. The kitchen includes a corner double sink and a wrap-around snack bar. The fireplace in the family room gives a warm feeling to the living area. A secondary bedroom or study is privately located in the left rear corner of the home, with direct access to a full bath. The master suite is decorated by a tray ceiling in the bedroom and a vaulted ceiling in the master bath. This plan is available with a basement or crawl space foundation. Please specify when ordering. No materials list is available for this plan. Design by Frank Betz Associates, Inc.

First floor — 1,103 sq. ft.
Second floor —
759 sq. ft.
Basement — 1,103 sq. ft.
Garage — 420 sq. ft.

Total living area:
1,862 sq. ft.

FIRST FLOOR
No. 98473

50'-4"
35'-0"

Bedroom 4/ Study 10⁰ x 11⁷
Bath
PANTRY
Breakfast
FRENCH DOOR
Family Room 17² x 13²
FPL
Garage 19⁸ x 20⁴
RANGE
DW.
Kitchen
REF.
COATS
STAIRS DN.
STAIRS UP
OPEN RAIL
Dining Room 10⁰ x 11⁰
Two Story Foyer
Living Room 10⁶ x 10⁰
Covered Porch

SECOND FLOOR

Vaulted M.Bath
SH.WR.
TRAY CLG.
Master Suite 17² x 13²
PLANT SHELF ABOVE
W.i.c.
LINEN
W.i.c.
Bath
STAIRS DN.
LINEN
W.i.c.
Bedroom 2 10⁰ x 10²
OPEN RAIL
Foyer Below
Bedroom 3 10² x 10⁰
PLANT SHELF

Refer to **Pricing Schedule C** on the order form for pricing information

Design 96468

MAKING LIFE EASIER

Not only does this home live bigger than its 1,864 square feet, but it also lives easier. The space flows easily from the sunlit foyer into a generous Great room with cathedral ceiling, while interior accent columns define the open kitchen and breakfast bay. The master bedroom, located off the Great room, features a tray ceiling and back porch access, and the well-appointed master bath is separated from the bedroom by closets. A new design twist puts two more bedrooms just steps away from the bonus room, creating a great children's wing. Design by Donald A. Gardner Architects, Inc.

Main floor — 1,864 sq. ft.
Garage & storage — 503 sq. ft.
Bonus room — 319 sq. ft.

Total living area:
1,864 sq. ft.

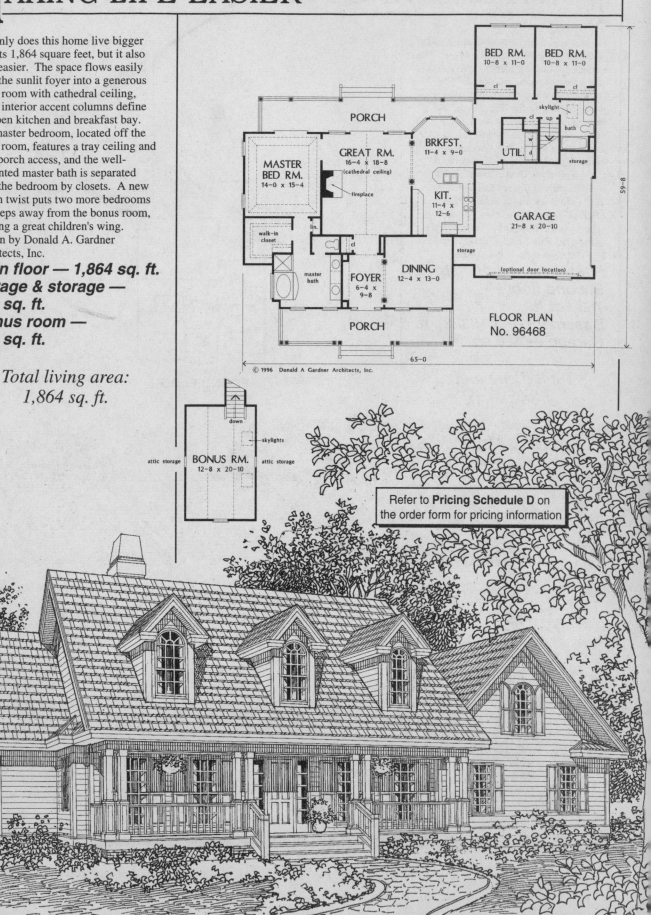

FLOOR PLAN No. 96468

© 1996 Donald A Gardner Architects, Inc.

Refer to **Pricing Schedule D** on the order form for pricing information

B. NATHAN

Design 98221

OUTSTANDING MASTER SUITE

A vaulted ceiling, a see-through fireplace with built-in shelving, arched entry into a private sitting area, huge walk-in closet and a stupendous master bath combine to create this outstanding master suite. The parlor, located to the left of the foyer, includes French doors separating it from the family room. This arrangement allows for quiet conversation while children enjoy themselves in the family room. The breakfast room is enhanced by a bay window and flows from the kitchen. An extended counter provides a snack bar for meals on the go. The formal dining room is easily accessed from the kitchen for ease in serving. This plan is available with a basement or slab foundation. Please specify when ordering. No materials list is available for this plan. Design by Archival Designs

First floor — 1,113 sq. ft.
Second floor — 1,148 sq. ft.
Basement — 1,113 sq. ft.
Garage — 529 sq. ft.

Total living area: 2,261 sq. ft.

Refer to **Pricing Schedule D** on the order form for pricing information

WIDTH 66'-0"
DEPTH 31'-0"

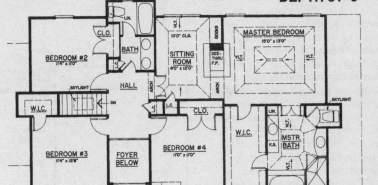

SECOND FLOOR PLAN

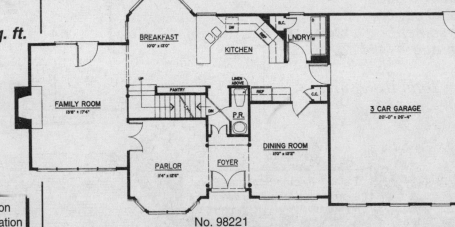

No. 98221
FIRST FLOOR PLAN

GRAND ENTRANCE

Design 98418

The grand arched window above the entrance of this home attracts immediate attention. Inside natural light streams into the two-story foyer. To the right of the entry way, the living room and dining room adjoin into a large area for entertaining. The boxed columns defining the two rooms have been outfitted with shelves. The kitchen is conveniently situated between the formal dining room and breakfast area. The family room is highlighted by a fireplace and includes stairs to the second floor. The second floor master suite features a vaulted ceiling topping the lavish bath and a huge walk-in closet. The three additional bedrooms share the full bath in the hall. This plan is available with a basement or crawl space foundation. Please specify when ordering. Design by Frank Betz Associates, Inc.

First floor — 1,424 sq. ft.
Second floor —
1,256 sq. ft.
Basement — 1,424 sq. ft.
Garage — 494 sq. ft.

Total living area:
2,680 sq. ft.

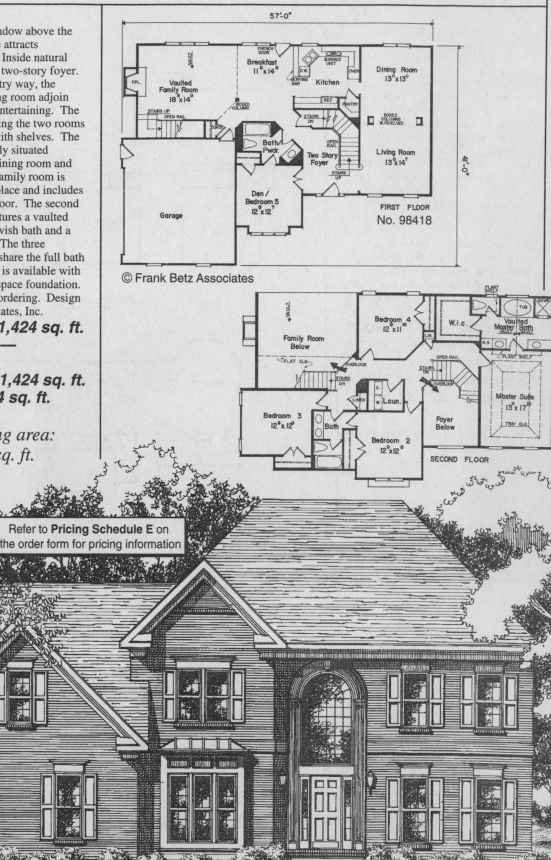

© Frank Betz Associates

No. 98418

FIRST FLOOR

SECOND FLOOR

Refer to **Pricing Schedule E** on the order form for pricing information

ELEGANT BRICK VENEER

Design 98003

Arched and oval windows accent the elegant brick veneer of this three bedroom executive home. The open, formal dining room is defined by columns and capped by a graceful tray ceiling. A deep tray ceiling adds space to the generous Great room which features rear clerestory dormers. The kitchen and breakfast bay share a vaulted ceiling and access to the wrapping back porch. The vaulted master suite includes a walk-in closet and a lavish bath with tray ceiling and back porch access. The bonus room has attic storage and a cozy window seat. Design by Donald A. Gardner Architects, Inc.

Main floor — 2,198 sq. ft.
Bonus room — 325 sq. ft.
Garage — 588 sq. ft.

Total living area:
2,198 sq. ft.

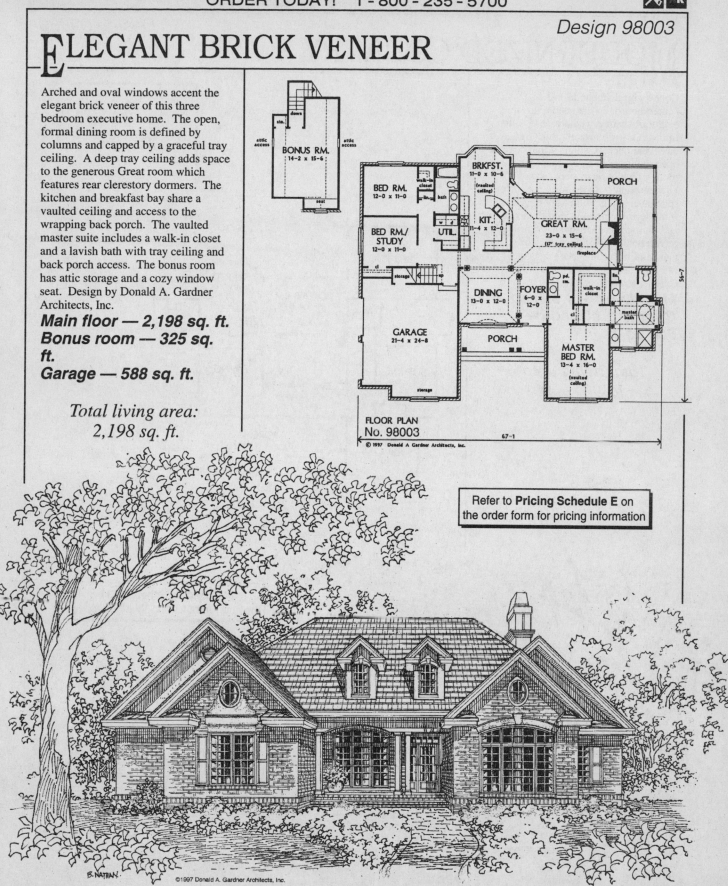

FLOOR PLAN
No. 98003

© 1997 Donald A Gardner Architects, Inc.

Refer to **Pricing Schedule E** on the order form for pricing information

Weather Shield
Windows & Doors

www.weathershield.com

Weather Shield Windows and Doors offers project planning guides for your remodeling or new home project. FREE. Specify "Remodeling" or "New Home" Planning Guide by calling

1-800-477-6808

226

Design 99850

MODERNIZED COUNTRY

Country on the outside and contemporary on the inside, this three-bedroom charmer celebrates Country life with a wrap-around porch and a large rear deck. Columns dramatically open the foyer to a generous Great room which in turn opens to the kitchen/breakfast area for a feeling of spaciousness. Natural light penetrates from dormer windows into the foyer and dining room. The master suite is privately located at the rear, while two front bedrooms share a second full bath. Design by Donald A. Gardner Architects, Inc.

Main floor — 1,590 sq. ft.
Garage & storage — 506 sq. ft.

Total living area:
1,590 sq. ft.

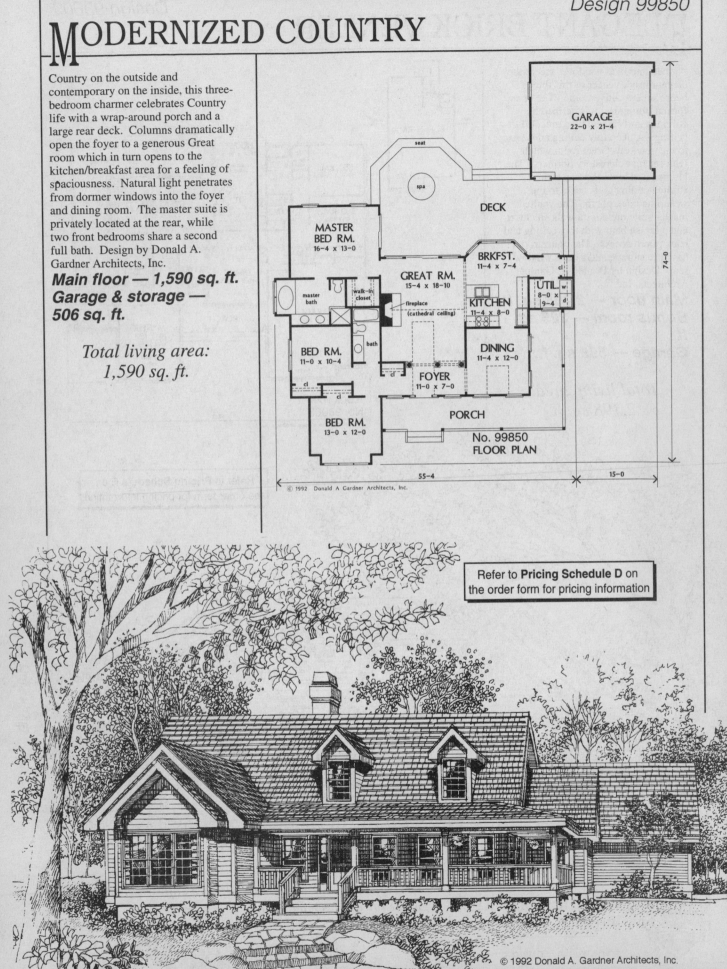

GARAGE
22-0 x 21-4

seat

spa

DECK

MASTER BED RM.
16-4 x 13-0

BRKFST.
11-4 x 7-4

cl

GREAT RM.
15-4 x 18-10

UTIL.
8-0 x 9-4

w
d

master bath

walk-in closet

fireplace
(cathedral ceiling)

KITCHEN
11-4 x 8-0

bath

BED RM.
11-0 x 10-4

DINING
11-4 x 12-0

cl

cl

FOYER
11-0 x 7-0

d

BED RM.
13-0 x 12-0

PORCH

No. 99850
FLOOR PLAN

74-0

55-4

15-0

© 1992 Donald A Gardner Architects, Inc.

Refer to **Pricing Schedule D** on the order form for pricing information

FIRMLY ESTABLISHED

Design 93602

Our home says a lot about our lives. This home gives the impression of a solid, established individual. In today's busy world, an established individual would need a home that efficiently fills his needs, yet pampers him. This home does just that. The formal living room and dining room adjoin with elegant columns defining the rooms. The well-appointed kitchen has plenty of cabinet space, an island with a double sink, dishwasher and a built-in pantry and planning desk. A sunny breakfast bay gives a cheery start to the day. The spacious two-story Great room has a beautiful fireplace enhancing the room's appearance and mood. The sleeping quarters are all located on the second floor. The master bedroom adds to its architectural interest with a tray ceiling. The private master bath pampers the owner with the luxury of an oval tub, double vanity, step-in shower and a huge walk-in closet. Three additional bedrooms share a full hall bath with a double vanity. No materials list is available for this plan. Design by Garrell Associates, Inc.

**First floor — 1,209 sq. ft.
Second floor — 1,202 sq. ft.
Basement — 1,209 sq. ft.
Garage — 370 sq. ft.**

Total living area: 2,411 sq. ft.

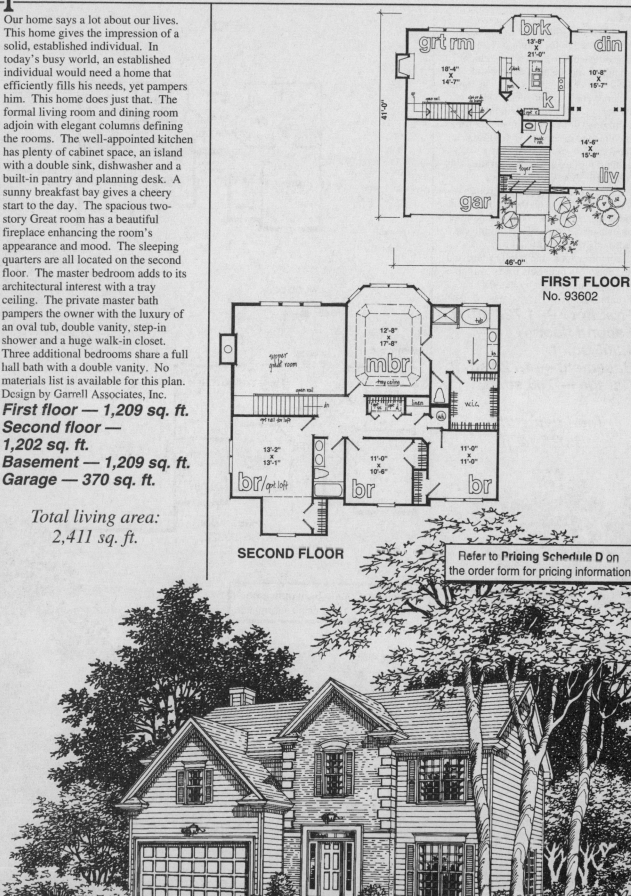

FIRST FLOOR
No. 93602

SECOND FLOOR

Refer to **Pricing Schedule D** on the order form for pricing information

SPLENDOR AND DISTINCTION

The expansive kitchen in this home is sure to be a hub for activity. The cooktop island includes a convenient eating bar and a corner double sink looks out over the rear yard. The built-in pantry and planning desk add to its efficiency. The expansive family room is equipped with a built-in wetbar for convenience in serving your guests. The formal living room boasts a second fireplace and a view of the front yard. A bay window adds elegance to the formal dining room. The master suite is on the second floor and its private master bath will pamper the owner in luxury. Three additional bedrooms share a full hall bath. A balcony overlooks the family room and the foyer. No materials list is available for this plan. Design by Patrick Morabito A.I.A.

First floor — 1,720 sq. ft.
Second floor — 1,305 sq. ft.
Basement — 1,720 sq. ft.
Garage — 768 sq. ft.

Total living area:
3,025 sq. ft.

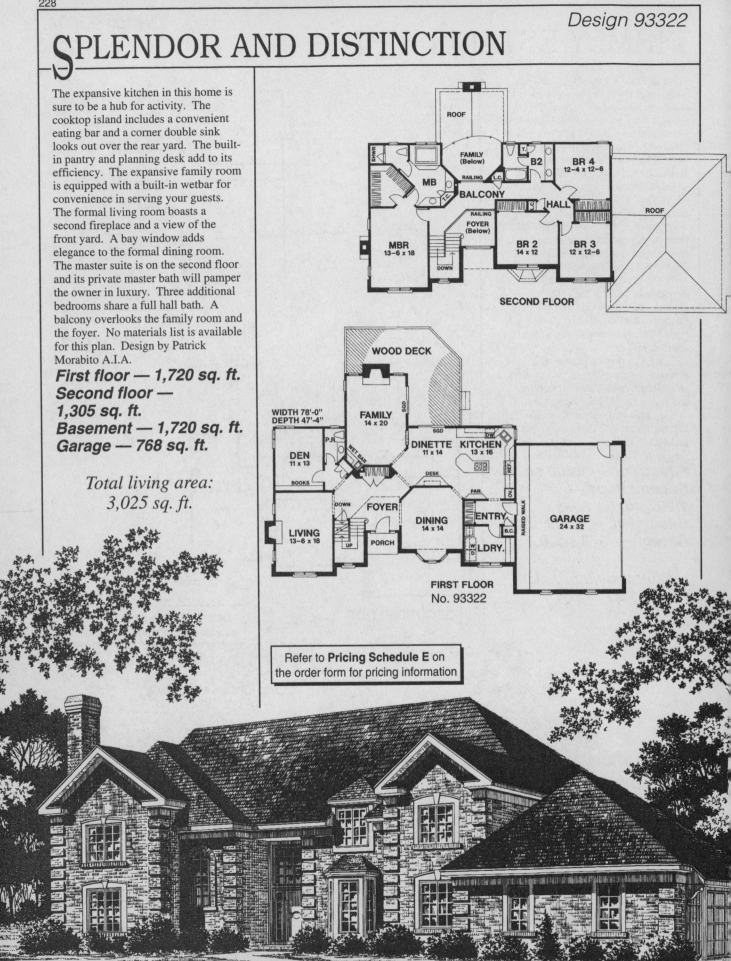

SECOND FLOOR

FIRST FLOOR
No. 93322

Refer to **Pricing Schedule E** on the order form for pricing information

Design 99804

COUNTRY COTTAGE

We hardly wasted an inch creating a spacious interior for this dormered and gabled country cottage that lives much bigger than it looks. The front bedroom, master bedroom, and open Great room/kitchen gain vertical space from cathedral ceilings while the open foyer pulls the dining room and Great room together visually. A wrap-around front porch, a breakfast bay window, and a skylit back porch add charm and expand living space. The master bath pampers the owner with a whirlpool tub, a separate shower and a double vanity. A bonus room adds flexibility to the plan. Design by Donald A. Gardner Architects, Inc.

Main floor —1,815 sq. ft.
Bonus room —
336 sq. ft.
Garage — 522 sq. ft.

Total living area:
1,815 sq. ft.

Refer to **Pricing Schedule D** on the order form for pricing information

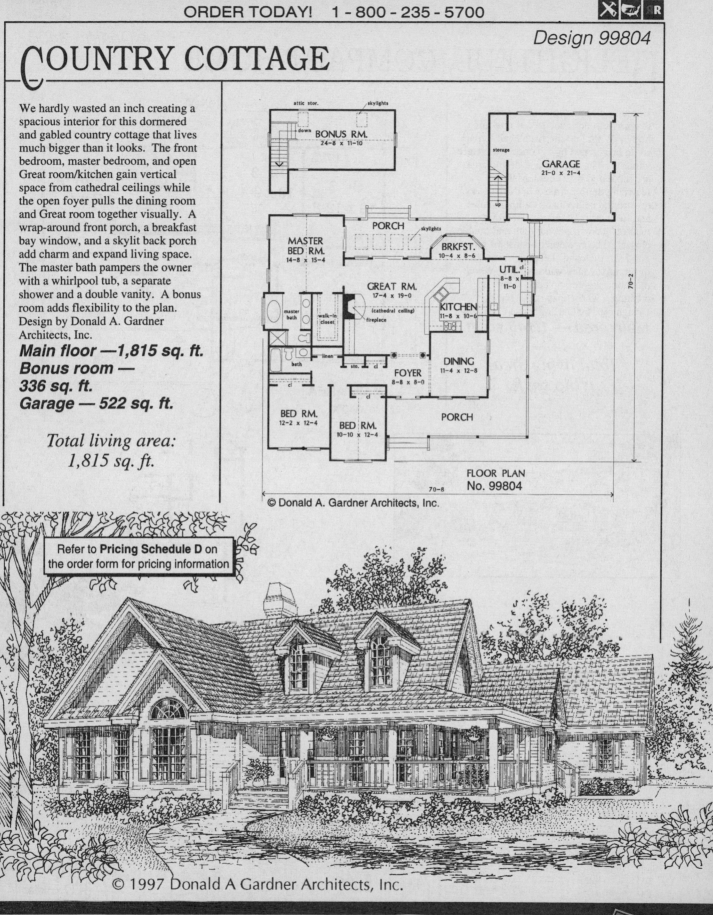

FLOOR PLAN
No. 99804

© Donald A. Gardner Architects, Inc.

© 1997 Donald A Gardner Architects, Inc.

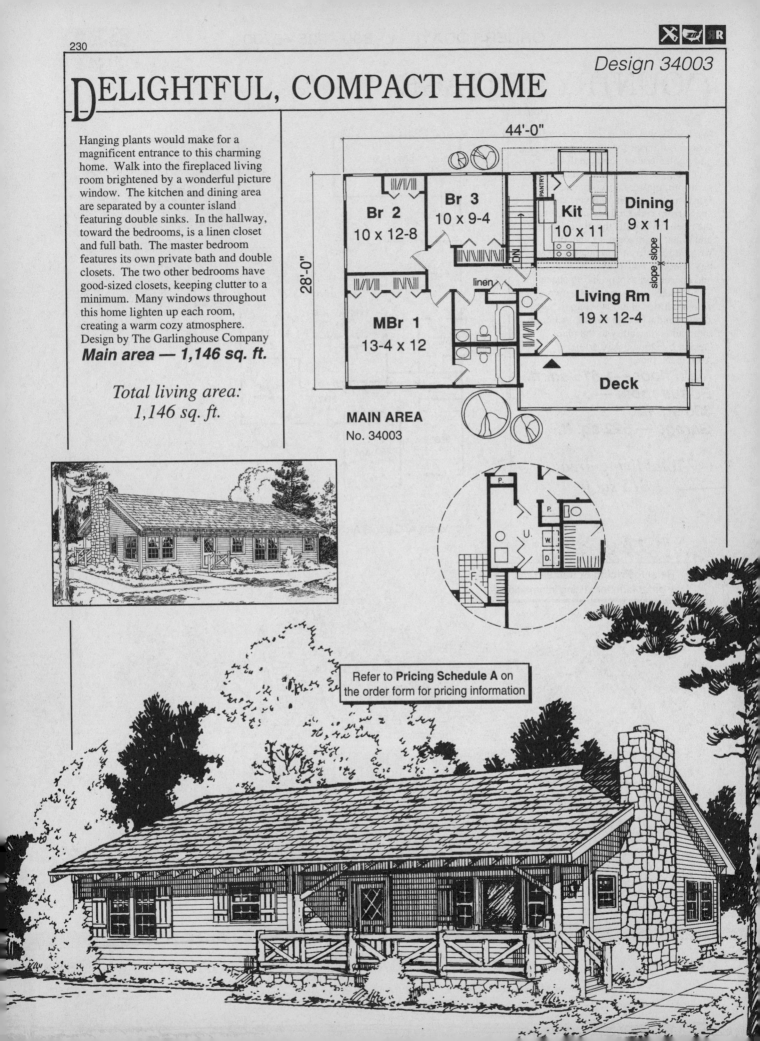

DELIGHTFUL, COMPACT HOME

Design 34003

Hanging plants would make for a magnificent entrance to this charming home. Walk into the fireplaced living room brightened by a wonderful picture window. The kitchen and dining area are separated by a counter island featuring double sinks. In the hallway, toward the bedrooms, is a linen closet and full bath. The master bedroom features its own private bath and double closets. The two other bedrooms have good-sized closets, keeping clutter to a minimum. Many windows throughout this home lighten up each room, creating a warm cozy atmosphere.
Design by The Garlinghouse Company

Main area — 1,146 sq. ft.

Total living area:
1,146 sq. ft.

44'-0"

28'-0"

Br 2
10 x 12-8

Br 3
10 x 9-4

Kit
10 x 11

Dining
9 x 11

PANTRY

DN

linen

MBr 1
13-4 x 12

slope slope

Living Rm
19 x 12-4

Deck

MAIN AREA

No. 34003

P.

P.

U.

W.

D.

F.

Refer to **Pricing Schedule A** on the order form for pricing information

GREAT ROOM ENHANCED BY FIREPLACE

An attractive presence in any neighborhood, this home boasts a volume entry. A formal dining room with bayed window and hutch space opens to the entry. A see-through fireplace serves both the hearth room and the expansive Great room. Further enhancing the Great room are the arched windows and French doors to the private den. Laid out in an open format, the kitchen, hearth room and bayed breakfast room includes an island counter, corner walk-in pantry, planning desk, wet bar and a cathedral ceiling over the breakfast area. A large master bedroom shows off the beautiful arched window arrangement and adjoins with a whirlpool bath. Three generous secondary bedrooms share a compartmented bath. Design by Design Basics, Inc.

First floor — 1,963 sq. ft.
Second floor — 778 sq. ft.
Basement — 1,963 sq. ft.
Garage — 658 sq. ft.

Total living area: 2,741 sq. ft.

Refer to **Pricing Schedule E** on the order form for pricing information

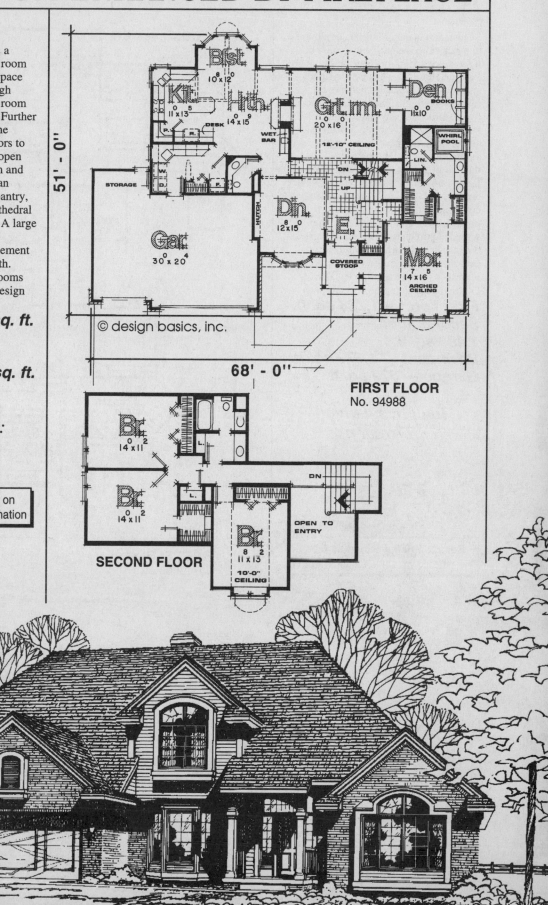

© design basics, inc.

FIRST FLOOR
No. 94988

SECOND FLOOR

Design 10686

A LIBRARY IN EVERY ROOM

Spectacular is one word you could use to describe the remarkable quality of light and space in this four-bedroom family home. Well-placed skylights and abundant windows bathe every room in sunlight. The huge, two-story foyer features an angular, open staircase that leads to the bedrooms, and divides the space between the vaulted living and dining rooms. At the rear of the house, the wide-open family area includes the kitchen, dinette, and fireplaced family room complete with built-in bar and bookcases. Vaulted ceilings in the screened porch are mirrored upstairs in the master suite, which features two walk-in closets, double vanities, and a luxurious jacuzzi. Design by The Garlinghouse Company

First floor — 1,786 sq. ft.
Second floor — 1,490 sq. ft.
Basement — 1,773 sq. ft.
Garage — 579 sq. ft.

Total living area:
3,276 sq. ft.

Refer to **Pricing Schedule F** on the order form for pricing information

SECOND FLOOR

- JACUZZI
- B.
- C.
- SHWR.
- CAB. ABV.
- LIN.
- C.
- DOWN
- BOOKS
- H.
- OPEN TO FOYER
- C.   BOOKS
- M. BEDROOM 18'-0"x17'-8" VAULTED CEILING
- B.
- BOOKS   BOOKS
- BEDROOM 4 11'-4"x15'-4"   C
- BEDROOM 3 11'-4"x12'-4"
- BEDROOM 2 11'-0"x14'-4"
- SCREENED PORCH VAULTED CEILING

FIRST FLOOR
No. 10686

- DINING RM. 14'-8"x14'-0"
- KITCHEN 12'-6"x14'-6"
- DINETTE 10'-6"x13'-0"
- FAMILY ROOM 18'-0" x 22'-0"
- BOOKS
- SKYLT.
- PANT.   PANT.
- DESK   BAR
- DN
- H.
- HIP VAULT CEILING
- BENCH
- SINK   W.   ST.
- B.   D.
- SKYLT.
- UP
- C.
- LAUNDRY/ SEWING 11'-2"x11'-2"
- CABINETS
- GARAGE 23'-8"x25'-7"
- VAULT   FOYER OPEN TO ABOVE
- LIVING RM. 14'-6"x16'-0"
- P.
- DEN/STUDY 11'-0"x12'-4"
- BOOKS
- DRIVEWAY
- 55'-6"
- 69'-0"

EASY FAMILY LIVING

Convenience in a design does not mean that you have to sacrifice style. This home has been designed for today's lifestyle. The Great room is open to the dining room, which is open to the kitchen. This large open living space is perfect for family interaction. The Great room has a two-story ceiling and is further enhanced by a fireplace. The peninsula counter in the efficient kitchen may serve as a breakfast bar for meals on the go. Upstairs are three bedrooms. The master suite includes a private master bath. The two additional bedrooms share the full hall bath. Design by Alan Mascord Design Associates

**First floor — 663 sq. ft.
Second floor —
740 sq. ft.**

*Total living area:
1,403 sq. ft.*

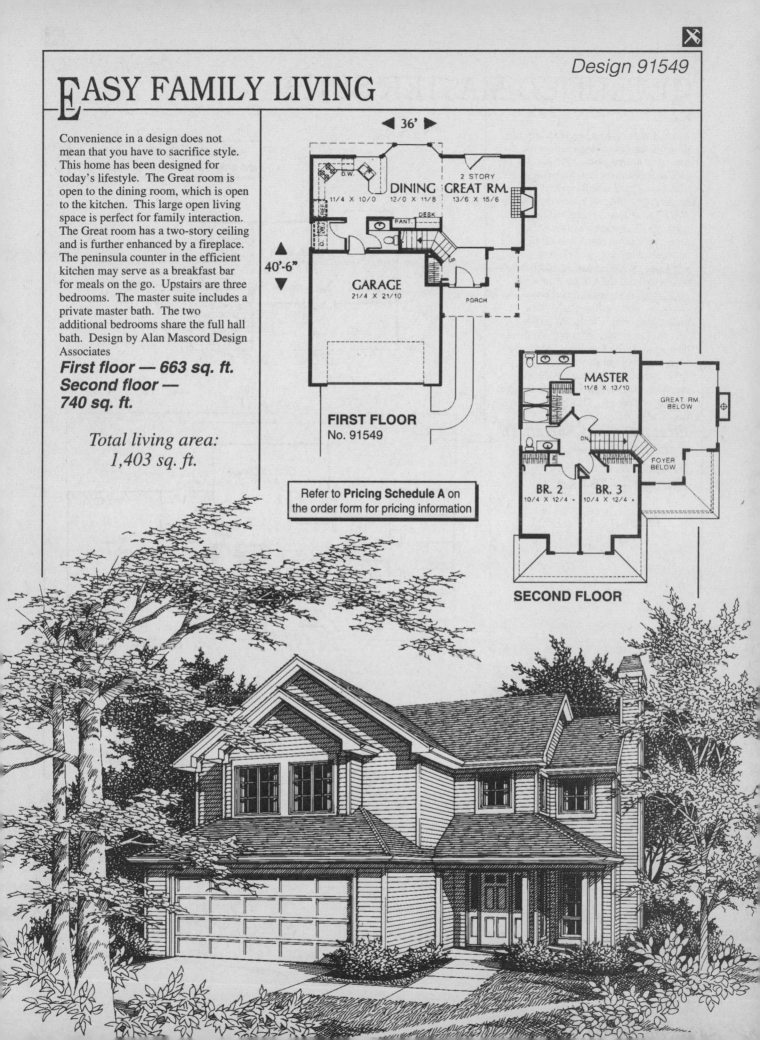

36'

40'-6"

D.W.

11/4 X 10/0   DINING   GREAT RM.
12/0 X 11/8   13/6 X 15/6

2 STORY

DESK

PANT.

UP

GARAGE
21/4 X 21/10

PORCH

FIRST FLOOR
No. 91549

MASTER
11/8 X 13/10

GREAT RM.
BELOW

DN.

BR. 2
10/4 X 12/4

BR. 3
10/4 X 12/4

FOYER
BELOW

SECOND FLOOR

Refer to **Pricing Schedule A** on the order form for pricing information

SECLUDED MASTER SUITE

Inside this plan, find bright quarry tile floors in the entryway, kitchen, family room and utility room. Outside, a tile roof shelters its owners for many years to come. Plants will flourish in the bright kitchen/family room, doubled in size by an attached prefabricated solarium. The entryway and living room are vaulted to the second floor and bathed in light by wide bay windows. With the simple addition of a door to the right, off the front entry deck, the bright, vaulted den could easily become a home office. The master bedroom is secluded on the second floor, away from two identical bedrooms on the first floor. Skylights bring natural light into the spa and water closet, and the huge walk-in closet provides ample room for storage as well as clothing. Design by Landmark Design, Inc.

First floor — 1,856 sq. ft.
Second floor —
618 sq. ft.
Garage — 704 sq. ft.

Total living area:
2,474 sq. ft.

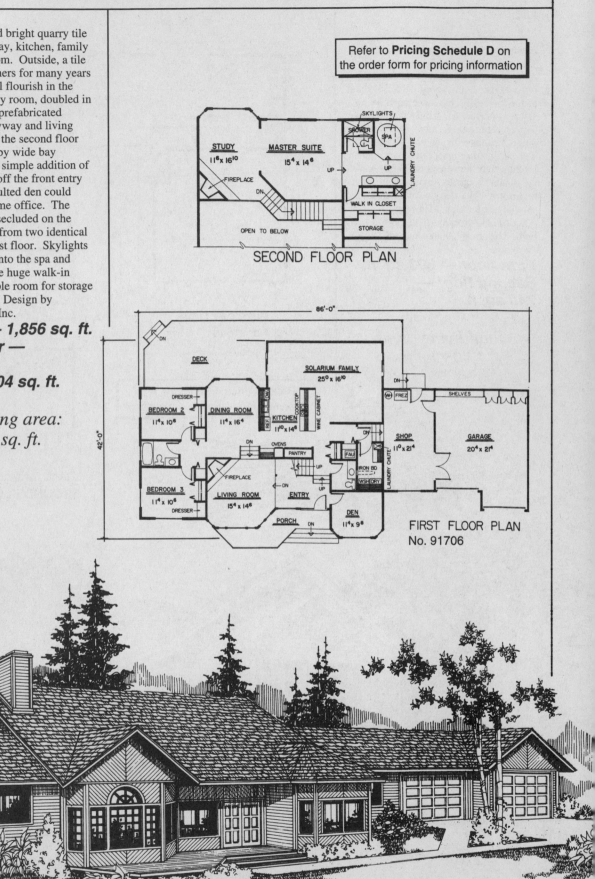

Refer to **Pricing Schedule D** on the order form for pricing information

SECOND FLOOR PLAN

FIRST FLOOR PLAN
No. 91706

Design 92053

STATELY TWO-STORY

This stately two-story home has the most desired features the home buyer is looking for in today's new construction. The exterior has a refined colonial styling with just enough brick to give it a rich look. Arched porch and a boxed out window complete the picture. As you enter the home you step into a roomy foyer that sets the tone for a warm, inviting and open plan. There is a dining room to the left that also has another doorway to the breakfast, kitchen and family room area that are on the rear of the house. This plan also features a first floor den and laundry room. The master suite has an enormous walk-in closet next to the luxurious bath with double sinks, separate tub and shower and enclosed toilet. The master suite also features a tray ceiling and a sitting area. Design by Urban Design Group

**First floor — 1,514 sq. ft.
Second floor —
1,386 sq. ft.
Basement — 1,514 sq. ft.**

*Total living area:
2,900 sq. ft.*

No. 92053

53'-4"

44'-4"

FAMILY ROOM
10'6" CEILING
21'x14'6"

DECK

KIT

DEN
11'6"x11'6"

BRK'FST
10'9"x15'6"

LAUNDRY

B4

DINING
11'x12'6"

GARAGE
21'8"x22'

ENTRY

LIVING
12'x16'5"

PORCH

MAIN FLOOR

Br4
11'6"x12'5"

B2

Br3
11'6"x12'10"

B1

MBR
TRAY CEILING
17'6"x15'6"

B3

Br2
12'x11'

SITTING

SECOND FLOOR

Refer to **Pricing Schedule E** on the order form for pricing information

Weather Shield
Windows & Doors

www.weathershield.com

Weather Shield Windows and Doors offers project planning guides for your remodeling or new home project. FREE. Specify "Remodeling" or "New Home" Planning Guide by calling

1-800-477-6808

WEATHER SHIELD
WINDOWS & DOORS
MEDFORD, WI
®

COMPACT CONTEMPORARY

Here's a beautiful little dream house with your budget in mind. With soaring ceilings and dramatic window treatments, you'll enjoy solar savings and delightful views from all the main living areas and sleeping loft. The main floor location of the bedroom and full bath makes one floor living simple. But with a half-bath, sleeping room and loft upstairs, there's room for more. Design by Living Designs

Main level — 808 sq. ft.
Upper level — 288 sq. ft.

Total living area:
1,096 sq. ft.

Refer to **Pricing Schedule A** on the order form for pricing information

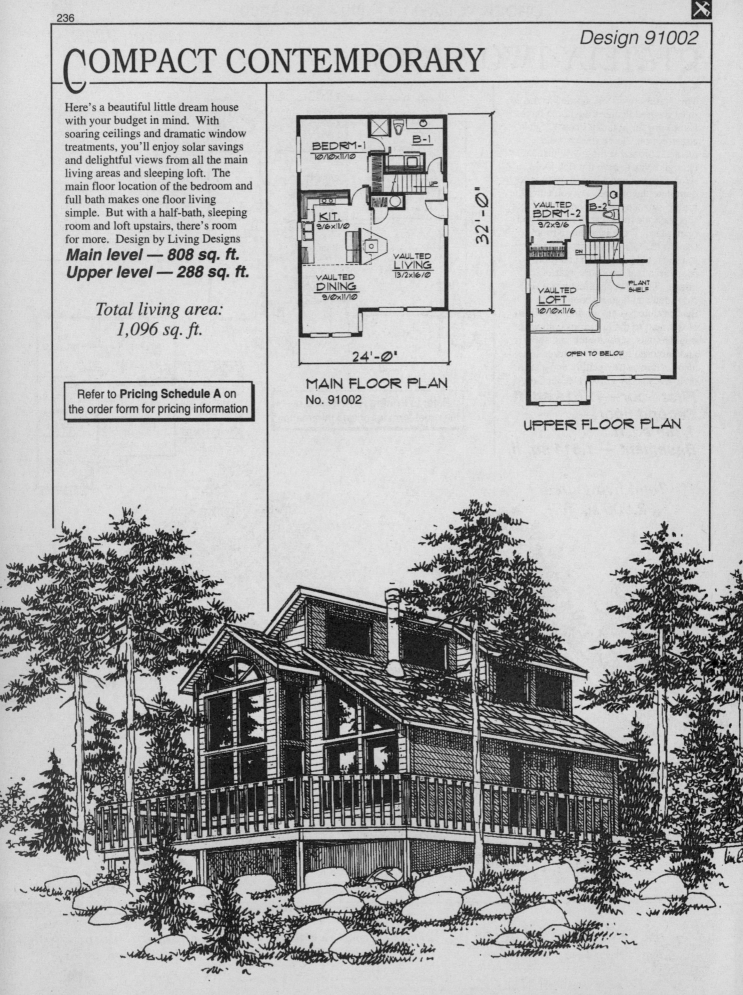

BEDRM-1
10/10x11/10

B-1

KIT.
9/6x11/0

VAULTED LIVING
13/2x16/0

VAULTED DINING
9/0x11/10

32'-0"

24'-0"

MAIN FLOOR PLAN
No. 91002

VAULTED BDRM-2
9/2x9/6

B-2

VAULTED LOFT
10/10x11/6

PLANT SHELF

OPEN TO BELOW

UPPER FLOOR PLAN

DETAILED ELEVATION

Design 98447

This lovely elevation is highlighted by stucco, stone and detailing around the arched windows. Vaulted ceilings elegantly top the Great room, breakfast room and keeping room. A fireplace further enhances the Great room. A second fireplace in the keeping room gives a cozy atmosphere to the living space. The efficient kitchen is separated from the breakfast room and keeping room only by counter space creating the feeling of spaciousness. The first floor master suite is crowned in a tray ceiling and pampered by a lavish master bath and huge walk-in closet. This plan is available with a basement or crawl space foundation. Please specify when ordering. Design by Frank Betz Associates, Inc.

First floor — 1,628 sq. ft.
Second floor —
527 sq. ft.
Bonus — 207 sq. ft.
Basement — 1,628 sq. ft.
Garage — 440 sq. ft.

Total living area:
2,155 sq. ft.

© Frank Betz Associates

FIRST FLOOR PLAN
No. 98447

54'-0"

46'-10"

Master Suite 13⁰ x 17³
Tray Ceiling
Vaulted M.Bath
Radius Window
Linen
Plant Shelf Above
Pwdr.
W.i.c.
Two Story Foyer
French Door
Closet
Vaulted Great Room 16⁰ x 18⁵
Open Rail
Stairs Dn.
Open Rail
Dining Room 11⁰ x 12³
Covered Porch
Vaulted Breakfast
Serving Bar
D.W.
Range
Kitchen
Ref.
Pantry
W.
Vaulted Keeping Room 12⁶ x 15⁰
Plant Shelf Above
Laund.
Garage 19⁵ x 21⁹

SECOND FLOOR PLAN

Breakfast Below
Keeping Room Below
Vault
Great Room Below
Bath
Linen
W.i.c.
Plant Shelf
Vault
Open Rail
Stairs Dn.
Foyer Below
Plant Shelf Below
Bedroom 2 11⁰ x 12³
Linen
W.i.c.
W.i.c.
Bedroom 3 12⁰ x 12⁸
Opt. Bonus Room 11⁵ x 15⁹

Refer to **Pricing Schedule C** on the order form for pricing information

Design 99456

STUCCO ACCENTS

Stucco accents and graceful window treatments enhance the front of this home. The double doors open to the private den with brilliant bayed windows. The French doors open to a large screened-in veranda ideal for outdoor entertaining. The open living room and handsome curved staircase add drama to the entry area. The gourmet kitchen, spacious bayed dinette and voluminous family room flow together for easy living. The elegant bayed master bedroom with a ten foot vaulted ceiling is situated to the back of the home for privacy. Two walk-in closets, his-n-her vanity, corner whirlpool and compartment shower highlight the master dressing area. This plan is available with a basement or slab foundation. Please specify when ordering. Design by Design Basics, Inc.

First floor — 1,631 sq. ft.
Second floor — 1,426 sq. ft.
Basement — 1,631 sq. ft.
Garage — 681 sq. ft.

Total living area:
3,057 sq. ft.

FIRST FLOOR
No. 99456

Refer to **Pricing Schedule E** on the order form for pricing information

SECOND FLOOR

RELAXING RETREAT

Take a vacation from the everyday stresses you endure in a home that takes your cares away. All the living area of this home is on one floor. The fireplaced living room is a nice size and flows easily into the dining and kitchen areas. These open areas create a feeling spaciousness. The wrap-around deck in the front of the home has a built in barbeque for easy outdoor cooking. The glass, double door entry with floor-to-ceiling glass on either side lets you enjoy the outdoors from inside while allowing lots of natural light to flow in. The bedrooms are a nice size and have ample closet space. Storage space could also include the loft area. This home could easily be turned into a retirement residence. Design by The Garlinghouse Company

Main area — 789 sq. ft.
Loft — 108 sq. ft.

Total living area:
897 sq. ft.

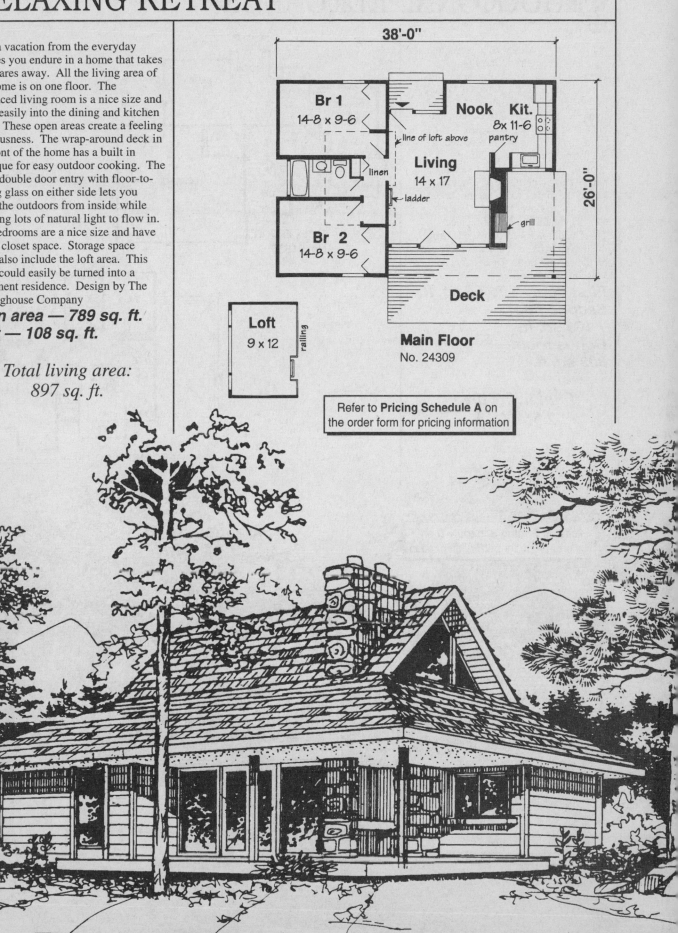

38'-0"

26'-0"

Br 1
14-8 x 9-6

Nook **Kit.**
8x 11-6
pantry

line of loft above

linen

Living
14 x 17

ladder

grill

Br 2
14-8 x 9-6

Deck

Loft
9 x 12
railing

Main Floor
No. 24309

Refer to **Pricing Schedule A** on the order form for pricing information

Design 91535

TRADITIONAL ELEGANCE

A lovely foyer area with an attractive staircase greets the visitor upon entering this home. A private den area with a double door entrance is located to the right of the entrance. A formal living room is located to the left, and enhanced by a fireplace and a decorative ceiling that is repeated in the formal dining room. A large cooktop island kitchen, with a built-in pantry and planning desk, efficiently serves the dining room and nook. A family room flows from the kitchen area and features a cozy fireplace. Three additional bedrooms, one being the master suite, and a bonus room are on the second floor. Design by Alan Mascord & Associates

First floor — 1,465 sq. ft.
Second floor — 1,103 sq. ft.
Bonus room — 303 sq. ft.

Total living area: 2,568 sq. ft.

Refer to **Pricing Schedule D** on the order form for pricing information

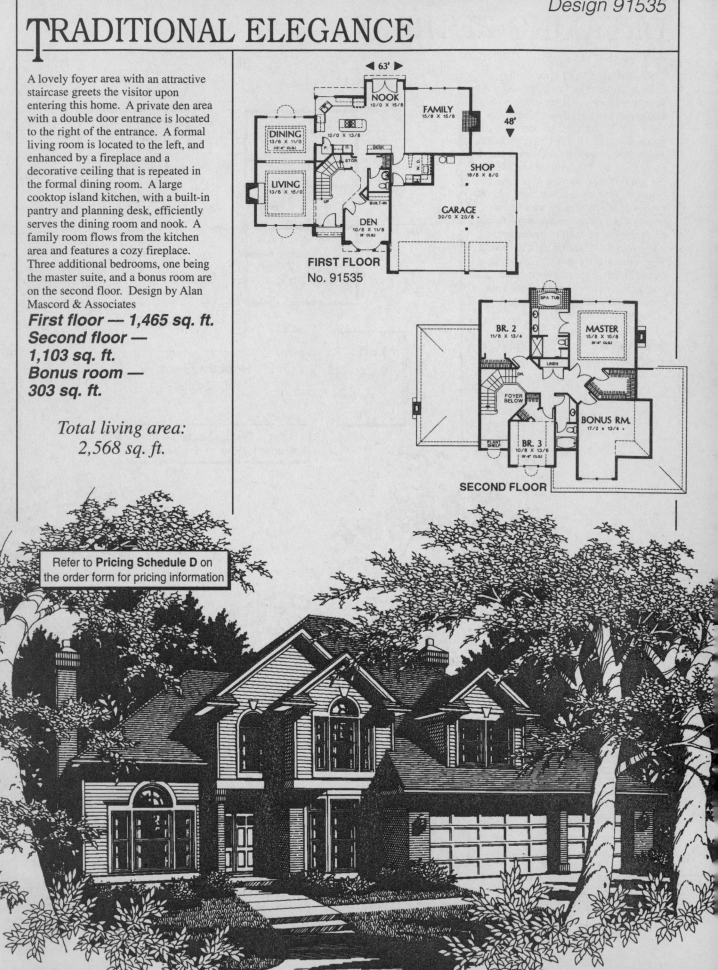

FIRST FLOOR
No. 91535

SECOND FLOOR

SKYLIGHTS BRIGHTEN TUDOR

Design 10673

Step from the arched fieldstone porch into the two-story foyer, and you can see that this traditional four bedroom home possesses a wealth of modern elements. Behind double doors lie the library and fireplaced living room, bathed in sunlight from two skylights in the sloping roof. Step out to the brick patio from the laundry room or bay-windowed breakfast room. The master bedroom suite contains a whirlpool tub. One bedroom boasts bay windows; another features a huge walk-in closet over the two car garage. Design by The Garlinghouse Company

First floor — 1,265 sq. ft.
Second floor — 1,210 sq. ft.
Basement — 1,247 sq. ft.
Garage — 506 sq. ft.

Total living area: 2,475 sq. ft.

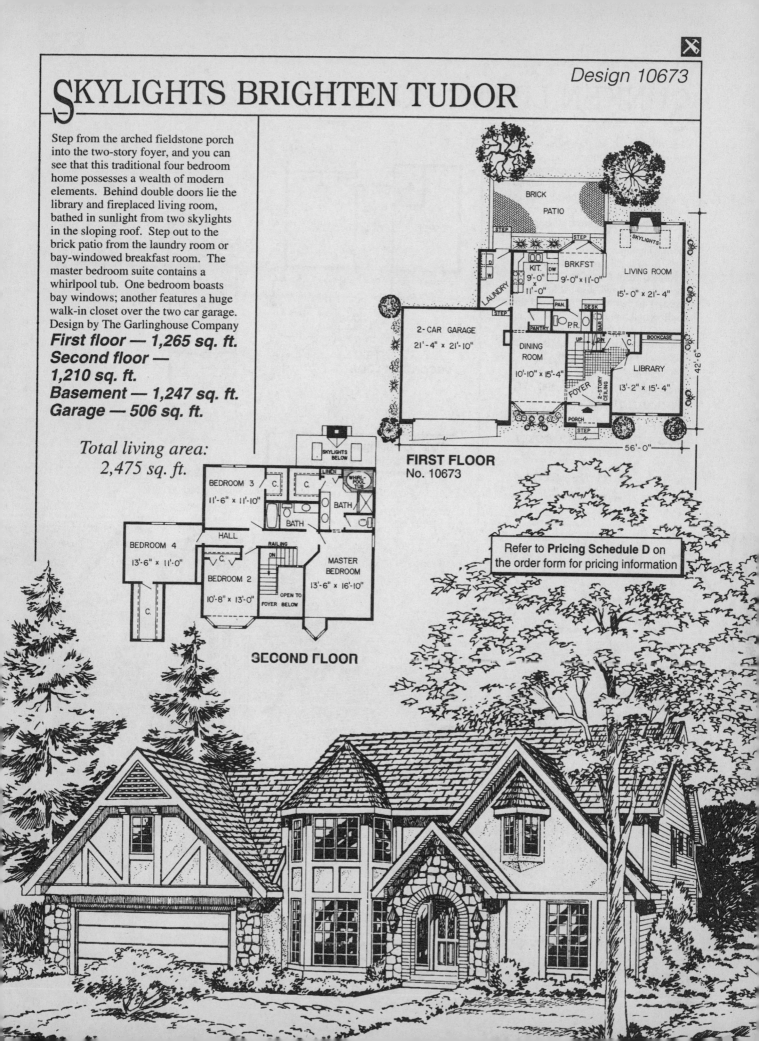

FIRST FLOOR
No. 10673

Refer to **Pricing Schedule D** on the order form for pricing information

SECOND FLOOR

Design 26112

SUNKEN LIVING ROOM FEATURED

Generous use of southern glass doors and windows, an air lock entry, skylights and a living room fireplace reduce energy needs. R-26 insulation is used for floors and sloping ceilings. Decking rims the front of the home and gives access through sliding glass doors to a bedroom-den area and living room. The dining room lies up several steps from the living room and is separated from it by a half wall. The dining room flows into the kitchen through an eating bar. A second floor landing balcony overlooks the living room. Two bedrooms, one with its own private deck, and a full bath finish the second floor. Design by The Garlinghouse Company

First floor — 911 sq. ft.
**Second floor —
576 sq. ft.**
Basement — 911 sq. ft.

*Total living area:
1,487 sq. ft.*

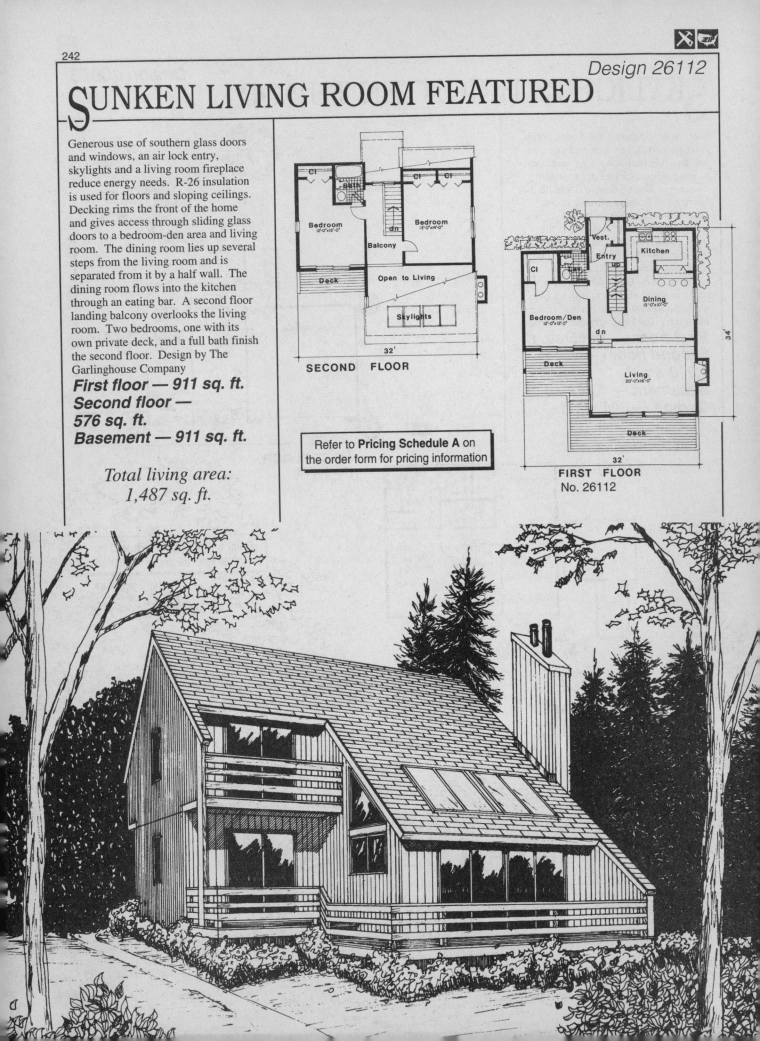

SECOND FLOOR

Cl · Bath · Bedroom 12'-0"x12'-0" · Deck · Balcony · Cl · Cl · Bedroom 13'-0"x14'-0" · dn · Open to Living · Skylights · 32'

Refer to **Pricing Schedule A** on the order form for pricing information

FIRST FLOOR
No. 26112

Vest. · Entry · Kitchen · Cl · Lav. · up · Dining 13'-0"x10'-0" · Bedroom/Den 12'-0"x12'-0" · dn · Deck · Living 20'-0"x16'-0" · Deck · 32' · 34'

IMPRESSIVE OPEN FOYER

Design 94622

Creating a terrific first impression, the foyer of this home is open to the second floor. The formal areas are located to either side of the foyer. Casual, informal living is comfortably accommodated for in the large Great room. A fireplace enhances this spacious room. The kitchen will please the gourmet of the family. A cook top island, ample storage and work space have been provided. The breakfast room adjoins the kitchen. The expansive master suite includes a private sitting room and a master bath. This plan is available with a crawl space or slab foundation. Please specify when ordering. No materials list is available for this plan. Design by Chatham Home Planning, Inc.

First floor — 2,033 sq. ft.
Second floor — 1,116 sq. ft.

Total living area: 3,149 sq. ft.

WIDTH 66'-0"
DEPTH 56'-0"

FIRST FLOOR
No. 94622

SECOND FLOOR

Refer to **Pricing Schedule E** on the order form for pricing information

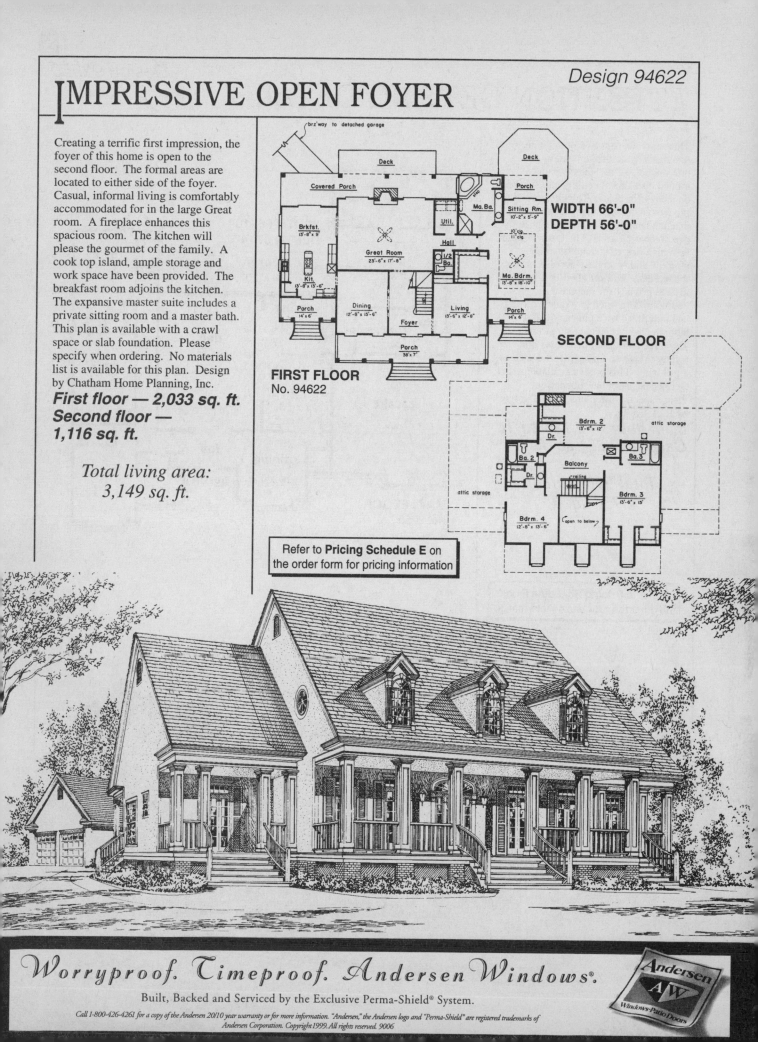

Design 92550

ATTENTION GETTING DETAIL

This spacious four bedroom home features a formal foyer leading directly into the den. The den is expansive, topped by a raised ceiling, and focuses on a cozy fireplace. The kitchen has a modern floor plan, using an angled extended counter, and flows into the den and eating area. The formal dining area includes an elegant boxed bay window and is directly accessed from the kitchen. The split bedroom plan insures privacy for the master bedroom. Crowned in a raised ceiling and pampered by a plush, whirlpool bath, the master suite is sure to please. The three additional bedrooms are roomy in size and have direct access to a full bath. This plan is available with a crawlspace or slab foundation. Please specify when ordering. Design by Rick Garner

Main floor — 2,735 sq. ft.
Garage — 561 sq. ft.

Total living area:
2,735 sq. ft.

Refer to **Pricing Schedule F** on the order form for pricing information

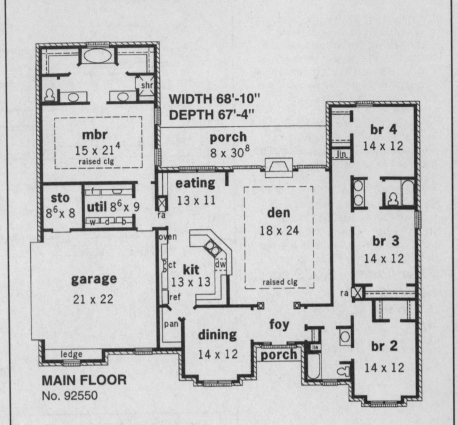

WIDTH 68'-10"
DEPTH 67'-4"

mbr
15 x 21⁴
raised clg

porch
8 x 30⁸

br 4
14 x 12

eating
13 x 11

den
18 x 24
raised clg

br 3
14 x 12

sto
8⁶ x 8

util 8⁶ x 9

garage
21 x 22

kit
13 x 13

dining
14 x 12

foy

br 2
14 x 12

porch

ledge

MAIN FLOOR
No. 92550

Design 34043

A HOME FOR TODAY AND TOMORROW

This convenient, one-level plan is perfect for the modern family with a taste for classic design. Traditional Victorian touches in this three-bedroom beauty include a romantic, railed porch and an intriguing breakfast tower just off the kitchen. But, the step-saving arrangement of the kitchen between the breakfast and formal dining rooms, the wide-open living room with sliders to a rear deck, and the handsome master suite with its skylit, compartmentalized bath make this a home you'll love today and long into the future. Notice the convenient laundry location on the bedroom hall. Design by The Garlinghouse Company

Main area — 1,583 sq. ft.
Basement — 1,573 sq. ft.
Garage — 484 sq. ft.

Total living area:
1,583 sq. ft.

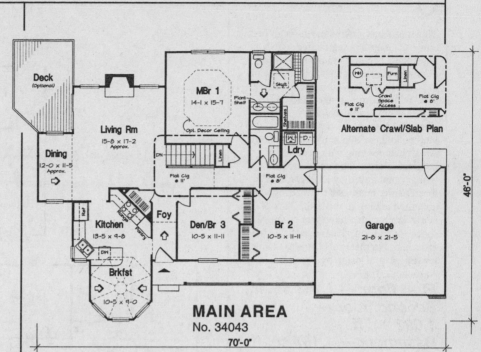

MAIN AREA
No. 34043
70'-0"

Refer to **Pricing Schedule B** on the order form for pricing information

Design 97215

STUNNING ENTRY

This home has a two-story high arched entry. The arch is segmented with a keystone. The large glass above the door and the sidelights to either side of the door naturally illuminate the foyer. The living room is sunken and the dining room is showcased by a step up. The breakfast room is open to the kitchen and the two-story family room. An arched opening with decorative columns defines the family room which is enhanced by a fireplace. The master suite features a tray ceiling with a vaulted ceiling in the bath. This plan is available with a basement or crawl space foundation. Please specify when ordering. No materials list is available for this plan. Design by Frank Betz Associates, Inc.

First floor — 1,167 sq. ft.
Second floor —
1,092 sq. ft.
Basement — 1,167 sq. ft.
Garage — 428 sq. ft.

Total living area:
2,259 sq. ft.

© Frank Betz Associates

47'-4"

39'-0"

FIRST FLOOR PLAN

Laund.
LAUNDRY SINK
RANGE
DW.
ISLAND
Breakfast
FRENCH DOOR
DECORATIVE COLUMNS
Two Story Family Room
18⁰ x 15⁰
Kitchen
DESK
PANTRY
REF.
ARCHED OPENING
ARCHED OPENING
Dining Room
12⁵ x 11⁰
STAIRS DN.
STEP DN.
Pwdr.
Garage
19⁵ x 21²
Living Room
12⁵ x 11²
Two Story Foyer
STEP DN.
COATS

SECOND FLOOR PLAN
No. 97215

TRAY CEILING
Master Suite
13⁷ x 17⁰
Bedroom 4
10⁴ x 11⁸
RADIUS WINDOW
Family Room Below
LIN.
OPEN RAIL
OPEN RAIL
STAIRS DN.
OVERLOOK
Bath
Vaulted M.Bath
SHWR.
Foyer Below
Bedroom 3
11² x 13⁰
Bedroom 2
11⁰ x 10⁶
PLANT SHELF ABOVE
LINEN
W.i.c.
9'-0" HIGH CLG.

Design 99058

OLD SOUTHERN STYLE

Both styling and space characterized the old Southern home. Here, the balanced design of an imposing facade, with hip roof and twin chimneys, is extended by an appendage in the traditional manner, in this case, a garage with a porch atop. Details of the exterior are also traditional; a semicircular colonnade dominates the entrance, and shutters and double hung windows provide the finishing touches. The large living and dining rooms flank the central foyer, and both have fireplaces, with the dining room chimney furnishing a grill for the kitchen and the living room chimney housing a barbecue for the porch. The family room is convenient for informal dining or supervision of children. On the second floor, the two larger bedrooms have doors to the deck over the garage. Design by National Home Planning Service

**First floor — 1,202 sq. ft.
Second floor —
1,351 sq. ft.
Basement — 1,202 sq. ft.**

*Total living area:
2,553 sq. ft.*

Refer to **Pricing Schedule D** on the order form for pricing information

second floor plan

first floor plan
No. 99058

Everything You Need...
...to Make Your Dream Come True!

❧

You pay only a fraction of the original cost for home designs by respected professionals.

❧

You've Picked Your Dream Home!

You can already see it standing on your lot... you can see yourselves in your new home... enjoying family, entertaining guests, celebrating holidays. All that remains ahead are the details. That's where we can help. Whether you plan to build-it-yourself, be your own contractor, or hand your plans over to an outside contractor, your Garlinghouse blueprints provide the perfect beginning for putting yourself in your dream home right away.

We even make it simple for you to make professional design modifications. We can also provide a materials list for greater economy.

For over 90 years, homeowners and builders have relied on us for accurate, complete, professional blueprints. Our plans help you get results fast... and save money, too! These pages will give you all the information you need to order. So get started now... I know you'll love your new Garlinghouse home!

EXTERIOR ELEVATIONS

Elevations are scaled drawings of the front, rear, left and right sides of a home. All of the necessary information pertaining to the exterior finish materials, roof pitches and exterior height dimensions of your home are defined.

CABINET PLANS

These plans, or in some cases elevations, will detail the layout of the kitchen and bathroom cabinets at a larger scale. This gives you an accurate layout for your cabinets or an ideal starting point for a modified custom cabinet design. Available for most plans. You may also show the floor plan without a cabinet layout. This will allow you to start from scratch and design your own dream kitchen.

TYPICAL WALL SECTION

This section is provided to help your builder understand the structural components and materials used to construct the exterior walls of your home. This section will address insulation, roof components, and interior and exterior wall finishes. Your plans will be designed with either 2x4 or 2x6 exterior walls, but most professional contractors can easily adapt the plans to the wall thickness you require.

FIREPLACE DETAILS

If the home you have chosen includes a fireplace, the fireplace detail will show typical methods to construct the firebox, hearth and flue chase for masonry units, or a wood frame chase for a zero-clearance unit. Available for most plans.

FOUNDATION PLAN

These plans will accurately dimension the footprint of your home including load bearing points and beam placement if applicable. The foundation style will vary from plan to plan. Your local climactic conditions will dictate whether a basement, slab or crawlspace is best suited for your area. In most cases, if your plan comes with one foundation style, a professional contractor can easily adapt the foundation plan to an alternate style.

ROOF PLAN

The information necessary to construct the roof will be included with your home plans. Some plans will reference roof trusses, while many others contain schematic framing plans. These framing plans will indicate the lumber sizes necessary for the rafters and ridgeboards based on the designated roof loads.

TYPICAL CROSS SECTION

A cut-away cross-section through the entire home shows your building contractor the exact correlation of construction components at all levels of the house. It will help to clarify the load bearing points from the roof all the way down to the basement. Available for most plans.

DETAILED FLOOR PLANS

The floor plans of your home accurately dimension the positioning of all walls, doors, windows, stairs and permanent fixtures. They will show you the relationship and dimensions of rooms, closets and traffic patterns. The schematic of the electrical layout may be included in the plan. This layout is clearly represented and does not hinder the clarity of other pertinent information shown. All these details will help your builder properly construct your new home.

STAIR DETAILS

If stairs are an element of the design you have chosen, the plans will show the necessary information to build these, either through a stair cross section, or on the floor plans. Either way, the information provides your builders the essential reference points that they need to build the stairs.

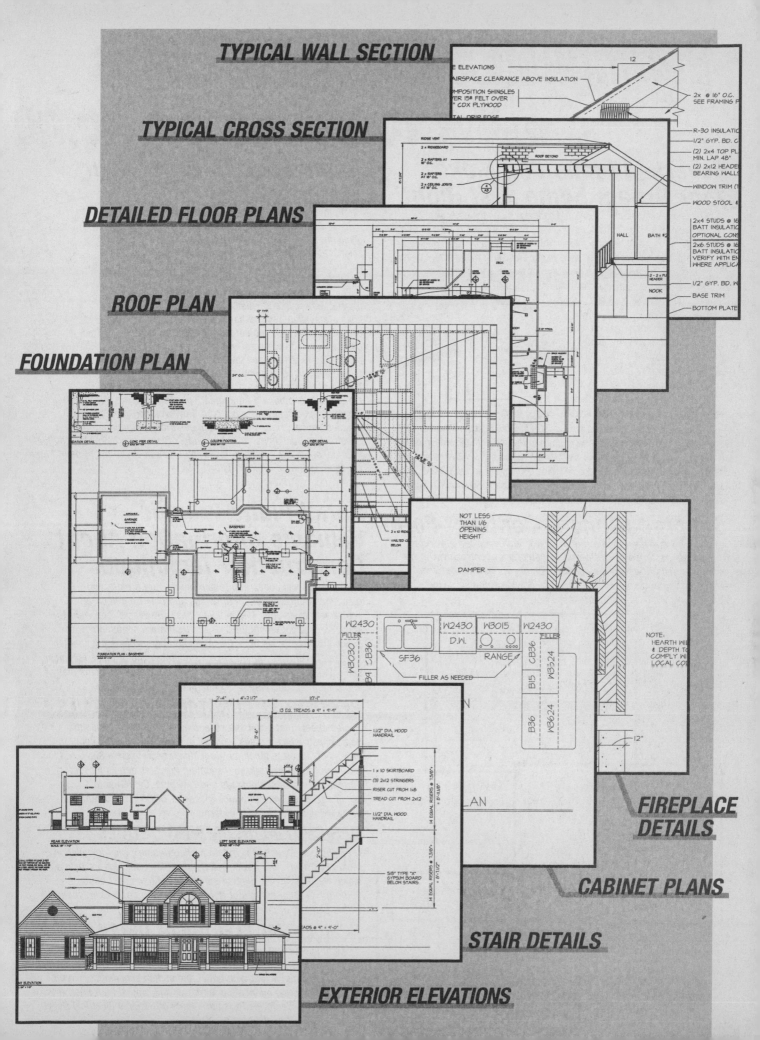

TYPICAL WALL SECTION

TYPICAL CROSS SECTION

DETAILED FLOOR PLANS

ROOF PLAN

FOUNDATION PLAN

FIREPLACE DETAILS

CABINET PLANS

STAIR DETAILS

EXTERIOR ELEVATIONS

Garlinghouse Options & Extras ...Make Your Dream A Home

Reversed Plans Can Make Your Dream Home Just Right!

"That's our dream home...if only the garage were on the other side!"

You could have exactly the home you want by flipping it end-for-end. Check it out by holding your dream home page of this book up to a mirror. Then simply order your plans "reversed." We'll send you one full set of mirror-image plans (with the writing backwards) as a master guide for you and your builder.

The remaining sets of your order will come as shown in this book so the dimensions and specifications are easily read on the job site...but most plans in our collection come stamped "REVERSED" so there is no construction confusion.

We can only send reversed plans with multiple-set orders. There is a $50 charge for this service.

As Shown   Reversed

Some plans in our collection are available in Right Reading Reverse. Right Reading Reverse plans will show your home in reverse, with the writing on the plan being readable. This easy-to-read format will save you valuable time and money. Please contact our Customer Service Department at (860) 343-5977 to check for Right Reading Reverse availability. There is a $150 charge for plan series 998, 964, & 980. $125 for all other plans.

Specifications & Contract Form

We send this form to you free of charge with your home plan order. The form is designed to be filled in by you or your contractor with the exact materials to use in the construction of your new home. Once signed by you and your contractor it will provide you with peace of mind throughout the construction process.

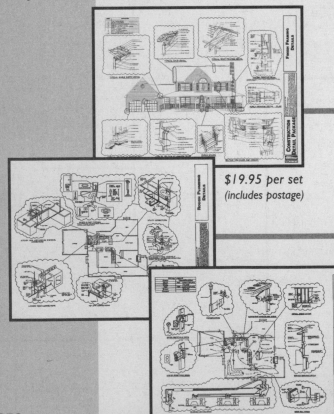

$19.95 per set
(includes postage)

Remember To Order Your Materials List

It'll help you save money. Available at a modest additional charge, the Materials List gives the quantity, dimensions, and specifications for the major materials needed to build your home. You will get faster, more accurate bids from your contractors and building suppliers — and avoid paying for unused materials and waste. Materials Lists are available for all home plans except as otherwise indicated, but can only be ordered with a set of home plans. Due to differences in regional requirements and homeowner or builder preferences... electrical, plumbing and heating/air conditioning equipment specifications are not designed specifically for each plan. However, non-plan specific detailed typical prints of residential electrical, plumbing and construction guidelines can be provided. Please see below for additional information. If you need a detailed materials cost you might need to purchase a Zip Quote. (Details follow)

Detail Plans Provide Valuable Information About Construction Techniques

Because local codes and requirements vary greatly, we recommend that you obtain drawings and bids from licensed contractors to do your mechanical plans. However, if you want to know more about techniques — and deal more confidently with subcontractors — we offer these remarkably useful detail sheets. These detail sheets will aid in your understanding of these technical subjects. The detail sheets are not specific to any one home plan and should be used only as a general reference guide.

RESIDENTIAL CONSTRUCTION DETAILS

Ten sheets that cover the essentials of stick-built residential home construction. Details foundation options — poured concrete basement, concrete block, or monolithic concrete slab. Shows all aspects of floor, wall and roof framing. Provides details for roof dormers, overhangs, chimneys and skylights. Conforms to requirements of Uniform Building code or BOCA code. Includes a quick index and a glossary of terms.

RESIDENTIAL PLUMBING DETAILS

Eight sheets packed with information detailing pipe installation methods, fittings, and sized. Details plumbing hook-ups for toilets, sinks, washers, sump pumps, and septic system construction. Conforms to requirements of National Plumbing code. Color coded with a glossary of terms and quick index.

RESIDENTIAL ELECTRICAL DETAILS

Eight sheets that cover all aspects of residential wiring, from simple switch wiring to service entrance connections. Details distribution panel layout with outlet and switch schematics, circuit breaker and wiring installation methods, and ground fault interrupter specifications. Conforms to requirements of National Electrical Code. Color coded with a glossary of terms.

Modifying Your Favorite Design, Made EASY!

OPTION #1

Modifying Your Garlinghouse Home Plan

Simple modifications to your dream home, including minor non-structural changes and material substitutions, can be made between you and your builder by marking the changes directly on your blueprints. However, if you are considering making significant changes to your chosen design, we recommend that you use the services of The Garlinghouse Co. Design Staff. We will help take your ideas and turn them into a reality, just the way you want. Here's our procedure!

When you place your Vellum order, you may also request a free Garlinghouse Modification Kit. In this kit, you will receive a red marking pencil, furniture cut-out sheet, ruler, a self addressed mailing label and a form for specifying any additional notes or drawings that will help us understand your design ideas. Mark your desired changes directly on the Vellum drawings. NOTE: Please use only a **red pencil** to mark your desired changes on the Vellum. Then, return the redlined Vellum set in the original box to The Garlinghouse Company at, 282 Main Street Extension, Middletown, CT 06457. **IMPORTANT:** Please **roll** the Vellums for shipping, **do not fold** the Vellums for shipping.

We also offer modification estimates. We will provide you with an estimate to draft your changes based on your specific modifications before you purchase the vellums, for a $50 fee. After you receive your estimate, if you decide to have The Garlinghouse Company Design Staff do the changes, the $50 estimate fee will be deducted from the cost of your modifications. If, however, you choose to use a different service, the $50 estimate fee is non-refundable. (Note: Personal checks cannot be accepted for the estimate.)

Within 5 days of receipt of your plans, you will be contacted by a member of The Garlinghouse Co. Design Staff with an estimate for the design services to draw those changes. A 50% deposit is required before we begin making the actual modifications to your plans.

Once the design changes have been completed to your vellum plan, a representative from The Garlinghouse Co. Design Staff will call to inform you that your modified Vellum plan is complete and will be shipped as soon as the final payment has been made. For additional information call us at 1-860-343-5977. Please refer to the Modification Pricing Guide for estimated modification costs. Please call for Vellum modification availability for plan numbers 85,000 and above.

OPTION #2

Reproducible Vellums for Local Modification Ease

If you decide not to use The Garlinghouse Co. Design Staff for your modifications, we recommend that you follow our same procedure of purchasing our Vellums. You then have the option of using the services of the original designer of the plan, a local professional designer, or architect to make the modifications to your plan.

With a Vellum copy of our plans, a design professional can alter the drawings just the way you want, then you can print as many copies of the modified plans as you need to build your house. And, since you have already started with our complete detailed plans, the cost of those expensive professional services will be significantly less than starting from scratch. Refer to the price schedule for Vellum costs. Again, please call for Vellum availability for plan numbers 85,000 and above.

IMPORTANT RETURN POLICY: Upon receipt of your Vellums, if for some reason you decide you do not want a modified plan, then simply return the Kit and the unopened Vellums. Reproducible Vellum copies of our home plans are copyright protected and only sold under the terms of a license agreement that you will receive with your order. Should you not agree to the terms, then the Vellums may be returned, **unopened,** for a full refund less the shipping and handling charges, plus a 15% restocking fee. For any additional information, please call us at 1-860-343-5977.

MODIFICATION PRICING GUIDE

CATEGORIES	ESTIMATED COST
KITCHEN LAYOUT — PLAN AND ELEVATION	$175.00
BATHROOM LAYOUT — PLAN AND ELEVATION	$175.00
FIREPLACE PLAN AND DETAILS	$200.00
INTERIOR ELEVATION	$125.00
EXTERIOR ELEVATION — MATERIAL CHANGE	$140.00
EXTERIOR ELEVATION — ADD BRICK OR STONE	$400.00
EXTERIOR ELEVATION — STYLE CHANGE	$450.00
NON BEARING WALLS (INTERIOR)	$200.00
BEARING AND/OR EXTERIOR WALLS	$325.00
WALL FRAMING CHANGE — 2X4 TO 2X6 OR 2X6 TO 2X4	$240.00
ADD/REDUCE LIVING SPACE — SQUARE FOOTAGE	QUOTE REQUIRED
NEW MATERIALS LIST	QUOTE REQUIRED
CHANGE TRUSSES TO RAFTERS OR CHANGE ROOF PITCH	$300.00
FRAMING PLAN CHANGES	$325.00
GARAGE CHANGES	$325.00
ADD A FOUNDATION OPTION	$300.00
FOUNDATION CHANGES	$250.00
RIGHT READING PLAN REVERSE	$575.00
ARCHITECTS SEAL (Available for most states.)	$300.00
ENERGY CERTIFICATE	$150.00
LIGHT AND VENTILATION SCHEDULE	$150.00

Questions?

Call our customer service department at **1-860-343-5977**

"How to obtain a construction cost calculation based on labor rates and building material costs in <u>your</u> Zip Code area!"

ZIP-QUOTE!
HOME COST CALCULATOR

ZIP QUOTE
HOME COST CALCULATOR

WHY?

Do you wish you could quickly find out the building cost for your new home without waiting for a contractor to compile hundreds of bids? Would you like to have a benchmark to compare your contractor(s) bids against? **Well, Now You Can!!,** with **Zip-Quote** Home Cost Calculator. Zip-Quote is only available for zip code areas within the United States.

HOW?

Our new **Zip-Quote** Home Cost Calculator will enable you to obtain the calculated building cost to construct your new home, based on labor rates and building material costs within your zip code area, without the normal delays or hassles usually associated with the bidding process. Zip-Quote can be purchased in two separate formats, an itemized or a bottom line format.

"How does **Zip-Quote** actually work?" When you call to order, you must choose from the options available, for your specific home, in order for us to process your order. Once we receive your **Zip-Quote** order, we process your specific home plan building materials list through our Home Cost Calculator which contains up-to-date rates for all residential labor trades and building material costs in your zip code area. "The result?" A calculated cost to build your dream home in your zip code area. This calculation will help you (as a consumer or a builder) evaluate your building budget. This is a valuable tool for anyone considering building a new home.

All database information for our calculations is furnished by Marshall & Swift, L.P. For over 60 years, Marshall & Swift L.P. has been a leading provider of cost data to professionals in all aspects of the construction and remodeling industries.

OPTION 1

The **Itemized Zip-Quote** is a detailed building material list. Each building material list line item will separately state the labor cost, material cost and equipment cost (if applicable) for the use of that building material in the construction process. Each category within the building material list will be subtotaled and the entire Itemized cost calculation totaled at the end. This building materials list will be summarized by the individual building categories and will have additional columns where you can enter data from your contractor's estimates for a cost comparison between the different suppliers and contractors who will actually quote you their products and services.

OPTION 2

The **Bottom Line Zip-Quote** is a one line summarized total cost for the home plan of your choice. This cost calculation is also based on the labor cost, material cost and equipment cost (if applicable) within your local zip code area.

COST

The price of your **Itemized Zip-Quote** is based upon the pricing schedule of the plan you have selected, in addition to the price of the materials list. Please refer to the pricing schedule on our order form. The price of your initial **Bottom Line Zip-Quote** is $29.95. Each additional **Bottom Line Zip-Quote** ordered in conjunction with the initial order is only $14.95. **Bottom Line Zip-Quote** may be purchased separately and does NOT have to be purchased in conjunction with a home plan order.

FYI

An **Itemized Zip-Quote** Home Cost Calculation can ONLY be purchased in conjunction with a Home Plan order. The **Itemized Zip-Quote** can not be purchased separately. The **Bottom Line Zip-Quote** can be purchased separately and doesn't have to be purchased in conjunction with a home plan order. Please consult with a sales representative for current availability. If you find within 60 days of your order date that you will be unable to build this home, then you may exchange the plans and the materials list towards the price of a new set of plans (see order info pages for plan exchange policy). The **Itemized Zip-Quote** and the **Bottom Line Zip-Quote** are NOT returnable. The price of the initial **Bottom Line Zip-Quote** order can be credited towards the purchase of an **Itemized Zip-Quote** order only. Additional **Bottom Line Zip-Quote** orders, within the same order can not be credited. Please call our Customer Service Department for more information.

Zip-Quote is available for plans where you see this symbol. Please call for current availability.

SOME MORE INFORMATION

The Itemized and Bottom Line Zip-Quotes give you approximated costs for constructing the particular house in your area. These costs are not exact and are only intended to be used as a preliminary estimate to help determine the affordability of a new home and/or as a guide to evaluate the general competitiveness of actual price quotes obtained through local suppliers and contractors. However, Zip-Quote cost figures should never be relied upon as the only source of information in either case. Land, sewer systems, site work, landscaping and other expenses are not included in our building cost figures. The Garlinghouse Company and Marshall & Swift L.P. can not guarantee any level of data accuracy or correctness in a Zip-Quote and disclaim all liability for loss with respect to the same, in excess of the original purchase price of the Zip-Quote product. All Zip-Quote calculations are based upon the actual blueprint materials list with options as selected by customer and do not reflect any differences that may be shown on the published house renderings, floor plans, or photographs.

Ignoring Copyright Laws Can Be
A $1,000,000 Mistake

Recent changes in the US copyright laws allow for statutory penalties of up to **$100,000** per incident for copyright infringement involving any of the copyrighted plans found in this publication. The law can be confusing. So, for your own protection, take the time to understand what you can and cannot do when it comes to home plans.

••• WHAT YOU CANNOT DO •••

You Cannot Duplicate Home Plans

Purchasing a set of blueprints and making additional sets by reproducing the original is **illegal**. If you need multiple sets of a particular home plan, then you must purchase them.

You Cannot Copy Any Part of a Home Plan to Create Another

Creating your own plan by copying even part of a home design found in this publication is called "creating a derivative work" and is **illegal** unless you have permission to do so.

You Cannot Build a Home Without a License

You must have specific permission or license to build a home from a copyrighted design, even if the finished home has been changed from the original plan. It is **illegal** to build one of the homes found in this publication without a license.

What Garlinghouse Offers

Home Plan Blueprint Package

By purchasing a multiple set package of blueprints or a vellum from Garlinghouse, you not only receive the physical blueprint documents necessary for construction, but you are also granted a license to build one, and only one, home. You can also make simple modifications, including minor non-structural changes and material substitutions, to our design, as long as these changes are made directly on the blueprints purchased from Garlinghouse and no additional copies are made.

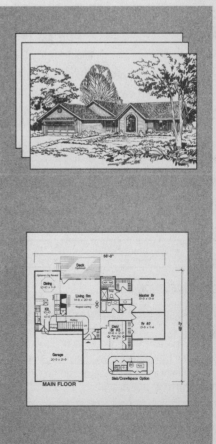

Home Plan Vellums

By purchasing vellums for one of our home plans, you receive the same construction drawings found in the blueprints, but printed on vellum paper. Vellums can be erased and are perfect for making design changes. They are also semi-transparent making them easy to duplicate. But most importantly, the purchase of home plan vellums comes with a broader license that allows you to make changes to the design (ie, create a hand drawn or CAD derivative work), to make copies of the plan, and to build one home from the plan.

License To Build Additional Homes

With the purchase of a blueprint package or vellums you automatically receive a license to build one home and only one home, respectively. If you want to build more homes than you are licensed to build through your purchase of a plan, then additional licenses may be purchased at reasonable costs from Garlinghouse. Inquire for more information.

Order Code No. H9NH1

Order Form

Plan prices guaranteed until 8/1/00 — After this date call for updated pricing

_____ set(s) of blueprints for plan #_____ $_____

_____ Vellum & Modification kit for plan #_____ $_____

_____ Additional set(s) @ $35 each for plan #_____ $_____

_____ Mirror Image Reverse @ $50 each $_____

_____ Right Reading Reverse (see page 250 for cost) $_____

_____ Materials list for plan #_____ $_____

_____ Detail Plans @ $19.95 each

     ❑ Construction   ❑ Plumbing   ❑ Electrical $_____

_____ Bottom line ZIP Quote@$29.95 for plan #_____ $_____

_____ Additional Bottom Line Zip Quote

     @ $14.95 for plan(s) #_____

_____ $_____

_____ Itemized ZIP Quote for plan(s) #_____ $_____

Shipping (see charts on opposite page) $_____

Subtotal $_____

Sales Tax(CT residents add 6% sales tax, KS residents add
6.15% sales tax) (Not required for other states) $_____

TOTAL AMOUNT ENCLOSED $_____

Send your check, money order or credit card information to:
(No C.O.D.'s Please)

Please submit all United States & Other Nations orders to:

Garlinghouse Company
P.O. Box 1717
Middletown, CT. 06457

Please Submit all Canadian plan orders to:

Garlinghouse Company
60 Baffin Place, Unit #5
Waterloo, Ontario N2V 1Z7

ADDRESS INFORMATION:

NAME:_____

STREET:_____

CITY:_____

STATE:_____ ZIP:_____

DAYTIME PHONE:_____

Credit Card Information

Charge To: ❑ Visa   ❑ Mastercard

Card # | | | | | | | | | | | | | | | | |

Signature _____ Exp. _____ / _____

IMPORTANT INFORMATION TO READ BEFORE YOU PLACE YOUR ORDER

How Many Sets Of Plans Will You Need?

The Standard 8-Set Construction Package

Our experience shows that you'll speed every step of construction and avoid costly building errors by ordering enough sets to go around. Each tradesperson wants a set — the general contractor and all subcontractors; foundation, electrical, plumbing, heating/air conditioning and framers. Don't forget your lending institution, building department and, of course, a set for yourself. * Recommended For Construction *

The Minimum 4-Set Construction Package

If you're comfortable with arduous follow-up, this package can save you a few dollars by giving you the option of passing down plan sets as work progresses. You might have enough copies to go around if work goes exactly as scheduled and no plans are lost or damaged by subcontractors. But for only $50 more, the 8-set package eliminates these worries.
* Recommended For Bidding *

The Single Study Set

We offer this set so you can study the blueprints to plan your dream home in detail. They are stamped "study set only-not for construction", and you can-not build a home from them. In pursuant to copyright laws, it is *illegal* to repro-duce any blueprint.

Our Reorder and Exchange Policies:

If you find after your initial purchase that you require additional sets of plans you may purchase them from us at special reorder prices (please call for pricing details) provided that you reorder within 6 months of your original order date. There is a $28 reorder processing fee that is charged on all reorders. For more information on reordering plans please contact our Customer Service Department at (860) 343-5977.

We want you to find your dream home from our wide selection of home plans. However, if for some reason you find that the plan you have purchased from us does not meet your needs, then you may exchange that plan for any other plan in our col-lection. We allow you sixty days from your original invoice date to make an exchange. At the time of the exchange you will be charged a processing fee of 15% of the total amount of your original order plus the difference in price between the plans (if appli-cable) plus the cost to ship the new plans to you. Call our Customer Service Department at (860) 343-5977 for more information. Please Note: Reproducible vel-lums can only be exchanged if they are unopened.

Important Shipping Information

Please refer to the shipping charts on the order form for service availability for your specific plan number. Our delivery service must have a street address or Rural Route Box number — never a post office box. (PLEASE NOTE: Supplying a P.O. Box number *only* will delay the shipping of your order.) Use a work address if no one is home during the day.

Orders being shipped to APO or FPO must go via First Class Mail. Please include the proper postage.

For our International Customers, only Certified bank checks and money orders are accepted and must be payable in U.S. currency. For speed, we ship internation-al orders Air Parcel Post. Please refer to the chart for the correct shipping cost.

Important Canadian Shipping Information

To our friends in Canada, we have a plan design affiliate in Kitchener, Ontario. This relationship will help you avoid the delays and charges associated with ship-ments from the United States. Moreover, our affiliate is familiar with the building requirements in your community and country. We prefer payments in U.S. Currency. If you, however, are sending Canadian funds please add 40% to the prices of the plans and shipping fees.

An Important Note About Building Code Requirements:

All plans are drawn to conform to one or more of the industry's major national building standards. However, due to the variety of local building regulations, your plan may need to be modified to comply with local requirements — snow loads, energy loads, seismic zones, etc. Do check them fully and consult your local building officials.

A few states require that all building plans used be drawn by an architect registered in that state. While having your plans reviewed and stamped by such an architect may be prudent, laws requiring non-conforming plans like ours to be completely redrawn forces you to unnecessarily pay very large fees. If your state has such a law, we strongly recommend you contact your state representative to protest.

The rendering, floor plans, and technical information contained within this publication are not guaranteed to be totally accurate. Consequently, no information from this publication should be used either as a guide to constructing a home or for estimating the cost of building a home. Complete blueprints must be purchased for such purposes.